SIN, IMPURITY, SACRIFICE, ATONEMENT

Hebrew Bible Monographs, 2

Series Editors
David J.A. Clines, J. Cheryl Exum

Editorial Board
A. Graeme Auld, Marc Brettler, David M. Carr, Paul M. Joyce,
Francis Landy, Lena-Sofia Tiemeyer, Stuart D.E. Weeks

Sin, Impurity, Sacrifice, Atonement
The Priestly Conceptions

Jay Sklar

Sheffield Phoenix Press
2015

Copyright © 2005, 2015 Sheffield Phoenix Press

First published in hardback, 2005
First published in paperback, 2015

Published by Sheffield Phoenix Press
Biblical Studies, University of Sheffield
45 Victoria Street
Sheffield S3 7QB

www.sheffieldphoenix.com

All rights reserved.
No part of this publication may be reproduced or transmitted in any
form or by any means, electronic or mechanical, including
photocopying, recording or any information storage or retrieval
system, without the publisher's permission in writing.

A CIP catalogue record for this book
is available from the British Library

Typeset by Forthcoming Publications Ltd
Printed by Lightning Source Inc.

ISBN 978-1-909697-88-1 (paperback)
ISBN 978-1-905048-12-0 (hardback)

ISSN 1747-9614

To Ski

Contents

Preface	ix
Abbreviations	x
Introduction: Approaches to כִּפֶּר in General	1

Part I
כִּפֶּר IN CONTEXTS OF SIN

Chapter 1
THE CONSEQUENCES OF SIN IN THE PRIESTLY LITERATURE — 11
1.1. The Connection between Sin and Punishment — 11
1.2. The Consequences of Sin in the Priestly Literature — 13
1.3. Summary and Comparison of the Penalties for Sin — 41

Chapter 2
כִּפֶּר DEFINED — 44
2.1. כִּפֶּר Defined — 48
2.2. Survey of Previous Definitions and Renderings of כִּפֶּר — 67
2.3. Summary — 77

Chapter 3
THE VERB כִּפֶּר IN CONTEXTS OF SIN — 80
3.1. כִּפֶּר in Contexts of Sin — 80
3.2. Summary — 99

Part II
כִּפֶּר IN CONTEXTS OF IMPURITY

Chapter 4
THE VERB כִּפֶּר IN CONTEXTS OF IMPURITY — 105
4.1. Purification and כִּפֶּר — 106
4.2. Consecration and כִּפֶּר — 116
4.3. Purification, Consecration, and כִּפֶּר — 125
4.4. כִּפֶּר, Purgation, and כִּפֶּר — 127
4.5. Summary — 134

Part III
SIN, IMPURITY, AND כִּפֶּר

Chapter 5
THE RELATIONSHIP BETWEEN SIN AND IMPURITY
AND ITS RELEVANCE TO כִּפֶּר   139
   5.1. Approaches to the Relationship between Sin and Impurity   141
   5.2. כִּפֶּר in the Priestly Literature   153
   5.3. Summary   158

Part IV
כִּפֶּר AND THE ROLE OF BLOOD

Chapter 6
A CONSIDERATION OF THE ROLE OF BLOOD IN SACRIFICIAL
ATONEMENT, WITH SPECIAL REFERENCE TO LEVITICUS 17.11   163
   6.1. Leviticus 17.11   164
   6.2. Summary and Conclusion   181

Chapter 7
CONCLUSION   183

Appendix
כִּפֶּר AND ITS SYNTAGMATIC RELATIONS IN THE PRIESTLY LITERATURE   188

Bibliography   194
Index of References   200
Index of Authors   211

Preface

This work is a revision of a PhD dissertation completed at the University of Gloucestershire in Cheltenham, England. It is a sincere delight for me to express my thanks and appreciation to several people who have been instrumental in helping this work become a reality. I came to study at Cheltenham because of Gordon Wenham, who has set a model of biblical scholarship that I can only hope to emulate. As my supervisor, he provided wise counsel and guidance in the preparation of the original dissertation, for which I thank him profoundly.

I also wish to thank my second reader Dr Walter Houston, whose perceptive critiques rescued me from many an error. Naturally, I alone bear responsibility for the deficiencies that remain.

Thanks are also due to the University of Gloucestershire for funding that enabled me to undertake studies in the first place. In this same regard I am grateful to the Overseas Research Students Council of the United Kingdom for an award that was likewise very helpful in funding my research.

I am very grateful for the help given to me by several of my students in preparing indices, in formatting the work, and in other related matters. To Donna Reinhard, Michael Quillen, Kristofer Holroyd, Bill Connors, and Brady Shuman I express my thankfulness.

Three editorial comments are in order. First, while the work interacts with German and French scholars, no knowledge of these languages is needed to follow the flow of the argument. Where these languages are cited, it is in the footnotes and then always to illustrate a point already made in the text above.

Second, the focus of this work is upon a synchronic reading of the text. Consequently, the terms 'priestly', 'priestly literature' or 'priestly texts' are used in a general way to refer to those texts in Exodus 25 to Numbers which deal with issues related to the cult of ancient Israel.

Third, when Hebrew and English versifications differ, the Hebrew is listed first followed by the English in parentheses, for example, Lev. 5.20 (6.1).

A final word of thanks is in order. It has been saved for last because it is the one that is the greatest joy for me to give. Ski, throughout this entire process you have been an unflagging support, a constant source of encouragement, and above all, my best friend. I am so thankful that you are my wife. It is with sincere thanksgiving, admiration, and love that I dedicate this work to you.

ABBREVIATIONS

AB	Anchor Bible
AfO	*Archiv für Orientforschung*
AHw	Wolfram von Soden, *Akkadisches Handwörterbuch* (Wiesbaden: Otto Harrassowitz, 1959–81)
ArOr	*Archiv orientální*
AV	Authorized Version
BASOR	Bulletin of the American Schools of Oriental Research
BDB	Francis Brown, S.R. Driver, and Charles A. Briggs, *A Hebrew and English Lexicon of the Old Testament* (Oxford: Clarendon Press, 1907)
BEvT	Beiträge zur evangelischen Theologie
BHS	*Biblia hebraica stuttgartensia*
Bib	*Biblica*
BKAT	Biblischer Kommentar: Altes Testament
CAD	*The Assyrian Dictionary of the Oriental Institute of the University of Chicago*
CahRB	Cahiers de la Revue biblique
CAT	Commentaire de l'Ancien Testament
CBC	Cambridge Bible Commentary
CBQ	*Catholic Biblical Quarterly*
CE	Codex Eshnunna
CH	Codex Hammurabi
DCH	David J.A. Clines (ed.), *The Dictionary of Classical Hebrew* (Sheffield: Sheffield Academic Press, 1993–), 5 vols. to date.
ET	English translation
EvQ	*Evangelical Quarterly*
EvT	*Evangelische Theologie*
FRLANT	Forschungen zur Religion und Literatur des Alten und Neuen Testaments
GKC	*Gesenius' Hebrew Grammar* (ed. E. Kautzsch, revised and trans. A.E. Cowley; Oxford: Clarendon Press, 1910)
HALAT	Ludwig Koehler *et al.* (eds.), *Hebräisches und aramäisches Lexikon zum Alten Testament* (5 vols.; Leiden: E.J. Brill, 1967–95)
HAT	Handbuch zum Alten Testament
HUCA	*Hebrew Union College Annual*
ICC	International Critical Commentary
IDB	George Arthur Buttrick (ed.), *The Interpreter's Dictionary of the Bible* (4 vols.; Nashville: Abingdon Press, 1962)
JB	Jerusalem Bible
JJS	*Journal of Jewish Studies*
JNSL	*Journal of Northwest Semitic Languages*
Joüon	P. Joüon, *A Grammar of Biblical Hebrew* (trans. T. Muraoka; Rome: Pontificio Istituto Biblico, 1993)

JPS	Jewish Publication Society
JPSV	Jewish Publication Society Version
JSJ	*Journal for the Study of Judaism in the Persian, Hellenistic, and Roman Periods*
JSOT	*Journal for the Study of the Old Testament*
JSOTSup	Journal for the Study of the Old Testament Supplement Series
MTZ	*Münchener theologische Zeitschrift*
NASV	New American Standard Version
NCBC	New Century Bible Commentary
NEB	New English Bible
NICOT	New International Commentary on the Old Testament
NIDOTTE	*New International Dictionary of Old Testament Theology and Exegesis*
NIV	New International Version
OTL	Old Testament Library
RB	*Revue biblique*
RSV	Revised Standard Version
SBLDS	Society of Biblical Literature Dissertation Series
SBLMS	Society of Biblical Literature Monograph Series
SBLSP	*Society of Biblical Literature Seminar Papers*
SJLA	Studies in Judaism in Late Antiquity
TDNT	Gerhard Kittel and Gerhard Friedrich (eds.), *Theological Dictionary of the New Testament* (trans. Geoffrey W. Bromiley; 10 vols.; Grand Rapids: Eerdmans, 1964–)
TDOT	G.J. Botterweck and H. Ringgren (eds.), *Theological Dictionary of the Old Testament* (trans. John T. Willis; 6 vols.; Grand Rapids: Eerdmans, 1990–)
THAT	Ernst Jenni and Claus Westermann (eds.), *Theologisches Handwörterbuch zum Alten Testament* (Munich: Chr. Kaiser Verlag, 1971–76)
TLOT	E. Jenni and C. Westermann (eds.), *Theological Lexicon of the Old Testament* (trans. Mark E. Biddle; 3 vols.; Peabody, MA: Hendrickson, 1997)
TOTC	Tyndale Old Testament Commentary
TWNT	Gerhard Kittel and Gerhard Friedrich (eds.), *Theologisches Wörterbuch zum Neuen Testament* (11 vols.; Stuttgart: W. Kohlhammer, 1932–79)
UT	Cyrus H. Gordon, *Ugaritic Textbook* (Analecta orientalia, 38; Rome: Pontifical Biblical Institute Press, 1965)
VTSup	Vetus Testamentum Supplements
W&O	Bruce K. Waltke and M. O'Connor, *An Introduction to Biblical Hebrew Syntax* (Winona Lake, IN: Eisenbrauns, 1990)
WBC	Word Biblical Commentary
ZAW	*Zeitschrift für die alttestamentliche Wissenschaft*
ZNW	*Zeitschrift für die neutestamentliche Wissenschaft*
ZTK	*Zeitschrift für Theologie und Kirche*

INTRODUCTION:
APPROACHES TO כִּפֶּר IN GENERAL

The main title of this study—*Sin, Impurity, Sacrifice, Atonement*—reflects the fact that sacrifices of atonement address sin in some contexts, and impurity in others, and in so doing lead to atonement (כִּפֶּר) for the one presenting the sacrifice. In contexts of sin, this atonement results in forgiveness. In contexts of impurity, it results in purification or consecration.[1] In both instances, however, it is an atoning sacrifice that is required, and in both instances the priest is said to make atonement for the offerer: וְכִפֶּר עָלָיו הַכֹּהֵן.

These brief observations, however, already raise questions. In particular, why is atonement required in *both* of these contexts? While it might not be surprising that it is needed in sin contexts, where the law of the LORD has been breached, it is not as clear why it is required in contexts of impurity, which is often the result of completely amoral processes, such as giving birth (Lev. 12). This question may be focused with a consideration of different approaches to the term כִּפֶּר.

The literature on כִּפֶּר is vast, and a full survey is beyond the range of the present study.[2] Nonetheless, the various approaches to כִּפֶּר in the priestly literature may be conveniently grouped into two main camps. The first of these translates כִּפֶּר with 'to atone/expiate' or 'to make atonement/expiation' in all priestly occurrences. The second camp follows the first in some

---

1. As discussed in §4.3, consecration is also a type of purification.
2. A more thorough review of the literature can be found in Bernd Janowski, *Sühne als Heilsgeschehen. Studien zur Sühnetheologie der Priesterschrift und zur Wurzel KPR im Alten Orient und im Alten Testament* (Neukirchen–Vluyn: Neukirchener Verlag, 1982), pp. 1-26 (15-25). See also references in N. Kiuchi, *The Purification Offering in the Priestly Literature* (JSOTSup, 56; Sheffield: JSOT Press, 1987), p. 94 and notes; Baruch J. Schwartz, 'The Prohibitions Concerning the "Eating" of Blood in Leviticus 17', in Gary A. Anderson and Saul M. Olyan (eds.), *Priesthood and Cult in Ancient Israel* (JSOTSup, 125; Sheffield: JSOT Press, 1991), pp. 34-66 (51 n. 3); and, for important earlier works, Johannes Herrmann, *Die Idee der Sühne im Alten Testament. Eine Untersuchung über Gebrauch und Bedeutung des Wortes kipper* (Leipzig: J.C. Hinrichs, 1905), pp. 7-31.

instances, but also translates כִּפֶּר with renderings such as 'to purify/effect purgation' in other instances. Each of these two main camps will be considered in turn.

Traditionally, כִּפֶּר has been translated in the priestly literature with renderings such as 'to atone/make atonement' or 'to expiate/make expiation'.³ While these renderings have generally been agreed upon, there has been a diversity of opinion as to the exact nature of this atonement. Many scholars, especially in the nineteenth century and beginning half of the twentieth, argued that כִּפֶּר is related to Arabic *kafara* ('to cover'), and that atonement thus refers to a covering over of sin or the sinner.⁴ Others have argued that the connection between כִּפֶּר and כֹּפֶר I ('ransom') is significant, and that atonement is therefore characterized by the payment of a ransom or the appeasement that results from such payment.⁵ Still others, on the basis of theological and contextual observations, emphasize the positive aspects of atonement, describing it as a process by which the worshipper symbolically dedicates their life to the holy.⁶

Which of these understandings finds support in the text is considered in more detail in Chapter 2. For the moment, however, it is enough to note that despite these differences, there is basic agreement that כִּפֶּר refers to sin being dealt with in such a way that the broken relationship between the LORD and the sinner is mended. That this is a plausible understanding of

3. AV; RSV; NASV; NIV; NEB; JB.
4. See references in Janowski, *Sühne*, pp. 20-22; Schwartz, 'Prohibitions', p. 54 n. 2. For a full defense of this view see Johann Jakob Stamm, *Erlösen und Vergeben im alten Testament. Eine begriffsgeschichtliche Untersuchung* (Bern: A. Francke, 1940), pp. 61-66 and references cited there; see also Johann Heinrich Kurtz, *Sacrificial Worship of the Old Testament* (trans. James Martin; Edinburgh: T. & T. Clark, 1863), pp. 67-71; Karl Elliger, *Leviticus* (HAT, 4; Tübingen: J.C.B. Mohr, 1966), p. 71. For an evaluation of this view, see Chapter 2, n. 2.
5. Herrmann, *Die Idee der Sühne*, pp. 99, 101-102; idem, 'ἱλάσκομαι, ἱλασμός', in *TDNT*, III, pp. 301-10 (303); Herbert Chanan Brichto, 'On Slaughter and Sacrifice, Blood and Atonement', *HUCA* 47 (1976), pp. 19-55 (26-27, 34-35); Adrian Schenker, '*kōper* et expiation', *Bib* 63 (1982), pp. 32-46. See further references in the introduction to Chapter 2, especially nn. 8-13. For an evaluation of this view, cf. §2.1 and §2.2 with §3.1.
6. Janowski, *Sühne*, pp. 185-276. Janowski's work follows and develops that of his mentor, Hartmut Gese. See Hartmut Gese, 'Die Sühne', in *Zur biblischen Theologie. Alttestamentliche Vorträge* (BEvT, 78; Munich: Chr. Kaiser Verlag, 1977), pp. 85-106 (ET 'The Atonement', in *Essays on Biblical Theology* [trans. K. Crim; Minneapolis: Fortress Press, 1981], pp. 93-116). For an evaluation of this view, see §2.2.1, especially n. 71 and references there.
One may further mention the debate between the translation 'expiation' and 'propitiation', a brief summary of which is found in B. Lang, 'כִּפֶּר *kipper*', in *TDOT*, VII, pp. 283-303 (293). For a fuller discussion see Norman H. Young, 'C.H. Dodd, "Hilaskesthai" and his Critics', *EvQ* 48.2 (1976), pp. 67-78.

כִּפֶּר is self-evident in the priestly literature, for it is used in sin contexts to describe taking care of the negative effects of sin in order to bring about reconciliation between the sinner and the LORD. For this reason, it is often said that a person is forgiven after atonement has been effected on their behalf: 'And the priest shall make atonement for [the leader] in regard to his sin, and he shall be forgiven' (Lev. 4.26b).

As noted above, however, this understanding of כִּפֶּר appears problematic in purification contexts, where no obvious sin has been committed. The woman who has had a baby, for example, offers a purification offering, by which the priest makes atonement (כִּפֶּר) for her. Moreover, the result in this instance is not forgiveness, as one would expect with atonement, but rather, purification: 'and the priest will atone for her and she will be pure (וְכִפֶּר עָלֶיהָ הַכֹּהֵן וְטָהֵרָה)' (Lev. 12.8b; see also 14.20b, 53b). Finally, in several instances sancta appear to be the direct object of כִּפֶּר (e.g. Lev. 16.20, 33; Ezek. 43.20, 26), and one may legitimately ask what the sense of 'atoning sancta' might be.

Recognizing these difficulties, several authors have proposed that כִּפֶּר can refer to purification, like Akkadian *kuppuru*, 'to wipe off, to purify', and can thus be translated 'to purify/purge/effect purgation'.[7] This understanding of

---

7. The principal authors holding to this are Baruch A. Levine, *In the Presence of the Lord: A Study of Cult and Some Cultic Terms in Ancient Israel* (SJLA, 5; Leiden: E.J. Brill, 1974), pp. 56-61 (Levine further notes [p. 56] that a connection between כִּפֶּר and *kuppuru* was favored by Gray; see George Buchanan Gray, *Sacrifice in the Old Testament* [Oxford: Clarendon Press, 1925], pp. 67-73); and Jacob Milgrom, *Leviticus 1–16* (AB, 3; New York: Doubleday, 1991), pp. 1040, 1080-82. Though not appealing to the Akkadian, Gerleman understands כִּפֶּר to refer to a rite of sprinkling or washing ('streichen, sprengen; [ab]wischen'); see Gillis Gerleman, 'Die Wurzel *kpr* im Hebräischen', in *Studien zur alttestamentlichen Theologie* (Heidelberg: Schneider, 1980), pp. 11-23.

For a summary of the discussion on *kapāru* (D stem *kuppuru*), as well as a survey of relevant texts, see Janowski, *Sühne*, pp. 29-60. With regard to the meaning of the verb, von Soden (*AHw*, pp. 442-43) originally suggested a *kapāru* I form, 'abschälen; abwischen', and a *kapāru* II form, denominated from *kupru* '(Trocken-) Asphalt', which meant 'mit Asphalt übergießen'. A different breakdown was proposed by Benno Landsberger (*The Date Palm and its By-Products according to the Cuneiform Sources* [AfO Beiheft, 17; Graz: Weidner, 1967]), who questioned the rendering 'abschälen' for *kapāru* I (proposing instead [p. 30] 'to trim, to clip, to strip off' [Ger. 'stutzen, kappen, abtakeln']), separated the 'abwischen' occurrences into 'auswischen' and 'ausschmieren' (though he does note [p. 32] that in some contexts these are impossible to distinguish), and stated that *kapāru* III (= *AHw*, II, 'mit Asphalt überschmieren') 'can not be a denominative because it occurs also with other substances than *kupru*: CT 40, 2, 47, dupl. CT 38, 17, 92: *šumma bītu ittâ agurra gaṣṣa qadūta ka-pi-ir* "if a house is smeared with raw or refined asphalt, clay, mortar, gypsum, or river sand"' (Landsberger, *Date Palm*, p. 32). The *CAD* entry on *kapāru*, an early draft of which was used by Landsberger (p. 30 n. 87),

כִּפֶּר finds support in three avenues. First, it would clarify the above problems; that is, translating כִּפֶּר with 'to purge/effect purgation' would fit in well in contexts of impurity, the results of which are the purification or consecration of the offerer or sancta. Second, this understanding of כִּפֶּר finds support in the fact that the priestly literature uses words for purification, such as טהר and חטא, right alongside of כִּפֶּר: 'For on this day he will effect purgation for you to purify you (כִּי־בַיּוֹם הַזֶּה יְכַפֵּר עֲלֵיכֶם לְטַהֵר אֶתְכֶם)' (Lev. 16.30a).[8] Finally, as mentioned above,[9] Akkadian attests *kuppuru* ('to purify'), which is not only similar to כִּפֶּר in form (D stem of √*kpr*), it is also used in cultic texts in a way analogous to כִּפֶּר.[10]

These authors do not claim that כִּפֶּר should always be translated with 'to purify' or 'to effect purgation'. Recognizing that this translation does not work in every context, they translate it with 'to purify/effect purgation' in some instances, and with 'to atone/expiate' or 'to make atonement/expiation' in other instances.

Even here, however, it is not always easy to choose between these two translations, as evidenced by certain tensions in the work of those in this second camp. Levine, for instance, argues, '*Kippēr* in biblical cultic texts reflects two distinct verbal forms: (1) *kippēr* I, the primary *Pi''ēl*, and (2) *kippēr* II, a secondary denominative, from the noun *kōper* "ransom, expiation gift"'.[11] Levine translates the *kippēr* I form, which he holds is related to *kuppuru*, with 'to purify' when it is followed by a direct object, and with 'to perform rites of expiation' or 'to make expiation' when it is followed by a preposition such as עַל.[12] At the same time, he also translates *kippēr* II with 'to make expiation', though with a fundamental difference. With *kippēr* I,

---

proposes a *kapāru* A (1. to wipe off; 2. to smear on [a paint or liquid]; 3. *kuppuru* to wipe off, to clean objects, to rub, to purify magically; 4. IV to be rubbed, to be smeared [passive to mngs. 1 and 2]) and a *kapāru* B (1. to strip, clip, to trim down; 2. *kuppuru* [same mngs.]; 3. II/2 to be terminated). It may be noted that von Soden apparently agreed with this analysis, stating in an entry on *kapāru* I in the 'Berichtigungen und Nachträge' of the third volume, 'wohl mit CAD 2 Verben!' (*AHw*, p. 1566).

8. See also Lev. 14.52-53: 'Thus [the priest] shall decontaminate (וְחִטֵּא) the house with the blood of the bird and with the running water...so he shall כִּפֶּר for the house (וְכִפֶּר עַל־הַבַּיִת), and it shall be clean (וְטָהֵר)'.

9. See above, n. 7.

10. After laying out the meanings of *kuppuru* as found in *CAD*, Levine (*Presence of the Lord*, p. 60) proceeds to argue that the 'biblical usage of *kippēr* almost exactly parallels the evidence available for Akkadian *kuppuru*', though Janowski (*Sühne*, pp. 29-60), following his extensive listing and discussion on pp. 29-57, identifies five major differences between the terms on pp. 57-60.

11. Levine, *Presence of the Lord*, p. 67; *kippēr* I in this instance refers to purification.

12. Levine, *Presence of the Lord*, pp. 64-65; idem, *Leviticus* (JPS; Philadelphia: Jewish Publication Society of America, 1989), p. 23.

expiation refers primarily to a *cleansing*. Thus in his comments on Lev. 4.20, where the priest performs the כִּפֶּר-rite for the inadvertent sin of the whole community, Levine states:

> The Akkadian verb *kuppuru*, which corresponds to Hebrew *kipper*, means 'to wipe off, burnish, cleanse'. In cultic terms this means that expiation is conceived of as cleansing, as wiping away impurity, contamination, and, by extension, sinfulness itself... The Levitical texts use the verb *kipper* to express the concept that through expiation one is 'wiped clean' of impurities that adhere or cling to a person—infect him, we might say.[13]

And though the context of Lev. 4.20 concerns an inadvertent sin, and not a major impurity, Levine can maintain this cleansing aspect of כִּפֶּר here because in his understanding sinfulness is a type of impurity.[14]

With *kippēr* II, on the other hand, expiation refers not to cleansing but to the *ransom* of a life. This is seen most clearly in his comments on the formula 'to atone for your lives' (לְכַפֵּר עַל־נַפְשֹׁתֵיכֶם) in Lev. 17.11: 'Literally, this formula means "to serve as *kofer* (ransom) for your lives". God accepts the blood of the sacrifices in lieu of human blood.'[15] He then goes on to state, however, that 'substitution was allowed only in cases of inadvertence'.[16] This creates a tension, though, since the context of כִּפֶּר in Lev. 4.20—which he characterized as meaning 'to cleanse'—is exactly that of an inadvertence, and where we would therefore expect כִּפֶּר to refer to the ransom principle.

The simple solution, perhaps, would be to suggest that Levine is mistaken in his comments on 4.20, and that here too כִּפֶּר refers to the ransom principle. This is possible, and in Chapter 3 it will be argued that כֹּפֶר does indeed play a major role in the meaning of כִּפֶּר in the sin contexts of Leviticus 4 and 5. At the same time, however, it may also be questioned: Should the tension illustrated in Levine's work be solved by deciding between ransom and cleansing, *or should elements of both ransom and cleansing be held together?*

A second scholar who translates כִּפֶּר with 'to effect purgation' in some instances and with 'to atone/expiate' or 'to make atonement/expiation' in

---

13. Levine, *Leviticus*, p. 23
14. This is hinted at in the quote above ('In cultic terms this means that expiation is conceived of as cleansing, as wiping away impurity, contamination, and, *by extension*, sinfulness itself') and stated explicitly in his comments on 16.16: 'Uncleanness is equated with sinfulness; thus, according to the biblical conception, sinfulness was regarded as a form of impurity. The verb *ḥiṭṭe'*, literally "to remove the sin", effectively means "to purify", as in 14.52' (Levine, *Leviticus*, p. 105).
15. Levine, *Presence of the Lord*, p. 115.
16. Levine, *Presence of the Lord*, p. 115.

others is Jacob Milgrom.¹⁷ Whenever כפר occurs in conjunction with the purification offering—which Milgrom understands to be for the sole purpose of cleansing the sanctuary and not the worshipper—he translates it with 'to effect purgation'. In a second series of texts, however, which concern averting the wrath of God, it is the ransom principle (כֹּפֶר) that is operative:

> (1) The function of the census money (Exod. 30.12-16) is *lĕkappēr 'al-napšōtêkem* 'to ransom your lives' (Exod. 30.16; cf. Num. 31.50): here the verb *kippēr* must be related to the expression found in the same pericope *kōper napšô* 'a ransom for his life' (Exod. 30.12). (2) The same combination of the idiom *kōper nepeš* and the verb *kippēr* is found in the law of homicide (Num. 35.31-33). Thus in these two cases, *kippēr* is a denominative from *kōper*, whose meaning is undisputed: 'ransom' (cf. Exod. 21.30). Therefore, there exists a strong possibility that all texts that assign to *kippēr* the function of averting God's wrath have *kōper* in mind: [guilty] life spared by substituting for it the [innocent] parties or their ransom.¹⁸

Finally, there is a third series of texts where כפר has the more 'figurative notion "atone" or "expiate"', for example, in the scapegoat rite (Lev. 16.10, 21), or 'in the incense offering by which Aaron stops the plague, thus expiating on Israel's behalf (Num. 17.11)¹⁹... The meaning here is that the offerer is cleansed of his impurities/sins and becomes reconciled, "at one", with God.'²⁰ Thus to Milgrom, כפר can refer to a straight cleansing of the sanctuary, to the payment of ransom, or to an expiation which is characterized by a cleansing of the person and reconciliation between that person and God.

The same tension that was evident above with Levine is also manifest in Milgrom's presentation. Numbers 35.31-33, for example, states that no act of כפר can be made for land defiled by bloodshed, except the shedding of the slayer's blood. Milgrom places this text in category two (כפר refers to the ransom principle), which seems justified on the basis of כפר in vv. 31 and 32.²¹ And yet the text could not be clearer that shed blood pollutes (חנף, hiphil; v. 33) and defiles (טמא, piel; v. 34) the land, suggesting that the act of כפר must not only ransom, but also cleanse, a point to which we return in some detail below.²² Once more, the simple solution would be to state that

---

17. Milgrom, *Leviticus 1–16*, pp. 1079-84.
18. Milgrom, *Leviticus 1–16*, p. 1082 (the last line reads differently in the original, for which see Chapter 2, n. 15).
19. Milgrom, *Leviticus 1–16*, p. 1083. He further states that 'atonement is also one of the functions of the *'ōlâ* (1.4...), the *minhâ* (14.20...), and the sole function of the *millī'îm*, the priestly consecration ram (Exod. 29.33) and the *'āšām* (5.16, 18, 26)'.
20. Milgrom, *Leviticus 1–16*, p. 1083.
21. Milgrom, *Leviticus 1–16*, p. 1082.
22. See §5.2.

this passage has been put in the wrong category. But it may again be questioned: Should the tension between ransom and cleansing be solved one way or the other, *or are there elements of both involved in the concept of* כִּפֶּר*?*

There are, then, two main approaches to the translation and understanding of כִּפֶּר in the priestly literature: (1) those who translate it simply with words such as 'to atone/make atonement' or 'to expiate/make expiation'; and (2) those who translate it in some instances with 'to atone/make atonement' (primarily understood as 'to ransom'), and in other instances with 'to purify/ effect purgation'. It was seen that the first approach is suitable in many instances, especially those in which כִּפֶּר addresses the results of sin, but that it appears less suitable in contexts of impurity. In this regard, the second approach fared better, allowing for the translation of 'to atone/make atonement' (i.e. 'to ransom') in sin contexts and 'to purify/effect purgation' in cleansing or consecration contexts. At the same time, however, it was noted that deciding between 'to ransom' and 'to purify' is not always easy, as demonstrated by the tensions present in both Levine and Milgrom. As a result, it was questioned: Does the tension between ransom and purification need to be decided one way or the other, *or is* כִּפֶּר *better understood as holding both of these together?*

It is argued in this study that this last question in particular holds the key to understanding the nature of atonement in the priestly literature. In order to establish this position, it will be necessary to consider how כִּפֶּר functions in sin contexts, how it functions in impurity contexts, as well as how these contexts relate to one another. Further, if it is the case that the כִּפֶּר-rite effects ransom and purification, it will be important to identify how the כִּפֶּר-rite as a whole is able to accomplish both. In view of these goals, this work comprises four parts.

In Part I (Chapters 1 to 3) we look at כִּפֶּר in sin contexts. Chapter 1 sets the context of the discussion by considering the consequences of both intentional and inadvertent sin in the priestly literature, the latter of which in particular is the occasion for the כִּפֶּר-rite. Having set this context, we then turn to consider כִּפֶּר more carefully. Anticipating that כִּפֶּר is related to the meaning of כֹּפֶר in these contexts, Chapter 2 provides a thorough analysis of the term כֹּפֶר. Chapter 3 then establishes that the meaning of כִּפֶּר is indeed related to that of כֹּפֶר in contexts of sin through a consideration of a key term and key phrase that occur in conjunction with כִּפֶּר, namely, סָלַח and נָשָׂא עָוֹן. Having established the meaning of כִּפֶּר in contexts of sin, we then turn in Part II (Chapter 4) to consider its meaning in contexts of impurity. This is done through a comparison of the verb כִּפֶּר with the three other verbs it occurs in conjunction with in these contexts, namely, טהר, חטא, and קדשׁ. In Part III (Chapter 5), we consider why it is that כִּפֶּר occurs in contexts of both sin and impurity. This question is answered through a comparison of sin and impurity that draws together the conclusions from the first two sections. Finally, Part IV (Chapter 6) considers one question that remains in the light of the conclusions of the Parts I–III, namely: Why is the כִּפֶּר-rite able to fulfill the dual role of ransom and purification?

Part I

כִּפֶּר IN CONTEXTS OF SIN

1

THE CONSEQUENCES OF SIN
IN THE PRIESTLY LITERATURE

As noted in the Introduction, the verb כִּפֶּר occurs in conjunction with sacrifice in contexts of sin as well as purification and consecration. We will begin by considering the first of these, namely, contexts of sin. Since the purpose of atoning sacrifice in these contexts is remedial (i.e. to address the negative situation that sin gives rise to) it is important to begin by identifying the priestly understanding of the consequences of sin.

1.1. *The Connection between Sin and Punishment*

We may begin more generally by noting that in the world-view of the Old Testament, as well as of the ancient Near East in general, sin is followed by a negative consequence and this consequence is a punitive judgment from the divine.[1] The priestly literature is no exception in this regard, as demonstrated

---

1. In short, there is a 'sin–disaster connection' (a *Sünde–Unheil-Zusammenhang*), with the disaster coming as God's judgment for the sin. Supporting references are extensive; the following is a representative cross-section: Gen. 6.5-7; 19.13-14; Exod. 32.1-10; Lev. 10.1-3; 18.25; 26.14-33; Num. 11.1; 12.9-11; 14.11-12, 22-23, 28-37; 16.25-35; 21.5-6; Deut. 4.25-28; 6.14-15; 7.4; 28.15-68; Judg. 2.13-15; 3.7-8; 1 Sam. 2.27-32; 2 Sam. 12.9-14; 1 Kgs 2.32; 8.31-40; 9.6-9; 11.9-11; 2 Kgs 17.6-18; 1 Chron. 21.1-15; 2 Chron. 7.13-14; Ezra 9.13-14; Neh. 9.26-28; Pss. 5.11 (10); 11.5-6; Prov. 12.2; Isa. 3.16-17; 9.13-14; 10.5-6; Jer. 3.1-3a; 4.4; 5.3; Lam. 3.42-47; Ezek. 7.3, 8-9; 11.6-12; 14.7-8; 22.4, 13-15; Hos. 1.4-5; 2.10-15 (8-13); 8.13b-14; 10.1-2; Amos 1.3–2.5; 3.2; Mic. 1.3-7; 6.13-16; Zeph. 1.2-6.

This understanding of divine retribution was radically challenged by Klaus Koch in his article, 'Gibt es ein Vergeltungsdogma im Alten Testament?', *ZTK* 52 (1955), pp. 1-42. In brief, Koch agrees on the one hand that there is an inviolable connection between sin and consequence (pp. 26-27), but disagrees on the other hand that this connection is due to divine retribution. To Koch, the consequence of an action is inherent within it (much as fruit is inherent within the seed [p. 10]), and does not result from an external judgment of the LORD. Indeed, the LORD may be involved in the process but not in a judicial sense. Instead, he compares the LORD to a midwife who helps to bring about something that

by two factors. First, as will become evident in the following, the priestly literature is similar to the rest of the Old Testament in using terms for sin or guilt to refer not only to the wrong itself, but also to the consequences of the wrong. For example, the phrase נָשָׂא עָוֹן ('to bear sin') frequently refers to bearing a *punishment* for some sin (see §1.2.3.1 below), and the verb אָשַׁם often refers to *suffering the consequences* of guilt (see §1.2.4.4 below).[2]

    previous human action has already begun (p. 5; he later compares the LORD to the catalyst in a chemical reaction [p. 21]). Instead of divine retribution, then, he holds that the relationship between deed and consequence is better described with the phrase *schicksalwirkende Tatsphäre*.

    Koch's thesis, while innovative, fails on many counts, not least of which being the large number of verses that explicitly describe the negative consequence following sin as a judgment from the LORD (see the initial paragraph of this note; it may be observed in this regard that Koch does not really address these types of verses, building his thesis instead upon places where the negative consequence that follows sin is not *explicitly* stated to be the judgment of the LORD). Other fundamental critiques have been leveled against Koch. John Barton ('Natural Law and Poetic Justice', *JTS* NS 30 [1979], pp. 1-14 [10]) notes the affinities which Koch's view has with deism, a surprising correspondence given the pre-rational worldview of the ancient Near East. Rolf Knierim (*Die Hauptbegriffe für Sünde im Alten Testament* [Gütersloher Verlagshaus: Gerd Mohn, 1965], p. 83) also notes that the impression from Koch is that the LORD plays a secondary role. Knierim (p. 77), while accepting Koch's description of the relationship between sin and consequence as *schicksalwirkende Tatsphäre*, disagrees that this should be divorced from the legal realm (*Hauptbegriffe*, p. 78), and argues instead that God accomplishes the deed–consequence relationship *by means of* a legal act (see his comments on Ps. 7.9-17 [8-16] [p. 79] and Hos. 5.12, 14 [p. 88]). Patrick D. Miller Jr (*Sin and Judgment in the Prophets: A Stylistic and Theological Analysis* [SBLMS, 27; Chico, CA: Scholars Press, 1982], p. 134) picks up this same critique in his study of sin and judgment in the prophets, concluding that the relationship between sin and its punishment 'is perceived as resting in the divine decision and not happening apart from that decision's decree'. For further critiques of Koch see the literature cited in Barton, 'Natural Law and Poetic Justice', p. 11 n. 3.

    For ancient Near Eastern material addressing the connection between sin and punishment see K. van der Toorn, *Sin and Sanction in Israel and Mesopotamia: A Comparative Study* (Assen: Van Gorcum, 1985), pp. 41-55. Van der Toorn also notes, however, that not all misfortune in the ancient Near East was interpreted as punishment; for example, physical ailments could be attributed simply to natural causes (pp. 67, 69-70). The same may be seen in the Old Testament; thus it is not until the *third* year of a famine that David inquires of the LORD to see if it is due to sin (2 Sam. 21.1).

    2.   See n. 41 below for other examples of terms for sin or guilt being used in this manner. This use of terms for sin to denote punishment is well explained as an example of metonymy, that is, the use of one name or noun (here, 'sin') for that of another (here, 'punishment') to which it stands in a certain relation (see here the extensive examples in E.W. Bullinger, *Figures of Speech Used in the Bible* [repr.; Grand Rapids: Baker Book House, 1898], pp. 538-608 [550-51]). It is the close relationship between the two terms that allows the one to be used for the other, for example, the relationship between work

The second factor is simply that the priestly literature explicitly and consistently conjoins sin and its punishment and understands this punishment as coming directly from the LORD, or, in some cases, as executed by the covenant community on behalf of the LORD.

There are four main consequences for sin detailed in the priestly literature: death, *kareth*, 'bearing one's sin' (עָוֹן נָשָׂא), and 'suffering guilt's consequences' (אָשֵׁם).[3] Each of these four penalties will now be considered. This will in turn prove important for the understanding of how the כִּפֶּר-rite functions to address these consequences in sin contexts.[4]

1.2. *The Consequences of Sin in the Priestly Literature*

1.2.1. *Death*[5]

Death is the most frequently prescribed penalty for sin in the priestly literature.[6] As becomes evident in the following two sections, it is often synonymous with the *kareth* penalty and is a common gloss on the phrase 'to bear sin' (עָוֹן נָשָׂא). Whether, however, death occurs in these contexts, or whether it occurs on its own, it is most commonly described with the verb מוּת in either the hophal (i.e. the sinner 'will be put to death') or the qal (i.e. the sinner 'will die'). A closer examination of these occurrences reveals that

---

and pay in Jer. 22.13: 'Woe to him who builds his house by unrighteousness, and his upper rooms by injustice; who makes his neighbor serve him for nothing, and does not give him his *work* (וּפֹעֲלוֹ לֹא יִתֶּן־לוֹ) (בְּרֵעֵהוּ יַעֲבֹד חִנָּם וּפֹעֲלוֹ לֹא יִתֶּן־לוֹ) [i.e. his *pay*]'. In the same way, the relationship between sin and punishment is such that terms for one can be used in place of terms for the other.

3. For this understanding of אָשֵׁם, see §1.2.4 below, especially §1.2.4.4.

Other penalties are also mentioned in the priestly literature: for example, leprosy for Miriam when she rebels against Moses (Num. 12.10) and the prohibition on Moses from entering the Promised Land for his failure to treat the LORD as holy (Num. 20.10-12; note the possible allusion to intentional sin as described in Num. 15: 'Then Moses *lifted up his hand* [יָד + רוּם] and struck the rock' [Num. 20.11; cf. Num. 15.30]). The four considered in the present chapter, however, are by far the most common.

4. As noted below in §1.3, the first three consequences for sin (viz. death, *kareth*, and 'bearing one's sin' [עָוֹן נָשָׂא]) occur in the context of intentional sin, for which a כִּפֶּר-rite is ordinarily not prescribed (for the few exceptions see n. 46 below). It is nonetheless necessary to consider them in order to gain as complete a picture as possible of the priestly understanding of sin's consequences. Moreover, as also discussed in §1.3 below, it does not appear that in the priestly system the *potential* consequences of inadvertent sin differ from the consequences of intentional sin.

5. Distribution: Exod. 28.35, 43; 30.20-21; 31.14, 15; 32.25-28, 35; 35.2; Lev. 8.35; 10.1-2, 6-7, 9; 15.31; 16.2, 13; 20.2, 9, 10, 11, 12, 13, 14, 15, 16, 20, 27; 21.9; 22.9; 24.14, 16, 17, 21, 23; Num. 1.51; 3.10, 38; 4.15, 19, 20; 14.1-37; 15.32-36; 16.31-33, 35; 17.11-14 (16.46-49); 17.25 (10), 28 (13); 18.3, 7, 22, 32; 21.6; 25.1-9; 35.16-21, 30, 31.

6. Cf. n. 5 with nn. 13, 38, 47.

the choice of the hophal or the qal appears to be determined on the basis of who executes the penalty—that is, whether the penalty is executed by the covenant community or the LORD himself.[7]

When מות appears in the hophal,[8] it is used to describe the death of the sinner at the hands of the covenant community. This is evidenced by parallel expressions which detail that the covenant community is to perform the execution: 'One who blasphemes the name of the LORD *shall surely be put to death* (מוֹת יוּמָת); all the congregation *shall certainly stone that one*' (Lev. 24.16a); and, 'If there is a woman who approaches any animal to mate with it, *you shall kill* the woman and the animal; *they shall surely be put to death* (מוֹת יוּמָתוּ). Their bloodguiltiness is upon them' (Lev. 20.16).[9] The methods of execution mentioned in such instances include both stoning (Lev. 20.2, 27; 24.16, 23; Num. 15.35) and burning (Lev. 20.14; 21.9), though at other times the method is not identified (Lev. 20.9, 10, 11, 12, 13, 15, 16; 24.17, 21, etc.). What these instances do share in common, though, is that the brazen sinner is executed at the hands of the covenant community.

When מות is used in the qal, however, it describes the death of the individual at the hands of the LORD.[10] In this regard, it appears that the individual is slain by an immediate and miraculous judgment of the LORD. The best-known example is that of Nadab and Abihu in Lev. 10.1-2:

> Now Nadab and Abihu, the sons of Aaron, each took his censer, and put fire in it, and laid incense on it, and offered unholy fire before the LORD, such as he had not commanded them. And fire came forth from the presence of the LORD and devoured them, and they died (וַיָּמֻתוּ) before the LORD.[11]

---

7. A point also noted by Milgrom; see Jacob Milgrom, *Studies in Levitical Terminology: The Encroacher and the Levite, the Term 'Aboda* (Berkeley: University of California Press, 1970), pp. 5-8.

8. See Exod. 31.14, 15; 35.2; Lev. 19.20; 20.2, 9, 10, 11, 12, 13, 15, 16, 27; 24.16, 17, 21; 27.29; Num. 1.51; 3.10, 38; 15.35; 18.7; 35.16, 17, 18, 21, 31.

9. See also Lev. 20.2, 27; 24.16; Num. 15.35-36; 35.16-18 (cf. vv. 19, 21). In other instances it is not specified that the covenant community is to carry out the execution, though this can be safely implied from the preceding texts; see Exod. 31.14-15; 35.2 (cf. Num. 15.35-36); Lev. 20.9-16 (cf. 20.2, 27); 24.17, 21 (cf. 24.16); Num. 1.51; 3.10, 38; 18.7 (for these last four texts see Milgrom, *Studies in Levitical Terminology*, pp. 16-59; a summary can be found in his *Numbers* [JPS; New York: Jewish Publication Society of America, 1990], pp. 423-24).

10. See Exod. 28.35, 43; 30.20, 21; Lev. 8.35; 10.2, 6, 7, 9; 15.31; 16.2, 13; 22.9; Num. 4.15, 19, 20; 14.37; 17.25 (10), 28 (13); 18.3, 22, 32. A possible exception is Lev. 20.20 (cf. 20.10-13, 15-16).

11. Given that the LORD is the one who executes this penalty directly, it is not surprising that the majority of instances where this type of death occurs or is threatened appears in the context of the tabernacle. See comments further below.

Indeed, the majority of instances of מות in the qal appear in a similar context, namely, where inappropriate contact with sancta results in an immediate judgment by the LORD: 'But [the Kohathites] shall not go in to see the holy objects even for a moment, lest they die (וָמֵתוּ)' (Num. 4.20); 'Tell Aaron your brother not to come whenever he chooses into the holy place within the veil, before the mercy seat which is upon the ark, lest he die (וְלֹא יָמוּת); for I will appear in the cloud upon the mercy seat' (Lev. 16.2); 'And henceforth the people of Israel shall not come near the tent of meeting, lest they bear sin and die (לָשֵׂאת חֵטְא לָמוּת)' (Num. 18.22).[12] Other instances where the LORD judges directly, though not because of the direct profanation of sancta, include that of the rebellious spies who died by a plague before the LORD (Num. 14.37) and that of the people of Israel who blamed Moses and Aaron for the deaths of Korah and his followers and who also died by a plague before the LORD (Num. 17.6-15 [16.41-50]; cf. 17.25 [17.10] with 17.14 [16.49]).

In sum, מות is used to describe the execution of the brazen sinner, be it at the hands of the covenant community (hophal) or at the hands of the LORD directly (qal).

1.2.2. *Kareth*[13] (כרת)

A second penalty prescribed for sin is commonly referred to as the *kareth* penalty (from the Heb. כָּרַת), that is, the 'cutting off' of the sinner.[14] There are generally two points of debate concerning this penalty: (1) what the penalty consists of; and (2) who executes the penalty.

In modern scholarship, three main proposals have been proposed for the nature of the penalty:[15] excommunication from the covenant community,[16]

---

12. See also Exod. 28.43; 30.20-21; Lev. 8.35; 10.9; 15.31; 16.13; 22.9; Num. 18.3, 32. Comparable in this regard is Uzzah, who was immediately slain by the LORD for touching the ark (2 Sam. 6.6-7).

13. Distribution: Exod. 30.33, 38; 31.14; Lev. 7.20, 21, 25, 27; 17.4, 9, 10, 14; 18.29; 19.8; 20.3, 5, 6, 17, 18; 22.3; 23.29; Num. 9.13; 15.30, 31; 19.13, 20.

14. Various qualifiers follow the verb כָּרַת: 'cut off from their people' (Exod. 30.33, 38; Lev. 7.20, 21, 25, 27, etc.); 'cut off from among their people' (Lev. 17.4, 10; 20.3, 6, etc.); 'cut off in the sight of their people' (Lev. 20.17); 'cut off from before me' (Lev. 22.3); 'cut off from Israel' (Num. 19.13); and 'cut off from the midst of the assembly' (Num. 19.20). Leviticus 17.14 simply has 'cut off' (but see vv. 4, 9, 10 where the qualifier 'from [among] their people' is included), and Num. 4.18, referring to the Kohathites, has 'cut off from the Levites'.

15. For a discussion of *kareth* in earlier Jewish literature, see Milgrom, *Numbers*, p. 405, who lists five separate explanations.

16. Philip J. Budd, *Leviticus* (NCBC; Grand Rapids: Eerdmans, 1996), p. 122; René Péter-Contesse, *Lévitique 1–16* (Geneva: Labor et Fides, 1993), p. 119 (where he suggests that the phrase could have originally referred to death as well, but that now, at least in the priestly literature, this is no longer the case); John I. Durham, *Exodus* (WBC, 3;

(premature) death,[17] and extinction of the lineage.[18] A fourth proposal, suggested by a few scholars, is that *kareth* could also refer to punishment in the afterlife.[19] These will be considered in turn.

Support for understanding *kareth* as excommunication comes primarily from the fact that a person is said to be 'cut off *from their people*',[20] which is taken as a reference to excommunication from the covenant community. While this seems a plain enough meaning of the phrase 'to be cut off from one's people', it does not do justice to the various texts which link *kareth* with death.[21]

More support can be found for understanding *kareth* as referring to the premature death of the sinner, as evidenced from the conjunction of the two in several texts. Thus Exod. 31.14 reads, 'Therefore you are to observe the Sabbath, for it is holy to you. Everyone who profanes it *shall surely be put to death*; for whoever does any work on it, that person *shall be cut off* from among their people'. Similarly, Num. 4.18-20 states, 'Do not let the tribe of the families of the Kohathites *be cut off from* among the Levites. But do this to them that *they may live and not die* when they approach the most holy [objects]...they shall not go in to see the holy [objects] even for a moment, *lest they die*.' In this way the *kareth* penalty seems to be synonymous with death.

The third understanding of *kareth*, which is complementary to the second, is that it refers to the extinction of the sinner's name from the covenant community. This understanding of *kareth* is especially suggested from non-priestly literature. After sinning against David and then realizing that David would be king, Saul cries out to him, 'So now swear to me by the LORD that *you will not cut off* (אִם תַּכְרִית) my seed after me, and that *you will not destroy my name* from my father's household!' (1 Sam. 24.22 [21]). Similarly, Boaz states that he has married Ruth 'in order to raise up the name of the deceased on his inheritance, *so that the name* of the deceased *may not be cut off* (וְלֹא יִכָּרֵת) from his brothers or from the court of his [birth] place...'

Waco, TX: Word Books, 1987), p. 406; Martin Noth, *Exodus* (trans. J.S. Bowden; London: SCM Press, 1966), p. 238 (originally published as *Das zweite Buch Moses, Exodus* [Das Alte Testament Deutsch, 5; Göttingen: Vandenhoeck & Ruprecht, 1959]).

17. Gordon J. Wenham, *Leviticus* (NICOT, 3; London: Hodder & Stoughton, 1979), pp. 125, 242; J.R. Porter, *Leviticus* (CBC; Cambridge: Cambridge University Press, 1976), p. 139.

18. Donald J. Wold, 'The *kareth* Penalty in P: Rationale and Cases', *SBLSP* 1 (1979), pp. 1-45 (5-6) (followed by David P. Wright, *The Disposal of Impurity* [SBLDS, 101; Atlanta: Scholars Press, 1987], p. 164 n. 2); Milgrom, *Numbers*, pp. 406-407.

19. Wenham, *Leviticus*, p. 242; Milgrom, *Numbers*, p. 407. Milgrom (*Numbers*, p. 405) also points out that this view was anticipated by earlier exegetes.

20. See above, n. 14.

21. See next paragraph.

(Ruth 4.10).[22] Other texts describe various peoples or households being cut off and specify that all of the males are killed, which would naturally result in the extinction of that family name.[23] Support for this understanding, however, can also be found in the priestly literature. In Num. 4.18-20, cited above, we read that if the Kohathites approach the most holy objects, they would be 'cut off' from the tribe of Levi (Num. 4.18), that is, their branch of the tribe of Levi would be extinguished (through death, v. 19). Leviticus 20.20-21 may also be noted in this regard, where one of the penalties for illicit sexual relationships is that the couple will die childless, thus not allowing the line of the sinner to carry on.[24]

As noted above, this third understanding of *kareth* is actually complementary to the second (premature death). That is to say, the significance of the *kareth* penalty was not simply that the sinner would die prematurely, but further that the sinner's name might be cut off, a consequence abhorred by the ancient Israelites.[25]

A fourth possibility is that *kareth* could also refer to punishment in the afterlife. This might be suggested by Lev. 20.2-3a, where the text could be interpreted to read that there is a double penalty, namely, being stoned *and* being cut off: 'You shall also say to the Israelites, "Any man from the Israelites or from the aliens sojourning in Israel, who gives any of his offspring to Molech, shall surely be put to death; the people of the land shall stone him with stones. I will also set my face against that man and will cut him off from among his people..."'[26] In further support, Wenham notes:

> Death in the Old Testament is often referred to as sleeping with one's fathers (e.g., 1 K. 1.21) or being buried with the fathers (1 K. 14.31). It appears, therefore, that [the phrase 'cut off from one's people'] may not only refer to premature death at the hand of God, but hint at judgment in the life to come. Offenders will be cut off from their people forever.[27]

---

22. See also Pss. 37.28, 38; 109.13.

23. See 1 Kgs 11.16; 14.10; 21.21. Wold ('The *kareth* Penalty in P', p. 14) also suggests that the Achan incident (Josh. 7), in which he and his entire family are killed, is a narrative example of *kareth*.

24. Though *kareth* is not mentioned here, see the parallel laws (Lev. 18.14, 16) which are subsumed under the *kareth* penalty (18.29). Note further that 20.17-21 are one unit and that vv. 17 and 18 of this unit do specify the *kareth* penalty for an illicit sexual relationship.

25. The word 'might' acknowledges the fact that a person might already have progeny that could carry on their name.

26. So Wenham, *Leviticus*, p. 278; Milgrom, *Numbers*, pp. 407-408. But see n. 35 below.

27. Wenham, *Leviticus*, p. 242 (though Wenham holds that the premature death of the sinner is the primary meaning of *kareth*; see n. 17 above). Picking up on a different phrase, Milgrom (*Numbers*, p. 407) argues that the opposite idiom of *kareth*, that is,

This could be correct and would only underscore the severity of the *kareth* penalty. In most instances, however, the immediate reference seems to be the (premature) death of the sinner with the possible consequence of the extinction of the sinner's lineage within Israel.

It now remains to discuss who executed the penalty, that is, whether *kareth* was carried out by people or by God. Many commentators hold that *kareth* is executed by God himself.[28] There are three lines of support for this. Most obviously, there are several texts where the LORD himself states that he will execute *kareth*; for example, Lev. 20.6: 'As for the person who turns to mediums and to spiritists, to play the harlot after them, I will also set my face against that person and will cut that person off from among their people'.[29] Second, Wenham has noted that many of the sins punishable by *kareth* were 'secret sins', that is, they would have been known only to the offender and to the LORD (as in eating sacrificial meat while unclean; Lev. 7.20).[30] The threat of *kareth* in such a situation implies that God himself would execute the penalty, even if undiscovered by others. Finally, after classifying the various occurrences of *kareth* in the priestly texts, Milgrom concludes:

> All fall within the category of religious law not civil law; that is, they are deliberate sins against God not against man.[31] Given the cardinal postulate of the priestly legislation that sins against God are punishable by God—and not by man—it follows that the punishment of *kareth* is executed solely by the Deity.[32]

By way of clarification, it should be noted that the first two points support the fact that there are at least *some* instances where the LORD executes *kareth*, whereas the third point argues that *kareth* is *always* executed by him. The first two points require little defense: it is obvious from the first that there are instances where the LORD executes *kareth* and this finds further support in the second. The third point, however, requires some modification.

'being gathered to one's kin/fathers' (see Gen. 25.8, 17; 35.29; 49.33), suggests reunion with one's relations in the afterlife. The inference, then, is that being cut off from one's kin/fathers relates to the afterlife as well (Milgrom cites here B. Alfrink, 'L'expression *ne'esap 'el 'amayw*', *OTS* 5 [1948], pp. 115-28 [128]).

28. Levine, *Leviticus*, pp. 241-42; Milgrom, *Numbers*, pp. 405-408; *idem*, *Leviticus 1–16*, pp. 424, 457-60; Wold, 'The *kareth* Penalty in P', p. 24; Wenham, *Leviticus*, pp. 125, 241.

29. See also Lev. 17.10; 20.3, 5.

30. Wenham, *Leviticus*, p. 242.

31. Similarly, Wold classifies the *kareth* offenses as violations against sacred time or substance, failure to perform purification rituals, illicit worship, illicit sexual relations (said to 'pollute'), and blasphemy. See Wold, 'The *kareth* Penalty in P', pp. 3-24.

32. Milgrom, *Numbers*, p. 406.

1. *The Consequences of Sin*

Leaving aside for the moment the question of whether there is a strict distinction between civil and religious law in the priestly system, one can note instances where 'sins against God' are committed that the LORD does indeed punish by means of human agency. This seems to be the best explanation, for example, of Exod. 31.14, where the use of the hophal of מות indicates that the covenant community carries out the execution,[33] which is then in turn explicated by the *kareth* penalty: 'Therefore you are to observe the Sabbath, for it is holy to you. Everyone who profanes it shall surely be put to death (מוֹת יוּמָת); for (כִּי) whoever does any work on it, that person shall be cut off from among their people.' Milgrom explains this verse in the same way as Lev. 20.2-3, that is, this text is prescribing two penalties: death (at the hands of the covenant community) plus *kareth* (at the hands of God).[34] While this is possible, though not necessary, for Lev. 20.2-3,[35] it is unlikely here, for the presence of כִּי suggests an interpretation of the one by the other: *kareth* is carried out by capital punishment.

This understanding finds further confirmation in the well-known passage about the 'high-handed sin' in Numbers 15. Verses 27-31 of this chapter describe two types of sin: unintentional sin, which may be forgiven by means of sacrifice (vv. 27-29), and intentional ('with a high hand') sin, which results in the person being cut off:

> But the person who does anything with a high hand, whether a native or a sojourner, reviles the LORD, and that person shall be cut off (וְנִכְרְתָה הַנֶּפֶשׁ הַהִוא) from among their people. Because of having despised the word of the LORD, and broken his commandment, that person shall be utterly cut off (הִכָּרֵת תִּכָּרֵת הַנֶּפֶשׁ הַהִוא); their iniquity shall be upon them. (vv. 30-31)

Significantly, this passage is immediately followed by a case in which a man is found gathering sticks on the Sabbath (v. 32). When it is inquired what is to be done with the man, the LORD responds, 'The man shall be put to death (מוֹת יוּמַת הָאִישׁ); all the congregation shall stone him with stones outside the camp' (v. 35). Occurring immediately after the prescription of the *kareth* penalty for high-handed sin, v. 35 provides a narrative illustration of someone suffering *kareth* for such sin, namely, being stoned to death by the covenant community.

---

33. See §1.2.1 above.
34. Milgrom, *Numbers*, pp. 407-408.
35. It is also possible that Lev. 20.3 is an explication of 20.2; thus: 'Any man of the people of Israel, or of the strangers that sojourn in Israel, who gives any of this children to Molech shall be put to death; the people of the land shall stone him with stones. Thus I myself will set my face against that man (וַאֲנִי אֶתֵּן אֶת־פָּנַי בָּאִישׁ הַהוּא), and will cut him off from among his people…'

Thus, while the LORD could (and did) carry out the *kareth* penalty by himself, he also used his people to implement the *kareth* penalty on those that were apostate.

When confronted with the *kareth* penalty, then, the sinner would expect to die prematurely—either by the LORD directly or at the hands of the covenant community—with the possible result of their line being extinguished from the people of Israel.

1.2.3. *To Bear Sin* (נָשָׂא עָוֹן)

The phrase נָשָׂא עָוֹן occurs in three distinct contexts.[36] In the first context, the sinner is the subject of the verb; in the second context, the one wronged—be it the LORD himself or a human—is the subject of the verb; and in the third context, a third party—neither the sinner nor the one wronged—is the subject of the verb. It is the first of these that is relevant to the present discussion and to which we now turn.[37]

1.2.3.1. *Sinner as subject*.

Most frequently it is the sinner who is the subject of the phrase נָשָׂא עָוֹן.[38] In these instances, different offenses are listed and the one who commits them is said to 'bear their sin': 'You shall not uncover the nakedness of your mother's sister or of your father's sister, for that is to make naked one's near kin; they shall bear their sin (עֲוֹנָם יִשָּׂאוּ)' (Lev. 20.19).

A survey of the verses using this phrase strongly suggests that it is a general statement of punishment, that is, the guilty party would face some sort of punishment for their sin. This is demonstrated by the fact that the phrase is frequently explicated by a more particular punishment that the sinner was to face:

---

36. נָשָׂא is actually conjoined with various terms for sin. In the first context of the phrase, נָשָׂא is conjoined with either עָוֹן or חֵטְא (see n. 38 below), in the second context with עָוֹן, חַטָּאת, חֲטָאָה, and פֶּשַׁע (see n. 28 below in §3.1.2.1), and in the third context solely with עָוֹן (see §3.1.2.2 below, though cf. Lev. 16.21 [where Aaron confesses sin (עָוֹן), rebellion (פֶּשַׁע), and transgression (חַטָּאת)] with 16.22 [where the goat bears away the sin (עָוֹן)]). For the sake of simplicity, the phrase נָשָׂא עָוֹן is referred to in the above, since this is common to all three contexts.

37. We return to the second and third contexts below in §3.1.2.

38. In this first usage, נָשָׂא is conjoined with either עָוֹן (Exod. 28.43; Lev. 5.1, 17; 7.19; 17.16; 19.8; 20.17, 19; 22.16; Num. 5.31; 14.34; 18.1 [× 2], 23 [for these two verses see §3.1.2 n. 27]; 30.16 [15]) or חֵטְא (Lev. 19.17; 20.20; 22.9; 24.15; Num. 9.13; 18.22, 32); it is difficult in these contexts to detect any difference in meaning between these two terms for sin. See especially the laws concerning sexual immorality in Lev. 20.17, 19, 20: two of these laws use נָשָׂא עָוֹן (vv. 17, 18) whereas the other uses נָשָׂא חֵטְא (v. 20), with no apparent distinction in meaning. Cf. also Lev. 22.9 (נָשָׂא חֵטְא) with 22.16 (נָשָׂא עָוֹן), and Num. 18.22 (נָשָׂא חֵטְא) with 18.23 (נָשָׂא עָוֹן). For verses outside the priestly literature that have the sinner as the subject of the phrase see Gen. 4.13; Isa. 53.12; Ezek. 14.10; 18.19-20; 23.49; 44.10, 12.

1. *The Consequences of Sin*

> And you shall make for [Aaron and his sons] linen breeches to cover their naked flesh…and they shall be upon Aaron, and upon his sons, when they go into the tent of meeting, or when they come near the altar to minister in the holy place; lest they *bear sin* and *die* (וְלֹא־יִשְׂאוּ עָוֹן וָמֵתוּ)… (Exod. 28.42-43a)

> If [the peace offering] is eaten at all on the third day, it is an abomination… and every one who eats it shall *bear their iniquity* (עֲוֹנוֹ יִשָּׂא)…and that person *shall be cut off* (וְנִכְרְתָה הַנֶּפֶשׁ הַהִוא) from their people. (Lev. 19.7-8)

> If a man lies with his uncle's wife, he has uncovered his uncle's nakedness; they shall *bear their sin* (חֶטְאָם יִשָּׂאוּ), *they shall die childless* (עֲרִירִים יָמֻתוּ). (Lev. 20.20)

> Bring out of the camp him who cursed; and let all who heard him lay their hands upon his head, and let all the congregation *stone him* (וְרָגְמוּ אֹתוֹ). And say to the people of Israel, Whoever curses their God shall *bear their sin* (וְנָשָׂא חֶטְאוֹ). (Lev. 24.14-15)

> But the person who is clean and is not on a journey, yet refrains from keeping the Passover, that person *shall be cut off* from their people (וְנִכְרְתָה הַנֶּפֶשׁ הַהִוא מֵעַמֶּיהָ), because they did not offer the LORD's offering at its appointed time; that person shall *bear their sin* (חֶטְאוֹ יִשָּׂא הָאִישׁ הַהוּא). (Num. 9.13)[39]

As summarized by Brichto, then, 'The expression *wenāśā' 'ăwōnō/ḥeṭ'ō* again and again refers to an indeterminate penalty/ punishment implemented by people or God'.[40]

This understanding of the phrase is not at all surprising given that terms for sin are often used as a metonymy for the punishment that results from them. Thus:

> And if the family of Egypt do not go up and present themselves, then upon them shall come the plague with which the LORD afflicts the nations that do not go up to keep the feast of booths. This shall be the punishment (חַטַּאת) to Egypt and the punishment (וְחַטַּאת) to all the nations that do not go up to keep the feast of booths. (Zech. 14.18-19)

> When morning dawned, the angels urged Lot, saying, 'Arise, take your wife and your two daughters who are here, lest you be consumed in the punishment (בַּעֲוֹן) of the city'. (Gen. 19.15)

> The woman said to him, 'Surely you know what Saul has done, how he has cut off the mediums and the wizards from the land. Why then are you laying a snare for my life to bring about my death?' But Saul swore to her by the LORD, 'As the LORD lives, no punishment (עָוֹן) shall come upon you for this thing'. (1 Sam. 28.9-10)

---

39. See also Lev. 7.18; 17.16; 19.17; 20.17, 19; 22.9, 16; Num. 5.31; 14.34; 18.1, 22, 23, 32; 30.16 (15).
40. Brichto, 'On Slaughter and Sacrifice', p. 24 n. 11. See also n. 43 below.

22   *Sin, Impurity, Sacrifice, Atonement*

As other commentators have noted, then, the connection between sin and punishment in the Bible is so strong that the writers often use terms for sin when referring to the punishment that the sin warrants.[41]

In short, נָשָׂא עָוֹן in these contexts is a general verdict, a way of saying that a person will suffer the consequences of their sin, whatever those consequences might be.[42] As with the first two penalties for sin, this judgment is

---

41. So Milgrom (*Leviticus 1–16*, p. 339): 'It has long been recognized that the biblical terms for good and bad behavior also connote their respective reward and punishment... Thus *ḥēṭ'* (Num. 32.33 [*sic*; read 32.23]; Isa. 53.12; Zech. 14.18-19; Prov. 10.16; Lam. 3.39; 4.6); *pešaʻ* (Isa. 24.20; Ps. 39.9); *ʻāwōn* (Gen. 4.13; 1 Sam. 25.24); *rāʻâ* (Jer. 4.18; 18.8, 11; Lam. 3.38), *inter alia*, stand not only for evil, but for its inherent punishment.'

See also the commentators listed in n. 43. For ancients who recognized this, see Ibn Ezra on Gen. 4.13 (Milgrom, *Leviticus 1–16*, p. 339). For a further discussion of medieval authorities, see Baruch J. Schwartz, '"Term" or Metaphor: Biblical נשׂא עון/פשע/חטא', *Tarbiz* 63 (1994), pp. 149-71 (Hebrew). Other modern scholars that have the same understanding are cited by Milgrom (*Leviticus 1–16*, p. 339): Walther Zimmerli, 'Die Eigenart des prophetischen Rede des Ezechiel', *ZAW* 66 (1954), pp. 1-26 (9-19); Klaus Koch, *Die Priesterschrift von Exodus 25 bis Leviticus 16. Eine überlieferungs-geschichtliche und literarische Untersuchung* (FRLANT, 71; Göttingen: Vandenhoeck & Ruprecht, 1959); Gerhard von Rad, *Old Testament Theology* (2 vols.; trans. D.M.G. Stalker; New York: Harper & Row, 1962–65), I, pp. 262-72. See also the references in Baruch J. Schwartz, 'The Bearing of Sin in the Priestly Literature', in D.P. Wright, D.N. Freedman, and A. Hurvitz (eds.), *Pomegranates and Golden Bells: Studies in Biblical, Jewish and Near Eastern Ritual, Law and Literature in Honor of Jacob Milgrom* (Winona Lake, IN: Eisenbrauns, 1995), pp. 3-21 (8 n. 18), and the seminal work of K.Hj. Fahlgren, 'Die Gegensätze von *ṣĕdāqā* im Alten Testament', in Klaus Koch (ed.), *Um das Prinzip der Vergeltung in Religion und Recht des Alten Testaments* (repr., Darmstadt: Wissenschaftliche Buchgesellschaft, 1972 [1932]), pp. 87-129 (104, 111, 113). See also my discussion of אשׁם below, especially §1.2.4.4.

One may further note that this is not unique to the Old Testament, but is also attested in Akkadian literature. Thus Janowski (*Sühne*, p. 36) notes that various Akkadian terms for sin, such as *arnu*, *ḫīṭu/ḫiṭītu* and *šē/īrtu*, refer to both sin and its penalty (see Janowski, *Sühne*, p. 36 n. 39 for further bibliography, as well as references in Milgrom, *Leviticus 1–16*, p. 339).

42. The strongest voice of dissent for this understanding of נָשָׂא עָוֹן is that of Baruch Schwartz, who argues that when the sinner is the subject of the phrase, it 'is a metaphor for the sinner's unrelieved *guilt*. It is at most an oblique way of saying that the sinner deserves punishment; *it is never indicative of punishment per se*' (Schwartz, 'Bearing of Sin', p. 9 [emphasis added]). In support, Schwartz surveys all of the occurrences of the phrase in the priestly literature and adduces six arguments in support of his thesis, the first two of which are the strongest: (1) sometimes 'the offense is to be punished by death by human agency', while at other times it is by divine agency or *kareth*, while other instances 'imply no punishment at all' (e.g. Lev. 5.1, 17). 'The fact that all of these alike are said to "bear their sin" means that the phrase is a metaphor for what they have in common: being guilty. They may or may not suffer punishment' (Schwartz, 'Bearing of

1. *The Consequences of Sin*

carried out either by the LORD directly (e.g. Exod. 28.42-43a [מות in qal]) or the covenant community on his behalf (e.g. Lev. 24.14-15). A translation such as 'to bear punishment' is thus an accurate representation of the usage of this phrase here.[43]

Sin', pp. 12-13). (2) 'If "bearing sin" and punishment were coextensive, we should expect one or the other but not both to be mentioned in a single context. The fact that this is not the case is an indication that the penalty and the sin-bearing are two separate phenomena: the sin-bearing is the culpability before God; the penalty may or may not follow' (Schwartz, 'Bearing of Sin', p. 13).

In response to his first point it may be noted that Schwartz has overstated the case by saying that some texts 'imply no punishment at all'. At most, it may be said that some texts *mention* no punishment at all (e.g. Lev. 19.17). However, given that the phrase נָשָׂא עָוֹן is frequently followed by a statement of punishment (see n. 39 above and attendant discussion; Schwartz himself ['Bearing of Sin', pp. 12-13] holds that seventeen of the twenty cases he mentions either state or imply punishment), it is more natural to assume that this phrase would have implied punishment to an ancient Israelite, even if none were mentioned. In particular, one may note that while texts such as Lev. 20.19 do not mention any specific punishment, 20.17 and 20.20—which discuss similar sins (sexual immorality in all three cases)—have both נָשָׂא עָוֹן/חֵטְא and a more specific punishment (cf. also Lev. 7.18 with 19.8). This naturally suggests that a punishment is assumed in 20.19 as well (which Schwartz himself recognizes; Schwartz, 'Bearing of Sin', p. 12 n. 35), and it would be erroneous to conclude that texts such as 5.1 'imply no punishment' simply because one is not specified (see also n. 105 in this regard). All of these observations put the burden of proof upon those who deny that any punishment is in view in those instances where it is not mentioned.

Moreover, both of these points may be responded to with reference to the above argument that the phrase נָשָׂא עָוֹן is a *general* statement that the sinner will be punished, which is then explicated by a more *specific* penalty (e.g. *kareth*, death). This invalidates the assumption of his first point, namely, that because different penalties are mentioned in these contexts the only thing they can have in common is being guilty. Rather, it is equally the case that all have punishment in common (נָשָׂא עָוֹן), though this can manifest itself in different ways (e.g. *kareth*, death, sacrifice). With reference to his second point, it may be noted that it is in fact because נָשָׂא עָוֹן is a more general expression of punishment that some specification is expected to follow, that is, both נָשָׂא עָוֹן and a more specific punishment are expected in the same context. For a fuller response to Schwartz see Jacob Milgrom, *Leviticus 17–22* (AB, 3A; New York: Doubleday, 2000), pp. 1488-90.

43. Cf. Baruch A. Levine (*Numbers 1–20* [AB, 4a; New York: Doubleday, 1993], p. 294) on Num. 9.13: 'That person must bear the punishment for his offense'; Milgrom (*Leviticus 1–16*, p. 292) on Lev. 5.1: '...then he must bear his punishment'; August Dillmann (*Die Bücher Exodus und Leviticus* [Leipzig: F. Hirzel, 3rd edn, 1880], p. 428) on Lev. 5.1: 'Vielmehr נָשָׂא עֲוֹנוֹ oder נָשָׂא חֶטְאוֹ meint...: in der Sünde auch ihre Folgen d. h. Schuld und Strafe auf sich nehmen (Gen. 4.13; Lev. 7.18; 17.16; 19.8, 17)...' See also NRSV on Lev. 5.1, 17, and NASV on 5.17. Even those who stick with a more literal rendering (e.g. 'he will bear his sin') note that the consequences of the sin are also in view. See Wenham, *Leviticus*, p. 100; Péter-Contesse, *Lévitique 1–16*, p. 86; Philip. J.

1.2.4. *To Suffer Guilt's Consequences* (אָשֵׁם)[44]

The fourth result of sin to consider is that expressed in the priestly literature by the verb אָשֵׁם. This verb is especially significant for the present study insofar as it occurs in contexts where atonement (כִּפֶּר) for sin also occurs; for example, the inadvertent sins of Leviticus 4 and 5. For this reason we will consider אָשֵׁם in some detail.

Leviticus 4 and 5 are the two chapters which deal the most extensively with the occasions requiring a purification (חַטָּאת) or guilt (אָשָׁם) offering. In the majority of instances, the sins described here are inadvertent (שָׁגַג/שְׁגָנָה)[45] and are in some way hidden from (וְנֶעְלַם מִמֶּנּוּ) or otherwise unknown to (וְלֹא יָדַע) the sinner.[46] This of course leads to the question: How can an offering be brought for a sin that is hidden from—or otherwise unknown to—the sinner? It is argued in this section that the answer to this question lies in the verb אָשֵׁם.

There are thirteen occurrences of this verb in the priestly literature, eleven of which are found in Leviticus 4 and 5, and another two in Numbers 5.[47]

Budd, *Numbers* (WBC, 5; Waco, TX: Word Books, 1984), p. 65; Knierim, *Hauptbegriffe*, pp. 52, 221.

Milgrom (*Leviticus 1–16*, p. 295) has further argued that this phrase 'always implies that the punishment will be meted out by God, not by man', though this falters at Lev. 24.14-15: 'Bring out of the camp him who cursed; and let all who heard him lay their hands upon his head, and let all the congregation *stone him* (וְרָגְמוּ אֹתוֹ). And say to the people of Israel, Whoever curses their God shall *bear their sin* (וְנָשְׂאוּ חֶטְאוֹ)' (to this Baruch Schwartz ['Bearing of Sin', p. 12 n. 35] adds Lev. 20.17, 19, 20, arguing that 'the presence of the death penalty in Lev. 20.9-16 must mean that it is to be inferred in vv. 17-21').

44. Though the forms אָשֵׁם and אָשָׁם are both attested, the secondary literature has tended to refer simply to אָשָׁם, and this convention is adopted in the following discussion.

45. See Lev. 4.2 (heading up all of Lev. 4; see also 4.13, 22, 27); 5.15, 18.

46. See Lev. 4.13-14 (cf. vv. 23, 28, where the sin must be made known to the sinner); 5.2-4, 17-18. Possible exceptions here include Lev. 5.1, 20-26 (6.1-7) (cf. Num. 5.5-8), and Lev. 19.20-22, which would appear to be intentional sins that are nonetheless expiable after confession (5.5, 26 [6.7]; 19.22). There is some question as to how these sins relate to Num. 15.30-31. Jacob Milgrom (*Cult and Conscience: The ASHAM and the Priestly Doctrine of Repentance* [SJLA, 18; Leiden: E.J. Brill, 1976], pp. 109-10) suggests that this passage is barring sacrificial atonement 'to the *unrepentant* sinner', and that the phrase 'with a high hand' is a literary image that describes 'the brazen sinner who commits his acts in open defiance of the LORD (cf. Job 38.15). The essence of this sin is that it is committed flauntingly' (Milgrom, *Numbers*, p. 12).

47. See Lev. 4.13, 22, 27; 5.2, 3, 4, 5, 17, 19 (× 2), 23 (6.4); Num. 5.6, 7. To these thirteen can be added the occurrences of the form אַשְׁמָה (Lev. 4.3; 5.24, 26 [6.5, 7]; see also 22.16). There is some debate on the form this word represents. An infinitival form is favored by GKC 45d; Milgrom, *Leviticus 1–16*, pp. 231, 338; and Rolf Rendtorff, *Leviticus* (BKAT, 3; 3 vols.; Neukirchen–Vluyn: Neukirchener Verlag, 1990), II, p. 152. Paul Joüon ('Notes de lexicographie hébraïque', *Bib* 19 [1938], pp. 454-59 [457]) takes it

The translations that have been proposed for אָשֵׁם within the priestly literature fall into four categories: (1) 'to be/become guilty', 'to incur guilt', 'to be/become liable for guilt'; (2) 'to feel guilt'; (3) 'to realize guilt'; and (4) 'to suffer guilt's consequences'. The merits and shortcomings of each will be considered in turn.

1.2.4.1. *'To be/become guilty', 'to incur guilt', 'to be/become liable for guilt'*. Traditionally, the verb אָשֵׁם has been understood as an objective statement of guilt, that is, 'to be/become guilty'[48] or 'to incur guilt'.[49] The RSV rendering of Lev. 4.22 serves as an example: 'When a ruler sins, doing unwittingly any one of all the things which the LORD his God has commanded not to be done, and is guilty (וְאָשֵׁם)…'[50] This rendering of אָשֵׁם does find support outside of the priestly literature, for example, Ezek. 22.4a, where 'being/becoming guilty' is parallel to 'being/becoming defiled': 'You have become guilty (אָשַׁמְתְּ) by the blood that you have shed, and defiled (טָמֵאת) by the idols that you have made'.[51]

as a nominal form with a verbal idea: '…le substantif אַשְׁמָה…est proprement le *nomen actionis*'. And W&O (36.1.1d) note, 'All CVCCâ infinitives can be identified as independent nouns rather than infinitives, and the dictionaries vary on this point…' In either case, it is usually translated verbally. Of the occurrences of אַשְׁמָה, 4.3 is discussed below (see especially §1.2.4.4) as is 5.26 (6.7) (see n. 99). 5.24 (6.5) could be using אַשְׁמָה to refer to the presentation of a guilt offering (so RSV, NASV, NIV), though it is equally possible to translate it with one of the renderings for אָשֵׁם proposed below, for example, 'on the day/when he suffers guilt's consequences' (see also Milgrom, *Leviticus 1–16*, pp. 319, 338; René Péter-Contesse and John Ellington, *A Handbook on Leviticus* [New York: United Bible Societies, 1992], pp. 77-78). אַשְׁמָה in the phrase עֲוֹן אַשְׁמָה in 22.16 is difficult, as indicated by the differences among translations: 'punishment for guilt' (NASV); 'iniquity and guilt' (RSV); 'guilt requiring payment' (NIV); 'the penalty of reparation' or 'the penalty of punishment' (Milgrom, *Leviticus 17–22*, pp. 1844, 1869; Milgrom favors the former); 'guilt requiring reparation' (John E. Hartley, *Leviticus* [WBC, 4; Waco, TX: Word Books, 1992], pp. 352-53). A consequential rendering ('the penalty of bearing sin's consequences') would be in keeping with the use of אַשְׁמָה in 4.3, namely, the priest causing the people to bear sin's consequences (on 4.3 see n. 95 below and the attendant discussion). While certainty on the translation of אַשְׁמָה is difficult in 22.16, it is possible to take אַשְׁמָה here in any of the senses identified immediately above without affecting the overall argument of this chapter.

48. AV; RSV; Joüon, 'Notes', p. 455; Péter-Contesse, *Lévitique 1–16*, p. 71 (Péter-Contesse later states that 'to feel guilty' is possible in some instances [pp. 96, 98]).

49. Levine, *Leviticus*, pp. 22-23.

50. Within this same category may be placed those renderings that include the idea of being guilty and also emphasize the fact that guilty deeds have consequences, for example, 'to be/become liable for guilt' (Janowski, *Sühne*, pp. 256-57; Rolf P. Knierim, 'אָשֵׁם', in *THAT*, I, pp. 251-57 [255]), or 'to be held responsible (for sin)' (van der Toorn, *Sin and Sanction*, p. 92 [on Lev. 5.2]).

51. See also Ezek. 25.12.

Table 1. *Various Approaches to the Verb* אָשֵׁם

Leviticus 4.3	
	אִם הַכֹּהֵן הַמָּשִׁיחַ יֶחֱטָא לְאַשְׁמַת הָעָם
'to be/become guilty'[52]	'…if it is the anointed priest who sins, thus bringing guilt on the people…'
'to realize guilt'[53]	'If it is the anointed priest who has incurred guilt, so that blame falls upon the people…'
'to feel guilt'[54]	'If it is the anointed priest who so does wrong to the detriment of the people…'
'to suffer guilt's consequences'[55]	'If it is the anointed priest who sins so that the people suffer guilt's consequences…'[56]

52. RSV's translation.
53. Though Kiuchi provides the most substantial argument in favor of this rendering (see §1.2.4.2 below) he does not provide a translation of many of the relevant verses. For this reason, the verses cited above are those of the JPSV, which also renders אָשֵׁם with 'to realize guilt'.
54. Milgrom, *Leviticus 1–16*, pp. 226-27. See §1.2.4.3 below.
55. Author's translations.
56. אַשְׁמַת could also be taken as an objective genitive (see translations). In this instance the translation would be: 'If it is the anointed priest who sins so that guilt's consequences fall upon the people…' Whether subjective or objective genitive, though, the end point is the same: the people suffer the consequences of guilt that arise from the sin of the high priest. For the relationship between the sin of the high priest and the suffering of the people see n. 95 below and the attendant discussion.

	Leviticus 4.13-14a
	וְאִם כָּל־עֲדַת יִשְׂרָאֵל יִשְׁגּוּ וְנֶעְלַם דָּבָר מֵעֵינֵי הַקָּהָל וְעָשׂוּ אַחַת מִכָּל־מִצְוֹת יְהוָה אֲשֶׁר לֹא־תֵעָשֶׂינָה וְאָשֵׁמוּ׃ (14) וְנוֹדְעָה הַחַטָּאת אֲשֶׁר חָטְאוּ עָלֶיהָ...
'to be/become guilty'	'If the whole congregation of Israel commits a sin unwittingly and the thing is hidden from the eyes of the assembly, and they do any one of the things which the LORD has commanded not to be done and are guilty; (14) when the sin which they have committed becomes known…'[57]
'to realize guilt'	'If it is the whole community of Israel that has erred and the matter escapes the notice of the congregation, so that they do any of the things which by the LORD'S commandments ought not to be done, and they realize their guilt—(14) when the sin through which they incurred guilt becomes known…'[58]
'to feel guilt'	'If it is the whole community of Israel that has erred inadvertently and the matter escapes the notice of the congregation, so that they violate one of the LORD'S prohibitive commandments, and they feel guilt (14) when the wrong that they committed in regard to it becomes known…'[59]
'to suffer guilt's consequences'	'If the whole congregation of Israel inadvertently sins and the matter is hidden from the eyes of the assembly, and they do one from among any of the LORD'S commands which are not to be done and they suffer guilt's consequences—(14) when the sin which they sinned in this regard becomes known…'[60]

57. See n. 59.
58. See n. 59.
59. For ו as 'when', see Milgrom, *Leviticus 1–16*, p. 243 (Milgrom cites Gen. 42.30 [sic; read 47.30] and Exod. 22.4 as other examples).
60. See n. 59. For a plausible explanation of the shift from ו in v. 14 to אוֹ in vv. 23 and 28, as well as the shift from the niphal of יָדַע (v. 14) to the hiphil (vv. 23, 28), see Milgrom, *Leviticus 1–16*, pp. 243-44. Alternately, the ו may be translated as 'or'. Thus Bernard M. Levinson ('The Case for Revision and Interpolation', in idem [ed.], *Theory and Method in Biblical and Cuneiform Law: Revision, Interpolation and Development* [JSOTSup, 181; Sheffield: Sheffield Academic Press, 1994], pp. 37-59 [46-47]) notes, 'In many instances in biblical law, or in quasi-legal authoritative pronouncements, *waw* functions to introduce alternatives ("either A or B") into a protasis or an apodosis', for example, 'You shall not see your countryman's ox or his sheep straying away, and pay no attention to them; you shall certainly bring them back to your countryman. (2) And if your countryman is not near you, *or* if you do not know him (וְאִם־לֹא קָרוֹב אָחִיךָ אֵלֶיךָ וְלֹא יְדַעְתּוֹ)…' (Deut. 22.1-2a) (see also Exod. 12.5; 20.4; 22.9a; Lev. 2.4b; Deut. 13.3 [2]). Thus with the fourth translation above: '…and they suffer for their guilt (14) or the sin which they sinned is made known…' This would have the advantage of maintaining consistency with the אוֹ of the following verses, though it would not be as apparent why a ו was used instead of אוֹ (for which again see Milgrom, *Leviticus 1–16*, pp. 243-44).

Leviticus 4.22-23a

	‏אֲשֶׁ֨ר נָשִׂ֜יא יֶחֱטָ֗א וְעָשָׂ֨ה אַחַ֜ת מִכׇּל־מִצְוֺ֞ת יְהֹוָ֧ה אֱלֹהָ֛יו אֲשֶׁ֥ר לֹא־תֵעָשֶׂ֖ינָה בִּשְׁגָגָ֑ה וְאָשֵֽׁם׃ (23) א֚וֹ־הוֹדַ֣ע אֵלָ֔יו חַטָּאת֖וֹ אֲשֶׁ֣ר חָטָ֣א בָּ֑הּ...
'to be/become guilty'	'When a ruler sins, doing unwittingly any one of all the things which the LORD his God has commanded not to be done, and is guilty, (23) if the sin which he has committed is made known to him…'
'to realize guilt'	'In case it is a chieftain who incurs guilt by doing unwittingly any of the things which by the commandment of the LORD his God ought not to be done, and he realizes his guilt—(23) or the sin of which he is guilty is brought to his knowledge…'
'to feel guilt'	'When the chieftain does wrong by violating any of the LORD'S prohibitive commandments inadvertently, and he feels guilt (23) or he is informed of the wrong he committed…'
'to suffer guilt's consequences'	'If a ruler sins and inadvertently does one from among any of the commands of the LORD his God which should not be done and suffers guilt's consequences (23) or his sin which he sinned in this regard is made known to him…'

Leviticus 4.27-28a

	‏וְאִם־נֶ֧פֶשׁ אַחַ֛ת תֶּחֱטָ֥א בִשְׁגָגָ֖ה מֵעַ֣ם הָאָ֑רֶץ בַּ֠עֲשֹׂתָ֠הּ אַחַ֨ת מִמִּצְוֺ֧ת יְהֹוָ֛ה אֲשֶׁ֥ר לֹא־תֵעָשֶׂ֖ינָה וְאָשֵֽׁם׃ (28) א֚וֹ הוֹדַ֣ע אֵלָ֔יו חַטָּאת֖וֹ אֲשֶׁ֣ר חָטָ֑א...
'to be/become guilty'	'If any one of the common people sins unwittingly in doing any one of the things which the LORD has commanded not to be done, and is guilty, (28) when the sin which he has committed is made known to him…'
'to realize guilt'	'If any person from among the populace unwittingly incurs guilt by doing any of the things which by the LORD'S commandments ought not to be done, and he realizes his guilt—(28) or the sin of which he is guilty is brought to his knowledge…'
'to feel guilt'	'If any person from among the populace does wrong inadvertently by violating any of the LORD'S prohibitive commandments and he feels guilt (28) or he is informed of the wrong he committed…'
'to suffer guilt's consequences'	'If any person from the populace sins inadvertently by doing any of the LORD'S commands which are not to be done and suffers guilt's consequences (28) or his sin which he sinned is made known to him…'

Leviticus 5.21-23aα (6.2-4aα)	
	... כִּי־תֶחֱטָא וּמָעֲלָה מַעַל בַּיהוָה וְכִחֵשׁ בַּעֲמִיתוֹ ... (23) אֲשֶׁר גָּזָל ...
'to be/become guilty'	'If any one sins and commits a breach of faith against the LORD by deceiving his neighbor in a matter of deposit or security, or through robbery, or if he has oppressed his neighbor (22) or has found what was lost and lied about it, swearing falsely—in any of all the things which men do and sin therein, (23) when one has sinned and become guilty, he shall restore what he took by robbery...'
'to realize guilt'	'When a person sins and commits a trespass against the LORD by dealing deceitfully with his fellow in the matter of a deposit or pledge, or through robbery, or by defrauding his fellow, (22) or by finding something lost and lying about it; if he swears falsely regarding any one of the various things that one may do and sin thereby—(23) when one has thus sinned and, realizing his guilt, would restore that which he got through robbery...'
'to feel guilt'	'When a person sins by committing a sacrilege against the LORD in that he has dissembled to his fellow in the matter of a deposit or investment or robbery; or having withheld from his fellow (22) or having found a lost object he has dissembled about it; and he swears falsely about any one of the things that a person may do and sin thereby—(23) when one has thus sinned and, feeling guilt, he shall return that which he robbed...'
'to suffer guilt's consequences'	'When a person sins and acts unfaithfully against the LORD, and deceives his companion in regard to a deposit or a security entrusted to him, or through robbery, or if he has extorted from his companion, (22) or has found what was lost and lied about it and sworn falsely regarding any one of the things a person may do and sin thereby; (23) and it will be, when he sins and suffers the consequences of guilt, that he shall restore what he took by robbery...'

While this translation is certainly a possibility for אָשֵׁם, it does run into difficulty in the context of Leviticus 4 and 5.[61] This manifests itself in two ways.

First, the traditional translation 'to be/become guilty' runs into difficulties in Leviticus 4, particularly in the transitions between vv. 13-14 and 2-23, as well as in the translation of אָשֵׁם in Lev. 5.23 (6.4). For ease of reference, the relevant verses from chs. 4 and 5 and their proposed renderings have been tabulated (see preceding pages).[62]

As can be noted above, there is a difference in the transition between vv. 13 and 14, vv. 22 and 23, and vv. 27 and 28, insofar as v. 14 begins with a ו while vv. 23 and 28 begin with אוֹ. It is at this juncture that the traditional rendering, 'to be/become guilty', runs into the most difficulties. The natural rendering of 'or' for אוֹ in vv. 23 and 28, adopted by all of the other translations above, is not possible for the traditional rendering of אָשֵׁם. This is because the sin is hidden from the sinner; as a result it would make no sense to say that 'if anyone sins, and is guilty *or* is told what their sin is, *then* he or she shall bring an offering', for in the first instance the sinner is not aware of their sin and would thus not even know to bring a sacrifice.[63] Thus a different rendering of the אוֹ is required. The RSV, however, fumbles at this point. Not only does it propose two different translations for the אוֹ in vv. 23 and 28 (even though the construction and context of the verses are exactly the same), neither of its proposals are likely renderings of the particle אוֹ ('if' [v. 23] and 'when' [v. 28]).[64]

---

61. Exceptions are Lev. 5.19 and, in Numbers, Num. 5.7, where אָשֵׁם is followed by לְ plus a personal object. In these instances a rendering such as 'to incur liability to' is justified. So Milgrom (*Leviticus 1–16*, p. 339), who comments, 'When [the verb *'āšām*] is followed by *l* and a personal object it means "to incur liability to" someone for reparation...' Thus Lev. 5.19 is translated: 'It is a reparation offering, he has incurred liability to the LORD' (Milgrom, *Leviticus 1–16*, p. 319; see also Péter-Contesse [*Lévitique 1–16*, p. 92], '...l'homme était effectivement coupable envers YHWH', and Rendtorff [*Leviticus*, II, p. 141], 'Er hat gegenüber Jhwh Schuld auf sich geladen'). This rendering is not only contextually appropriate, it also finds further support in the similar construction in 2 Chron. 19.10a.

62. This table does not contain every instance of אָשֵׁם in these chapters, since the critique of the rendering 'to be guilty' in Lev. 4, for example, will also apply to several instances of the verb in Lev. 5 (e.g. Lev. 5.2-5, 17). Even where verses are not included in the table, however, they are included at the appropriate points in the following discussion.

63. The same critique applies to the traditional rendering of אָשֵׁם in Lev. 5.2-5, 17, where the sinner is again unaware of their sin.

64. None of the major lexicons (BDB, *HALAT*, *DCH*) list 'when' as a translational option for אוֹ. It may be noted that it is possible to translate אוֹ with 'if' in the sense of 'but if', for example, Exod. 21.35-36: 'When one man's ox hurts another's, so that it dies, then they shall sell the live ox and divide the price of it; and the dead beast also they shall divide. But if (אוֹ) it is known that the ox has been accustomed to gore in the past, and its

By way of contrast, the other translations are able to render אוֹ with 'or' in both vv. 23 and 28, and in so doing provide an answer to the question of how the sinner even knows to bring a sacrifice. Thus sinners, who are unaware of what their sin is: (1) bring an offering either because they recognize their sin and subsequently feel guilty *or* have their sin made known to them;[65] (2) simply realize their sin *or* have their sin made known to them;[66] or, (3) realize their sin because of suffering *or* have their sin made known to them.[67] All of these have in common that sinners come to realize their sin in some way and then bring the offering.[68]

A second problem with the traditional rendering occurs in Lev. 5.23 (6.4). The context of the verse is as follows:

> If any one sins and commits a breach of faith against the LORD by deceiving his neighbor in a matter of deposit or security, or through robbery, or if he has oppressed his neighbor or has found what was lost and lied about it, swearing falsely—in any of all the things which men do and sin therein, when one has sinned and become guilty (וְהָיָה כִּי־יֶחֱטָא וְאָשֵׁם), he shall restore what he took by robbery...and he shall bring to the priest his guilt offering to the LORD... (Lev. 5.21-23a, 25a [6.2-4a, 6a] RSV)

As noted above, the majority of passages in Leviticus 4 and 5 that contain the verb אשׁם deal with a sin that is either inadvertent or perhaps committed and then forgotten.[69] The sinner does bring an offering, but only after being

---

owner has not kept it in, [the owner] shall pay ox for ox, and the dead beast shall be [the owner's]'. This would then give the following translation in Lev. 4.22-23: '...and they shall be guilty. But if the sin which they committed is made known...' Against this possibility, however, it would remain unclear why the law of vv. 13-14 assumes that the sin is made known ('*when* the sin which they have committed becomes known') (so RSV), while in vv. 22-23 and 27-28 it only remains a possibility that the sin becomes known ('But *if* the sin which he committed becomes known'). The other three renderings above, however, are consistent in this regard, understanding that the sin is discovered in each instance in Lev. 4.

65. So Milgrom; see §1.2.4.3 below.
66. So Kiuchi; see §1.2.4.2 below.
67. See §1.2.4.4 below.
68. These renderings would also, therefore, explain the use of אשׁם in Lev. 5.2-5 (cf. n. 63 and the attendant discussion) and the translations 'to realize guilt' and 'to suffer guilt's consequences' would also explain 5.17 (though 'to feel guilty' struggles here; see below, §1.2.4.3). The main differences of the three translations of אשׁם in cases of unknown sin are that Milgrom understands אשׁם to refer to the guilt that comes from realizing the sin, whereas Kiuchi understands אשׁם to refer primarily to the recognition of the sin. The proposal of the current writer differs still, in that it understands אשׁם to refer to the suffering that comes because of the sin, which in turn prompts a recognition that some sin has been done (e.g. 2 Sam. 21; see §1.2.4.4 below).
69. For the latter, see Lev. 5.2-4 and the comments of Wenham (*Leviticus*, pp. 92-93) and Milgrom (*Leviticus 1–16*, pp. 298-300); an overview of different approaches to Lev. 5.1-4 can be found in Kiuchi (*Purification Offering*, pp. 27-31).

told the sin or becoming aware of it on their own. In the situation above, however, neither the vocabulary of inadvertence nor that of forgetfulness occurs. Indeed, it is evident that the person is fully aware of their sin from the outset.[70] What then prompts the sinner to return what was stolen and to bring the guilt offering? It cannot simply be their guilt, as the above translation suggests, for the sinner would be aware of their guilt from the outset. Some other factor must be involved.

Exegetes both modern and ancient have recognized the difficulty of this point. Thus Milgrom lists no less than fifteen sources—including Hellenistic, rabbinic, medieval, and some modern commentators—that have translated אשם differently here, for example, with the sense 'to feel guilty'.[71] Indeed, either of the translations 'to feel guilty', or, more generally, 'to suffer guilt's consequences', make better sense here, since they explain why sinners—who were aware of their sin from the outset—finally restore the stolen property and bring an offering: they are prompted to do so by their guilty conscience or some more general type of suffering brought on by their sin.

In sum, the traditional rendering of 'to be/become guilty' for the verb אשם struggles with the transitions in Lev. 4.22-23 and 4.27-28 and fails to do justice to the flow of thought in Lev. 5.23. As has also become evident in the above discussion, the three other renderings that have been proposed for אשם avoid at least some of these problems. It is to these renderings that we now turn.

1.2.4.2. *'To realize guilt'*. N. Kiuchi argues that the proper rendering of the verb אשם is 'to realize guilt'.[72] Kiuchi's argument runs as follows. To begin, it is clear that the sins considered in Leviticus 4 are done inadvertently (בִּשְׁגָגָה). A study of this root leads Kiuchi to the conclusion that it 'presumes the unconsciousness of a sin', that is, the sinner is not aware that he or she has done wrong.[73] But if the sinner is unconscious of his act, how can he or she be told to bring an offering? The answer of 4.23 and 4.28 is that the sinner is told their sin. But this is only one alternative (note the אוֹ of vv. 23 and 28). The other alternative, found in 4.22 and 4.27 and described with the verb אשם, must be that the sinner becomes aware of their sin (i.e. realizes it). Thus the translation, 'In case it is a chieftain who incurs guilt by doing

---

70. Milgrom argues that the sin that is being addressed in this instance is not that of thievery, but that of swearing falsely. For details see Milgrom, *Leviticus 1–16*, pp. 365-67.

71. Milgrom, *Leviticus 1–16*, p. 344.

72. Kiuchi, *Purification Offering*, pp. 31-34. See also Hartley, *Leviticus*, pp. 44-45, 72-73 (though he states [p. 62] that 'to become culpable' is another option for this verb), Rendtorff, *Leviticus*, II, p. 152, and the JPSV.

73. Kiuchi, *Purification Offering*, p. 31; his argument for this can be found on pp. 25-31.

unwittingly (בִּשְׁגָגָה) any of the things which by the commandment of the LORD his God ought not to be done, and he realizes his guilt (וְאָשֵׁם)—or the sin of which he is guilty is brought to his knowledge... (אוֹ־הוֹדַע אֵלָיו חַטָּאתוֹ אֲשֶׁר חָטָא בָּהּ)' (4.22-23a).[74] In short, the consciousness of sin that is missing from the root שׁגג must be expressed by the verb אָשֵׁם: 'Since the root שׁגג presumes the unconsciousness of sin, the consciousness of sin must be included in *'āšēm*.[75]

Kiuchi's rendering—like the renderings 'to feel guilty' and 'to suffer guilt's consequences'—does well in that it provides an answer to the question raised by the fact that the majority of sins dealt with in these chapters are not only inadvertent, they are also hidden from, or in some way unknown to, the sinner. The question this raises is as follows: How do sinners know to bring an offering if their sin was unintentional and they are unaware of it (or it is otherwise unknown to them)? Kiuchi's answer is simply that they become aware of their sin in some way; they realize it. This in turn opens the way for them to bring the appropriate offering.

Kiuchi's translation, like the third and fourth above, also does well in explaining the transitions between Lev. 4.13 and 4.14, 4.22 and 4.23, and 4.27 and 4.28.[76]

Nonetheless, this proposal is not without some difficulties. To begin, Kiuchi's first argument above is based on the hypothesis that the absence of consciousness of sin from the root שׁגג implies it must be contained in the verb אָשֵׁם.[77] While Kiuchi is correct in identifying that sinners must become aware of their sin in such passages as Leviticus 4 (otherwise how could they bring an offering?), it does not follow that the verb אָשֵׁם *must* contain the idea of consciousness of sin as part of its semantic domain (i.e. 'to realize guilt'). It is also possible that אָשֵׁם refers to the suffering caused by the sin which in turn *leads* to a realization of the sin. אָשֵׁם would then express the *results* of the sin ('suffering guilt's consequences'), as it does frequently outside of the priestly literature,[78] not the realization of the sin itself. Alternatively, it is possible that one could realize their sin, which would *then* lead to feelings of guilt. אָשֵׁם would then express the *results* of realizing one's sin, not the realization itself (so Milgrom).[79] In either case, the verb

---

74. Kiuchi (*Purification Offering*, pp. 33-34) also addresses the relationship between אָשֵׁם and יָדַע in vv. 13-14, arguing that יָדַע is an explication of אָשֵׁם. For the grammatical possibility of this see the translation of v. 14 in the chart above and especially n. 61.
75. Kiuchi, *Purification Offering*, p. 33.
76. See nn. 65, 66, 67, and the attendant discussion.
77. 'Since the root שׁגג presumes the unconsciousness of sin, the consciousness of sin must be included in *'āšēm*' (Kiuchi, *Purification Offering*, p. 33).
78. See §1.2.4.4.
79. See §1.2.4.3.

אָשֵׁם does not need to contain consciousness of sin as part of its semantic domain.

Second, this translation is not able to maintain consistency in its rendering of אָשֵׁם in 4.3 and 4.13, since it would not make sense in 4.3 to say, 'If the high priest sins so as to make the people realize their guilt…'.[80] It is for this reason not surprising that the JPSV translates אָשֵׁם differently in 4.3: 'If it is the anointed priest who has incurred guilt, so that blame falls upon the people…' Given that the sacrificial rite is exactly the same in 4.3-12 and 4.13-21, however, and given that the verb אָשֵׁם follows the sin and precedes the sacrifice in both instances, it is not clear why it should be translated differently from 4.3 to 4.13.[81] As discussed in more detail below, this problem is avoided if אָשֵׁם is translated with a general consequential rendering in each verse.[82]

1.2.4.3. *'To feel guilt'*.

A third understanding of the verb אָשֵׁם in the priestly literature was proposed by Jacob Milgrom, who argued that it should be rendered with 'to feel guilt' whenever it does not have an object.[83] Milgrom offers two main arguments in support of this rendering of אָשֵׁם.

The first argument may be presented as follows.

Proposition One: The root אָשֵׁם has a consequential meaning, that is, it refers to both the wrong and the retribution:

> It has long been recognized that the biblical terms for good and bad behavior also connote their respective reward and punishment… Thus *ḥēṭ'* (Num. 32.33 [*sic*; read 32.23]; Isa. 53.12; Zech. 14.18-19; Prov. 10.16; Lam. 3.39; 4.6); *pešaʿ* (Isa. 24.20; Ps. 39.9); *ʿāwōn* (Gen. 4.13; 1 Sam. 25.24); *rāʿă* (Jer. 4.18; 18.8, 11; Lam. 3.38), inter alia, stand not only for evil, but for its inherent punishment… The same can be shown for *'āšām*. It connotes both the wrong and the retribution.[84]

---

80. This problem could be avoided if הָעָם is taken to be a subjective genitive: 'If the high priest sins so that/with the result that the people realize their guilt (לְאַשְׁמַת הָעָם)…' While this is possible grammatically (cf. the consequential rendering of אָשֵׁם in Lev. 4.3 in the last column of the chart above), the sense is somewhat awkward for this definition of אָשֵׁם (and perhaps for this reason the JPSV translates differently at this point; see the comments above).

81. This critique is elaborated upon below with reference to Milgrom's proposal; see n. 94 and attendant discussion.

82. See §1.2.4.3 and especially §1.2.4.4.

83. Originally in Milgrom, *Cult and Conscience*, pp. 3-12. Milgrom repeats this argument with only the slightest changes in Milgrom, *Leviticus 1–16*, pp. 339-45. The more recent work (*Leviticus 1–16*) is referred to in the following. As mentioned above, Milgrom (*Leviticus 1–16*, p. 344) also notes that his translation of אָשֵׁם with 'to feel guilt' was anticipated by earlier commentators in at least some instances (most notably Lev. 5.23).

84. Milgrom, *Leviticus 1–16*, p. 339.

1. *The Consequences of Sin*

He supports this by citing several texts both outside of the priestly literature and within it that use the root אשם to refer to some form of retribution.[85]

Proposition Two: 'The consequential *'āšām* also has a psychological component'.[86] He supports this by arguing:

> The ancients did not distinguish between emotional and physical suffering; the same language describes pangs of conscience and physical pains (e.g., Jer. 17.14; Pss. 38.2-11, 18-19; 102.4-11; 149.3; cf. 34.19). That is why in the penitential psalms it is difficult to determine whether the speaker is suffering, on the one hand, from natural disease, economic want, or political persecution; or, on the other, from mental torment or guilt (Pss. 6, 32, 38, 41, etc.).[87]

In short, it was possible for the ancient Israelites to use the same term to refer to both emotional and physical suffering, which they understood to be related.

First Conclusion: These propositions lead Milgrom to his first conclusion:

> Thus it is logical to expect that a language that, as observed, will express the consequential syndrome of sin–punishment by a single word will also have at least one root in its lexicon to express another consequential relationship, that which exists between sin–punishment and guilt feelings.[88]

Having arrived at this conclusion, he suggests that the single word which fits this description is the root אשם.

His second argument may be presented as follows.

Proposition One: Non-legal texts speak of the feelings of guilt metaphorically, for example, 'David's heart smote him' (1 Sam. 24.5; 2 Sam. 24.10); 'a stumbling [offense] of the heart' (1 Sam. 25.31); 'my kidneys have whipped me' (Ps. 16.7).[89]

Proposition Two: Cultic and legal texts prefer precise, not metaphorical language.[90]

Second Conclusion: Thus one precise term would be necessary to describe guilt feelings in the cultic and legal texts: 'In the cultic and legal texts… where metaphors are eschewed, a precise term would be essential to pinpoint the existence of guilt…'[91] Once more, Milgrom suggests that this is to be found in the root אשם, and more specifically for the priestly texts, in the verb אָשֵׁם.

---

85. Milgrom, *Leviticus 1–16*, pp. 340-42; see Gen. 26.10; Lev. 4.3; 5.6; 1 Chron. 21.3; Ps. 34.22-23; Jer. 51.5b; Hos. 5.15; Zech. 11.5.
86. Milgrom, *Leviticus 1–16*, p. 342.
87. Milgrom, *Leviticus 1–16*, p. 342.
88. Milgrom, *Leviticus 1–16*, p. 343.
89. Milgrom, *Leviticus 1–16*, p. 343; he cites further Ps. 38.3-6 (2-5), 19 (18).
90. Milgrom, *Leviticus 1–16*, p. 343.
91. Milgrom, *Leviticus 1–16*, p. 343.

These two arguments then lead Milgrom to his main conclusion:

> Thus, contrary to usual translations, *'āšām* without an object does not refer to a state of guilt; rather, in keeping with its consequential meaning, it denotes the suffering brought on by guilt, expressed now by words such as qualms, pangs, remorse, and contrition. *'āšām* would then mean to be conscience-smitten or guilt-stricken, and henceforth it will be rendered as 'feel guilt'.[92]

Milgrom's thesis has many points to commend it. As noted above, the translation 'to feel guilt' explains the use of אָשֵׁם in Lev. 5.23 very well: the person returns what is stolen and brings a guilt offering because of a smitten conscience and feelings of guilt. It was also noted above that this translation explains the transitions between Lev. 4.13 and 4.14, 4.22 and 4.23, and 4.27 and 4.28.[93] Moreover, Milgrom also does well in recognizing that אָשֵׁם, like other terms for sin, can have a consequential meaning. The question that remains is whether this consequential meaning should be limited to being 'conscience-smitten or guilt-stricken' and hence rendered as 'to feel guilt'. Two observations suggest that this limitation is problematic.

First, it was seen above in the table of translations on Leviticus 4 that one of the differences came in the rendering of the particles at the beginning of vv. 14, 23 and 28. A second difference concerns the translation of לְאַשְׁמַת הָעָם in Lev. 4.3. With the RSV and JPSV, a majority of translators have rendered this phrase in terms of bringing guilt upon the people.[94] While this is entirely possible, Milgrom has noted that the sin of the priest does not simply make the people guilty, it also endangers them: 'That priestly misconduct can harm the community is explicitly stated: "Do not dishevel your hair and do not rend your clothes, lest you die and *anger strike the whole community*" (10.6; cf. Gen. 20.9, 17-18)'.[95] This then weighs in favor of a rendering such as 'to the detriment of the people' (so Milgrom),[96] in which אָשֵׁם is understood in a consequential sense to refer to general suffering, and not just to emotional suffering.[97]

At the same time, however, the offering of the priest in vv. 3-12 and that of the congregation in vv. 13-21 is exactly the same, which in turn suggests that the sin is just as grave in each instance.[98] This being the case, it would

---

92. Milgrom, *Leviticus 1–16*, p. 343.
93. As a result it would also explain the use of אָשֵׁם in Lev. 5.2-5. See above, n. 68.
94. Cf. Péter-Contesse (*Lévitique 1–16*, p. 71): '…entraînant ainsi le peuple dans la culpabilité'; Hartley (*Leviticus*, p. 44): '…bringing guilt on the people'; Dillmann (*Exodus und Leviticus*, p. 419): '…zur Verschuldung des Volks d. h. so, dass es diesem zur Verschuldung gereicht'; Wenham (*Leviticus*, p. 84): '…bringing guilt on the people'.
95. Milgrom, *Leviticus 1–16*, p. 232.
96. Milgrom, *Leviticus 1–16*, pp. 231-32.
97. For this use of the verb, see references in n. 85 above; see further §1.2.4.4 below.
98. The exact nature of the sin in either instance is not clear. For different possibilities on the priest's sin, see Milgrom, *Leviticus 1–16*, p. 232; for different possibilities on

also follow that the consequence of the sin—expressed by אָשֵׁם in both passages—would be the same in each instance, namely, general suffering. Surprisingly, it is at this very point that Milgrom changes his rendering of אָשֵׁם in 4.13 from one which includes the idea of general suffering ('to the detriment of the people') to one which emphasizes their subjective reaction to the sin ('they feel guilty'). It would seem more natural, however, to understand the verb to have the same meaning in each instance.[99] In short, if the sin of the high priest is to the general detriment of the people, it is natural to expect that the sin of the people is to their general detriment as well.

Second, it may be observed that Milgrom's rendering appears problematic with regard to his understanding of Lev. 5.17-19. Milgrom holds that this passage is like Leviticus 4 in dealing with a sin that is inadvertent; unlike Leviticus 4, however, where the sins were eventually discovered, this passage addresses an inadvertent sin that is never discovered.[100] Thus he translates the relevant verses as follows: 'If, however, a person errs by violating any of the LORD's prohibitive commandments without knowing it and he feels guilt, he shall bear his responsibility by bringing to the priest an unblemished ram…' (vv. 17-18a).[101] This raises the obvious question: Why would people feel guilty if they were unaware of their sin? Milgrom answers:

> Indeed, *wĕ 'āšēm* in v. 17 can serve as a showcase for the psychological component of the consequential *'āšām*: the subject is experiencing psychical (and perhaps even physical) suffering that, for lack of knowledge concerning its cause, he attributes to an unwitting offense against God… The law of 5.17-19 is thus the legal formulation of the psychological truth that he who does not know the exact cause of his suffering imagines the worst: he has affronted the deity; he has committed sacrilege against the sancta and 'incurred liability to the LORD' (v. 19).[102]

---

the sin of the congregation and/or assembly (as well as whether there is a difference between the two terms), cf. Wenham, *Leviticus*, pp. 98-99, with Milgrom, *Leviticus 1–16*, pp. 241-43.

99. One may also compare 5.26, where לְאַשְׁמָה occurs again and where Milgrom (*Leviticus 1–16*, p. 319) does translate it with 'to feel guilty': 'The priest shall effect expiation on his behalf before the LORD so that he may be forgiven for whatever he has done to feel guilt thereby [לְאַשְׁמָה בָהּ]'. Such a rendering would of course not work in 4.3 ('If the anointed priest sins to make the people feel guilty…'), and thus Milgrom translates 4.3 with a more general consequential suffering. It may be noted, however, that the general consequential translation of 4.3 works just as well in 5.26 ('…and [the sinner] shall be forgiven for any of the things which one may do and thereby suffer guilt's consequences') and would also maintain consistency in the renderings of this term.

100. See also Wenham, *Leviticus*, pp. 107-108; Levine, *Leviticus*, pp. 31-32. For a different understanding of this passage, see Kiuchi, *Purification Offering*, p. 33.

101. Milgrom, *Leviticus 1–16*, p. 319.

102. Milgrom, *Leviticus 1–16*, pp. 332-33.

And yet this explanation goes against his understanding of אשם elsewhere, where he sees the guilt as a result of recognizing sin, that is, the 'psychical suffering' is a response to the knowledge of the sin.[103] In this instance, however, there is no knowledge of the sin; why then is there guilt? Why does the sinner suspect that he or she has done wrong? If Milgrom's understanding of the passage as a whole is correct, then a more logical reading of אשם is to take it as a reference to suffering in general (a reading which Milgrom himself hints at).[104] In other words, the person is undergoing some sort of general suffering, suspects that it is because of sin, and therefore brings a guilt offering. Thus: 'If a person sins and does any of the commands of the LORD which are not to be done—though he or she did not know it—and suffers guilt's consequences and bears punishment for their sin,[105] then that person will bring to the priest a blameless ram from the flock...' (5.17-18a).

A third observation may now be added, namely, careful attention to Milgrom's arguments reveals that, at most, he opens up the *possibility* that אשם could refer to emotional suffering. In his first argument, for example, he states, 'Thus it is logical *to expect* that a language that, as observed, will express the consequential syndrome of sin–punishment by a single word will also have at least one root in its lexicon to express another consequential relationship, that which exists between sin–punishment and guilt feelings'.[106] Naturally, one could expect such a word to exist, but this is different than showing that such a word does indeed exist. Similarly, in his second argument he states, 'In the cultic and legal texts…where metaphors are eschewed, a precise term would be essential to pinpoint the existence of guilt…'[107] This assumes, of course, that these cultic-legal texts had need of such a word, an assumption which is of course possible but not proven. Proof of the possibility would have to come in part from whether or not the proposed

---

103. See n. 65 above and the attendant discussion.

104. '[T]he subject is experiencing psychical (*and perhaps even physical*) suffering…' (Milgrom, *Leviticus 1–16*, p. 332 [emphasis added]).

105. It is possible to take the phrase וְנָשָׂא עֲוֹנוֹ as the beginning of the apodosis and translate, 'If a person sins and does any of the commands of the LORD which are not to be done—though he or she did not know it—and suffers guilt's consequences, then [that person] will bear the penalty of their sin, and will bring to the priest…' (cf. Milgrom, *Leviticus 1–16*, p. 319 [though his translation of וְנָשָׂא עֲוֹנוֹ with 'he shall bear his responsibility' is too weak a rendering for עָוֹן; see Chapter 3 n. 36 and attendant discussion). This translation understands the bearing of sin to consist of the bringing of the sacrifice. Alternatively, the phrase וְנָשָׂא עֲוֹנוֹ is parallel to וְאָשֵׁם (so above), that is, both phrases describe the general suffering that is brought about by sin. This possibility finds support in Lev. 5.1-4, which consists of four parallel laws, the first of which uses the phrase נָשָׂא עָוֹן (5.1), while the next three use the verb אָשֵׁם (vv. 2-4). This again suggests that נָשָׂא עָוֹן is being used to describe the general suffering that is brought on by sin.

106. Milgrom, *Leviticus 1–16*, p. 343 (emphasis added).

107. Milgrom, *Leviticus 1–16*, p. 343.

rendering of אשם fits well in its various contexts. The first two observations above, however, suggest that the rendering 'to feel guilt' is at the least inconsistent (cf. 4.3 and 4.13) and at the most problematic (5.17).

In short, Milgrom has done well in identifying the consequential aspect of the verb אשם. It does not seem, however, that this consequential aspect should be limited to being 'conscience-smitten or guilt-stricken' and hence translated as 'to feel guilt'. As intimated in the above, a more general consequential understanding of אשם would seem to do better justice to this verb in the priestly literature. It is to this final understanding of the verb that we now turn.

1.2.4.4. *'To suffer guilt's consequences'*. The fourth proposal for אשם is 'to suffer guilt's consequences'.[108] The legitimacy of such a translation is grounded not only in the fact that terms for sin in general have a consequential meaning,[109] but more specifically in the fact that several texts outside of the priestly literature use אשם consequentially. Thus אשם is often explicated with the description of the punishment it describes:

> Evil will slay the wicked and those who hate the righteous *will be condemned* (יאשמו). (Ps. 34.22 [34.21])

> Their heart is smooth; now they will *suffer for their guilt* (יאשמו): he himself will break down their altars, destroying their pillars. (Hos. 10.2)

> Samaria *shall suffer for her guilt* (תאשם), because she has rebelled against her God; they shall fall by the sword, their little ones shall be dashed in pieces, and their pregnant women ripped open. (Hos. 14.1 [13.16])

> Therefore a curse devours the earth, and its inhabitants *suffer for their guilt* (ויאשמו); therefore the inhabitants of the earth are scorched, and few men are left. (Isa. 24.6)

> Israel is holy to the LORD, the first of his harvest; all who eat of it *will suffer for their guilt* (יאשמו): evil will come upon them, declares the LORD. (Jer. 2.3)[110]

---

108. This has been suggested by K. van der Toorn for Lev. 4.22-26 and 4.27-31, though in other instances (e.g. Lev. 5.2) he translates with 'to be held responsible (for sin)'. See van der Toorn, *Sin and Sanction*, p. 92.

109. See above, n. 41.

110. See further Ps. 5.11 (10) (hiphil); Ezek. 6.6; Joel 1.18 (niphal). It is not impossible that אשם in some of the above verses may be translated with 'to incur guilt' or 'to be guilty', but the context of these verses, together with the fact that other terms for sin denote both the sin and the consequence, make it most likely that אשם should be translated consequentially in these instances. See also discussion in Milgrom, *Leviticus 1–16*, pp. 340-41. The editor of *BHS* suggests that the versions are reading the root שמם instead of אשם in both Ezek. 6.6 and Joel 1.18, though it is equally possible that the versions simply translated אשם with its consequential meaning.

Not only does this consequential understanding of the verb find support outside of the priestly literature, there are also several other considerations which commend this as the most appropriate rendering of אשם within the priestly literature.

To begin, as noted above, this rendering of the verb is like Kiuchi's and Milgrom's in that it works well with the transitions from 4.22 to 4.23 and from 4.27 to 4.28, that is, it allows for the או to be translated in its most normal fashion.[111]

Second, this rendering of אשם explains well how people who were unaware that they had sinned became aware of it, namely, their suffering prompted them to seek out what they had done wrong. It was not uncommon in the ancient Near East for those who suffered to assume that they had done something wrong.[112] One biblical example of this comes from 2 Sam. 21.1: 'Now there was a famine in the days of David for three years, year after year; *and David sought the presence of the* LORD. And the LORD said, "It is for Saul and his bloody house, because he put the Gibeonites to death".' In this instance, in the third year of famine David suspects that some sin might be behind it. He in turn seeks the LORD and discovers that this suffering is indeed a result of sin, namely, the sin of Saul. Hence an unknown sin is discovered because the suffering it produced prompted David to seek the LORD.[113] This is the same situation envisioned by the use of אשם in the priestly texts: an unknown sin has been committed, and the sinner becomes aware of it only because of some sort of suffering that results from the sin.[114] The sinner is then in a position to seek the LORD and discover what their sin might be.

Third, a consequential understanding of the verb also makes good sense of Lev. 5.23, where a person who has sinned—and who was aware of their sin—returns what was stolen and brings a guilt offering. Translating אשם with 'to suffer guilt's consequences' explains well what it is that may have

---

111. See above, nn. 65, 66, 67, and the attendant discussion.

112. For a discussion of the ancient Near Eastern context see especially van der Toorn, *Sin and Sanction*. A classic example from the ancient Near East can be found in the *šurpu* collection of incantations (E. Reiner, *Šurpu* [*AfO* Beiheft, 11; Graz: Im Selbstverlage des Herausgebers, 1958]), where someone who is suffering has a priest recite a litany of possible sins that the sufferer might have done to bring about their suffering.

113. It is not stated how this was done. Anderson notes, 'According to a rabbinic tradition (*Yebamoth*, 78b), David consulted Yahweh by means of lots; this is possible but other means are equally likely' (A.A. Anderson, *2 Samuel* [WBC, 11; Waco, TX: Word Books, 1989], p. 249). Hertzberg, however, thinks it more likely that the question was put to a prophet or a priest (see Hans Wilhelm Hertzberg, *I & II Samuel* [trans. J.S. Bowden; London: SCM Press, 1964], p. 382).

114. This is true not only of Lev. 4, but also of Lev. 5.2-5 and 5.17.

prompted the person to bring this offering, namely, the sinner began to suffer the consequences of their wrong.

Finally, unlike Milgrom's and Kiuchi's renderings, translating אשם with 'to suffer guilt's consequences' allows for consistency of translation from 4.3 to 4.13. As mentioned above, if the inadvertent sin of the high priest causes the people to experience some sort of general suffering (אשם) (4.3), then one would expect that the inadvertent sin of the people themselves—which requires the exact same sacrificial rite as is required by the sin of the high priest—would also result in some sort of general suffering (אשם) (4.13). For this reason it is not surprising to find the verb אשם occurring in each of these cases to describe the consequences of the sin, and it seems most natural to render it similarly in each instance, that is, 'to suffer guilt's consequences'.[115]

In sum, the most appropriate translation for אשם in the priestly literature is a general consequential one; that is, it refers to the general consequences brought on by the guilt of sin and may be translated with 'to suffer guilt's consequences'.

1.3. *Summary and Comparison of the Penalties for Sin*

In summarizing and comparing the above penalties for sin, it is helpful to begin with the first three (death, *kareth*, נָשָׂא עָוֹן), which occur consistently in the context of intentional sin, before turning to consider the fourth (אשם), which occurs consistently in the context of sin that may be atoned for.[116]

The terms death, *kareth*, and נָשָׂא עָוֹן, then, are found in the context of intentional sin.[117] Three facts are of particular note. First, each of these three penalties refers to the death of the sinner. This is obviously the case with the first, where the death of the sinner is described or prescribed, and is equally the case with the second (*kareth*), which was argued above to refer to the premature death of the sinner. Moreover, while the third penalty above (נָשָׂא עָוֹן) was seen to be a general statement that the sinner would bear the consequence of their sin, whenever that consequence is specified it is specified either with death (Exod. 28.43; Lev. 20.20; 22.9; 24.15 [with v. 16]; Num.

---

115. See the last column of the chart above in §1.2.4.1.

116. 'Sin that may be atoned for' and not 'inadvertent sin' since אשם occurs in the context of sins that may be atoned for and yet appear to be intentional (Lev. 5.20-26 [6.1-7]; see above, n. 46).

117. As a general statement of penalty, נָשָׂא עָוֹן also occurs in Lev. 5.17 in the context of inadvertent sin, where one is able to avoid the penalty of death by bringing a guilt offering. It also occurs once in the context of sin which appears to be intentional but which is expiable, this time by means of a purification offering (Lev. 5.1).

18.1 [with v. 3], 22, 32) or *kareth* (Lev. 19.8; 20.17; Num. 9.13),[118] and it can safely be assumed that this is the case even when death is not specified.[119] Second, while the connection between intentional sin and death need not imply that every intentional sin had to be followed by death,[120] as a rule it is death, not forgiveness by means of atonement, that is expected in the context of these intentional sins. Third, this penalty is carried out by the LORD directly or by the covenant community acting on behalf of the LORD. In this regard sin is considered first and foremost an affront to the LORD.

The fourth consequence of sin (אָשָׁם) occurs in the context of sin that may be atoned for. Once more, three factors are worthy of note. First, because the sins in these instances may be atoned for, sacrifice is prescribed. When these sacrifices are properly offered, the person is then forgiven for their sin (e.g. Lev. 4.27-31). Second, the consequences of sin that may be atoned for are never described as death (מוֹת) or with the term *kareth*. If a consequence is stated, aside from the sacrifice itself, it is with אָשָׁם. As argued above, this term refers to some sort of general suffering that prompts sinners either to seek out what sin they might have inadvertently committed (Lev. 4; 5.2-4, 17) or to confess that sin which they have tried to hide (5.20-26 [6.1-7]). The assumption of the text is that the sinner ends up bringing the appropriate sacrifice; as a result of this sacrifice the sinner is forgiven and no further consequences of their sin are forthcoming. Third, unlike penalties for intentional sin which are executed by the LORD or the covenant community on his behalf, the consequences referred to by אָשָׁם are only brought about by the LORD. This is due to the nature of these sins as those which are hidden from the sinner (or, in a few instances, as those which the sinner hides from others).[121]

It is important to make a qualification, however, especially with reference to inadvertent sin (Lev. 4; 5.2-4, 17), since the fact that death is not mentioned in these contexts could be taken to mean that the life of the inadvertent sinner is never at risk.[122] Instead, one may say at most that death never

---

118. For Lev. 5.1, 17, see n. 105. Numbers 14.34 refers to the Israelites bearing their sins forty years in the desert. The punishment here is not simply the wilderness wandering, however, but also that their 'corpses shall fall in the wilderness' (v. 32), that is, death before entry into the Promised Land.

119. Cf. Lev. 20.19, which does not specify the penalty, with vv. 17 and 20, which specify the penalty of *kareth* (v. 17; see also v. 18) or death (v. 20). Cf. also Lev. 7.18, which does not specify the penalty, with 19.7-8, where the penalty is specified as *kareth*.

120. For example, Lev. 5.1, 20-26 (6.1-7); see above, n. 46.

121. For example, Lev. 5.20-26 (6.1-7).

122. Thus Milgrom (Jacob Milgrom, Review of Bernd Janowski, *Sühne als Heilsgeschehen*, *JBL* 104 [1985], pp. 302-304 [303]), in critique of Janowski's understanding that Lev. 17.11 refers to expiatory sacrifice in general, writes, 'Moreover, Janowski seems not a whit disturbed by the morality of a system which purportedly posits that the

had to be the consequence of inadvertent sin, but this is only because the sinner could present a sacrifice and be forgiven. Three factors suggest, though, that death still *could be* the result if the sin were not properly addressed. First, as argued above on the term אָשֵׁם, the text envisions situations in which someone commits an inadvertent sin but does not bring a sacrifice because they are unaware of it and because no one tells them of it. As a result, they begin to suffer some sort of negative consequence for this sin (אָשֵׁם), *even though it is inadvertent*, which then prompts them to seek the sin out and then bring the requisite offering. Inadvertent sin, therefore, does not mean the absence of punitive consequences. Second, the fact that these punitive consequences could eventually lead to death (or *kareth*) is suggested by Lev. 17.11. This verse states that the blood of atoning sacrifice serves to ransom the life of the sinner,[123] which naturally implies that the life of the sinner is at risk. Since the context of atoning sacrifice is inadvertent sin, though, the implication is that it is the life of the inadvertent sinner that is at risk. In further support it may finally be noted that it was possible to commit inadvertent sins that would result in death if done intentionally, for example, eating the meat of peace offerings while unclean (Lev. 7.20). If one committed such a sin inadvertently and was then made aware of it or became aware of it, but refused to bring the appropriate sacrifice, the natural inference is that such a person would suffer the consequences that this sin normally calls for, namely, *kareth*. One does not *have* to suffer *kareth* if this is done inadvertently, but this is only because a sacrifice may be offered instead. If the sacrifice is not offered, however, the burden of proof is upon those who would maintain that the penalty of *kareth* (i.e. premature death) would not apply.

In sum, there is a strong connection in the priestly literature between sin and death. Intentional sins are most often accompanied by one of three capital penalties: death, *kareth*, or נָשָׂא עָוֹן. It is death, not atonement and forgiveness, that is the expectation in these contexts. In contexts that use the verb אָשֵׁם, however, the sinner may escape death by means of sacrificial atonement (כִּפֶּר). It is to a deeper understanding of sacrificial atonement that we now turn.

---

inadvertent wrongdoer (Lev. 4) and the new mother (Lev. 12) are deserving of death' (for discussion of Lev. 17.11, including how an understanding in keeping with Janowski's relates to Milgrom's comments on the new mother, see §6.1.5 below). See more recently Milgrom, *Leviticus 17–22*, p. 1475, for a critique of which see again the discussion in §6.1.5.

123. See §6.1.3 below.

2
כִּפֶּר DEFINED

In the last chapter it was seen that sin, be it intentional or inadvertent, eventually leads to death. At the same time, it was also seen that death did not have to be the result if sacrificial atonement was allowed. In these instances, the sinner was able to present a sacrifice, by which the priest effected atonement and the sinner received forgiveness: וְכִפֶּר עָלָיו הַכֹּהֵן וְנִסְלַח לוֹ (Lev. 4.31b).

As noted in the Introduction, כִּפֶּר in these situations has been translated traditionally with 'to atone/expiate' or 'to make atonement/expiation'. The exact nature of this atonement, however, has been variously understood. Earlier scholars, appealing especially to Arabic *kafara*, understood atonement to be rooted in the idea of 'covering', that is, the priest covers the sin or the sinner so that the sinner does not have to face the wrath of God.[1] This approach has been critiqued on both linguistic and exegetical grounds, however, and has largely fallen out of favor.[2]

---

1. For those holding to the view that atonement is related to the idea of covering, see the Introduction, n. 4.
2. Proponents of this view base their conclusion upon the following arguments: (1) כִּפֶּר is related to Arabic *kafara* ('to cover'), and shows the same semantic development as this verb (Stamm, *Erlösen und Vergeben*, pp. 61, 63-66); (2) the phrase כִּפֶּר עַל עָוֹן in Jer. 18.23 is paralleled in Neh. 3.37 (4.5) with כִּסָּה עַל עָוֹן (Stamm, *Erlösen und Vergeben*, p. 63; see Dionys Schötz, *Schuld und Sündopfer im Alten Testament* [Breslau: Müller & Seiffert, 1930], p. 103); (3) in Gen. 32.21 (20), where Jacob says of Esau, 'I will appease him (אֲכַפְּרָה פָנָיו) with the present that goes before me', the sense of כִּפֶּר here perhaps goes back to the idea of 'covering' someone's face. Possible support is found in the phrase כְּסוּת עֵינַיִם ('to cover the eyes') in Gen. 20.16, which describes the effect of the gift that Abimelech gave to Abraham for wronging Sarah ('Hier [i.e. in Gen. 32.21 (20)] bedeutet כִּפֶּר פָּנִים בַּמִּנְחָה wohl in der Tat "das Antlitz mit dem Geschenk bedecken", was den Sinn von versöhnen hat' [Stamm, *Erlösen und Vergeben*, p. 62 and references cited there]). The meaning of 'to cover' for כִּפֶּר is then seen to have developed to express atonement. Stamm (*Erlösen und Vergeben*, p. 66), for example, holds that while the original meaning of כִּפֶּר was 'to cover', its meaning developed to express 'to atone' (*sühnen*) and 'to forgive' (*vergeben*) in a manner similar to the development evident with Arabic *kafara*. This brings us to the fundamental critique of this position,

2. כִּפֶּר Defined

A second approach, put forward by Hartmut Gese and then developed by his student Bernd Janowski, is that the emphasis of atonement is upon the worshipper symbolically dedicating their life to the holy through the atonement process. As such, atonement is positive in nature, in contrast to penal understandings which might be more negative in nature. Moreover, people

however, insofar as the focus upon the 'original' meaning of the word in order to determine the word's meaning in a later context is based in large part upon a nineteenth-century methodology of lexical analysis that emphasized the diachronic over the synchronic in determining meaning (as this relates to כִּפֶּר, see Janowski, *Sühne*, pp. 15-18). This methodology has since been severely critiqued, and modern linguists hold the diachronic perspective to be largely secondary to that of the synchronic (the seminal work in this whole discussion is that of Ferdinand de Saussure, *Cours de linguistique générale* [Paris: Payot, 3rd edn, 1969 (1st edn 1916)], in turn applied to biblical studies by James Barr, *The Semantics of Biblical Language* [Oxford: Oxford University Press, 1961]). Apart from this methodological shortcoming, however, the view that 'to cover' was the original meaning of כִּפֶּר is itself vulnerable to several problems, and the points cited above in favor of this view may be responded to seriatim. First, Richard E. Averbeck ('כפר', in *NIDOTTE*, II, pp. 689-710 [692]) observes that the etymological evidence becomes confused 'when Arab. is cited in its base stem meaning (= Heb. q.) and then compared to the Akk. D stem and the Heb. pi. stem'. (Stamm [*Erlösen und Vergeben*, p. 63] does note that there are fourteen occurrences of *kaffara* in the Koran with the meaning 'to cover' or 'to atone'. Unlike the priestly literature, however, the subject is never a human, but Allah [×13] or almsgiving, which in turn mitigates the relevance of the observation.) Second, the parallel between כִּפֶּר and כִּסָּה in Jer. 18.23 and Neh. 3.37 (4.5) by no means proves that they are synonymous. To begin, words in parallel phrases will often describe the same result even if the words do not have the same meaning. For example, the phrase 'and do not cover (וְאַל־תְּכַם) their sin' in Neh. 3.37 (4.5) is immediately followed by the phrase 'and let not their sin be blotted out (אַל־תִּמָּחֶה) from your sight'. In this instance, 'cover' and 'blot out' do not have the same meaning; they do, however, describe the same result: the sin of the guilty not being punished. It is equally possible to explain the parallel between כִּפֶּר and כִּסָּה in Jer. 18.23 and Neh. 3.37 (4.5) in the same way. Indeed Lang ('כִּפֶּר', p. 289), citing Levine (*Presence of the Lord*, pp. 57-58), further notes, '…since [כִּסָּה] often means "forgive (guilt or sin)" (Pss. 32.1; 85.3 [2]), it is unlikely that Neh. 3.37 (4.5) involves a consciously etymologizing variant'. Moreover, the interchange between כִּפֶּר and כִּסָּה is put into further perspective when it is pointed out that verbs other than כִּסָּה are interchanged with כִּפֶּר that certainly do not mean 'to cover'—for example, חָטָא (cf. Lev. 16.20 [וְכִלָּה מִכַּפֵּר...וְהִקְרִיב] with Ezek. 43.23 [בְּכַלּוֹתְךָ מֵחַטֵּא תַּקְרִיב]). Stamm offers no comment in this regard. Third, Gen. 32.20b in its entirety reads as follows: 'I will appease his face (אֲכַפְּרָה פָנָיו) with the present that goes before me. Then afterward I will see his face (אֶרְאֶה פָנָיו); perhaps he will lift up my face.' It seems peculiar to postulate a root meaning of 'to cover' for כִּפֶּר here when Jacob immediately proceeds to say that the כִּפֶּר action will result in him *seeing* Esau's face. And while the use of כִּסָּה in Gen. 20.16 is noteworthy, the parallel would be more exact if כִּסָּה were followed by פָּנִים instead of עֵינַיִם. For further critique of this understanding of כִּפֶּר, see also Levine, *Presence of the Lord*, pp. 57-59.

are able to accomplish atonement only because of the gracious gift of God in providing a means of atonement. For this reason, atonement does not find its roots in human achievement, but in God's initiative and gracious provision. As discussed below, the emphasis on God's initiative in atonement is well-supported from the text and should be maintained.[3] At the same time, however, this view overemphasizes the positive aspects of atonement at the expense of more negative elements that are central to כִּפֶּר.[4]

A third approach understands atonement to be characterized by cleansing in at least some sin contexts, including, for example, the inadvertent sins of Leviticus 4 and 5.[5] This approach is indeed partially correct insofar as sin is defiling.[6] It has been noted above, however, that sin consistently calls for the LORD's judgment in the priestly literature, and it will be argued below that this situation calls for a 'ransom' (כֹּפֶר) to be paid on behalf of the sinner.[7]

A fourth approach, then, is to understand atonement in terms of כֹּפֶר, that is, 'ransom'. That כִּפֶּר is used in this manner in at least some instances enjoys abroad consensus among biblical scholars. Thus Johannes Herrmann,[8] Herbert Brichto,[9] Baruch Levine,[10] Adrian Schenker,[11] Bernd Janowski,[12] and Jacob Milgrom[13] all aver that כִּפֶּר does occur with a meaning denominative

---

3. See §2.1.2.2 below, as well as Chapter 6 and n. 4.

4. See comments below in §2.2.1.

5. See Introduction, n. 7.

6. See end of §3.1.1 below.

7. See Chapter 3.

8. Herrmann, 'ἱλάσκομαι, ἱλασμός', p. 303, notes: 'Many students rightly assume that there is a close connection between כִּפֶּר and כֹּפֶר'; and 'At Is. 47.11 כִּפֶּר means "to pay כֹּפֶר", "to raise a כֹּפֶר", "to avert by כֹּפֶר"' (p. 303).

9. Brichto's general conclusion on the meaning of the verb is as follows: 'To offer/ make composition [i.e. a כֹּפֶר], to accept composition—is the basic force of *kipper*' (Brichto, 'On Slaughter and Sacrifice', p. 35; see also pp. 26-27, 34, and the discussion in §2.2.3).

10. '*Kippēr* in biblical cultic texts reflects two distinct verbal forms: (1) *kippēr* I, the primary *Pi''ēl*, and (2) *kippēr* II, a secondary denominative, from the noun *kôper* "ransom, expiation gift"' (Levine, *Presence of the Lord*, p. 67).

11. See Schenker, '*kōper*', pp. 32-46, as well as discussion in §2.2.2.

12. 'Im Interesse einer sachgemäßen Erfassung nicht nur der einzelnen Bedeutung-saspekte der Wurzel כפר, sondern auch der alttestamentlichen Sühnetheologie wird darum zu fragen sein, ob die alttestamentlichen כֹּפֶר-Belege nicht auf eine Bedeutung der Wurzel כפר hinweisen, die—bei aller sonstigen Differenz!—gerade für die כִּפֶּר-Belege im kultischen und außerkultischen Bereich konstitutiv ist. Der älteste כֹּפֶר-Beleg (Ex 21,30), der diesen Terminus unzweifelhaft als "ein Wort von bürgerlich-juristischer Natur" ausweist, vermag eine erste, positive Antwort auf diese Frage zu geben' (*Sühne*, p. 154).

13. Milgrom (*Leviticus 1–16*, pp. 1082-83) lists no less than seven different contexts in which he sees כִּפֶּר functioning as a denominative of כֹּפֶר.

2. כִּפֶּר Defined

of כֹּפֶר in at least some passages.[14] Significantly, some of the clearest examples of this come from the priestly literature, which is well illustrated by Milgrom's comments on the connection between כִּפֶּר and כֹּפֶר:

> There are...cases in which the ransom [i.e. כֹּפֶר] principle is clearly operative. (1) The function of the census money (Exod. 30.12-16) is *lĕkappēr 'al-napšōtêkem* 'to ransom your lives' (Exod. 30.16; cf. Num. 31.50): here the verb *kippēr* must be related to the expression found in the same pericope *kōper napšô* 'a ransom for his life' (Exod. 30.12). (2) The same combination of the idiom *kōper nepeš* and the verb *kippēr* is found in the law of homicide (Num. 35.31-33). Thus in these two cases, *kippēr* is a denominative from *kōper*, whose meaning is undisputed: 'ransom' (cf. Exod. 21.30). Therefore, there exists a strong possibility that all texts that assign to *kippēr* the function of averting God's wrath have *kōper* in mind: guilty life spared by substituting for it the innocent parties or their ransom.[15]

There thus seems no question that כִּפֶּר is related to כֹּפֶר in some instances, and it will be argued in the next chapter that this is indeed the case for the use of כִּפֶּר in contexts of sin. For this reason, it is important to identify the usage of כִּפֶּר as exactly as possible. This chapter therefore begins with a concept-oriented approach to כִּפֶּר in which an exegesis of the passages where the term occurs is provided in an attempt to identify those elements that are basic to its sense. We then turn to consider the term from a field-oriented approach in which it is compared and contrasted with words derived from two roots that are part of the same semantic field as כִּפֶּר, namely, פדה and גאל. Finally, we survey renderings of the term that others have proposed in order to determine the English word that is most similar to כִּפֶּר in denotation.

---

14. Stamm (*Erlösen und Vergeben*, p. 62), citing Procksch (Otto Procksch, 'λύω', in *TWNT*, IV, pp. 329-37 [330]), argues against the relationship between כִּפֶּר and כֹּפֶר on the basis of the difference in their sphere of use, namely, that כִּפֶּר belongs to the cultic–sacral realm while כֹּפֶר is a word of civil law. This fails, however, to address the fact that the two clearly are related in various passages (see quote from Milgrom above). Thus Janowski (*Sühne*, p. 154) notes in response to Stamm: 'Die Ausklammerung der כֹּפֶר-Belege ist allerdings...schon deshalb nicht gerechtfertigt, weil einige כִּפֶּר-Texte der Sache nach deutlich auf die כֹּפֶר-Problematik anspielen (2Sam 21,3f.) und es umgekehrt כֹּפֶר-Belege gibt, in denen dieses Wort seinem Sinngehalt nach einem bestimmten Bedeutungsaspekt von כִּפֶּר nahesteht (Prov 6,35) oder in einem Kontext erscheint, der traditionell dem כִּפֶּר-Begriff vorbehalten ist (Interzession: Hi 33,24; 36,18).'

15. Milgrom, *Leviticus 1–16*, p. 1082. The last line of the above actually reads as follows: 'Therefore, there exists a strong possibility that all texts that assign to *kippēr* the function of averting God's wrath have *kōper* in mind: innocent [*sic*] life spared by substituting for it the guilty [*sic*] parties or their ransom'. In a private communication, Milgrom states that he inadvertently switched the words 'innocent' and 'guilty' in the original, for which reason they are switched back in the above.

2.1. כֹּפֶר Defined[16]

To begin, then, the definition of the word כֹּפֶר will be discussed by means of a concept-oriented approach and a field-oriented approach.[17] With a concept-oriented approach, we will seek to identify those elements central to the sense of כֹּפֶר through careful exegesis of passages that contain this term. The focus here will be on how כֹּפֶר is functioning within its immediate contexts.[18] With a field-oriented approach, the term כֹּפֶר will be contrasted with words from two roots which are part of the same semantic field, namely, גאל and פדה. In identifying when כֹּפֶר is interchangeable with terms stemming from these roots, and when it is unique, the goal is again to identify those elements that are central to the sense of כֹּפֶר itself.

2.1.1. Concept-Oriented Approach

One of the greatest dangers of the concept-oriented approach is the difficulty in distinguishing the actual lexical sense of the word from concepts that are present in any given context in which the word is used.[19] While this danger is real, it is to go too far to state, as E. Nida has, that 'The correct meaning of any term is that which contributes least to the total context'.[20] As Hugenberger notes,

---

16. In this chapter all references to כֹּפֶר are to כֹּפֶר I in BDB, that is, 'ransom, bribe, composition'. Other meanings for כֹּפֶר include '(unwalled) village' (1 Sam. 6.18), 'bitumen, asphalt' (Gen. 6.14), and 'henna, henna bushes' (Song 1.14; 4.13).

17. For the distinction between 'concept-oriented' and 'field-oriented' approaches, see the discussion in Peter Cotterell and Max Turner, *Linguistics and Biblical Interpretation* (London: SPCK, 1989), pp. 145-81 (145-55). The same basic approach is also espoused by Moisés Silva, who uses the terms 'syntagmatic' and 'paradigmatic' instead of 'concept-oriented' and 'field-oriented'. For his general distinction between the two see Moisés Silva, *Biblical Words and Their Meaning: An Introduction to Lexical Semantics* (Grand Rapids: Zondervan, 1983), pp. 119-20. Silva discusses the paradigmatic approach in Chapter 5 (pp. 119-35) and the syntagmatic approach in Chapter 6 (pp. 137-69; in this regard, Silva is taking a very broad approach to what constitutes a syntagm, namely, the wider context as a whole). For a brief definition and discussion of syntagmatic and paradigmatic relationships between words see John Lyons, *Semantics* (2 vols.; Cambridge: Cambridge University Press, 1977), I, pp. 240-42.

18. For a lucid model of defining a term by means of a concept-oriented approach, consult Hugenberger's definition of בְּרִית in Gordon P. Hugenberger, *Marriage as a Covenant: A Study of Biblical Law and Ethics Governing Marriage, Developed from the Perspective of Malachi* (VTSup, 52; Leiden: E.J. Brill, 1994). The following discussion is modeled upon Hugenberger's approach.

19. Cotterell and Turner, *Linguistics*, p. 151.

20. Eugene A. Nida, 'The Implications of Contemporary Linguistics for Biblical Scholarship', *JBL* 91 (1972), pp. 73-89 (86) (cited in Anthony C. Thiselton, 'Semantics and New Testament Interpretation', in I. Howard Marshall [ed.], *New Testament Interpretation: Essays on Principles and Methods* [Carlisle: Paternoster Press, 1992], pp. 75-104 [84]).

While this principle [of Nida] offers an important corrective for certain past interpretative excesses, it appears to overstate the case and has recently been criticized and replaced by a more nuanced approach offered by A. Wierzbicka and P. Cotterell and M. Turner.[21] Offering the English word 'bicycle' as an example, Cotterell and Turner note that any English speaker would recognize as anomalous the sentence: 'It's a bicycle, but you steer it with handlebars'. This is so because the possession of handlebars is properly part of the sense or lexical concept of the term 'bicycle', even if handlebars are not normally a contextually focused element for 'bicycle'.[22]

Similarly, not every lexical concept of the term כֹּפֶר need be contextually focused in each passage in which it occurs in order to be a part of its sense. A definition of the term, therefore, may include elements that are not contextually focused in every passage.

Ideally, one would be able to test which lexical concepts are properly a part of the sense of כֹּפֶר by constructing diagnostic sentences and having a native speaker state whether the sentence was semantically anomalous or not. The following sentence would be just one possible example: 'It was a כֹּפֶר and it appeased the injured party'. Naturally, the absence of any native speakers of Biblical Hebrew makes such an exercise impossible. As a second choice—and one that must remain more tentative by the very nature of the case—one may do a careful exegesis of the passages containing the word כֹּפֶר and then look for those elements that show up consistently across a variety of passages.[23] This will be the methodology in the following discussion. Rather than give an exhaustive exegesis of each passage, only those points relevant to the understanding of כֹּפֶר will be addressed. The exegesis of these passages is then followed by a summary (§2.1.2) and a definition of כֹּפֶר (§2.1.3).

---

21. He cites here Anna Wierzbicka, *Lexicography and Conceptual Analysis* (Ann Arbor, MI: Karoma, 1985); Cotterell and Turner, *Linguistics*, pp. 122-23.

22. See Cotterell and Turner, *Linguistics*, pp. 148-49. The quote is from Hugenberger, *Marriage*, pp. 175-76.

23. Identifying 'those elements that show up consistently across a variety of passages' is important in order to avoid 'illegitimate totality transfer'. As described by James Barr (*Semantics*, p. 218), illegitimate totality transfer is committed when 'the "meaning" of a word (understood as the total series of relations in which it is used in the literature) is read into a particular case as its sense and implication there'. Stated differently, illegitimate totality transfer occurs 'when the semantic value of a word as it occurs in *one context* is *added* to its semantic value in *another context*; and the process is continued until the *sum* of these semantic values is then *read into a particular case*' (Thiselton, 'Semantics and New Testament Interpretation', p. 84 [emphasis his]). Cotterell and Turner (*Linguistics*, p. 152), citing Beekman *et al.*, discuss this in terms of confusing the 'lexical concept' with the 'discourse concept'; see John Beekman, John Callow, and Michael Kopesec, *The Semantic Structure of Written Communication* (Dallas, TX: Summer Institute of Linguistics, 5th edn, 1981), pp. 41ff.

2.1.1.1. *Exodus 21.28-32*. This is the well-known case of the goring ox.[24] The form of the case follows that of others in the Covenant Code, with כי introducing the main case (v. 28) and אם introducing variations on the main case (vv. 29, 30, 32).[25] The main case stipulates that an ox that kills someone must be stoned, though its owner is free from punishment. Verse 29 then considers a variation on this case, namely, the owner of the ox knew that the ox was in the habit of goring and yet did not guard it carefully enough. In this instance, the owner is also held liable for the death of the person and both ox and owner are killed. An exception, however, was possible: a כֹּפֶר could be placed upon the owner in lieu of death, in which case the owner was obligated to pay whatever sum was demanded (v. 30). Further attention to vv. 29-30 reveals several elements relevant to an understanding of כֹּפֶר.

The context concerns a severe wrong which results in the guilty party (i.e. the negligent owner of the ox) being condemned to death (v. 29). This can of course be avoided with the payment of a mitigated penalty, namely, the כֹּפֶר

---

24. There is extensive discussion in the literature on this case. Aside from the commentaries, see especially F.C. Fensham, 'Liability of Animals in Biblical and Ancient Near Eastern Law', *JNSL* 14 (1988), pp. 85-90; J.J. Finkelstein, *The Ox That Gored* (Philadelphia: American Philosophical Society, 1981); Bernard S. Jackson, 'The Goring Ox', in *idem* (ed.), *Essays in Jewish and Comparative Legal History* (SJLA, 10; Leiden: E.J. Brill, 1975), pp. 108-52; Janowski, *Sühne*, pp. 154-59; Meir Malul, *The Comparative Method in Ancient Near Eastern and Biblical Legal Studies* (Neukirchen–Vluyn: Neukirchener Verlag, 1990), pp. 113ff.; Eckart Otto, *Rechtsgeschichte der Redaktionen im Kodex Ešnunna und im 'Bundesbuch': Eine Redaktionsgeschichtliche und rechtsvergleichende Studie zu altbabylonischen und altisraelitischen Rechtsüberlieferungen* (Göttingen: Vandenhoeck & Ruprecht, 1989), pp. 123ff., 137ff.; *idem, Körperverletzungen in den Keilschriftrechten und im Alten Testament: Studien zum Rechtstransfer im Alten Orient* (Neukirchen–Vluyn: Neukirchener Verlag, 1991), pp. 147ff.; Shalom M. Paul, *Studies in the Book of the Covenant in the Light of Cuneiform and Biblical Law* (VTSup, 18; Leiden: E.J. Brill, 1970), pp. 78ff.; Adrian Schenker, *Versöhnung und Widerstand. Bibeltheologische Untersuchung zum Strafen Gottes und der Menschen, besonders im Lichte von Exodus 21–22* (Stuttgart: Katholisches Bibelwerk, 1990), pp. 61ff.; A. van Selms, 'The Goring Ox in Babylonian and Biblical Law', *ArOr* 18 (1950), pp. 321-30; Raymond Westbrook, *Studies in Biblical and Cuneiform Law* (CahRB, 26; Paris: J. Gabalda, 1988), pp. 40, 60f., 68, 83ff.; R. Yaron, 'The Goring Ox in Near Eastern Law', in H.H. Cohn (ed.), *Jewish Law in Ancient and Modern Israel: Selected Essays* (New York: Ktav, 1971), pp. 50-60. For ancient Near Eastern parallels see CH 250-52 and CE 54, 55. Westbrook (*Studies*, p. 83) notes that the discussion tends to focus on two points: '(1) the unusual nature of the ox's execution, not being ordinary slaughter but stoning coupled with a prohibition on eating its flesh; (2) the absence of any reference to the fate of the ox in the parallel laws of CH and CE'. These questions, however, are incidental to the understanding of כֹּפֶר as found in this passage and are therefore outside the scope of the present discussion.

25. Verse 31, which begins with או, is not a separate law as much as a further clarification of the preceding laws.

2. כֹּפֶר Defined

(v. 30). The decision on whether the owner dies or pays a כֹּפֶר instead, however, is not within their control! Verse 30 begins, 'If כֹּפֶר *is placed* upon him (אִם כֹּפֶר יוּשַׁת עָלָיו)', and this decision rests solely with the one who places the כֹּפֶר.

The text does not identify who places the כֹּפֶר; is it the family of the slain or is it a judicial court? While the latter is not impossible, it seems that the family of the slain is in view here.[26] In support of this is Exod. 21.23bα, which comes in the midst of a case concerning a pregnant woman who is struck during a fight, resulting in some type of injury (Exod. 21.22-25). While several details of the case remain obscure,[27] it is clear that the husband has some direct say in the punishment that is meted out: '...and [the guilty party] will be punished according as the husband of the woman *places upon him* (עָנוֹשׁ יֵעָנֵשׁ כַּאֲשֶׁר יָשִׁית עָלָיו בַּעַל הָאִשָּׁה)' (v. 22bα).[28] Significantly, the phrase 'places upon him' (עַל + שִׁית) is again used in Exod. 21.30 (this time in the passive) for the placing of the כֹּפֶר upon the guilty. As it was the family of the injured woman in v. 22 that places the punishment upon the guilty, it seems most likely that it is also the family of the slain that places the כֹּפֶר upon the ox-owner in v. 30 (if they choose to!). In short, the life of the ox-owner has been forfeited through their wrong into the hands of the family of the slain and their only hope of deliverance is for that family to choose to place a כֹּפֶר upon them.

As a final point, the above discussion makes clear that the wrong of the guilty party has ruptured their relationship with the injured party, and to such an extent that the latter may very well demand their death! Thus the acceptance of a כֹּפֶר instead of death not only rescues the life of the guilty, it also serves to mollify the injured party and bring peace to the damaged relationship.

---

26. So Westbrook, *Studies*, p. 85; Jackson, 'The Goring Ox', p. 127.

27. For a helpful overview see Raymond Westbrook, 'Lex Talionis and Exodus 21, 22-25', *RB* 93 (1986), pp. 52-69; see more recently, Cornelis Houtman, *Exodus* (trans. Sierd Woudstra; 4 vols.; Leuven: Peeters, 2000), III, pp. 160-71.

28. The last phrase of v. 22b has proven particularly difficult for translators. As a whole, v. 22b reads as follows: '...and he will be punished according as the husband of the woman places upon him and he will give בִּפְלִלִים (עָנוֹשׁ יֵעָנֵשׁ כַּאֲשֶׁר יָשִׁית עָלָיו בַּעַל הָאִשָּׁה וְנָתַן בִּפְלִלִים)'. Many of the ancient versions (LXX, Vulg., TO) took the term בִּפְלִלִים as a reference to judges or to the activity of judges, an idea reflected in the AV translation: '...and he shall pay as the judges determine'. This appears problematic, however, in two regards. First, as Westbrook ('Lex Talionis', pp. 58-61) notes, other occurrences of the root פלל run into serious (if not intractable) problems when the rendering 'judge' is used, for example, Deut. 32.30-31. Second, it seems curious that after stating the husband decides the punishment, the guilty party then pays according to the judges. While the exact meaning of פְּלִלִים remains obscure, various renderings have been proposed which avoid one or both of the above problems posed by the rendering 'judge' (see Houtman, *Exodus*, pp. 162-63, for an extensive overview of various approaches to this word).

In sum, the life of the ox-owner is forfeit: having participated via their negligence in the death of another person, their punishment is death (v. 29). This punishment, however, may be avoided by a mitigated penalty: a כֹּפֶר may be given instead, effectively ransoming their life (it is a פִּדְיֹן נַפְשׁוֹ) and re-establishing peace with the injured party. But it is not up to the guilty to decide. Their only hope of deliverance is with the family of the slain, into whose hands their life is forfeit: if they choose to extend to the guilty the option of כֹּפֶר, the guilty may escape death; if not, death is the expected result.

2.1.1.2. *Exodus 30.11-16.* This passage contains laws related to taking a census of Israelite men over the age of twenty. The reason for the census is not stated.[29] What is clear, however, is the severity of the situation, for census-taking in Israel was an exercise fraught with danger.[30] The reason for the danger remains a matter of debate.[31] The severity of the danger, however, is perfectly evident: those counted in a census risked suffering a plague from the LORD (v. 12), an event which was always accompanied by disease or

---

29. The passage simply begins in the normal manner of case law ('When [כִּי] you take a census...' [v. 12]); it has been observed, however, that the totals of this census (Exod. 38.25-28) are the same as those of Num. 1.46, which is clearly a census for war (Num. 1.3).

30. See the story of David's census in 2 Sam. 24. The danger accompanying a census was not unique to Israel in the ancient Near East; see E.A. Speiser, 'Census and Ritual Expiation in Mari and Israel', *BASOR* 149 (1958), pp. 17-25; Milgrom, *Numbers*, pp. 336-37.

31. In his well-known article, 'Census and Ritual Expiation in Mari and Israel', E.A. Speiser suggests that the recording of names in a census would have been ominous to an ancient Near Easterner because of its similarity to the actions of the gods in recording names in the 'cosmic' books of life and death for the purpose of deciding who would live and who would die. As a precautionary measure, then, the one being counted would offer some form of propitiation (pp. 23-25). While interesting, this explanation is largely speculative, insofar as it cannot be proved that an ancient Near Easterner would have made a cognitive connection between the writing down of their name and the cosmic books of life and death. Moreover, the census passage we are considering states that the כֹּפֶר is offered to avoid a plague, which always came about because of some wrong—whether moral or ritual—on the part of the people (in this regard, the taking of the census in 2 Sam. 24 is instructive in that David does not see the action as simply dangerous, but dangerous because it was sinful [v. 10]). This stands in contrast to Speiser's suggestion, which holds that a census was dangerous not due to any wrong but rather because of its correspondence with the divine books of life. It is unlikely, then, that Speiser's suggestion applies to the biblical material. More recently, Houtman (*Exodus*, pp. 562-63) has argued that knowing the number is equal to having power over the counted persons and thus infringing on the authority of God. If this were the case, however, one would expect that only those taking the census—and not those counted—would be guilty; in our text, though, it is the ones counted who must give the כֹּפֶר.

death.³² In order to avoid this plague, each person had to give a כֹּפֶר of one-half shekel of silver as a contribution for the work of the tabernacle (vv. 13-16). This would in turn serve as a memorial before the LORD, making atonement for their lives (v. 16).³³

The main observations relevant to כֹּפֶר made in the comments above on Exod. 21.28-32 are also relevant here. To begin, an act is described (i.e. the taking of a census) that will result in severe consequences for those involved, namely, a plague from the LORD. While it is not as clear as in Exodus 21 why the deed is wrong (reasons of pollution? infringement upon the property of the LORD?), the end result is the same: one party has offended another and is liable to severe consequences at the hand of the offended.³⁴ Second, in place of this severe consequence, a mitigated penalty is offered: the payment of a כֹּפֶר. This payment serves to rescue (otherwise forfeited) life from certain doom. Third, the כֹּפֶר not only rescues the life of the guilty, it also functions to appease the injured party, restoring peace to the relationship.³⁵ Finally, the offer of כֹּפֶר is extended at the initiative of the 'injured' party, that is, the LORD. While in Exod. 21.30 the offer of כֹּפֶר was determined on a case-by-case basis, in the present passage the LORD makes clear that כֹּפֶר

---

32. See Num. 17.11-14 (16.46-49); 25.1-9; 1 Sam. 5.6-10; 2 Sam. 24.15-17.

33. Literally לְכַפֵּר עַל־נַפְשֹׁתֵיכֶם. The important role that כֹּפֶר plays in the context of a census or plague is underscored with reference to other passages including either of these. Most similar to our present passage is Num. 31.48-54. Here a census is taken after a battle to determine if any men have been lost. Having taken the census, the officers then come to Moses and bring a תְּרוּמָה (v. 52; cf. Exod. 30.13, 14, 15) in order to כַּפֵּר for themselves (נֶפֶשׁ + עַל + כַּפֵּר, v. 50; cf. Exod. 30.15, 16). The תְּרוּמָה is then taken to the tent of meeting (v. 54; cf. Exod. 30.13, 16) as a memorial before the LORD (זִכָּרוֹן + לִפְנֵי יְהוָה, v. 54; cf. Exod. 30.16). Similarly, 2 Sam. 24 records that 70,000 people died after the census of David (v. 15). Though the verb כִּפֶּר does not occur here, the passage does record that the plague was finally checked when David made burnt offerings and peace offerings, the former of which presumably functioned to accomplish כִּפֶּר (cf. Lev. 1.4). Even where a census was not involved, כִּפֶּר was still necessary for stopping a plague. The clearest example of this is Num. 17.11-14 (16.46-49) where a plague decimates the people (17.14 [16.49]) until Aaron effects כִּפֶּר for the people (17.12-13 [16.47-48]). See also Num. 8.14-19, where the Levites are taken in place of the first-born Israelites to כִּפֶּר on their behalf so that a plague from the LORD does not come upon them (v. 19).

34. That the LORD is the one offended is clear in our passage from the fact that it is a plague 'from the LORD'. Similarly, after David's census in 2 Sam. 24 we read that 'the LORD sent a pestilence upon Israel from the morning until the appointed time; and seventy thousand men of the people from Dan to Beersheba died' (v. 15).

35. A plague was considered evidence of the wrath of the LORD. During the plague of Num. 17, for example, Moses says to Aaron, 'Take your censer and put in it fire from the altar, and lay incense on it; then bring it quickly to the congregation and make atonement for them, for *wrath has gone forth from the Lord, the plague has begun!*' (17.11 [16.47]). See also references in n. 32.

is available whenever the situation arises. In both instances, however, the prerogative to grant כֹּפֶר lies in the hand of the offended.

2.1.1.3. Numbers 35.30-34. Numbers 35.9-34 is one of four passages which discuss the cities of refuge.[36] The passage begins by specifying who may use the city for refuge (viz. those who killed someone unintentionally; vv. 11, 15, 22-25) and who may not use the city for refuge (viz. those who murdered; vv. 16-21). Verses 26-29 then stipulate that those who kill unintentionally must remain in the city of refuge until the death of the high priest. If they leave the city before that time they are liable to death at the hands of the blood redeemer (vv. 26-27); it is only after the death of the high priest that they may leave with impunity (v. 28). This leads up to vv. 30-34, which consist of three major sections.

The first section, vv. 30-31, considers the case of murder. Verse 30 stipulates that at least two witnesses are necessary to condemn someone to death, and v. 31 that כֹּפֶר may not be accepted for those guilty of murder. The second section, v. 32, concerns those who have killed unintentionally and are living in a city of refuge. Here too it is stated that כֹּפֶר is unacceptable, that is, they may not pay a כֹּפֶר and leave the city of refuge; as noted above, it is only the death of the high priest that allows them to leave with impunity. The final section, vv. 33-34, provides the ground for the prohibition on כֹּפֶר in the previous two sections: the blood of the slain pollutes the land and the only way to כִּפֶּר the land is by the death of the slayer (v. 33). Without this the land would be defiled, an event which was unacceptable due to the fact that the LORD himself dwelt in the midst of it (v. 34).

This text differs from the first two considered above in that כֹּפֶר is not a viable option for the guilty party.[37] It also differs in that the reason for not

---

36. See also Exod. 21.13 (here 'place' [מָקוֹם] instead of 'city of refuge'); Deut. 19.1-13; Josh. 20.1-9.

37. Indeed, the *prohibition* of כֹּפֶר in this passage has led at least one scholar to conclude that the payment of a כֹּפֶר was *practiced* in Israel for homicide and was applicable in other homicide laws (even when it is not stated as an option). Thus Westbrook cites this text in support of his theory that the biblical system was consonant with other ancient Near Eastern systems of law with regard to allowing ransom in the case of intentional homicide. After looking at Exod. 21.12-14 and Deut. 19.1-14, in which he infers from other ancient Near Eastern sources that ransom was a possible, though unmentioned, alternative, Westbrook turns to Num. 35.9-34. After describing the similarities between this law and those in Exod. 21 and Deut. 19, he then states: '…what we have been forced to infer from the other two sources—the right of the avenger to take ransom-money instead of revenge—is revealed as an explicit assumption about the existing law. But it is at this point that Num. 35 parts company with the other two sources. For it assumes the existence of ransom only to forbid it entirely in the case of premeditated murder (v. 31) and for return of the killer from exile in other cases (v. 32)'

accepting a כֹּפֶר is clearly tied in with ideas of pollution, a point not made in Exod. 21.30 (though perhaps included in Exod. 30.11-16?). Despite these differences, however, the understanding of כֹּפֶר in this passage is more or less the same as in the above. To begin, there is a guilty party (the slayer) and an injured party (the blood redeemer, usually identified with the family of the slain[38]). Second, the life of the slayer is forfeited through his or her wrong into the hand of the blood redeemer. Thus vv. 19 and 21, addressing the case of intentional homicide, both state that it is the blood avenger that is to put the slayer to death, and v. 25, addressing the case of unintentional homicide, states that the congregation shall deliver the slayer *from the hand of* the blood avenger. From this one may infer that if ransom were a viable option, this choice would be completely in the power of the blood avenger. Third, this is again a situation where the כֹּפֶר—were it acceptable—would need to mollify the injured party, who would otherwise execute the guilty. Finally, it may be noted that if כֹּפֶר were possible here it would obviously be a mitigated penalty (damages as opposed to death) and would rescue the life of the slayer.

2.1.1.4. *Psalm 49.8-9 (7-8)*.[39]

In Psalm 49 the psalmist describes the general sinfulness of his enemies, who fear no consequences because of their riches

---

(Westbrook, *Studies*, pp. 79-80). In this way, Westbrook appears to suggest that Num. 35 is evidence that the payment of כֹּפֶר in the laws of Exod. 21 and Deut. 19 was an assumed right.

It may be granted with Westbrook that this law is most likely prohibiting an existing practice (and so note Bernard Jackson's comment ['Reflections on Biblical Criminal Law', in *idem* (ed.), *Essays in Jewish and Comparative Legal History*, pp. 25-63 (46)], cited by Westbrook [*Studies*, p. 80 n. 170]: 'A legislator does not waste his energy in condemnation of acts which are not done'). The fact that this might have been an existing practice at this time, however, does not at all indicate that this practice had been accepted as legitimate. ' "Thou shalt not kill, thou shalt not commit adultery, thou shalt not steal" imply that murder, adultery, and theft were all previously known, but not that they were permitted' (Jackson, 'Reflections', p. 46). For this reason, one cannot infer from Num. 35 that the payment of כֹּפֶר was an assumed right in the laws of Exod. 21 and Deut. 19. At most, one may say that it would appear in Num. 35 that ransom was being practiced for murder and that this was *ethically unacceptable* to the legislator; hence the need to specify that it must not be done.

38. See George Buchanan Gray, *Numbers* (ICC; Edinburgh: T. & T. Clark, 1903), pp. 470-71; Gordon J. Wenham, *Numbers* (TOTC; Leicester: InterVarsity Press, 1981), p. 236; Jeremiah Unterman, 'Redemption', in *ABD*, V, pp. 650-54 (651).

39. It is also possible to group Prov. 13.8 here since it too appears to deal with a situation that does not involve a specific sin. The verse reads as follows: 'The ransom (כֹּפֶר) of one's life is their riches, but the poor hears no rebuke'. This verse seems to be suggesting that the rich are subject to many threats due to the fact that they have money to buy their way out of danger, whereas the poor are ignored because they have nothing

and wealth (vv. 6 [5], 7 [6], 12 [11]). By considering the common fate of all people, however, the psalmist assures himself that he need not fear their adversity. After all, the wealthy have no ultimate advantage over him since not even their riches can rescue them from death: 'No man can by any means ransom (לֹא פָדֹה יִפְדֶּה) his brother or give to God a כֹּפֶר for him; for the ransom (פִּדְיוֹן) of his soul is costly...' (vv. 8-9a).

This passage differs from the others discussed above in that there is no one specific sin in view that is warranting death, for example, murder or census-taking; rather, it is the death that comes to all people that is being considered. At the same time, however, the contrast is between the consequence the *wicked* face in death (i.e. Sheol; v. 15 [14]) and that which the *righteous* face (i.e. redemption by the LORD; v. 16 [15]). In this regard, כֹּפֶר is operating in a similar context to the above passages: there is a guilty party, the wicked, who face a severe consequence (death). If anything could rescue them it would be a כֹּפֶר, which they could easily supply from their wealth. This decision, however, is not within their power to make; only God can decide whether כֹּפֶר is accepted or not, and in this case the decision is negative: no כֹּפֶר would suffice (v. 8 [7]).

2.1.1.5. *Proverbs 6.20-35.* This passage is a warning from father to son to avoid the adulteress. One of the many reasons he gives to his son for doing so comes in his description of the reaction of the husband who has been cheated on: 'For jealousy enrages a man, and he will not spare in the day of vengeance. He will not accept any כֹּפֶר, nor will he be content though you multiply the bribe (שֹׁחַד)' (Prov. 6.34-35).

As the passage in Numbers 35 raised the question of whether a כֹּפֶר was normatively accepted in the case of homicide, this passage has raised the question of whether a כֹּפֶר was acceptable in the case of adultery, even though it is explicitly stated elsewhere that death should be the result (e.g. Lev. 20.10). There are actually two points at issue here. The first, which can only be mentioned in passing, is a question concerning methodology in reading biblical law and can be stated as follows: Are we to read every case law at its face value, that is, the adulterer of Lev. 20.10 *must* die, or are we to understand that there could be unstated assumptions of the text that would have been well known to the society receiving the law, for example, adulterers could pay a legitimate כֹּפֶר and thus escape death?[40] If one holds that

to offer (so William McKane, *Proverbs* [OTL; London: SCM Press, 1970], p. 458). The context is not specific enough, however, to allow firm conclusions to be drawn.

40. The differences between the two approaches can be seen in Jackson's ('Reflections', pp. 25-63) critiques of Moshe Greenberg (Moshe Greenberg, 'Some Postulates of Biblical Criminal Law', in Menahem Haran [ed.], *Yehezkel Kaufmann Jubilee Volume* [Jerusalem: Magnes Press, 1960], pp. 5-28), Shalom M. Paul (*Studies*), and Anthony

case law should be read at face value, then the כֹּפֶר mentioned in Prov. 6.35 will be seen as an illegitimate payment. If not, then one will see the כֹּפֶר mentioned in Prov. 6.35 as a normal and legitimate option.

But this leads to the second issue, for even if one holds that case law can allow for unstated exceptions, it must still be determined if Prov. 6.35 is one of those exceptions or not. Stated differently, was the option of כֹּפֶר mentioned in Prov. 6.35 one that was legally sanctioned?

Those who argue that while death *could* be exacted in the case of adultery, it did not *need* to be, generally understand the word כֹּפֶר here as a reference to a legally legitimate payment (though in this case not accepted due to the wrath of the husband). Thus Jackson states:

> Prov. 6.32-35 condemns the adulterer as a fool. The husband will be jealous and will not accept *kofer*. His non-acceptance is the result of the human attribute of jealousy, not of any legal prohibition. The text is correctly viewed as evidence that adultery could be settled by payment of an agreed amount of compensation.[41]

On the other hand, those who argue that the law did not permit compensation in the case of adultery understand the word כֹּפֶר here as a reference to a 'bribe'. Thus Phillips points out, *contra* Jackson and McKeating, that while כֹּפֶר can refer to a legal payment of money it can also refer to a bribe (see 1 Sam. 12.3; Amos 5.12). That this is the case here finds support in the fact that כֹּפֶר is parallel to שַׁחַד, 'the normal Old Testament word for the payment of money to pervert the course of justice, and generally translated "bribe" '.[42]

Leaving aside the question of whether case law allowed for unstated exceptions, it is agreed with Phillips here that Jackson and McKeating have begged the question by assuming that כֹּפֶר refers to a legally legitimate payment. While Jackson correctly states that a כֹּפֶר was considered a possibility in this instance, the question that remains is whether this כֹּפֶר was an ethically acceptable payment in the mind of the writer or whether it was a bribe, 'hush money'. Neither Jackson nor McKeating adequately address this. Their argument is further weakened by failing to comment on the word שַׁחַד.

Phillips (*Ancient Israel's Criminal Law: A New Approach to the Decalogue* [Oxford: Basil Blackwell, 1970]). Greenberg, Paul, and Phillips tend toward reading the laws at their face value while Jackson is much more cautious of such an approach.

41. Jackson, 'Reflections', p. 60. See also Henry McKeating ('Sanctions against Adultery in Ancient Israelite Society, with Some Reflections on Methodology in the Study of Old Testament Ethics', *JSOT* 11 [1979], pp. 57-72 [59]): 'Though it is not stated, it may be that what the unappeased husband may do is to apply the full rigor of the law and demand the extreme penalty. What is manifest is that he is certainly not *obliged* to do any such thing. The penalty is evidently largely a matter for his discretion, and he can in principle be bought off.' See, however, the comments further below.

42. Anthony Phillips, 'Another Look at Adultery', *JSOT* 20 (1981), pp. 3-25 (17-18).

While this word need not always denote 'bribe', as Phillips himself notes,[43] it often appears with this sense, especially in a judicial context: 'A wicked person receives a bribe (שֹׁחַד) from the bosom to pervert the ways of justice' (Prov. 17.23; see further Exod. 23.8; Deut. 10.17; 16.19; 27.25; 1 Sam. 8.3, etc.). This would tip the evidence in favor of understanding כֹּפֶר to have a negative sense here, which, in turn, suggests that even if the giving of כֹּפֶר were practiced in Israel in the case of adultery, the law would have viewed this action as ethically unacceptable.

Though כֹּפֶר has a negative sense in this context, it still operates in a manner similar to those cases in which it is legally permissible: there is a guilty party and an injured party; the guilty party has forfeit himself to the injured party, who in turn decides whether the guilty party is punished or whether כֹּפֶר is accepted instead; the כֹּפֶר—were it accepted!—would serve to mollify the wrath of the injured party; and finally, the giving of the כֹּפֶר would be a less severe punishment than was otherwise expected.

2.1.1.6. *1 Samuel 12.1-5; Amos 5.12*.[44] In both of these passages כֹּפֶר is used in the same sense as in Prov. 6.35 above, that is, 'bribe'. In 1 Samuel 12, Samuel addresses the people before the confirmation of Saul as king. In so doing, he states his innocence in all matters related to his leading of the people: 'Here I am; bear witness against me before the LORD and his anointed. Whose ox have I taken, or whose donkey have I taken, or whom have I defrauded? Whom have I oppressed, or from whose hand have I taken a bribe (כֹּפֶר) to blind my eyes with it? I will restore it to you' (v. 3). This can be contrasted with the sinful behavior of the leaders in Amos 5.12, whom the LORD reproves as follows: 'For I know your transgressions are many and your sins are great, you who distress the righteous and accept a bribe (כֹּפֶר), and turn aside the poor in the gate'.

Though these passages provide far less contextual clues than others above, it is still evident that the כֹּפֶר is operating in a context in which one party (Samuel, the leaders) has power over another, as demonstrated by the fact that it is Samuel and the leaders who are offered the bribe. Further, the very fact that a bribe is offered implies that the one offering it is seeking to avoid the normal procedure of the law, which could refer simply to bending the law in their favor in a general sense, but which could also refer to disregarding the law so that they escape a punishment that the law requires. Finally, in those cases where it is a punishment they are seeking to escape, the כֹּפֶר would obviously be a lesser penalty, or else the guilty would not offer it in the first place.

---

43. Phillips, 'Another Look at Adultery', p. 18.
44. It is possible that Job 36.18 belongs here, though vv. 16-20 are extremely difficult and do not allow for any solid conclusions.

2.1.1.7. *Isaiah 43.3-4*.⁴⁵ Isaiah 43.3-4 differs from any of the above passages in that the כֹּפֶר is not given by the ones facing punishment; instead, it is given by the one who is wronged: the LORD himself! 'For I am the LORD your God, the Holy One of Israel, your Savior; I have given Egypt as your ransom (כֹּפֶר), Cush and Seba in your place. Since you are precious in my sight, since your are honored and I love you, I will give others in your place and other peoples in exchange for your life.' As a result, the כֹּפֶר in this instance results in no material loss for the guilty party, that is, for Israel. Nonetheless, in common with the above instances of כֹּפֶר is the fact that there is a guilty party (Israel) whose life is forfeit (i.e. they are in exile and have no hope of rescuing themselves). As well, the כֹּפֶר is the means by which they are relieved of this penalty. Moreover, as the exile of the people was the ultimate sign of the rupture between Israel and God, so the giving of the כֹּפֶר and the subsequent return of the people signals the appeasement of the LORD and the re-establishment of peace to the relationship. Finally, the offer of כֹּפֶר was completely at the discretion of the offended party. This is especially evident in this text as it is the injured party himself who provides the כֹּפֶר.

2.1.1.8. *Job 33.24*. This chapter is part of Elihu's speech to Job, in which he describes a man who is suffering (vv. 19-22) but who is then ransomed: 'If there is an angel as mediator for him, one out of a thousand, to remind a man what is right for him, then let him be gracious to him and say, "Deliver him from going down to the pit, I have found a ransom (כֹּפֶר)"' (vv. 23-24). After this occurs the sufferer prays to God for acceptance and then states to those around him, 'I have sinned and perverted what is right and it is not proper for me. He has ransomed (פָּדָה) my soul from going to the pit and my life shall see the light' (vv. 27-28).

Like other passages, the כֹּפֶר here functions to deliver someone from a severe threat, in this case 'going down to the pit' (v. 24). Moreover, this is a punishment that seems to be connected in some way with the sin of the one doomed to die (v. 27), and appears to have been accepted (v. 28), though the element of an injured party is not as much in focus here as elsewhere. Like Isa. 43.3-4 above, this text also differs from the other כֹּפֶר passages above in that it is a third party—in this case the angelic messenger (v. 23)—that provides the כֹּפֶר and not the one who is facing the negative consequence.

---

45. It is also possible to place Prov. 21.18 here, which is similar to Isa. 43.3-4 in its focus upon one party serving as a כֹּפֶר and thereby suffering some penalty or misfortune in place of another party: 'The wicked is a ransom (כֹּפֶר) for the righteous, and the treacherous is in the place of the upright'. The idea here appears to be that the righteous escape some form of punishment or misfortune through the substitution of the wicked as a כֹּפֶר. Once again, however, the context is not specific enough for more substantial conclusions to be drawn about the nature of כֹּפֶר.

2.1.2. Summary of Exegetical Findings

In view of the above exegesis, the following four elements of כֹּפֶר may be put forward as fundamental to the meaning of the term (focusing for the present on the positive sense of כֹּפֶר).

2.1.2.1. *Delivery of a guilty party from punishment.* That is to say, some wrong has been done and the כֹּפֶר is given in order to deliver the guilty party from the punishment that the wrong calls for. As will be seen below, this distinguishes it from a redemption payment, in which payment is given to redeem someone from the ownership of another though without any sense that the one being redeemed has done any wrong.[46]

2.1.2.2. *Dependence upon the one wronged to accept it.* This further clarifies the statement above, for it is not simply that a wrong has been done that requires punishment, but that the decision on whether a כֹּפֶר is accepted in lieu of punishment lies completely in the hands of the offended.

2.1.2.3. *Mitigation of the penalty.* This includes the idea that it is still a punishment, but that it is a lesser punishment than would have ordinarily been expected.

2.1.2.4. *Appeasement of the injured party.* The offense of the guilty party is such that it not only causes them to be subject to punishment, it also ruptures their relationship with the injured party. The כֹּפֶר thus not only rescues their life from the deserved punishment, it also functions to mollify the injured party and restore peace to the relationship.

2.1.3. Definition and Rendering of כֹּפֶר

The above summary leads to the following definition of כֹּפֶר. Positively, a כֹּפֶר is a legally or ethically legitimate payment that delivers a guilty party from a just punishment that is the right of the offended party to execute or to have executed. The acceptance of this payment is entirely dependent upon the choice of the offended party is a lesser punishment than was originally expected, and its acceptance serves both to rescue the life of the guilty and to appease the offended party, thus restoring peace to the relationship. We turn to consider which English word most closely denotes this understanding of the term כֹּפֶר in §2.2 below.

Slightly different is the negative sense of כֹּפֶר, which may be defined as a legally or ethically questionable payment which delivers a guilty party from a just punishment by the offended party or the forces of law, or which

---

46. See §2.1.5 below.

otherwise subverts the normal course of justice. Once more, acceptance of this payment is dependent upon the one to whom it is given (e.g. judges, elders in the city gate). As is generally agreed, this sense of כֹּפֶר is best rendered by the English word 'bribe'.

2.1.4. *Field-Oriented Approach*

Having identified the basic sense of כֹּפֶר using a concept-oriented approach, we may now attempt to clarify an understanding of this term further by comparing it with other terms that are within the same semantic field. To be specific, we will consider the nominal forms of two roots, namely, פדה and גאל.[47] Naturally, there are many other terms that could also be considered in the following. For example, one could consider all of those terms that occur in contexts where some item of value is given from one person to another, such as various words for 'gift' (אֶשְׁכָּר ;מִנְחָה ;מַתָּן, etc.). The justification for focusing upon the roots פדה and גאל is that they occur in contexts that are the most similar to כֹּפֶר, namely, in contexts where one party is being delivered from the authority of another through the giving of an item of value (as opposed to words for 'gift', which do not necessarily involve the idea of deliverance). This similarity in context is important in identifying the finer nuances of meaning, since the closer the contexts of two different terms are to one another, the finer the distinctions are between the way in which those two terms are used. Stated differently, the choice of two different terms to express more or less the same thing in more or less the same context signifies either that the terms are identical in meaning or that they are very similar in meaning and yet have some slight but distinct difference. As will be seen below, the latter is indeed the case with both פדה and גאל in relation to כֹּפֶר.

2.1.4.1. פדה. The root פדה witnesses the following nominal forms: פְּדוּיִם, פְּדְיוֹן, פִּדְיוֹם, and פְּדוּת.[48] These forms separate into three distinct usages. In the first usage is פְּדוּת, which is the most general of the three, occurring in Pss. 111.9 and 130.7.[49] In these passages it has the broad sense of 'rescue' or 'redemption' from some type of negative situation: 'He sent redemption to his people (פְּדוּת שָׁלַח לְעַמּוֹ); he has commanded his covenant for ever. Holy and terrible is his name!' (Ps. 111.9); 'O Israel, hope in the LORD! For with

---

47. The verbal uses of these roots more or less overlap with the nominal uses; they will be referred to below in conjunction with the discussion of the nominal uses.
48. This last word occurs only twice, and both times in construct. The absolute would perhaps have been *פִּדְיוֹן (cf. the construct of נִקְיוֹן in Amos 4.6: נִקְיוֹן שִׁנַּיִם; see also Joüon 88Mb). In the absence of certainty, however, the term פִּדְיוֹן will be used.
49. פְּדוּת also occurs in Exod. 8.19 (23), though a reading of *פְּלֻת would seem to fit the context better (cf. v. 18, where the root פלה occurs).

the LORD there is steadfast love, and with him is plenteous redemption (וְהַרְבֵּה עִמּוֹ פְדוּת)' (Ps. 130.7). Unlike כֹּפֶר, which refers to a type of payment, פְּדוּת is used in these verses more broadly to refer to the act of redeeming or rescuing someone. Indeed, this general sense of redeeming or rescuing from trouble is paralleled by the verb פָּדָה, which frequently occurs with this meaning (e.g. to redeem/rescue from troubles [Ps. 25.22], enemies [Ps. 55.19 (18)], or some other negative situation [2 Sam. 4.9; Job 5.20; 6.23; Pss. 26.11; 31.6 (5); Isa. 51.11; Jer. 15.21, etc.]). Unlike the contexts of כֹּפֶר, the person being redeemed or rescued in these situations has not necessarily done any wrong, nor does the decision on whether the person may be redeemed or rescued lie in the hand of the one from whom they are being redeemed.

Within the second usage are the nouns פְּדוּיִם and פִּדְיוֹם. These occur in Num. 3.40-51, which discusses the ransoming of the first-born. Both of these terms are similar to כֹּפֶר in that they refer to a payment. In the case of Numbers 3, this was the five-shekel payment that had to be given for the 273 first-born who were in excess of the number of the Levites: 'So Moses took the ransom money (וַיִּקַּח מֹשֶׁה אֵת כֶּסֶף הַפִּדְיוֹם) from those who were in excess...' (v. 49a); 'And Moses gave the ransom money (וַיִּתֵּן מֹשֶׁה אֶת־כֶּסֶף הַפְּדֻיִם) to Aaron and his sons...' (v. 51a; see also vv. 46, 48; Num. 18.16).

What is especially significant to note in Numbers 3 and other first-born passages are the contextual similarities and differences between these passages and the passages mentioning כֹּפֶר. To begin, it is important to note that the first-born child or animal did not belong first and foremost to its parents or owners but to God. Thus in Exodus 13, which uses the verb פָּדָה instead of the nominal forms, we read:

> And when the LORD brings you into the land of the Canaanites, as he swore to you and to your fathers, and shall give it to you, you shall set apart to the LORD all that first opens the womb. All the firstlings of your cattle that are males shall be the LORD's. Every firstling of a donkey you shall ransom (תִּפְדֶּה) with a lamb, or if you will not ransom it (וְאִם־לֹא תִפְדֶּה) you shall break its neck. Every first-born of man among your sons you shall ransom (תִּפְדֶּה). And when in time to come your son asks you, 'What does this mean?', you shall say to him, 'By strength of hand the LORD brought us out of Egypt, from the house of bondage. For when Pharaoh stubbornly refused to let us go, the LORD slew all the first-born in the land of Egypt, both the first-born of man and the first-born of cattle. Therefore I sacrifice to the LORD all the males that first open the womb; but all the first-born of my sons I ransom (אֶפְדֶּה).' (vv. 11-15; see also Lev. 27.26-27; Num. 18.15-17)

In short, the first-born belonged to the LORD. If it was an animal that was suitable for sacrifice, then it would be offered to the LORD. If not, it would be ransomed by means of a sacrificial animal. Similarly, a first-born son also had to be ransomed, and in this regard the LORD stipulates in Numbers 3 that the ransom was to be a Levite, or, failing that, a payment of five shekels. What is significant about this context is that the person or animal being ransomed belongs to the LORD and it is the LORD as the controlling party who must stipulate what the ransom will be. In this regard the context of the first-born is quite similar to that of כֹּפֶר, namely, one is not simply delivering a person or item from the power of another, one is doing so by means of a payment, and then only by such payment as stipulated by the controlling party.

What is even more significant, however, is the difference between the context of the first-born and that of כֹּפֶר, namely, whereas someone in need of a כֹּפֶר has done something wrong by which they have placed themselves under the authority of another, the first-born is guilty of no wrong at all. Indeed, while the term פִּדְיוֹן can be used parallel to כֹּפֶר in a context of wrong, as will be seen immediately below, the term כֹּפֶר does not occur in the various passages addressing the ransom of the first-born (the same is true of the verb כִּפֶּר). It is reserved instead for those passages in which some wrong has been committed.

This leads us to the third usage, that of פִּדְיוֹן. This term occurs only twice and both times it is used in close conjunction with כֹּפֶר. In the case of the goring ox in Exodus 21 we read, 'If a כֹּפֶר is placed upon [the guilty owner of the ox], then he shall give for the פִּדְיוֹן of his life whatever is placed upon him (אִם־כֹּפֶר יוּשַׁת עָלָיו וְנָתַן פִּדְיֹן נַפְשׁוֹ כְּכֹל אֲשֶׁר־יוּשַׁת עָלָיו)' (v. 30). It is difficult at this point to distinguish any difference at all between כֹּפֶר and פִּדְיוֹן. Indeed, not only are both words the passive subject of יוּשַׁת, but פִּדְיוֹן + נָתַן נַפְשׁוֹ here in v. 30 is paralleled by כֹּפֶר נַפְשׁוֹ + נָתַן in Exod. 30.12. These observations thus suggest that the terms are basically equivalent here; the choice of פִּדְיוֹן over כֹּפֶר would then perhaps be due to stylistic considerations. The second passage is Ps. 49.8-9 (7-8). Though the text has some difficulties, it is clear enough to show a similar interchange between כֹּפֶר and פִּדְיוֹן: 'No man can by any means ransom (לֹא־פָדֹה יִפְדֶּה) his brother, or give God a ransom (כֹּפֶר) for him; for the ransom (פִּדְיוֹן) of their life is costly, and he should cease forever'. Once again, there is no obvious difference in meaning between the two terms, and an explanation in terms of stylistic variation is even more probable given the poetic nature of the verse. In short, פִּדְיוֹן in these two instances seems to be used synonymously with כֹּפֶר; in this regard, it has the same sense as that identified above for כֹּפֶר (§2.1.3).

By way of summary, then, the nominal forms of the root פדה have three distinct usages. In the first, פְּדוּת refers generally to the act of redeeming or rescuing someone from danger; this overlaps with כֹּפֶר-contexts in only a very broad way. In the second, פִּדְיוֹם and פִּדוּיִם refer to a payment made to ransom a first-born man or animal. It was noted that this context was very similar to כֹּפֶר-contexts in that it involved not only ransoming someone, but ransoming them by means of a payment, and then only by such payment as stipulated by the controlling party. It was also noted, however, that this context differed in that the party in need of ransom had done nothing wrong, whereas כֹּפֶר is used only in contexts where some wrong has been done. This led to the third usage, in which פִּדְיוֹן is used synonymously with כֹּפֶר in Exod. 21.30 and Ps. 49.8-9 (7-8), thus having the same denotation in these passages as identified for כֹּפֶר above.

2.1.4.2. גאל. גאל[50] attests one nominal form, גְּאֻלָּה,[51] as well as a nominal use of the participle, namely, גֹּאֵל.

The first of these, גְּאֻלָּה, can refer either to the legal right of redemption (i.e. the right to release a person or object from the possession of another) or the action thereof, or it can also refer to the redemption price itself. These uses can be illustrated by the following verses:

(1) right of redemption:

> If a man sells a dwelling house in a walled city, he may redeem it within a whole year after its sale; for a full year he shall have the right of redemption (וְאִישׁ כִּי־יִמְכֹּר בֵּית־מוֹשַׁב עִיר חוֹמָה וְהָיְתָה גְּאֻלָּתוֹ עַד־תֹּם שְׁנַת מִמְכָּרוֹ יָמִים תִּהְיֶה גְאֻלָּתוֹ) (Lev. 25.29);

> As for the cities of the Levites, the Levites have a permanent right of redemption (גְּאֻלַּת עוֹלָם תִּהְיֶה לַלְוִיִּם) for the houses of the cities which are their possession (Lev. 25.32; see also vv. 24, 31, 48; Ruth 4.6; Jer. 32.7, 8);

(2) act of redemption:

> Now this was the custom in former times in Israel concerning the redemption and the exchange (וְזֹאת לְפָנִים בְּיִשְׂרָאֵל עַל־הַגְּאֻלָּה וְעַל־הַתְּמוּרָה): to confirm a transaction, the one drew off their sandal and gave it to the other, and this was the manner of attesting in Israel (Ruth 4.7);[52]

(3) redemption price:

> If there remain but a few years until the year of Jubilee, he shall make a reckoning with him; according to the years of service due from him he shall refund [the money for] his redemption (כְּפִי שָׁנָיו יָשִׁיב אֶת־גְּאֻלָּתוֹ) (Lev. 25.52; see also vv. 26, 51).[53]

---

50. All references are to גאל I in BDB. BDB lists a גאל II form meaning 'to defile', but this is semantically unrelated to גאל I.

51. Possibly also גְּאוּלַי in Isa. 63.4, though certainty on this point is difficult.

52. The verb גָּאַל, which occurs alongside of גְּאֻלָּה in Lev. 25 and Ruth 4, occurs frequently in this second sense, that is, to describe the act of redeeming a person or object.

53. It is possible that Ezek. 11.15 uses the term in a fourth way, namely, as a reference to close relatives.

In relation to כֹּפֶר-contexts, the following two similarities may be noted. First, the גְּאֻלָּה-contexts involve the release of one party or object from the authority of another; and second, this release occurs by means of a payment of some item of value. At the same time, these contexts also differ from כֹּפֶר-contexts in two significant ways. First, the person who is under the authority of another has done nothing wrong. In this regard, these contexts are similar to the first-born contexts of the root פדה above. Second, the permission of the person in charge of the property is not necessary in order for the act of redemption to proceed, since the one who does the redeeming has the right to do so. In this regard, these contexts differ from both those of כֹּפֶר and those of the first-born.

Finally, the term גֹּאֵל also has three uses. In the first it is similar to גְּאֻלָּה above insofar as it occurs in a legal context. In these instances it refers to a near relative of the person who was able to exercise the right of redemption on that person's behalf: 'If anyone among you becomes poor, and sells part of their property, then their next of kin (lit. redeemer) shall come and redeem what their relative has sold (וּבָא גֹאֲלוֹ הַקָּרֹב אֵלָיו וְגָאַל אֵת מִמְכַּר אָחִיו)' (Lev. 25.25; see also v. 26; Ruth 2.20; 3.9, 12). The second use also occurs in a legal context but refers this time to the 'avenger of blood', who is usually understood to be a close relative[54] of someone who was slain, and who thus had the right to execute the slayer: 'The avenger of blood (גֹּאֵל הַדָּם) is the one who shall put the murderer to death; when they meet, the avenger of blood shall execute the sentence' (Num. 35.19; see also vv. 21, 24, 25; Deut. 19.6, 12; Josh. 20.3, 5, 9; 2 Sam. 14.11). In the third use, גֹּאֵל is used more broadly to refer to the LORD as the one who rescues someone from a negative situation (akin to the broader sense of פְּדוּת above): 'I will make your oppressors eat their own flesh, and they shall be drunk with their own blood as with wine. Then all flesh shall know that I am the LORD your Savior, and your Redeemer (וְגֹאֲלֵךְ), the Mighty One of Jacob' (Isa. 49.26; see also Pss. 19.15 [14]; 78.35; Isa. 41.14; 43.14; 44.6, 24; 60.16; Jer. 50.34).[55]

Since the context of the first sense of גֹּאֵל above is the same as that of גְּאֻלָּה, the similarities and differences between this context and those involving כֹּפֶר are the same as the similarities and differences between the גְּאֻלָּה-contexts and כֹּפֶר-contexts identified above. The second sense of גֹּאֵל involves contexts that are unrelated to כֹּפֶר-contexts; the use of גֹּאֵל in these instances is perhaps prompted by the nearness of relation that the 'redeemer of blood' has to the slain party and not because the גֹּאֵל is redeeming anyone in these instances. The third sense occurs in contexts that have a general

---

54. See above, n. 38.
55. In keeping with the broader sense of פְּדוּת above, one may also note that פָּדָה and גָּאַל often occur in parallel with one another; see, e.g., Ps. 69.19 (18); Isa. 35.9-10; 51.10-11; Jer. 31.11; Hos. 13.14.

similarity to כֹּפֶר-contexts insofar as one party is being rescued from another, though unlike the first sense, and unlike the גְּאֻלָּה-contexts, this does not necessarily involve the payment of an item of value. The contexts of this third sense also differ, like the גְּאֻלָּה-contexts above, in that the party has not necessarily done anything wrong, nor is it up to the party who controls the item/person being redeemed whether or not redemption may take place.

2.1.5. *Summary and Conclusions concerning the Relationship of* כֹּפֶר *to* גְּאֻלָּה, פִּדְיוֹן, פְּדוּת, פִּדְיוֹם, פְּדוּיִם, *and* גָּאַל

In summarizing the relationship of כֹּפֶר to the nominal forms of the roots פדה and גאל, we may begin with the contexts of the root גאל, which are least like those of כֹּפֶר, and then proceed to the contexts of the root פדה, which fall somewhere in between those of גאל and those of כֹּפֶר.

To begin, the contexts of the term גְּאֻלָּה, and the first sense of the term גָּאַל, share in common with both כֹּפֶר-contexts and first-born contexts (פִּדְיוֹם, פְּדוּיִם) that they concern the delivery of one person (or object) from the authority of another by means of a payment of some item of value. Further, they are similar to first-born contexts, and differ from כֹּפֶר-contexts, in that the person being redeemed has not necessarily done anything wrong. Finally, they differ from both first-born and כֹּפֶר-contexts in that the person who does the redeeming has the automatic right of redemption and does not need the approval of the person from whom the person or object is being redeemed. Due to this last fact in particular, translators have properly rendered גְּאֻלָּה and גָּאַל with 'redemption' and 'redeemer' as opposed to 'ransom' and 'one who ransoms', since the root 'to redeem' is most appropriate to contexts where the one who does the redeeming has the right to do so, whereas the root 'to ransom' is most appropriate to contexts where the one who does the ransoming is in large part subject to the will of the one to whom the ransom is paid.

With reference to the nominal forms of the root פדה, it was noted above that one of these is used as a synonym of כֹּפֶר, namely, פִּדְיוֹן, while another is used in a more general way to refer to rescuing or redemption from trouble, namely, פְּדוּת. The terms that shed the most light upon an understanding of כֹּפֶר were פִּדְיוֹם and פְּדוּיִם, which occur in the context of ransoming the first-born. This context was seen to be similar to כֹּפֶר in three important ways: (1) it concerns delivering one party from the authority of another; (2) this is done by means of a payment of some item of value; and (3) the payment and subsequent deliverance of the one party is stipulated by the party in authority. As indicated directly above, this last aspect of the context in particular suggests that פִּדְיוֹם and פְּדוּיִם are best translated with terms from the 'ransom' word group and not the 'redemption' word group. This would also suggest that the term כֹּפֶר, which is similar to פִּדְיוֹם and

2. כֹּפֶר *Defined*

פְּדוּיִם in this regard, could helpfully be translated with the word 'ransom'. At the same time, however, it was also noted that there remains an important difference between first-born contexts and כֹּפֶר-contexts—namely, in the former the person being ransomed has done nothing wrong whereas in the latter the person has indeed done something wrong. As indicated in the concept-oriented study of כֹּפֶר above, this results in the need to appease the party in authority for the wrong done to them. This is turn leads to the question: If כֹּפֶר differs from פִּדְיוֹם and פְּדוּיִם in this important regard, and if פִּדְיוֹם and פְּדוּיִם are best translated with words from the 'ransom' word group, then is the best translation of כֹּפֶר also the word 'ransom' or is there another English term which more closely denotes the sense of כֹּפֶר? In order to answer this question we now turn to consider the definitions and renderings that others have given for the term כֹּפֶר.

2.2. *Survey of Previous Definitions and Renderings of* כֹּפֶר

As indicated in the above, any discussion of the term כֹּפֶר must address the *definition* of the word as well as which English term is the best *rendering* for it. As the following survey shows, the definitions of כֹּפֶר proposed by various scholars often overlap significantly even when they provide different renderings. Subtle distinctions and particular emphases do exist though, and it is in the different renderings given for כֹּפֶר where this becomes most apparent. The following discussion is therefore grouped according to the three main renderings of כֹּפֶר that have been proposed—namely, 'ransom' (or in a negative sense, 'bribe'), 'appeasement', and 'composition'.[56]

2.2.1. כֹּפֶר *as 'Ransom'*

In the lexicons and scholarly material, כֹּפֶר is most often rendered simply as 'ransom', or, in its negative sense, 'bribe'. Thus BDB: 'the price of a life, ransom';[57] J. Herrmann: 'At Num. 35.31, 32 כֹּפֶר is the ransom for the life (נֶפֶשׁ) of the murderer.... כֹּפֶר is again a ransom for the life of man at Job 33.24 and 36.18, and also at Prov. 13.8; 6.35; 21.18';[58] B. Levine: 'ransom, expiation, gift';[59] and J. Milgrom: '[its] meaning is undisputed: "ransom"'.[60]

---

56. Others have understood כֹּפֶר to refer to a 'covering', for critique of which see n. 2 above.
57. See also *HALAT*: 'Schweigegeld, Lösegeld'; *DCH*, IV: 'ransom, redemption payment...bribe'; F. Maass: 'Entschädigung, Lösegeld, Bestechungsgeld' ('כבר', in *THAT*, I, pp. 842-57 [844]).
58. Herrmann, 'ἱλάσκομαι, ἱλασμός', p. 303.
59. Levine, *Presence of the Lord*, p. 61.
60. Milgrom, *Leviticus 1–16*, p. 1082; see also Janowski (*Sühne*, p. 153): 'Lösegeld; Bestechungsgeld'. For further references see Schenker, '*kōper*', pp. 42-44.

Several authors, however, including some of the above, provide further definitions of the word 'ransom'. The definitions of Herrmann and Lang are among the most precise. Herrmann, for example, defines ransom as follows: 'It denotes a material expiation by which injury is made good and the injured party is reconciled, i.e., by which the hurt is covered and the guilty party is released from obligation'.[61] Similar to Herrmann's definition is that of Lang, who begins by stating, 'The noun *kōper* is a legal term. It denotes the material gift that establishes an amicable settlement between an injured party and the offending party.'[62] After a brief discussion of Exod. 21.30; Num. 35.31-34; and Prov. 6.35, this definition is further clarified as follows:

> These examples illustrate the various aspects of *kōper*: for the recipient, it...represents compensation, reparation, indemnification; from the perspective of the offender, it represents a ransom (cf. Ex. 21.30: *pidyōn napšô*, 'redemption of his life') for his own life, which is forfeit, a gift to propitiate the enraged injured party.[63]

In sum, the main elements common to both Herrmann and Lang are as follows: there is a guilty party and an injured party; the guilty party is under obligation to the injured party; and, the כֹּפֶר functions to reconcile the two parties. This understanding of כֹּפֶר, though more generally stated, is consonant with the conclusions arrived at above in §2.1.3. The question that remains is whether or not the English term 'ransom' is the word that best corresponds to this definition.

The Oxford English Dictionary defines the word 'ransom' as follows: 'The sum or price paid or demanded for the release of a prisoner or the restoration of captured property'.[64] In this regard, the English word 'ransom' does correspond to כֹּפֶר insofar as the כֹּפֶר-payment does release one person from the power of another, most often in the context of an imminent punishment. At the same time, however, כֹּפֶר occurs in contexts where a party *that has done wrong* is giving the כֹּפֶר to *the person that they have wronged*, by which they appease the injured party and are reconciled. By way of contrast, the English word 'ransom' does not signify that the one receiving the ransom payment has been wronged by the one giving it and needs to be appeased for that wrong, as when ransom is paid to a kidnapper who has in no way been wronged by their captive. Indeed, in this last example it is not the injured party who receives the ransom payment but the party who is doing wrong! In this way, the term כֹּפֶר includes elements which the English word

---

61. Herrmann, 'ἱλάσκομαι, ἱλασμός', p. 303. See also Herrmann, *Die Idee der Sühne*, pp. 38-43.
62. Lang, 'כֹּפֶר', p. 301.
63. Lang, 'כֹּפֶר', p. 301.
64. *The Oxford English Dictionary* (Oxford: Clarendon Press, 1971).

'ransom' does not necessarily include, most notably the idea of appeasement of the *injured* party.

Another author who typically translates כֹּפֶר with 'ransom' (*Lösegeld*) is Bernd Janowski. Janowski differs from Herrmann or Lang, however, in having a narrower focus in his understanding of כֹּפֶר. Since he provides a thorough discussion of the texts in which the term כֹּפֶר is found,[65] his view will be considered in some detail.

With regard to his discussion of כֹּפֶר in general, Janowski considers the occurrences of the term under two headings: legal uses of כֹּפֶר and theological uses. He begins his consideration of the legal uses with an examination of Exod. 30.12, then Exod. 21.30, and Num. 35.31-34. Each of these texts concern a life or death situation which only the כֹּפֶר can (or cannot [Num. 35.31-34]) resolve. Janowski argues that the emphasis of these texts is on the כֹּפֶר as that which rescues the life of the guilty from death. Stated differently, the כֹּפֶר is described *from the perspective of the guilty*: it is a ransom of *their* life, a פִּדְיֹן נַפְשׁוֹ (Exod. 21.30; cf. Num. 35.31; Exod. 30.12). Thus, while it may serve to compensate the victim, this is only secondary to its function of redeeming the life of the guilty. Janowski further notes that the choice between ransom and punishment is up to the offended party (see especially Exod. 21.28-32). As a result, if the offended party does choose to allow כֹּפֶר, then the guilty party would not perceive this as a penalty but as a gift: in the face of death, they are given life instead.[66]

Janowski next proceeds to consider the verses which he deems use כֹּפֶר in the theological (as opposed to legal) arena, namely, those texts in which God—and not a person—accomplishes the ransom.[67] The most obvious example here is Isa. 43.1-7, where the LORD himself places Egypt, Cush,

---

65. Janowski, *Sühne*, pp. 152-74.

66. See, for example, the conclusion to Janowski's (*Sühne*, pp. 156-58) discussion on Exod. 21.30: 'Für das Verständnis von כֹּפֶר in Ex 21,30 heißt dies: In einer Situation, die von seiten des (in der beschriebenen Weise) schuldig gewordenen Menschen irreparabel ist, so daß er dem Tode verfallen ist (יוּמָת Ex 21, 29bb), bewirkt die כֹּפֶר-Gabe (neben der Kompensation für das Leben des Getöteten) die *Lösung des eigenen Lebens aus Todesverfallenheit*: sie ist פִּדְיֹן נַפְשׁוֹ "Auslösung seines Lebens". Obwohl "von außen auferlegt", ist dieses כֹּפֶר dennoch weder eine *Buß*leistung (das wäre eher der verdiente Tod: Ex 21, 29bb) noch einfach eine dem Schuldigen auferlegte Geld*strafe*; vielmehr wird die כֹּפֶר-Summe, die Errettung vom drohenden Tode bewirkt, schon in diesem frühen Rechtstext nicht nur als eine die Schuld ausgleichende Ersatzgabe, sondern vor allem als *Auslösung des verwirkten Lebens* (פִּדְיֹן נַפְשׁוֹ) und d.h.: als *Existenzstellvertretung*, als *Lebensäquivalent* verstanden. Dieser Aspekt gab dem Terminus כֹּפֶר auch seinen über rein rechtliche Kategorien ("Schadensregulierung") hinausweisenden, traditionsgeschichtlich wirksam gewordenen Sinngehalt' (emphasis his).

67. Janowski states: 'Im Unterschied zur Verwendung von כֹּפֶר im Kontext rechtlicher Bestimmungen geht es im theologischen Verwendungsbereich dieses Wortes um die *Auslösung durch Gott*' (*Sühne*, p. 169 [emphasis his]).

and Seba as the כֹּפֶר for Israel (v. 3; cf. also v. 4), though Janowski holds that the angelic intercession in Job 33.24 is also comparable. Janowski maintains that כֹּפֶר in these texts is still similar to its use in legal texts insofar as it refers to the rescuing of a life from a situation of doom[68] by functioning as a substitute for the life of the guilty.[69] The only anomalous text is that of Ps. 49.8, where כֹּפֶר is not referring to salvation from an imminent crisis but rather from death in general, namely, the death that is inevitable for all people.[70]

What Janowski emphasizes more than Herrmann and Lang is the perspective of the guilty party, namely, that they are liable to severe consequences (death) for their wrong and are powerless to rescue themselves; their only hope is for the offended party to choose to receive כֹּפֶר so that they might escape capital punishment. So far this is in keeping with the conclusions made above on the meaning of כֹּפֶר. Janowski differs, however, in that he emphasizes the perspective of the guilty party to such an extent that he understands the term כֹּפֶר to refer primarily to redemption of the guilty and only secondarily to compensation of the victim.[71]

While this emphasis upon the perspective of the guilty party is helpful in highlighting an important element of כֹּפֶר, it is not justifiable to emphasize it to the extent that Janowski has, since a כֹּפֶר-payment always involves both the guilty party and the injured party.[72] In particular, there are two important

---

68. Thus he says, 'Nach den bisher untersuchten alttestamentlichen "Lösegeld"-Belegen bewirkt die Gabe eines כֹּפֶר immer die *Lösung des verwirkten Lebens aus einem den Schuldigen existentiell gefährdenden Unheilsgeschehen*…' (*Sühne*, p. 171 [emphasis his]).

69. Thus on Isa. 43.3-4 he comments, 'Der zentrale Aussagegehalt des כֹּפֶר-Begriffs liegt, wie das synonyme תַּחַת zeigt, im *Stellvertretungsgedanken*. Wo Lösegeld (כֹּפֶר) *an die Stelle* (תַּחַת) eines verwirkten Lebens tritt, erwirkt es die Lösung des Menschen aus Todesverfallenheit. Hierin bestätigt sich, daß כֹּפֶר als *Existenzstellvertretung*, als *Lebensäquivalent* zu verstehen ist' (*Sühne*, p. 170 [emphasis his]).

70. Janowski, *Sühne*, pp. 171-73.

71. This understanding of כֹּפֶר is in keeping with Janowski's larger argument on atonement, namely, that atonement is not the appeasement of God's anger through the execution of a penalty or the removal of sin, but a *positive* process, grounded in the activity of God, in which the offerer symbolically dedicates their life to the holy (see, e.g., Janowski, *Sühne*, pp. 1, 247). While Janowski is certainly correct in seeing the activity of God as the source of atonement (see §2.1.2.2 above, as well as Chapter 6 and n. 4), his thesis fails to account adequately for the perspective of the injured party in atonement (see critique immediately following), as well as for the cleansing elements central to כֹּפֶר (see n. 23 in Chapter 4 as well as §4.1 to §4.3 as a whole).

72. As noted above, Janowski appeals to the phrase פִּדְיוֹן נַפְשׁוֹ ('ransom of/for their life') to demonstrate that the function of the כֹּפֶר is to redeem a forfeited life. This seems completely justifiable. The problem, however, is that Janowski proceeds to say that the term כֹּפֶר must be understood *primarily* from the perspective of the guilty party. This,

elements of כֹּפֶר that do not feature in Janowski's discussion of the term. The first is the element of appeasement. As noted above, the כֹּפֶר-payment does not simply occur in a neutral legal situation, but one in which great harm has been done to the injured party: a family member has been killed (Exod. 21.30), a husband has been cheated (Prov. 6.35). The כֹּפֶר, therefore, must not only rescue the life of the guilty, it must do so by mollifying the injured party (which in some cases—such as the husband of Prov. 6.35—is impossible due to the greatness of the wrath).[73] In short, the element of appeasement appears to be an important part of a כֹּפֶר-payment.[74] The second element is that the כֹּפֶר-payment is still a punishment. While Janowski is correct in observing that from the perspective of the guilty party a כֹּפֶר-payment might not seem like a penalty (since anything less than death can indeed be looked upon as a gift), the fact remains that the injured party is choosing to allow a *mitigated* penalty to be given in place of the one deserved—that is, a כֹּפֶר-payment instead of death.

In sum, the above authors have correctly identified that an important element of כֹּפֶר is the release of one party from the power of another, often in the context of an imminent punishment. Moreover, Herrmann and Maass seem closer than Janowski to a proper understanding of the term, insofar as they also refer to elements relevant to the injured party and not just the offending party, namely, appeasement and penalty. At the same time, it has also been noted that the English word 'ransom' does not denote that the one

---

however, is a *non sequitur*. The phrase '*ransom* for their life' does not require that the word 'ransom' be understood primarily from the perspective of the guilty party any more than the phrase '*medicine* for their healing' requires that the word 'medicine' be understood primarily from the perspective of the one who is healed. Rather, the question is: What is medicine and *how does it function* to heal the sick? In this regard, one will need to speak not only of the sick person but also of the sickness that is being healed (and so note *The Oxford English Dictionary* definition of 'medicine': 'Any substance or preparation used in the treatment of disease…'). In the same way, the question that needs to be asked of כֹּפֶר is: What is כֹּפֶר and *how does it function* to ransom the life? In this regard one will need to speak not only of the ransomed life but also of the injured party that is appeased by the ransom payment (see the definition in §2.1.3 above).

73. In some instances the injured party has not been so much harmed by the wrong as angered (Exod. 30.11-16); here again, however, the כֹּפֶר must not only meet the requirement of punishment but do so in such a way that the angry party is appeased.

74. In a footnote responding to Adrian Schenker's understanding of כֹּפֶר as 'appeasement' (for which see immediately below, §2.2.2), Janowski does acknowledge that the idea of appeasement can at times be in the foreground (e.g. Prov. 6.35), though even here he maintains that the perspective of the guilty party is still in view, that is, their life is forfeit and the כֹּפֶר serves to rescue their life (see Janowski, *Sühne*, pp. 157-58 n. 268). As demonstrated above (§2.1.2), however, the elements of rescuing a forfeited life (so Janowski) and appeasing the offended party (so Schenker) are *both* central to כֹּפֶר.

receiving the ransom payment has been wronged by the ransomed party and is thus in need of appeasement for a wrong done to him or her, for example, a kidnapper. While the context may account for this deficiency in the English term 'ransom', it may also be asked whether there is another English term that is closer in its denotation to the understanding of כֹּפֶר outlined above. For this reason, we now turn to consider a second rendering of כֹּפֶר, namely, 'appeasement'.

2.2.2. כֹּפֶר as 'Appeasement'

One of the most thorough discussions of the term כֹּפֶר appears in Adrian Schenker's article 'kōper et expiation', in which he proposes that כֹּפֶר refers primarily to 'appeasement'.[75] Due to the attention that Schenker pays to this term, his argument is considered in some detail.

Schenker's goal in this essay is to determine the meaning of the term כֹּפֶר with a view to understanding better the nature of atonement. He begins his examination of כֹּפֶר with the case of the goring ox in Exod. 21.28-32, where כֹּפֶר clearly functions to rescue the owner of the ox from certain death. What is unclear, however, is the exact nature of this כֹּפֶר: Is it the redemption of a guilty life and thus the amount paid in replacement of that life? Is it a payment made to compensate for a person that has been killed? Is it the price paid to bring peace between two families?[76] Schenker acknowledges that these possible descriptions of כֹּפֶר are all different aspects of the arrangement that כֹּפֶר results in. What he wants to determine more specifically, however, is the particular aspect of this arrangement that the word כֹּפֶר signifies.[77]

Schenker notes that one possible approach for answering this question is to study the term פִּדְיוֹן ('ransom'), which appears parallel to כֹּפֶר in v. 30. He also states, however, that while these two terms could be synonymous, they need not necessarily be so, and the fact that they both occur in this context to refer to the same thing could suggest that they refer to two different aspects of the same reality.[78]

---

75. Schenker, 'kōper', pp. 32-46. See also Schenker, *Versöhnung und Widerstand*.
76. Schenker, 'kōper', p. 33.
77. 'Il ne faut pas objecter que ce ne sont là que des *aspects différents* de la *même et unique réalité* de l'accommodement, car c'est précisément notre question: quel est *l'aspect de l'accommodement* que le mot *kōper* signifie?' (Schenker, 'kōper', p. 33 [emphasis his]).
78. Schenker ('kōper', pp. 33-34) argues as follows: 'Un aspect de l'accommodement, c'est le rachat de la vie du coupable. La somme nécessaire à ce rachat s'appelle *pidyōn napšô* dans la proposition *principale* du v. 30. Faut-il conclure du fait que *kōper* se trouve à la place symétriquement correspondante dans la proposition subordonnée du même v. 30 qu'il a la même signification que *pidyōn napšô*, autrement dit, qu'il est synonyme de *kōper*?... Ce n'est pas impossible en effet, mais ce n'est pas certain non plus! Le seul

2. כֹּפֶר Defined

Instead of focusing on פִּדְיוֹן, therefore, Schenker proceeds by looking at two passages which are contextually comparable to Exod. 21.28-32. There are two criteria in particular that he notes. The first criterion is that there is a settlement that takes place that negotiates a peaceful solution instead of a violent one. The second criterion is that the verb כִּפֶּר is used in a profane sense, that is, the settlement of a conflict between people occurs. Schenker suggests that two passages meet these criteria, namely, Gen. 32.21 (20) and Prov. 16.14. In both of these passages there is a rupture in the relationship between the parties such that the injured party is ready to execute the offending party. In order to achieve peace, the guilty party '*kippers*' the injured party, which Schenker argues is best understood in these contexts as 'mollifying' or 'appeasing' him. In support, he notes that the sense of the verb in these instances cannot mean 'to ransom' since it is the offended party that is the object of כִּפֶּר and not the guilty party (and one does not 'ransom' the offended party). In an important step, Schenker then argues that since the contexts of Gen. 32.21 (20) and Prov. 16.14 are the same as that of Exod. 21.30, it is likely that the meaning of the verb in the former two and the meaning of the noun in the latter is the same. In short, the verb is 'to appease, to mollify' and the noun is 'appeasement, mollification'.[79]

Having reached this conclusion, Schenker proceeds to give a brief overview of all the passages containing the word כֹּפֶר, arguing that this sense of 'appeasement' is appropriate to the meaning of כֹּפֶר in each. This is followed by a survey of other views on כֹּפֶר, the majority of which conclude that it refers simply to 'ransom'. Schenker contrasts this understanding of the term with his own, emphasizing that the noun כֹּפֶר refers primarily to the appeasement that takes place when the guilty party gives the כֹּפֶר to the offended party; it is only indirectly a reference to buying back or ransoming one's life.[80] With this understanding of כֹּפֶר in place, Schenker concludes with seven brief implications for the theology of atonement.[81]

---

fait de deux termes différents pour le même prix payé au cours de l'arrangement pourrait suggérer que les deux termes signifient deux *aspects différents* d'une même somme. *kōper* et *pidyōn nepeš* désignent certainement la même somme versée, mais peut-être en exprimant chacun un aspect spécifique.' While this is possible, it was also noted above (§2.1.4.1) that פִּדְיוֹן נַפְשׁוֹ + נָתַן here in v. 30 is paralleled by כֹּפֶר נַפְשׁוֹ + נָתַן in Exod. 30.12, suggesting that כֹּפֶר and פִּדְיוֹן are more synonymous than not. See also discussion of Ps. 49.8-9 (7-8) in §2.1.1.4 above. For the insights into כֹּפֶר that one can gain from comparison with nominal forms of the root פדה see §2.1.4.1 and §2.1.5.

79. '[N]ous pouvons également conclure à une parenté de signification entre verbe et nom, cette signification étant "apaiser, adoucir" pour le verbe et "apaisement, adoucissement" pour le nom' (Schenker, '*kōper*', p. 37).

80. 'Il apparaît donc que l'interprétation aujourd'hui prédominante de *kōper* est celle de rachat où le coupable achète, légitimement ou illégitimement, sa vie, sa liberté, son innocence. Notre étude nous conduit cependant à penser que l'aspect exprimé par le

Schenker's essay goes beyond most discussions with regard to considering the links between כֹּפֶר and כִּפֶּר, a matter which is explored more fully in the next chapter. Of greater import for the present discussion is the distinction Schenker maintains between 'ransom' and 'appeasement' and how this distinction affects one's understanding of כֹּפֶר. In particular, the term 'ransom' signifies that a payment has been made which releases one person from the power of another, most often in the context of an imminent punishment. It does not, however, *necessarily* signify that there is any enmity or hostility between the two, or that the one being ransomed has wronged their captor, as when ransom is paid to a kidnapper who is not necessarily angry at their prisoner, nor has the prisoner done any wrong to their captor. By way of contrast, the term 'appease' contains as a fundamental element the fact that one person has wronged another and that the appeasement leads to a re-establishment of a peaceful relationship. Stated differently, the emphasis of 'appeasement' is upon the restoration of peace between the guilty party and the injured party, whereas the focus of 'ransom' is the release of one party from the power of another.

There can be no doubt that 'appeasement' is an important element of כֹּפֶר, for the biblical situations requiring a כֹּפֶר are those in which one party has wronged another, for example, by slaying one of their family members (Exod. 21.30; Num. 35.31-34). As noted above, these are therefore not simply situations in which the life of the guilty must be rescued ('ransomed'), but also those in which hostility between two parties must be resolved ('appeased'). This helps to highlight a potential deficiency in the term 'ransom'.

At the same time, however, it may be asked: Does כֹּפֶר refer *primarily* to appeasement and only *indirectly* to ransom, as Schenker maintains, or is it better to understand ransom and appeasement both to be central elements of כֹּפֶר? Three comments are relevant in this regard.

First, as noted above in the field-oriented study of כֹּפֶר (§2.1.4), what distinguishes כֹּפֶר from nouns built on the root גאל and some nouns built on the root פדה is that כֹּפֶר occurs in contexts where some wrong has been done which makes the offending party liable to penalty. It is indeed given to appease the wronged party, but in a context which is directly related to the rescue of the offending party. Thus Exod. 30.12: 'When you take a census of the Israelites to number them, then each one of them shall give a כֹּפֶר for himself to the LORD, when you number them, *that there may be no plague*

---

terme *kōper* est plutôt celui de l'apaisement d'un conflit où le coupable veut acheter, honnêtement ou malhonnêtement, la paix avec les personnes qu'il a lésées dans un de leurs droits et qui lui en veulent précisément pour cela. C'est le prix de l'accommodement, ce n'est qu'indirectement le rachat' (Schenker, '*kōper*', pp. 44-45).

81. Schenker, '*kōper*', pp. 45-46.

2. כֹּפֶר Defined

among them when you number them'.[82] In short, the goal of the כֹּפֶר is never appeasement alone, but always appeasement *for the sake of avoiding penalty*.

Second, the phrase כֹּפֶר נַפְשׁוֹ in Exod. 30.12 and the frequently occurring phrase כֹּפֶר + עַל + personal object (Exod. 30.15, 16; Lev. 1.4; 4.20, etc.) further confirm that the rescuing or ransoming of the guilty party is not simply an indirect aspect of כֹּפֶר. Rather, it is a כֹּפֶר *for their life*, it is כֹּפֶר *for them*. This does not mitigate the element of appeasement;[83] rather, it underscores again that the rescuing or ransoming of the guilty part is central to what a כֹּפֶר-payment accomplishes and not an indirect result.

These comments lead to a final observation. It was noted in the above that the word 'ransom' does not *necessarily* denote that the person to whom the ransom is paid is appeased of some wrong committed by the person paying the ransom, for example, when an innocent party pays a ransom to a kidnapper. In the same way, however, the word 'appeasement' does not *necessarily* denote that the guilty party is under the authority or power of the one they appease, as when one person appeases another who is angry with them and yet has no power or authority to punish them (let alone have them executed). Granted, it is still up to the injured party whether or not they accept appeasement, just as it is up to the injured party whether כֹּפֶר is allowed. The difference, however, is that a refusal to be appeased does not imply that punishment will follow in its stead (since an injured party is not necessarily in a position to have the offender punished), whereas the refusal to grant כֹּפֶר does imply that punishment will therefore follow (since a כֹּפֶר is given in lieu of a greater punishment).[84] Naturally, it might be quite clear from the context that punishment will follow if the injured party is not appeased (for example, the king in Prov. 16.14). As with the rendering 'ransom' above, however, what is to be noted is that the rendering 'appeasement' does not by itself denote all of the elements which are properly a part of the sense of כֹּפֶר, for example, the offending party being under the power of the injured party and subject to penalty.[85] Once more, then, it may still be asked whether

---

82. See further the discussion of texts in §2.1.1.
83. See §2.1.2.4 above.
84. And so compare the following two sentences: 'It was a ransom payment and its purpose was to release one party from the power of another'; 'It was an appeasement payment and its purpose was to release one party from the power of another'. The first sentence is semantically anomalous, for releasing one party from the power of another is fundamental to the meaning of 'ransom'. The second sentence, however, is not so; the fact that one person is released from the power of another provides us with information we could not have known from the phrase 'appeasement payment' itself.
85. By way of summary, then, while Schenker's study is helpful, the emphasis on appeasement (at the expense of 'ransom') may be questioned on two grounds. First, as demonstrated in §2.1 above, the element of 'ransom' is clearly an aspect of כֹּפֶר. Indeed, as mentioned in n. 78, it appears (*contra* Schenker) that פִּדְיוֹן and כֹּפֶר are more synonymous than not in Exod. 21.30. Thus the element of 'ransom' indicated by פִּדְיוֹן is also

there is an English term which more exactly represents the definition of כֹּפֶר given above.

Thus far we have considered two possible renderings of the term כֹּפֶר: 'ransom' and 'appeasement'. In both instances it was noted that these renderings did not denote all the elements of כֹּפֶר identified above. In particular, the term 'ransom' conveys that one party is under the authority of another (and most likely with severe consequences imminent) and that the כֹּפֶר releases them, but does not necessarily imply that any wrong has been committed by the captive party. The term 'appeasement' does convey that some wrong has been committed and that the כֹּפֶר mollifies the injured party, but does not necessarily imply that the guilty party is under the authority of the injured party or that the guilty party will be punished. It is with these facts in mind that we turn to consider the final rendering of כֹּפֶר proposed in the literature, namely, 'composition'.

2.2.3. כֹּפֶר *as 'Composition'*

The main proponent of the rendering 'composition' for כֹּפֶר is H. Brichto, who writes as follows:

> The biblical context of *kōper* is most closely approximated by the term 'composition' in its legal sense, the settling of differences. An imbalance between two parties (individuals, families, clans or larger social groupings) results from a damage or deprivation inflicted upon one by the other. Equilibrium is restored by a process which consists of a transfer of something of value (a person, an animal, or a commutation of such in the form of commodity or currency) from the injuring party to the injured. The acceptance of this value-item by the latter, itself termed 'the composition' (as is the process itself also), serves to 'compose' or settle the difference.[86]

What is especially significant about this suggestion for the translation of כֹּפֶר is that elements of both 'ransom' and 'appeasement' are fundamental to the meaning of 'composition'. Similar to 'ransom', the term 'composition' includes within it the fact that one party is subject to another party, for example, a debtor to their creditor.[87] The 'composition' functions to release the party for whom it is paid (e.g. the debtor) from the party which receives

---

likely an important element of כֹּפֶר (see especially §2.1.4.1). Second, the term 'appeasement' does not in and of itself denote this important aspect of the term כֹּפֶר. Thus while it may be agreed with Schenker, for example, that כִּפֶּר cannot be translated with 'to ransom' in Gen. 32.21 (20) and Prov. 16.14, it may also be noted that the rendering 'to appease' does not properly account for all of the dynamics of כִּפֶּר in these contexts either, and specifically, of the rescue from danger that כִּפֶּר effects.

86. Brichto, 'On Slaughter and Sacrifice', pp. 27-28.

87. 'An agreement for the payment (or the payment by agreement) of a sum of money, in lieu of the discharge of some other *obligation*, or in a different way from that *required* by the original contract...' (*The Oxford English Dictionary* [emphasis added]).

it (e.g. the creditor). Similar to 'appeasement', the term 'composition' also includes the fact that one party has wronged another and that the paying of the 'composition' is acceptable to the injured party as a settling of the difference. Moreover, like both 'ransom' and 'appeasement' in these contexts, the term 'composition' refers to a payment, the acceptance or refusal of which is ultimately dependent upon the party to whom it is offered. Finally, it may be noted that the term 'composition' can be used to refer to a *mitigated* payment.[88]

Despite these strengths, there are still two weaknesses of the term 'composition'. To begin, this term is used primarily in the context of financial offenses, for example, defaulting on a loan,[89] whereas the context of the כֹּפֶר references is either a breach of criminal law more generally or some offense against the LORD himself. This weakness is not necessarily fatal, however, since it is generally clear from the context what type of offense has been committed.

Perhaps a more serious problem, at least for the translator, is that the term 'composition' is so infrequently used in spoken or written English today that the majority who come across it will be unaware of its precise denotation. For this reason, it is perhaps best to use either 'ransom' or 'appeasement' when translating כֹּפֶר. While neither of these terms overlaps completely with כֹּפֶר in terms of denotation, the insufficiencies of the terms are usually accounted for by the context.[90]

2.3. *Summary*

Anticipating that the verb כִּפֶּר is related to the meaning of the noun כֹּפֶר in at least some sin contexts, this chapter focused upon the definition of the term כֹּפֶר. It began with a concept-oriented approach in which the texts containing the term כֹּפֶר were considered exegetically. The goal here was to

---

88. *The Oxford English Dictionary* continues, 'An agreement for the payment (or the payment by agreement) of a sum of money, in lieu of the discharge of some other obligation, or in a different way from that required by the original contract; a compounding; *spec.* an agreement by which a creditor accepts a *certain proportion* of a debt, in satisfaction, from an insolvent debtor' (emphasis added).

89. 'A sum paid and accepted by creditors to ward off bankruptcy' (William J. Stewart and Robert Burgess, *Collins Dictionary of Law* [Glasgow: Harper Collins: 1996]). See also nn. 87 and 88.

90. That is to say, the English term 'ransom' does not denote that the party in authority has been wronged by the one paying ransom, and the English term 'appeasement' does not denote that the one wronged has authority over the one who is appeasing, while the Hebrew word כֹּפֶר includes both of these ideas. Nonetheless, one may still use the terms 'ransom' or 'appeasement' because the context supplies what these terms lack in and of themselves.

identify those elements which were a part of the sense of the term in each passage. When the results coming from the various passages were compared, four main elements consistently came forward. This led to the following definition of the positive sense of כֹּפֶר: a legally or ethically legitimate payment which delivers a guilty party from a just punishment that is the right of the offended party to execute or to have executed. The acceptance of this payment is entirely dependent upon the choice of the offended party, it is a lesser punishment than was originally expected, and its acceptance serves both to rescue the life of the guilty as well as to appease the offended party, thus restoring peace to the relationship.[91]

This definition was followed by a consideration of the term from a field-oriented approach in which כֹּפֶר was compared and contrasted with the nominal forms of two roots from the same semantic field, namely, פדה and גאל. Nominal forms from the root גאל were found to be least like כֹּפֶר. In particular, it was noted that the one point of similarity held between the contexts of גְּאֻלָּה, the first sense of the term גאל, and the term כֹּפֶר, is that all three concern the delivery of one person (or object) from the authority of another by means of a payment of some item of value. They differ, however, in that the person being redeemed in the גְּאֻלָּה- and גאל-contexts has not necessarily done anything wrong, and further, in that the person who does the redeeming has an automatic right of redemption and does not need the approval of the one from whom the person or object is being redeemed.

With reference to the root פדה, it was seen that one of the nominal forms was a synonym of כֹּפֶר (viz. פִּדְיוֹן), while another referred to rescuing from trouble more generally (viz. פְּדוּת). The nominal forms shedding the most light on כֹּפֶר were פִּדְיוֹם and פְּדוּיִם, which occur in the context of the ransoming of the first-born (Num. 3). The first-born context is similar to the contexts of כֹּפֶר in three important ways: (1) it concerns delivering one party from the authority of another; (2) this is done by means of a payment of some item of value; and (3) the payment and subsequent deliverance of the one party is stipulated by the party in authority. This suggested that the terms פִּדְיוֹם and פְּדוּיִם are well translated with terms from the 'ransom' word group and not the 'redemption' word group. At the same time, however, it was noted that this context differed from כֹּפֶר-contexts in that the person being ransomed (the first-born) has done nothing wrong. This in turn raised the question of whether the 'ransom' word group was sufficient for translating the term כֹּפֶר or whether an alternate word group was preferable.

For this reason, different English renderings of the term כֹּפֶר were then considered. The first of these, 'ransom', was seen to work well insofar as it denotes the release of one party from another, often in a context of imminent

---

91. For the negative definition of כֹּפֶר (i.e. 'bribe'), see §2.1.3 above.

punishment, by means of an item of value. At the same time, however, the English term 'ransom' does not necessarily denote that the party being ransomed has done some wrong for which the injured party needs to be appeased.

This led to the second rendering, 'appeasement', which made up for the deficiency of 'ransom' in that it does denote that the party to whom the payment is made has been wronged in some way and needs to be mollified. At the same time, however, this term was also seen to be insufficient in that it does not necessarily denote that the injured party has authority over the one for whom the payment is made.

This in turn led to a third suggestion, 'composition', put forth by Brichto. This word has the advantage of combining elements of both 'ransom' and 'appeasement' that are central to כֹּפֶר-contexts: similar to 'ransom', the term 'composition' includes within it the fact that the party for whom the payment is made is subject to the party to whom it is made; similar to 'appeasement', it includes the fact that the party for whom the payment is made has in some way wronged the party to whom it is made, implying that the payment of the composition is acceptable to the injured party as a settling of the difference. Similar to both 'ransom' and 'appeasement', the payment it represents is accepted or rejected completely at the discretion of the injured party. In addition, it was noted that the term 'composition' can also be used to refer to a mitigated penalty. Due to the rarity of this word in English usage today, however, and due to the fact that the deficiencies in the terms 'ransom' and 'appeasement' can often be accounted for by the context, it was suggested that either of these last two terms might be preferable to translators.

3

THE VERB כִּפֶּר IN CONTEXTS OF SIN

The goal of Part I (Chapters 1 to 3) is to understand the verb כִּפֶּר in contexts of sin. It was shown in Chapter 1 that there is a connection between sin and death in the priestly literature, but that certain sins could be atoned for (כִּפֶּר) by means of sacrifice.[1] In this way, the sinner was able to avoid the penalty of death. Chapter 2 then began by noting that the idea of atonement (כִּפֶּר) is directly related to the noun כֹּפֶר in at least some instances. Anticipating that these instances included contexts of sin, the previous chapter concentrated on the usage and meaning of the term כֹּפֶר. It was concluded that a כֹּפֶר was a legally legitimate payment which delivered a guilty party from a just punishment that is the right of the offended party to execute or to have executed. By this means, a mitigated penalty could substitute for the original penalty that the sin deserved.[2]

We now turn in this chapter to consider whether this understanding of כֹּפֶר is indeed related to the meaning of כִּפֶּר in contexts of sin. This is done through an examination of the words that occur in conjunction with כִּפֶּר in sin contexts, namely, the verb סָלַח and the phrase נָשָׂא עָוֹן, each of which is considered in turn.

3.1. כִּפֶּר in Contexts of Sin

3.1.1. סָלַח

The verb סָלַח occurs thirteen times in the priestly literature. The majority of the occurrences (ten) are in the niphal in a context where a sin has been committed, for which a sacrifice has then been made.[3] Following the completion of the sacrifice, סָלַח occurs together with the verb כִּפֶּר in some variation of the well-known phrase, 'And the priest will atone for them (וְכִפֶּר עֲלֵהֶם הַכֹּהֵן)

---

1. See §1.3 above.
2. See §2.1.3 above for the full definition.
3. See Lev. 4.20, 26, 31, 35; 5.10, 13, 16, 18, 26 (6.7); 19.22; Num. 15.25 (cf. v. 26), 28. With the exception of Lev. 5.26 (6.7) and 19.22, all of the sins listed are unintentional. For the qal uses of סָלַח see n. 4.

3. *The Verb* כִּפֶּר *in Contexts of Sin* 81

and they will be forgiven (וְנִסְלַח לָהֶם)'.[4] We may begin by making some grammatical observations on this phrase as a whole and then turn to consider the meaning of סָלַח itself more closely.

The use of נִסְלַח in this phrase is unique to the priestly texts. The one granting the forgiveness is not identified, but it is commonly agreed that it is

---

4. The phrases are as follows: וְכִפֶּר עֲלֵהֶם הַכֹּהֵן וְנִסְלַח לָהֶם (Lev. 4.20); וְכִפֶּר עָלָיו (Lev. 4.31); וְכִפֶּר עָלָיו הַכֹּהֵן וְנִסְלַח לוֹ (Lev. 4.26); הַכֹּהֵן מֵחַטָּאתוֹ וְנִסְלַח לוֹ וְכִפֶּר עָלָיו הַכֹּהֵן מֵחַטָּאתוֹ אֲשֶׁר־חָטָא וְנִסְלַח לוֹ (Lev. 4.35); עַל־חַטָּאתוֹ אֲשֶׁר־חָטָא וְנִסְלַח לוֹ (Lev. 5.10); וְכִפֶּר עָלָיו הַכֹּהֵן עַל־חַטָּאתוֹ אֲשֶׁר־חָטָא מֵאַחַת מֵאֵלֶּה וְנִסְלַח לוֹ (Lev. 5.13); וְכִפֶּר עָלָיו הַכֹּהֵן עַל שִׁגְגָתוֹ אֲשֶׁר־שָׁגָג וְהוּא (Lev. 5.16); וְהַכֹּהֵן יְכַפֵּר עָלָיו בְּאֵיל הָאָשָׁם וְנִסְלַח לוֹ לֹא־יָדַע וְנִסְלַח לוֹ (Lev. 5.18); וְכִפֶּר עָלָיו הַכֹּהֵן לִפְנֵי יְהוָה וְנִסְלַח לוֹ (Lev. 5.26 [6.7]); וְכִפֶּר עָלָיו הַכֹּהֵן בְּאֵיל הָאָשָׁם לִפְנֵי יְהוָה עַל־חַטָּאתוֹ אֲשֶׁר חָטָא וְנִסְלַח לוֹ מֵחַטָּאתוֹ אֲשֶׁר חָטָא וְכִפֶּר הַכֹּהֵן (Lev. 19.22); וְכִפֶּר הַכֹּהֵן עַל־כָּל־עֲדַת בְּנֵי יִשְׂרָאֵל וְנִסְלַח לָהֶם (Num. 15.25); עַל־הַנֶּפֶשׁ הַשֹּׁגֶגֶת בְּחֶטְאָה בִשְׁגָגָה לִפְנֵי יְהוָה לְכַפֵּר עָלָיו וְנִסְלַח לוֹ (Num. 15.28). סָלַח also occurs three times in the qal in Num. 30 (vv. 6 [5], 9 [8], and 13 [12]). The situation here is one in which the vow of a woman is annulled by either her father (30.5 [6]) or her husband (30.9 [8], 13 [12]), in which case she is no longer liable to the vow and will be forgiven (וַיהוָה יִסְלַח־לָהּ). The context makes clear that the action of סָלַח includes the remission of penalty, since 30.16 (15) states that a husband who tries to nullify an oath belatedly will bear his wife's sin (וְנָשָׂא אֶת־עֲוֹנָהּ). The verb כִּפֶּר does not occur in these contexts, however, since no sacrifice is required. סָלַח also occurs twice in the qal in Num. 14, for which see discussion below and n. 12. Cognates to סָלַח exist in other ancient Near Eastern languages, though at our current state of knowledge these have shed little light upon the meaning of סָלַח. In Ugaritic we find the expression *slḥ npš* in a ritual text (*UT* 9.1), though the meaning is still obscure. Cyrus H. Gordon (*Ugaritic Literature* [Rome: Pontificio Istituto Biblico, 1949], p. 113]) translates as 'forgiveness of soul' but also suggests 'to sprinkle' as a possibility (*UT* 19.1757). John Gray ('Social Aspects of Canaanite Religion', in *The Legacy of Canaan: The Ras Shamra Texts and their Relevance to the Old Testament* [VTSup, 15; Leiden: Brill, 1965], pp. 170-92 [191]) relates Ugaritic *slḥ* to Arabic *slḥ* ('to unclothe' and 'to come to an end'; see Johann Jakob Stamm, 'סלח', in *THAT*, II, pp. 150-60 [150-51]). Akkadian yields *salāḫu*, which does occur in cultic (as well as medicinal) texts, but which means 'to sprinkle', as in with oil or water (see references in Stamm, *Erlösen und Vergeben*, p. 57; *AHw* 1013; *CAD* A, 1, a, b; 2). Some have nonetheless suggested that one may gain insight into the meaning of סָלַח with reference to *salāḫu*. So Milgrom (*Numbers*, p. 396): 'In Akkadian the verb *salāḫu* means "asperse", and it is the common term in rituals of healing. Thus when God extends man His boon of *salaḥ*, He thereby indicates His desire for reconciliation with man in order to continue His relationship with him...'; and Levine (*Leviticus*, p. 24): 'The verb *salaḥ* has been variously explained. Most likely, the proposed derivation from a verb meaning "to wash, sprinkle with water" (with attested cognates in Ugaritic and Akkadian) is correct. The basic concept would be that of cleansing with water, a concept then extended, of course, to connote God's forgiveness and acceptance of expiation.' These suggestions, however, involve substantial speculation with regard to the historical development of the term. At most, one can suggest with Stamm (*Erlösen und Vergeben*, p. 58) that סָלַח and *salāḫu* both go back to the same Semitic root, though they have developed differently over time.

the LORD, the one who is the subject of the verb everywhere else in the Old Testament.[5] It may be further observed that the passive form is not a requisite for stating the forgiveness of the LORD in the priestly material; for example, Num. 30.6 (5) reads: '…and the LORD will forgive her (וַיהוָה יִסְלַח־לָהּ)…' The reason the passive is used in the instances under consideration is not clear, but could be due to the fact that the qal might have implied that the priest was the one who had granted forgiveness: '…and the priest will atone for them and he will forgive them (וְכִפֶּר עֲלֵהֶם הַכֹּהֵן וְסָלַח לָהֶם)'. The use of the niphal, however, makes it clear that forgiveness is from the LORD.[6]

This leads to the subsequent observation that there is a change in subject from the first half of the phrase to the second: the performance of the כִּפֶּר-rite is carried out by the priest, while the granting of forgiveness lies in the hand of the LORD.[7] In short, the כִּפֶּר-rite carried out by the priest results in forgiveness being granted by the LORD to the sinner. This relationship can be presented as follows:

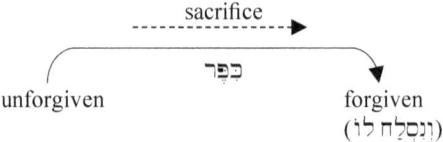

Since the כִּפֶּר-rite carried out by the priest results in סָלַח, it stands to reason that a closer examination of the nature of סָלַח will also yield insight into the nature of כִּפֶּר. For this reason, סָלַח is now considered more carefully.

---

5. As noted by Rendtorff (*Leviticus*, III, p. 176 [see also p. 179]). See also Hartley, *Leviticus*, pp. 62-63; Milgrom, *Leviticus 1–16*, p. 245; Péter-Contesse, *Lévitique 1–16*, p. 83; Janowski, *Sühne*, pp. 10-11, esp. pp. 251-52; Kiuchi, *Purification Offering*, pp. 36-37.

6. Alternatively, Christian Macholz ('Das "Passivum divinum", seine Anfänge im Alten Testament und der "Hofstil"', *ZNW* 81 [1990], pp. 247-53 [248-49, 251-53]) has suggested that the *passivum divinum* was originally a *passivum regium*, that is, the passive was commonly used when speaking to kings and that this was in turn used in speech concerning the deity. In either case, however, it is clear that the one who grants forgiveness is the LORD.

7. Milgrom, *Leviticus 1–16*, p. 245; Stamm, *Erlösen und Vergeben*, p. 129; 'סלח', pp. 151, 153; Rendtorff, *Leviticus*, III, pp. 176, 179-80; Janowski, *Sühne*, pp. 251-52. 'The fact that forgiveness lies in the hand of the LORD and not of the priest, however, does not imply that the sinner who brought the sacrifice was left to wonder whether or not it had achieved its goal. Indeed, the emphasis of the priestly literature is that the LORD Himself has provided these means so that the sinner could gain forgiveness' (Janowski, *Sühne*, p. 252; see also Stamm, *Erlösen und Vergeben*, pp. 61, 129).

The agreed upon rendering for סָלַח in the נִסְלַח-formula is 'to forgive'. The relevant entries from *The Oxford English Dictionary* define this verb as follows: 'to give up, cease to harbour (resentment, wrath)', or 'to give up resentment or claim to requital for, pardon (an offence, offender)'.[8] With the first entry, then, the emphasis of forgiveness lies primarily in the changed disposition of the offended party, who ceases to harbor resentment or wrath. The guilty party *could* benefit from this, insofar as they are no longer the object of resentment or wrath, but this is not the emphasis. With the second entry, however, the emphasis falls equally upon the change in the disposition of the one offended as well as upon the benefit that accrues to the guilty because of this change: a requital claimed for the wrong of the guilty is released, or an offense which the guilty has committed is pardoned. This latter sense of forgiveness also implies that the person granting the forgiveness has some authority over the guilty party, insofar as the guilty party is dependent upon this person's forgiveness in order to avoid the consequences of their wrong. It is in this second sense of forgiveness that סָלַח is used in the נִסְלַח-formulas (and, indeed, elsewhere in the Old Testament), for the guilty party has broken the LORD's law and can therefore expect punishment to follow; only by the LORD's granting of forgiveness could this penalty be avoided.[9]

Now it has already been seen in Chapter 2 that a deserved penalty could be avoided by means of a כֹּפֶר. This כֹּפֶר was placed upon the guilty party by the offended party as a *mitigated penalty*, that is, in place of a much harsher, yet deserved, penalty.[10] One might expect, then, that if pardon for sin (נִסְלַח) is granted when the LORD's law has been broken, it is because the offended party (the LORD) has agreed to allow for a כֹּפֶר in place of the deserved penalty,[11] that is, the כִּפֶּר-rite which results in forgiveness refers to the effecting of a כֹּפֶר-payment. This understanding of כִּפֶּר in contexts of sin will be strengthened if it can be shown: (1) that סָלַח does not necessarily refer to the remittal of all penalty, but does allow for a mitigated penalty (a כֹּפֶר); and (2) that כִּפֶּר—which is a consistent part of the נִסְלַח-formula—can refer to the paying of a כֹּפֶר. These two points will be considered in turn.

---

8. *The Oxford English Dictionary*, s.v.

9. See Chapter 1 for the connection between sin and punishment in the priestly literature.

10. See §2.1.1 above, and summary in §2.1.2. Specifically priestly texts are discussed in §2.1.1.2 (Exod. 30.11-16) and §2.1.1.3 (Num. 35.30-34).

11. This is not to say that a כֹּפֶר was always necessary, for in some instances the one offended could remit all punishment, for example, the LORD's forgiveness of the woman whose oath is annulled (Num. 30.6 [5], 9 [8], and 13 [12]). Nonetheless, the normative approach taken to avoid the original punishment is that of כֹּפֶר (Chapter 2).

The fact that סָלַח does not necessarily refer to the remittal of all penalty, but does allow for a mitigated one, finds support in Numbers 14, especially vv. 11-25.[12] This is the well-known story of the Israelite's reaction to the spies' report. Having just received 'an evil report' about the Promised Land from ten of the twelve spies (especially that the land 'devours its inhabitants' and that all the people in it were of 'great stature' [13.31-33]), the people of Israel wept all night, fearing that they and their little ones would fall by the sword (14.1-3). They thus decide to appoint a new leader and to return to Egypt (vv. 4-5), and when Joshua tries to dissuade them (vv. 6-9), they respond by declaring that he and the others should be stoned (v. 10a). It is at this point that the glory of the LORD appears at the tabernacle (v. 10b). Addressing Moses, the LORD says that he will strike the people with pestilence, disinherit them, and in turn make a great nation out of Moses (vv. 11-12). Moses pleads with the LORD not to do so, stating that if the people are destroyed, the other nations would conclude that the LORD was not strong enough to bring the people into the land he had promised them (vv. 13-16). Moses then prepares to ask for forgiveness, and in so doing appeals to the character of the LORD as a forgiving God, quoting the LORD's earlier self-description of Exodus 34: 'The LORD is slow to anger, and abounding in steadfast love, forgiving iniquity and transgression (נֹשֵׂא עָוֹן וָפֶשַׁע), but he will by no means clear the guilty, visiting the iniquity of fathers upon children, upon the third and upon the fourth generation' (Num. 14.18).[13] It is at this point that Moses then asks for forgiveness: 'Pardon the iniquity (סְלַח־נָא לַעֲוֹן) of this people, according to the greatness of your steadfast love, and according as you have forgiven this people (וְכַאֲשֶׁר נָשָׂאתָה לָעָם הַזֶּה), from Egypt even until now' (v. 19).[14] The LORD grants this request, stating, 'I have pardoned (סָלַחְתִּי), according to your word' (v. 20).

Significantly, however, this granting of pardon does not mean complete remission of penalty, as the LORD immediately proceeds to state that the people of Israel who doubted him would surely die before ever reaching the Promised Land (vv. 21-23). What is relevant to the present discussion, though, is that this is a mitigation of the original penalty. To be specific,

12. Traditionally, Num. 13–14 is seen as a mixture of JE and P, with 14.11-25 belonging to JE (see discussion and references in Katharine D. Sakenfeld, 'The Problem of Divine Forgiveness in Numbers 14', *CBQ* 37 [1975], pp. 317-30 [317-20]; see also the overview and critique of the traditional approach in Wenham, *Numbers*, pp. 124-26). 14.11-25 are still relevant to the present discussion, however, insofar as the putative P doublet of 14.11-25 (i.e. 14.26-39a) does not contradict or correct the idea of forgiveness presented there, but rather expands on the punishment mentioned in 14.23a. For further aspects of the unity of Num. 13–14, see Wenham, *Numbers*, pp. 124-26.

13. Cf. Exod. 34.6-7. For נֹשֵׂא עָוֹן as an expression of forgiveness, see §3.1.2.1 below.

14. An alternative translation of the last phrase is 'just as you have borne this people from Egypt until now', though this does not affect the present argument.

instead of the entire nation being immediately wiped out, it is only the adults who partook in the Exodus from Egypt that are affected: they are prohibited from entering the Promised Land and will eventually die in the wilderness.[15] This conjunction of divine forgiveness and a mitigated penalty is also noted by Wenham, who goes one step further in relating the forgiveness granted here in Numbers 14 to the sacrificial texts that contain the נִסְלַח-formula:

> The divine pardon does not mean Israel will escape all punishment for their sin, only that they will not suffer the total annihilation they deserve. A similar understanding of forgiveness is found in many sacrificial texts. After the worshipper has performed the full ritual involving very often the heavy expense of killing an animal, it is stated 'he shall be forgiven' (e.g. Lev. 4.20, 26, 31; 5.6, etc.). In other words, the man is restored to fellowship with God, but he has still paid for his offence by offering a sacrifice.[16]

Thus the LORD's statement that he has forgiven the people (v. 20) refers not to the removal of all penalty, but to his agreement to withhold the penalty that is deserved (being struck by the plague immediately) and to substitute a lighter penalty in its stead (non-entry into the Promised Land), thereby allowing the relationship between the LORD and Israel to continue. In this way, סָלַח is actually seen to be a statement of the כִּפֶּר-principle: the satisfaction of the connection between sin and punishment, through the payment of a mitigated penalty, resulting in a restored relationship between offender and offended. In short, by granting forgiveness (סָלַחְתִּי; v. 20), the LORD was agreeing to a כִּפֶּר-arrangement with the people.[17]

---

15. Stamm, *Erlösen und Vergeben*, p. 109.
16. Wenham, *Numbers*, pp. 122-23.
17. Admittedly, this understanding of forgiveness is broader than that conveyed by the English verb 'to forgive', which does include the idea of pardon for a punishment deserved, as well as the restoration of relationship, but which does not necessarily include the idea of a ransom (or composition) payment in the stead of the deserved penalty. Unfortunately, a more appropriate word is difficult to find. Thus the rendering 'to forgive' is maintained for סָלַח, with the proviso that it often includes the idea that a mitigated penalty is substituted for the deserved one. Other scholars argue that סָלַח does not refer to pardon as much as to the preservation of the people, or to reconciliation between them and God, or to God's forbearance of the people. Sakenfeld, for instance, defines forgiveness as 'God's preservation of the people of his own free decision and expected or hoped for on the basis of his self-declaration of his attitude toward the community ("as thou has spoken", 14.17, referring to Ex 34)' (Sakenfeld, 'The Problem of Divine Forgiveness in Numbers 14', p. 330; see also pp. 326-27). Jacob Milgrom (*Numbers*, p. 112), citing several ancient Jewish commentators, writes in a similar vein, 'Hebrew *salaḥ*, implying not the absolution of sin but the suspension of anger [Ibn Ezra, Sefer ha-Mivḥar, Abravanel]; that they not die immediately and their children may survive [Ramban]; that they live out their lives and their children inherit [Shadal]...' Milgrom (*Numbers*, p. 396) later concludes, 'Moses asks for reconciliation not forgiveness, for assurance that Israel will be brought to its land and not that the sin of the Exodus

This understanding of סָלַח, then, would support the supposition that when כִּפֶּר results in סָלַח in the verses using the וְנִסְלַח-formula, כִּפֶּר has a denominative reference, that is, it refers to the effecting of a כֹּפֶר-payment.[18] In addition, it was also noted above that this understanding of כִּפֶּר would be further strengthened if it could be shown that כִּפֶּר is indeed used to refer to the paying of a כֹּפֶר. In this regard the discussion in Chapter 2 may be noted, where it was seen that the use of כִּפֶּר to refer to the effecting of a כֹּפֶר-payment enjoys a broad consensus among biblical scholars, with the priestly literature containing some of the clearest examples.[19]

From the above, one may therefore suggest that כִּפֶּר does refer to the effecting of a כֹּפֶר-payment when it results in סָלַח. It is thus now possible to return to the original verses we were considering and translate accordingly: 'And the priest will effect a כֹּפֶר-payment for them (וְכִפֶּר עֲלֵהֶם הַכֹּהֵן)[20] and they will be forgiven (וְנִסְלַח לָהֶם)'.[21]

It is important to note, however, that this must remain a tentative translation, for while כִּפֶּר in these instances does refer to an act of כֹּפֶר, it could also refer to more than that. In particular, Jacob Milgrom has argued that inadvertent sins which require a purification offering, such as those occurring

generation will be exonerated'. While there is truth in these statements—the people are indeed preserved (Sakenfeld), there is reconciliation between Israel and the LORD (Milgrom)—it should be recognized that these authors are describing the *results* of the LORD's decision to pardon (סָלַח) the people, which is just one aspect of what it means to forgive. To state this more exactly: the preservation of the people and the reconciliation between them and the LORD are the results of the LORD's forgiveness, that is, his agreement to a mitigated penalty (non-entry into the Promised Land) in place of the one deserved (destruction of the people). In this regard, סָלַח is very much a pardoning of the original offense by means of a כֹּפֶר-arrangement that in turn allows the relationship between Israel and the LORD to continue.

18. This statement is not attempting to answer whether כִּפֶּר is a denominative of כֹּפֶר, or whether כֹּפֶר is derived from כִּפֶּר. It is simply noting an implication of the above, namely, that כִּפֶּר is used in these contexts to express verbally what כֹּפֶר expresses nominally.

19. See Chapter 2, nn. 8-13 and attendant discussion.

20. The כֹּפֶר-payment in this instance is clearly the sacrificial rite executed by the priest on behalf of the offerer (see diagram above on p. 82). For the translation of עַל, see the Appendix.

21. Several questions may be asked with reference to the exact way in which the sacrifice functioned as a כֹּפֶר-payment. For example, in what way did the sacrifice of an animal satisfy the connection between sin and punishment, that is, did the penalty consist in the cost of the animal or in something else? And further, did the sacrifice accomplish anything aside from the payment of a mitigated penalty, for example, did it also serve to purify the sanctuary? These questions will be considered in more depth below in the consideration of the meaning of Lev. 17.11 (Chapter 6) and in the consideration of the priestly notions of purity and impurity and how these relate to כִּפֶּר (Chapter 5).

3. *The Verb* כִּפֶּר *in Contexts of Sin* 87

with the נִסְלַח‎-formula in Lev. 4.1–5.13, pollute the sanctuary and its sancta, and that the purification offering—by which atonement (כִּפֶּר) is made—serves to cleanse these.[22] While this study will augment Milgrom's understanding of כִּפֶּר in these contexts,[23] he does seem correct in stating that

22. Milgrom, *Leviticus 1–16*, pp. 256-58; *idem*, 'Israel's Sanctuary: The Priestly Picture of Dorian Gray', *RB* 83 (1976), pp. 390-99 (391-94).

23. Milgrom (*Leviticus 1–16*, pp. 227-28) translates כִּפֶּר with 'to effect purgation' in these contexts. This translation is based upon his understanding of the purification offering, which is the primary means of effecting כִּפֶּר in these contexts and which he understands to result solely in the cleansing of the sanctuary and its sancta (pp. 254-58). In keeping with this understanding, Milgrom (pp. 254-58) states that *the sinner* is forgiven their sin through repentance, whereas *the sanctuary* is cleansed by the blood of the purification offering. As a result, Milgrom (p. 228) translates כִּפֶּר in Lev. 4–5 with 'to effect purgation': 'Thus the priest shall effect purgation on his behalf for the wrong he committed, that he may be forgiven' (Lev. 4.35b). One may ask at this point: If the sinner is forgiven through repentance, why does the text state that forgiveness comes as a result of the sacrificial rite? Milgrom's (p. 256) answer is that the wrong which the worshipper is forgiven of in these contexts is not the *original* inadvertence, but the *subsequent* wrong of defiling the tabernacle: the inadvertent offender needs forgiveness not because of his act per se—as indicated above, his act is forgiven because of the offender's inadvertence and remorse—but because of the consequence of his act. His inadvertence has contaminated the sanctuary, and it is his responsibility to purge it with a *ḥaṭṭā't*. While Milgrom seems correct that sins do defile the sanctuary (see above), and that the purification offering does serve to cleanse the sanctuary (see §4.4 below), it appears that he has introduced a false disjunction into the text by separating forgiveness of the original inadvertence from the כִּפֶּר-rite itself. The most straightforward reading of these texts is that the sinner has committed an inadvertent sin, becomes aware of it, and brings a purification offering in order to receive forgiveness *for that sin* (and not simply for the subsequent results of the sin in terms of the pollution of the sanctuary): 'If any person from among the populace *does wrong* inadvertently by violating any of the LORD's prohibitive commandments and he suffers the consequence of his guilt or he is informed *of the wrong he committed*, he shall bring as his offering a female goat without blemish *for the wrong he committed*... Thus the priest shall effect a כֹּפֶר-payment for him, that he may be forgiven' (Lev. 4.27-28, 31b); 'If the offering he brings is a sheep, he shall bring a female without blemish... Thus the priest shall effect a כֹּפֶר-payment for him *for the wrong he committed*, that he may be forgiven' (Lev. 4.32, 35b). Again, this is not to deny that the purification offering cleanses the sanctuary as well (see discussion above); it is simply to affirm that the focus of these texts appears to be on the forgiveness of the *original inadvertence* by means of the כִּפֶּר-rite, and that in such a context the verb most likely refers to the effecting of a כֹּפֶר-payment. How this understanding of the verb then relates to the element of purgation is discussed in §5.2 below. Finally, it may be noted that even if Milgrom were correct, it would not greatly affect the present argument, since the sinner would still be in need of a כֹּפֶר-payment to be made on his behalf. This is because the sinner would have defiled the sanctuary, which is a sin of great consequence in the priestly literature that results in liability to severe judgment. As argued in §4.4 below, the verb כִּפֶּר in this context refers not just to effecting purgation, but also to effecting a כֹּפֶר-payment (see §4.4 below for further details). Stated differently, it is not

inadvertent sins do result in the pollution of the sanctuary and its sancta. This finds support in two considerations. First, it is clear that sins which do not involve the direct defilement of the sanctuary can still lead to its pollution—for example, Lev. 20.3, where the LORD states that the one who gives their child to Molech is guilty of 'defiling (טִמֵּא) my sanctuary and profaning my holy name'.[24] It is therefore possible that the sins of Leviticus 4 and 5 also result in the defiling of the sanctuary. Second, given that one function of the purification offering is the cleansing of the sanctuary and its sancta (Lev. 16.16, 19, 33; see also 8.15), the requirement of the purification offering in contexts such as Lev. 4.1–5.13 suggests that the sins here have resulted in the pollution of the sanctuary, and that כִּפֶּר, at least in the context of the purification offering in Lev. 4.1–5.13, may also refer to the cleansing of the sanctuary. How this then relates to the understanding of כִּפֶּר as the effecting of a כֹּפֶר-payment will be considered further in Chapter 5 when the relationship between impurity, sin, and כִּפֶּר is examined.

Thus far we have seen that the verb כִּפֶּר, when occurring in conjunction with the verb סָלַח, can refer to the effecting of a כֹּפֶר-payment. This finds support in the fact that the forgiveness expressed by סָלַח is in keeping with the כֹּפֶר-principle (i.e. not the remission of all penalty but the substitution of a mitigated penalty), and in the fact that כִּפֶּר is clearly used elsewhere with a denominative meaning (i.e. referring to the effecting of a כֹּפֶר-payment). This understanding of כִּפֶּר as the effecting of a כֹּפֶר-payment finds further support in the phrase נָשָׂא עָוֹן, which occurs in conjunction with כִּפֶּר. For this reason we now turn to consider נָשָׂא עָוֹן more carefully.

3.1.2. נָשָׂא עָוֹן[25]

It has already been noted above that the phrase נָשָׂא עָוֹן occurs in the priestly literature in three distinct contexts.[26] In the first, the sinner is the subject of the verb; in the second, the person wronged—be it the LORD himself or another human—is the subject of the verb; and in the third, a third party—neither the sinner nor the one wronged—is the subject of the verb. Due to this change in subject, the phrase has to be translated differently in each of these three contexts. It was argued above that the phrase is best translated with 'to bear punishment' in the first context. Anticipating the conclusions of this chapter, the phrase may be translated in the next two contexts as

---

simply purgation that is effected in the context of defiling the sanctuary, but a very specific type of purgation, namely, כִּפֶּר-purgation (see §5.2).

24. Milgrom, *Leviticus 1–16*, p. 257.

25. נָשָׂא is actually conjoined with various terms for sin. For the sake of simplicity, the phrase נָשָׂא עָוֹן is referred to, since this is common to all three uses of the phrase. See Chapter 1, n. 36.

26. See §1.2.3.

3. *The Verb* כִּפֶּר *in Contexts of Sin* 89

follows: 'to forgive sin' (with offended party as subject); 'to bear away sin/punishment' (with third party as subject).²⁷ These last two contexts will now be considered in turn.

3.1.2.1. *Person wronged as subject.* In the second usage of the phrase נָשָׂא עָוֹן, the person wronged—be it the LORD or a person—is the subject of the verb, and the phrase is translated in these instances with 'to forgive'.²⁸ This usage occurs outside of the material traditionally classified as priestly, and a full treatment of it is thus outside the scope of this section. Nonetheless, because it might be related to the third usage (which does occur in the priestly material), and because this usage occurs in conjunction with כִּפֶּר in one instance (Exod. 32.30-32), it is important to provide a summary discussion of it.

By way of general summary, then, in this second usage of the phrase the subject is the offended party, which is either another person or the LORD himself. Thus we find the phrase used in appeals to other people when Joseph's brothers ask him for forgiveness (Gen. 50.17 [× 2]), when Pharaoh asks Moses for forgiveness (Exod. 10.17), when Saul asks Samuel for forgiveness (1 Sam. 15.25), and when Abigail asks David for forgiveness (1 Sam. 25.28). People ask the LORD to forgive their sin another four times: Moses asks the LORD to forgive the sin of the people after the golden calf incident (Exod. 32.32); Job asks why the LORD does not forgive his sin (Job 7.21); the Psalmist asks the LORD to forgive all his sins (Ps. 25.18); and Hosea instructs the people to ask the LORD for forgiveness (Hos. 14.3 [2]). Finally, the LORD is described as forgiving sin seven times: in his self-revelation (Exod. 34.7); in Moses' appeal after the people rebelled over the

---

27. Cf. Zimmerli, 'Die Eigenart', pp. 9-12. Zimmerli distinguishes the same three usages of the phrase as above but adds a fourth, namely, 'to be answerable for something' (Zimmerli, 'Die Eigenart', p. 10). He sees this to be the meaning in Num. 18.1 and 23 (as well as Ezek. 18.19-20), where the priests are said to 'bear the sin' of the sanctuary and of their priesthood, that is, 'to be answerable for' the sanctuary and their priesthood. Since Zimmerli's article, however, Jacob Milgrom has shown that these verses refer to the responsibility of the priests to guard the sanctuary from encroachment (for details see Milgrom, *Studies in Levitical Terminology*, pp. 16-59; a summary can be found in Milgrom, *Numbers*, pp. 423-24). If they did not, they would 'bear the sin', that is, be punished (cf. 18.3, where the LORD says to Aaron: '[The Levites] shall attend you and attend to all duties of the tent; but shall not come near to the vessels of the sanctuary or to the altar, lest they, *and you*, die'). Thus this usage of נָשָׂא עָוֹן is no different from that of the first category above: those who sinned—in this case, by not guarding the sanctuary—would suffer the consequences of it.

28. In this second usage נָשָׂא is followed by either עָוֹן (Exod. 34.7; Num. 14.18; Ps. 85.3 [2]; Isa. 33.24; Ezek. 4.4, 5, 6; Mic. 7.18; Hos. 14.3 [2]), חַטָּאת (Gen. 50.17; Exod. 10.17; 32.32; 1 Sam. 15.25; Pss. 25.18; 32.5), חַטָּאָה (Exod. 34.7), and/or פֶּשַׁע (Gen. 50.17 [× 2]; Num. 14.18; 1 Sam. 25.28; Job 7.21; Ps. 32.1).

spies' report (Num. 14.18); in Ps. 32.5, where the LORD forgives the Psalmist's sin, and in v. 1, where the LORD is the assumed subject who forgives sin; in Ps. 85.3 (2), where the LORD is described as having forgiven the iniquity of his people; in Isa. 33.24, where the sin of the people is forgiven; and in Mic. 7.18, where God is again described as the one who forgives sin.

One thing that is common in all of these verses is that there is some form of punishment in the immediate context. Thus in the first instances: Joseph's brothers were terrified at what Joseph might do to avenge their earlier misdeeds (Gen. 50.15-17); Pharaoh was already experiencing the plague of locusts (Exod. 10.12-17); Saul had just been told that his kingship was being taken away (1 Sam. 15.23-25); and Abigail knew that David and his men were preparing to destroy her husband (1 Sam. 25.14-31). In the instances where the LORD is asked for forgiveness: Moses knew that a punishment was coming (Exod. 32.32-33); Job was in the midst of severe suffering and expected it to end in death (Job 7.21); the Psalmist was in the midst of suffering and trials (Ps. 25.17-18); and the people of Israel in Hosea's day had been warned of the imminent judgment of the Lord (Hos. 13.15–14.1 [13.15-16]). Even the descriptions of the LORD as the one who forgives sin occur in a context involving punishment: in the context of Exod. 34.7 the people's sin had resulted in the LORD not being in their midst (33.2-3; 34.9); in Numbers 14 the people's rebellion had resulted in the LORD's threat to strike them with pestilence (v. 12); in Psalm 32 the hand of the LORD was heavy upon the psalmist (v. 4) until he confessed his sin and received the LORD's forgiveness (v. 5); in Psalm 85 the LORD's forgiveness (v. 3 [2]) is paralleled to the turning aside of his fury and burning anger (v. 4 [3]); in Isa. 33.24 forgiveness will mean a lack of sickness; and in Mic. 7.18 the LORD's forgiveness of sins is described against the backdrop of his judgments upon the people outlined in ch. 6.

In short, when sinners ask the offended to 'bear sin' for them, they are asking for a remission of the penalty that the sin deserves. In some of these instances they are asking for the remission of a penalty that has not yet come, for example, the request of Joseph's brothers to Joseph, or of Abigail to David.[29] In other instances they are asking for the remission of a penalty that they are currently experiencing, for example, with Pharaoh's request to

---

29. This is not to say that the sinner expected there to be no punishment; even in some of the above examples the principle of כֹּפֶר is evident. Thus the request of Joseph's brothers for forgiveness (Gen. 50.17) is immediately followed by their falling before him and indenturing themselves as his servants (v. 18; it may also be noted that in a certain sense he had already punished them [Gen. 42–44]), and Abigail's request of David for forgiveness (1 Sam. 25.28) follows immediately after she has presented a gift to him (v. 27). What the sinner was asking, however, was that the punishment the sin deserved would not come to pass.

Moses (Exod. 10.12-17), or the Psalmist's request to the LORD (25.17-18). In either case, however, a remission of the penalty which the sin deserved is in view.

Thus this second usage of the phrase is the converse of the first usage. It was seen with the first usage that when the sinner was the subject of the phrase, he or she was going to suffer the punitive consequences of their wrong; here, however, the sinner is asking the offended to forgive their sin so that they will not suffer the consequences of their wrong (if those consequences have not yet come), or so that they will stop suffering the consequences of their wrong (if they are currently suffering them).

One may further note that this second usage of עָוֹן נָשָׂא is consonant with the biblical understanding of forgiveness (סָלַח) discussed above (§3.1.1), especially with reference to the remission of the original penalty that the sin deserves. This consonance between נָשָׂא עָוֹן and סָלַח finds support in two avenues. The first is the fact that נָשָׂא עָוֹן and סָלַח can be used interchangeably. In Num. 14.18-19, for instance, Moses pleads for the LORD to forgive the people for doubting the LORD and believing the evil report from the ten spies. In so doing, he appeals to the character of the LORD as a forgiving God: 'The LORD is slow to anger, and abounding in steadfast love, forgiving iniquity and transgression (נֹשֵׂא עָוֹן וָפָשַׁע)...' (v. 18).[30] This is in turn followed by his request for forgiveness, where instead of using the phrase נָשָׂא עָוֹן he uses the word סָלַח: 'Pardon the iniquity (סְלַח־נָא לַעֲוֹן) of this people, I pray thee...' (v. 19). This similarity between נָשָׂא עָוֹן and סָלַח is illustrated again in Exodus 34, where the LORD's self-description as a God who forgives sin (נֹשֵׂא עָוֹן; v. 7) is once more followed by the request of Moses that the LORD forgive (סָלַח) his people: '...and pardon our iniquity and our sin (וְסָלַחְתָּ לַעֲוֹנֵנוּ וּלְחַטָּאתֵנוּ)...' (v. 9). Finally, in Exod. 32.32, Moses is again requesting that the LORD forgive his people. This time, however, instead of using סָלַח as he does in Num. 14.19 and Exod. 34.9, he uses the phrase נָשָׂא חַטָּאת: 'Alas, this people have sinned a great sin; they have made for themselves gods of gold. But now, if you will forgive their sin (אִם־תִּשָּׂא חַטָּאתָם)...' (vv. 31-32a).

A second fact which confirms the consonance between נָשָׂא עָוֹן and סָלַח is that there is a similar relationship between נָשָׂא עָוֹן and כִּפֶּר in Exodus 32 as there is between סָלַח and כִּפֶּר in the passages with the נִסְלַח-formula considered above. With the נִסְלַח-formula, the subject of כִּפֶּר is the priest and the result is described with סָלַח. In Exodus 32, the כִּפֶּר-action is performed by Moses, and the result is described with נָשָׂא עָוֹן. Thus when Moses says to the people, 'You have sinned a great sin. And now I will go up to the LORD; perhaps I can make atonement for your sin (אוּלַי אֲכַפְּרָה בְּעַד חַטַּאתְכֶם)

---

30. Cf. Exod. 34.6-7.

(v. 30), he expresses the hoped for result ('perhaps'!) with נָשָׂא עָוֹן: 'But now, if you will forgive their sin (אִם־תִּשָּׂא חַטָּאתָם)...' (v. 32a). As in Numbers 14, discussed above (§3.1.1), there is no specific atonement rite per se. Indeed, in the face of such open sin and rebellion, there was no priestly means by which to make atonement. Rather, Moses attempts to effect כִּפֶּר here by requesting the LORD's forgiveness, that is, that the LORD would agree not to execute the penalty which their sin deserved. As in Numbers 14, the Lord does forgive them: he does not wipe them out completely. It may also be noted, however, that this forgiveness does not mean the remission of all penalty. As in Numbers 14, a mitigated penalty is placed upon the people: instead of completely wiping them out, the LORD 'smites' some of them (Exod. 32.35).

Like סָלַח above, then, נָשָׂא עָוֹן in these contexts can be translated with 'to forgive', with the understanding that this refers to the remission of the original penalty. As with סָלַח, this does not imply that there would therefore be no penalty at all; Joseph's brothers, for example, ask for forgiveness and yet still offer themselves as slaves (Gen. 50.17-18), and the Israelites suffer a mitigated penalty in Exodus 32. In this regard the phrase is also similar to סָלַח in that it can be used in a way congruent with the כִּפֶּר-principle, that is, the placing of a mitigated penalty in lieu of the deserved one. At the least, however, the phrase נָשָׂא עָוֹן is most similar to סָלַח in that it is used in these contexts to refer to the remission of the original penalty.

3.1.2.2. *Third party as subject.* The third usage of the phrase נָשָׂא עָוֹן differs from the first and second usage above in that it is a third party, and not the sinner or the offended party, that is said to 'bear the sin'. This usage occurs three times in the priestly literature: Exod. 28.38; Lev. 10.17; and Lev. 16.22 (cf. vv. 10, 21).[31] The meaning here is that the third party in some way 'bears away' or 'removes' the sin of the guilty.[32] That the usage of נָשָׂא עָוֹן in these verses is relevant to how one understands atonement is indicated especially by Lev. 10.17 and Lev. 16.22, both of which use נָשָׂא עָוֹן in conjunction with

---

31. For Num. 18.1, 23, see above, n. 27.
32. Note, for example, the following translations of and comments on Exod. 28.38: 'And it shall be on Aaron's forehead, and Aaron shall take away the iniquity of the holy things (וְנָשָׂא אַהֲרֹן אֶת־עֲוֹן הַקֳּדָשִׁים) which the Israelites consecrate, with regard to all their holy gifts...' (NASV); Péter-Contesse (*Lévitique 1–16*, p. 167): 'L'expression נשא עון signifie...ici "ôter le péché" et non "porter le (poids du) péché"'; Levine (*Leviticus*, p. 63): 'The priests effectively removed the sins of the people by attending to the sacrifices of expiation. But they were not to be punished for the sins of the community'; Dillmann (*Exodus und Leviticus*, pp. 473-74): '...dass sie die Vergehung oder Schuld der Gemeinde...wegnehmen...'; Milgrom (*Leviticus 1–16*, p. 596): '...and he has assigned it to you to remove the iniquity of the community...' (see also pp. 622-25).

כִּפֶּר. The purpose of this section, therefore, is to consider more carefully what light this third usage throws on the meaning of כִּפֶּר.

3.1.2.2.1. Leviticus 10.17. Leviticus 10 begins with the Nadab and Abihu incident (vv. 1-7), and then proceeds to record further instructions for Aaron and his remaining sons for the execution of their duties (vv. 8-15). Following this, Moses looks for the goat of the purification offering which had been offered for the people (v. 16; cf. 9.15) but whose flesh had been burned (instead of eaten, as it should have been). Upon discovery of this, Moses becomes angry with Eleazar and Ithamar and asks them, 'Why have you not eaten the purification offering in the place of the sanctuary, since it is a thing most holy and has been given to you to bear away the sin of the congregation (לָשֵׂאת אֶת־עֲוֹן הָעֵדָה), to make atonement for them (לְכַפֵּר עֲלֵיהֶם) before the LORD?' (v. 17). The three issues that arise from this verse are the meaning and use of the infinitive in the phrase 'to bear away the sin' (לָשֵׂאת אֶת־עֲוֹן), the meaning of the phrase itself, and finally, its relation to the second infinitive phrase, 'to make atonement for them'. The first two of these will be looked at together, followed by a consideration of the third.

The ל in the phrase לָשֵׂאת אֶת־עֲוֹן הָעֵדָה has been understood in two different ways. A few scholars have understood נָשָׂא עֲוֹן here to refer to 'bearing the responsibility'.[33] In this case, the ל must be taken as indicating a clause that provides the grounds for the LORD giving the purification offering to the priests. Thus Milgrom, who initially followed Ehrlich, translated 'and I [*sic*] have given (the *ḥaṭṭā't*) to you for bearing the responsibility of the community by performing purgation rites before the LORD on their behalf'.[34] In short, the purification offering was given to them as a reward *because* they bore the responsibility of the community in purging the sanctuary.

This understanding of לָשֵׂאת אֶת־עֲוֹן, however, fails on two accounts. First, this is an unlikely use of ל, which is used to indicate a purpose, result, temporal, or epexegetical clause, but not typically to indicate a ground clause.[35]

---

33. Arnold B. Ehrlich, *Randglossen zur hebräischen Bibel. Zweiter Band: Leviticus, Numeri, Deuteronomium* (repr., Hildesheim: Georg Olms Verlagsbuchhandlung, 1908–14), p. 37 (noted by Kiuchi, *Purification Offering*, p. 47). Ehrlich states, 'נשׂא עון, wenn nicht Gott, sondern der Priester Subjekt ist, heisst immer, ohne Ausnahme, für das Vergehen eines andern gegen die Heiligtümer verantwortlich sein'. He further cites the use of עֲוֹן in Num. 18.1 in this regard, for which see discussion above, n. 27.

34. Jacob Milgrom, *Studies in Cultic Theology and Terminology* (SJLA, 36; Leiden: E.J. Brill, 1983), p. 70 (noted by Kiuchi, *Purification Offering*, p. 47). As noted below in n. 38, Milgrom has since changed his understanding of the text.

35. W&O 36.2.3c-e. Indeed, there are instances where the infinitive construct is used to introduce a ground clause: 'Why is the land ruined and laid waste like a wilderness, so that no one passes through? And the LORD says: "Because they have forsaken (עַל־עָזְבָם) my law..."' (Jer. 9.11b-12a [12b-13a]); 'Thus says the LORD: "For three transgressions

Second, Kiuchi, citing Knierim, notes simply that 'the meaning of עָוֹן is not as neutral as the modern term 'responsibility' implies'.[36]

These critiques also point the way to a more likely understanding of לָשֵׂאת אֶת־עֲוֹן, namely, with most scholars, to understand the ל in its customary function of indicating purpose, and to understand עָוֹן as having its normal meaning of 'sin' or 'guilt'.[37] This leads to the following translation: 'Why have you not eaten the purification offering in the place of the sanctuary, since it is a thing most holy, and he has given it to you *in order to* bear away the *sin* of the congregation (לָשֵׂאת אֶת־עֲוֹן הָעֵדָה), to make atonement for them (לְכַפֵּר עֲלֵיהֶם) before the LORD?' Exactly how this sin is borne away is greatly debated. As early as the LXX and rabbinic times, and down to modern times, the purpose clause of לָשֵׂאת אֶת־עֲוֹן has been related to the eating in v. 17a (i.e. the priests bore the sin away by eating the purification offering).[38] Others, however, understand the purpose clause of לָשֵׂאת אֶת־עֲוֹן to be related to the purification offering rite as a whole. Péter-Contesse, for instance, argues that the phrase 'to bear the sin of the congregation' is directly dependent upon the verb 'to give' and not the verb 'to eat'.[39] It does

---

of Edom, and for four, I will not revoke the punishment; because he pursued (עַל־רָדְפוֹ) his brother with the sword..."' (Amos 1.11a) (GKC 114r). Here, however, the infinitive construct is prefixed by עַל and not ל.

36. Kiuchi, *Purification Offering*, p. 50. See Knierim, *Hauptbegriffe*, p. 220 n. 88. Knierim was in turn criticizing Zimmerli, 'Die Eigenart', p. 10, and his understanding of Num. 18.1 and 23 (see above, n. 27).

37. See nn. 38 and 39 for those holding to this view. It may be questioned what particular sin the word עָוֹן refers to. Wenham (*Leviticus*, p. 149), noting that there is no specific sin mentioned in the larger context (see Lev. 9), states that the purpose of the purification offering here was 'not to atone for specific sins, but for the general sinfulness of the nation...' Similarly, Kiuchi (*Purification Offering*, p. 46) states, '...what the *hattat* in Leviticus 9 deals with, is not particular sins but rather general sinfulness or uncleanness, assumed in the encounter of man—whether he is a priest or not—with God on any special occasion...' (followed by Hartley, *Leviticus*, p. 122).

38. The LXX, for instance, inserts φαγεῖν into the verse: '...this he gave to you to eat, in order that you might bear...' (noted by Kiuchi, *Purification Offering*, p. 46), and the *Sipra* records the following: '"When the priests eat (the purification offering) the offerers are expiated" (Shemini 2.4)' (noted by Milgrom, *Leviticus 1–16*, p. 624). This understanding has been followed by some modern commentators as well, who see the eating of the purification offering as playing some role—though not necessarily an exclusive one—in the bearing of sin (Levine, *Leviticus*, pp. 63-64; Dillmann, *Exodus und Leviticus*, pp. 473-74). The most thorough discussion in favor of this position remains that of Milgrom, *Leviticus 1–16*, pp. 622-25 (see also pp. 635-40).

39. Péter-Contesse, *Lévitique 1–16*, p. 167. See also Janowski, *Sühne*, p. 239 n. 272; Elliger, *Leviticus*, p. 132. Kiuchi (*Purification Offering*, pp. 46-52, esp. pp. 48-52) provides a detailed discussion in which he argues that the bearing of sin does not refer to the consumption of the animal but to the rite as a whole, and in particular, to the blood manipulation.

not appear, however, that these different understandings of the *means* by which the sin is removed (viz. by the consumption of the animal or by the performance of the rite as a whole) need alter the general understanding of the results: the sin is removed so that the sinner no longer needs to suffer the consequences of their sin.

Finally, with reference to the relationship between לָשֵׂאת אֶת־עֲוֹן and לְכַפֵּר עֲלֵיהֶם, it seems best also to take this second infinitive phrase as a purpose or result clause. This is the case, for instance, in Lev. 8.34, where a finite verb is also followed by two consecutive infinitive constructs, the second of which is לְכַפֵּר: 'As has been done today, the LORD has commanded to be done to make atonement for you (צִוָּה יְהוָה לַעֲשֹׂת לְכַפֵּר עֲלֵיכֶם)'. Here the second infinitive construct states the purpose or result of the first, that is, the LORD has commanded them to do certain things for the purpose of accomplishing atonement (or, with the result that atonement will be accomplished). So also in Lev. 10.17: the priests are to bear away the sin of the congregation for the purpose of accomplishing atonement (or, with the result that atonement will be accomplished).[40]

What is particularly significant to note in this regard is that it is clear the means of bearing away the sin of the congregation (i.e. the purification offering) had been ordained by the LORD: 'Why have you not eaten the purification offering in the place of the sanctuary, since it is a thing most holy and he has given it to you (וְאֹתָהּ נָתַן לָכֶם) in order to bear away the sin of the congregation (לָשֵׂאת אֶת־עֲוֹן הָעֵדָה), in order to make atonement for them (לְכַפֵּר עֲלֵיהֶם) before the LORD?' This is in perfect keeping with the observations on כִּפֶּר above, insofar as it is the offended party (the LORD) who has agreed to a כֹּפֶר (the purification offering) by which sin is removed (נָשָׂא עָוֹן) so that the sinner no longer needs to face the consequences of their sin.

3.1.2.2.2. *Leviticus 16.10, 21-22.* These verses describe the scapegoat component of the Day of Atonement rites. The purpose of the scapegoat is first introduced in v. 10: '...but the goat on which the lot fell for Azazel shall be presented alive before the LORD to make atonement upon it by sending it

---

40. This understanding also fits in well with the use of נָשָׂא עָוֹן in Lev. 16.22, where atonement is accomplished when the goat bears away the sins of the people into the wilderness, and in Exod. 28.38, where sin is removed so that the Israelites may be accepted before the LORD (see further below). Alternatively, it is grammatically possible that the second infinitive phrase (לְכַפֵּר עֲלֵיהֶם) is expressing the means by which the first infinitive phrase (לָשֵׂאת אֶת־עֲוֹן) is accomplished, that is, the priests are to bear away the sin of the congregation *by* making atonement for it (so Janowski, *Sühne*, p. 239 n. 272; Elliger, *Leviticus*, p. 132; for this use of the infinitive see Joüon 124o, and discussion of Lev. 16.10 in following section). In either instance, however, the bearing away of sin and the effecting of atonement are two sides of the same coin.

away (לְכַפֵּר עָלָיו לְשַׁלַּח אֹתוֹ) into the wilderness to Azazel' (v. 10). Verses 21-22 then further elaborate on this account:

> And Aaron shall lay both his hands upon the head of the live goat, and confess over it all the iniquities of the people of Israel, and all their transgressions, all their sins; and he shall put them upon the head of the goat, and send it away into the wilderness by the hand of a man who is in readiness. The goat shall bear all their iniquities upon itself (וְנָשָׂא הַשָּׂעִיר עָלָיו אֶת־כָּל־עֲוֹנֹתָם) to a solitary land; and he shall let the goat go in the wilderness.

Relevant to how one understands the phrase נָשָׂא עָוֹן in v. 22 is the relationship between the phrases לְכַפֵּר עָלָיו and לְשַׁלַּח אֹתוֹ in v. 10. The RSV understands לְשַׁלַּח to be acting as a purpose clause here, that is, כִּפֶּר is made upon the goat *so that* it may then be sent into the wilderness: 'But the goat on which the lot fell for Azazel shall be presented alive before the LORD to make atonement over it, that it may be sent away into the wilderness to Azazel'. This translation thus implies that the כִּפֶּר-rite is complete *before* the goat is sent off, that is, the rite consists only of confessing and placing the sins of the people upon the head of the goat.

A second understanding of לְשַׁלַּח is that it should be taken as explicative of לְכַפֵּר עָלָיו, that is, he will perform atonement with the goat *by* sending it into the wilderness.[41] In this view, the כִּפֶּר-rite consists not only of

---

41. So Kiuchi, *Purification Offering*, p. 151; Milgrom, *Leviticus 1–16*, p. 1009; Péter-Contesse, *Lévitique 1–16*, pp. 248, 254 n. 26; Hartley, *Leviticus*, pp. 220, 236; NIV. Again, for this use of the infinitive construct see Joüon 124o. There is some debate over the meaning of עָלָיו in the phrase לְכַפֵּר עָלָיו. Levine (*Presence of the Lord*, p. 65) argues that כִּפֶּר + עַל can refer to a 'spatial process, that is, "to perform rites of expiation in proximity to, upon-" sacrificial animals, persons, places, etc.'. As a result, he translates v. 10 as follows: 'While the goat designated by lot for 'Azazel shall be stationed, alive, in the presence of Yahweh, to perform rites of expiation beside it, and to send it off to 'Azazel, to the wilderness' (p. 80). Levine's interpretation, however, is unlikely. As noted by Milgrom (*Leviticus 1–16*, p. 1023), 'There is no warrant whatever to read *'al* as "in proximity to"'. Indeed, Levine's earlier discussion in this regard (*Presence of the Lord*, p. 65) does not provide one single example where this is the case. A second view is that of Milgrom (*Leviticus 1–16*, p. 1023), who translates לְכַפֵּר עָלָיו as 'to perform expiation upon it', and who holds that עַל following כִּפֶּר can have this meaning when the direct object is non-human, for example, 'And [Aaron] will go out to the altar which is before the LORD and will perform כִּפֶּר upon it (וְכִפֶּר עָלָיו)' (Lev. 16.18; see also Exod. 30.10; Lev. 8.15; 16.16). In this regard, the goat in Lev. 16.10 'is treated as an inanimate object; hence *kippûr*…takes place upon it. Its meaning is not that the goat itself is purged but that the purgation of the sanctuary is completed when the goat, laden with the sanctuary's impurities, is dispatched to the wilderness' (Milgrom, *Leviticus 1–16*, p. 1023). As discussed in the Appendix, this understanding of כִּפֶּר + עַל + impersonal object is possible. It is also noted there, however, that it is equally possible to translate the עַל in these instances with 'for', that is, 'he will atone for…' This of course appears problematic in this context, however, since it would be awkward to have the goat as the

3. *The Verb* כִּפֶּר *in Contexts of Sin* 97

confessing the sins and placing them upon the head of the goat, but also in sending the goat into the wilderness.

While both of these are possible grammatically, the first view is logically questionable. While it is understandable that atonement is made *so that* people can be forgiven, or *so that* they can be purified, it is not as clear what it would mean that atonement is made *so that* the goat can then be sent into the wilderness. For this reason, the second translation is to be preferred, namely, that atonement (כִּפֶּר) is fully accomplished *by* sending the goat, bearing the sin (נָשָׂא עָוֺן), into the wilderness.

---

object of atonement! This leads to the third view. Kiuchi (*Purification Offering*, pp. 150-51) argues that this phrase is properly understood once it is realized that 'the third-person pronominal suffix in כפר עליו refers to Aaron, and that the agent of לכפר is the Azazel goat'. In support, Kiuchi notes that v. 10 stands apart from the preceding and following verses in that it alone is constructed in the passive. In particular, whereas the first goat has been the object in v. 9 and Aaron has been the subject (וְהִקְרִיב אַהֲרֹן אֶת־הַשָּׂעִיר אֲשֶׁר עָלָה עָלָיו הַגּוֹרָל לַיהוָה וְעָשָׂהוּ חַטָּאת), in v. 10 the passive is used, making the second goat the subject of the sentence (וְהַשָּׂעִיר אֲשֶׁר עָלָה עָלָיו הַגּוֹרָל לַעֲזָאזֵל יָעֳמַד־חַי לִפְנֵי יְהוָה לְכַפֵּר עָלָיו). This opens up the possibility that the subject–object relationship is switched in this verse, that is, that the goat is the subject and Aaron is the object. Thus Kiuchi (p. 151) translates, 'But the goat on which Azazel's lot comes up must be stood alive before the LORD to make atonement for him (Aaron) by sending it to Azazel to the Wilderness'. Moreover, this possibility is strengthened when Lev. 1.4 is considered. The verse reads as follows: וְסָמַךְ יָדוֹ עַל רֹאשׁ הָעֹלָה וְנִרְצָה לוֹ לְכַפֵּר עָלָיו. Kiuchi (p. 152) notes first that there is a thematic parallel, namely, 'the offerer who lays his hand on the sacrifice (v. 4a) becomes the beneficiary of the atonement made by the sacrifice (v. 4b). This relationship in the imposition of a hand between the offerer and the sacrifice perfectly suits Lev. 16.10, 21-22, where, we argue, the Azazel goat makes atonement for Aaron.' Second, he notes (p. 152) that there is also a syntactical parallel between these passages: '…Lev. 1.4b provides a fitting example in which לכפר (the *lamed* expressing purpose) is preceded by a passive verb, i.e. נרצה. This syntactical feature is common to Lev. 16.10, where לכפר is preceded by the passive יעמד. In the light of this parallel construction it may be inferred that, just as in Lev. 1.4b the agent of לכפר is the sacrifice, in Lev. 16.10 the agent of לכפר is the Azazel goat.' The most vocal critique of this view has come from Milgrom, who writes as follows: 'Kiuchi's proposal that "v 10 refers to Aaron in *'ālāyw*"…must be rejected on many counts, not the least of which is that, in view of the following *'ōtô* (referring to the goat), *'ālāyw* should have read *'al 'ahărōn*' (*Leviticus 1–16*, p. 1023; this is actually the only critique that Milgrom mentions). It appears, however, that Milgrom has overstated the case in saying that ' *'ālāyw should* [emphasis added] have read *'al 'ahărōn*', for this assumes that the specification of Aaron would have been necessary to the original audience in order to avoid confusion. As indicated in the above, however, the switch from the active to the passive could suffice in signaling that the goat is the subject, and Aaron the object, of the phrase לְכַפֵּר עָלָיו. Thus, while this view is at first glance the most surprising of the three, the lines of support that Kiuchi adduces for it suggest that it is the most likely.

As with Lev. 10.17 above, then, it may be noted that the understanding of כִּפֶּר here is also in keeping with the כֹּפֶר nature of atonement, for here too the offended party (the LORD) has agreed to a כֹּפֶר-arrangement (the scapegoat) by which sin may be removed (נָשָׂא עָוֹן) so that the guilty party no longer needs to face sin's consequences.

3.1.2.2.3. *Exodus 28.38*. Exodus 28 is a description of the holy garments that are to be made for Aaron (vv. 1-39) and for his sons (vv. 40-43). Among these garments is a plate, made of pure gold and inscribed with the words 'holy to the LORD' (קֹדֶשׁ לַיהוָה), which is to be fastened upon Aaron's turban with a blue cord (vv. 36-37). The purpose of this plate is described as follows: 'It shall be upon Aaron's forehead, and Aaron shall bear away the sin (וְנָשָׂא אַהֲרֹן אֶת־עֲוֹן) of the holy offerings which the people of Israel hallow as their holy gifts; it shall always be upon his forehead, that they may be accepted (לְרָצוֹן לָהֶם) before the LORD' (v. 38).

The situation envisaged by this passage appears to be as follows. An Israelite brings an offering before the LORD. In order for this offering to be accepted on his or her behalf, it must be blameless:

> Say to Aaron and his sons and all the people of Israel, 'When any one of the house of Israel or of the sojourners in Israel presents their offering...[then] for your acceptance (לִרְצֹנְכֶם) it must be a male without blemish, of the cattle or the sheep or the goats. You shall not offer anything that has a blemish, for it will not be acceptable for you (כִּי־לֹא לְרָצוֹן יִהְיֶה לָכֶם).' (Lev. 22.18-20)

Conceivably, however, an Israelite could unwittingly bring an animal that did have some blemish, with the result that the person bringing it would not be accepted before the LORD.[42] To safeguard against this, or any other punitive consequences, the LORD commanded for the golden plate to be made and attached to Aaron's turban. By wearing this plate Aaron was able to 'bear away the sin' of a blemished sacrifice (וְנָשָׂא אַהֲרֹן אֶת־עֲוֹן הַקֳּדָשִׁים), that is, to nullify the negative consequences of the sin. In this way, the regular benefits of the sacrificial animal still accrued to the worshipper, namely, acceptance before the LORD (לְרָצוֹן לָהֶם).[43]

---

42. While the priestly literature nowhere specifies a penalty for someone who brings a blemished animal, it can safely be assumed that this was considered an affront to the deity and therefore attended with severe consequences. See Mal. 1.6-11 and 2.1-3.

43. One may further inquire as to the exact role of the plate in this bearing away of sin. Houtman (*Exodus*, p. 517), for example, asks, 'Is power going out from the text [i.e. the inscription "holy to the LORD"], so that the plaque can be considered an amulet and its effect be called apotropaic? Or is the bearer of the plaque representative of Israel and is the inscription intended to signify that in respect of the sacred offerings "everything was intended to be *holy to the LORD*, and if aught was done irregularly, the intention at least was good" (Cassuto)?' Houtman himself (p. 516) understands the phrase 'holy to

Unlike Lev. 10.17 and 16.22, כִּפֶּר does not occur here in conjunction with נָשָׂא עָוֺן, perhaps because there is no specific rite that is carried out in this instance. As a result, this passage does not speak as directly to the understanding of כִּפֶּר as the others. At the same time, however, just as the LORD appoints a special means in Lev. 10.17 and 16.10, 21-22 for the removing of sins, so here too there is a special means appointed by the LORD to remove sin (נָשָׂא עָוֺן), namely, Aaron's wearing of the golden plate inscribed with the words 'Holy to the LORD'. How Aaron was able to remove sins for the people by wearing this plate is not entirely clear;[44] what is clear, however, is that in so doing sin was removed with the result that the people could be accepted by the LORD.

In sum, this third usage of the phrase refers to a third party bearing away sin by means of a כֹּפֶר-arrangement established by the offended party, namely, the LORD. In this way, this third usage of the phrase is completely compatible with the understanding of כִּפֶּר arrived at above, namely, that כִּפֶּר expresses a כֹּפֶר-arrangement. In these instances, the LORD—who is the offended party—has pre-emptively declared what the כֹּפֶר-arrangement should be, that is, the purification offering (Lev. 10.17), the scapegoat (Lev. 16.10, 21-22), and the wearing of the golden plate (Exod. 28.38). Each of these was a special means for bearing away sin (נָשָׂא עָוֺן) and the first two of these (Lev. 10.17; 16.22) expressly state that atonement (כִּפֶּר) is accomplished. In further keeping with the כֹּפֶר-principle, these means were also agreed to—and indeed, ordained by—the offended party, namely, the LORD.

3.2. *Summary*

This chapter began with a consideration of what insight the occurrences of the verb סָלַח in the priestly literature could give us into the meaning of the verb כִּפֶּר, and in particular, whether it supported the understanding that כִּפֶּר in sin contexts referred to the effecting of a כֹּפֶר. We thus began with the occurrences of סָלַח in the phrase 'and the priest will atone for them (וְכִפֶּר עֲלֵהֶם הַכֹּהֵן) and they will be forgiven (וְנִסְלַח לָהֶם)'. It was noted that the subject of כִּפֶּר was the priest, and that the performance of the כִּפֶּר-rite resulted in forgiveness being granted by the LORD (וְנִסְלַח לָהֶם). Due to the evident link in these references between the verbs כִּפֶּר and סָלַח, it was

---

the LORD' as a reference to Aaron and suggests (p. 517) that 'the high priest's consecration to YHWH is substitutionary for that of Israel (cf. Isa. 53.4 and Lev. 16)'. Whatever the conclusion as to the exact role of the plate here, the overall result of the phrase נָשָׂא עָוֺן remains relatively clear: to nullify the negative consequences of bringing a blemished animal so that the worshipper could be accepted before the LORD (Dillmann, *Exodus und Leviticus*, p. 310).

44. See n. 43.

argued that if the exact nature of forgiveness (סָלַח) could be clarified, it would yield insight into the meaning of כִּפֶּר.

We therefore turned to consider סָלַח more carefully through an examination of Numbers 14, where the LORD's decision to forgive (סָלַחְתִּי) the people was expressed in the substitution of a mitigated penalty (non-entry into the land) for a much more severe penalty (immediate destruction by plague). In this way, סָלַח was seen to be an expression of the כֹּפֶר-principle. This understanding of סָלַח, together with the fact that כֹּפֶר is used elsewhere to express the effecting of a כֹּפֶר-payment, led to the conclusion that the verb כִּפֶּר, when expressing the action of the priest, which results in forgiveness (סָלַח), refers to the execution of a כֹּפֶר on behalf of the sinner. It was also noted here, however, that it is likely that inadvertent sins also cause the defilement of sancta, and that כִּפֶּר—at least in the context of the purification offering in Lev. 4.1–5.13—might also refer to purification. How this relates to the overall understanding of כִּפֶּר is considered in Chapter 5 below.

We then turned to consider the phrase נָשָׂא עָוֹן, which, like סָלַח, also occurs in conjunction with כִּפֶּר in the priestly literature. It was noted that there are three distinct usages of the phrase. In the first usage, the sinner is the subject of the phrase, and it refers to their suffering the punishment due for their sin (see §1.2.3.1). In the second usage, which occurs outside of the priestly literature, the offended party is the subject of the phrase, and in bearing away the sin he or she grants forgiveness to the sinner, with the result that the sinner does not suffer the original penalty which their sin deserved.

The third usage of the phrase occurs within the priestly literature, namely, in Exod. 28.38, Lev. 10.17, and Lev. 16.22. It is similar to the second usage in that it again refers to the sin of the sinner being taken away so that the sinner does not suffer the original penalty which their sin deserves. It differs from the second usage in that the person taking away the sin is a third party, and not the party who was offended. Of the three texts that use the phrase in this way, Lev. 10.17 and 16.22 are especially significant to the present study in that the phrase occurs here in conjunction with כִּפֶּר. In these instances a third party removes the sin of the sinner by means of a special rite (the purification offering [Lev. 10.17], the scapegoat ritual [Lev. 16.10, 21-22]), by which atonement is accomplished and the sinner no longer has to face the consequences of their sin. Significantly, it was seen that this third usage of the phrase was consonant with the understanding of כִּפֶּר above, namely, that כִּפֶּר expresses a כֹּפֶר-arrangement. Thus in each instance the offended party (i.e. the LORD) prescribes a special means (i.e. a כֹּפֶר) by which the penalty of sin could be avoided. By executing the כִּפֶּר-rite (the purification offering [Lev. 10.17]; the scapegoat [Lev. 16.22]), or simply by wearing the golden plate (Exod. 28.38), the sin was borne away (נָשָׂא עָוֹן), and the guilty party no longer faced punishment for it.

From both the verb סָלַח and the phrase נָשָׂא עָוֹן, then, it may be concluded that the verb כִּפֶּר in sin contexts refers to the effecting of a כֹּפֶר on behalf of the guilty party.

In Part I (Chapters 1 to 3), we have considered the meaning of כִּפֶּר in contexts where it is addressing sin. It has been argued that the meaning of כִּפֶּר in these instances is related to כֹּפֶר, but that it might also refer to elements of purification. We now turn in Part II (Chapter 4) to consider the meaning of כִּפֶּר in contexts where it is addressing impurity, namely, in contexts of purification and consecration.

Part II

כִּפֶּר IN CONTEXTS OF IMPURITY

4

THE VERB כִּפֶּר IN CONTEXTS OF IMPURITY

In Part II (Chapter 4) we turn to consider the verb כִּפֶּר in contexts where it is addressing impurity, namely, in purification and consecration contexts.[1] By way of preface, it may be noted that there are three major categories in the priestly worldview: the impure (טמא), the pure (טהר), and the holy (קדשׁ).[2] The verb כִּפֶּר relates to these three categories insofar as it occurs when a person or item is moving in a positive direction, that is, when they are being purified, or when they are being consecrated.

Within these contexts there is a distinctive series of verbs which are used alongside of כִּפֶּר to describe this positive motion and which are therefore

1. For the relationship of purification to consecration, see §4.3 below.
2. On the basis of Lev. 10.10—which states that Aaron and his sons are 'to distinguish between the holy (הַקֹּדֶשׁ) and the common (הַחֹל), and between the unclean (הַטָּמֵא) and the clean (הַטָּהוֹר)'—some have proposed חֹל as a fourth category that is distinct from the other three. Thus Philip Peter Jenson (*Graded Holiness: A Key to the Priestly Conception of the World* [JSOTSup, 106; Sheffield: JSOT Press, 1992], p. 40) sees a parallelism between the first half of the verse and the second, namely, that 'holy' is close in meaning to 'clean', and 'common' is close in meaning to 'unclean' (see also the diagram reproduced by Jenson from James Barr, 'Semantics and Biblical Theology—A Contribution to the Discussion', in *Congress Volume: Uppsala, 1971* [VTSup, 22; Leiden: E.J. Brill], pp. 11-19 [15]). Others have understood the second half of the verse to explicate the word חֹל, that is, חֹל refers to that which is not holy, whether it be pure or impure: 'Everything that is not holy is common. Common things divide into two groups, the clean and the unclean' (Wenham, *Leviticus*, p. 19). The likelihood of the latter view is supported by the use of חֹל elsewhere in the Old Testament. Thus when David asks Ahimelech for bread, Ahimelech responds, 'There is no *ordinary* (חֹל) bread on hand, but there is *consecrated* (קֹדֶשׁ) bread…' (1 Sam. 21.5 [4]; see also v. 6 [5]). Similarly, we read in Ezek. 48.15 that an allotment of land 'shall be for *common* (חֹל) use for the city, for dwellings and for open spaces…' In both of these instances חֹל refers simply to that which is not holy, as opposed to that which is unclean. This understanding of חֹל finds further support in a later statement of Jenson (*Graded Holiness*, p. 45 n. 1) himself: 'Lyons…describes words with negative polarity as those which are regarded as lacking in some quality (e.g. small indicates lack of size). *ḥōl* may well imply a lack of holiness' (Jenson refers to Lyons, *Semantics*, I, p. 275).

important factors in understanding כִּפֶּר. In contexts of purification, these verbs are טהר and חטא, and in contexts of consecration the verb is קדשׁ. In the following, then, the focus is upon describing the usage of these verbs individually, and then comparing and contrasting them with each other and with כִּפֶּר. We will begin with the verbs for purification (טהר, חטא), looking at each individually, and then comparing them with כִּפֶּר. This will be followed by a consideration of the verb for consecration (קדשׁ), which will then also be followed by a comparison of it with כִּפֶּר. The concern throughout will not be to provide a thorough exegesis of each passage containing these terms, but to focus upon those points relevant to understanding the usage of these terms relative to one another and to כִּפֶּר. These points include: who the subjects and objects of the verbs are; whether they take direct objects or not; and, perhaps most importantly, what means are associated with the purification or consecration these verbs represent. The chapter then concludes by considering how the above observations relate to the translation of כִּפֶּר, and, in particular, whether the rendering 'to purify/effect purgation'—which has been suggested by others for כִּפֶּר in these contexts—is sufficient.

4.1. *Purification and* כִּפֶּר

4.1.1. טהר

טהר occurs in the priestly literature in the qal, piel, and hithpael. In the qal, טהר refers simply to being or becoming pure: '…and the priest shall make atonement for [the parturient] and she shall be pure (וְטָהֵרָה)' (Lev. 12.8); '…and [the one with a discharge] shall bathe his body in running water, and shall be pure (וְטָהֵר)' (Lev. 15.13); 'And every person that eats what dies of itself or what is torn by beasts…shall wash their clothes, and bathe in water, and be impure until the evening, and then shall be pure (וְטָהֵר)' (Lev. 17.15).[3] In each instance the person or article has begun in a state of impurity and has finished in a state of purity; the qal describes this final state of purity.

In the piel, טהר has two different uses. The first of these, which occurs in Leviticus 13 and 14, is a 'declarative' use, in which the priest declares a person to be pure. Thus we read of the person suspected of leprosy, 'And the priest shall examine him again on the seventh day, and if the diseased spot is dim and the disease has not spread in the skin, then the priest shall pronounce him pure (וְטִהֲרוֹ); it is only an eruption; and he shall wash his clothes, and be pure (וְטָהֵר)' (Lev. 13.6). The rendering 'to pronounce pure' is not only in keeping with the declarative use of the piel elsewhere,[4] it also finds

---

3. See also Lev. 11.32; 13.6, 34, 58; 14.8, 9, 20, 53, etc.
4. For example, גַּדְּלוּ לַיהוָה אִתִּי, 'Declare with me that the LORD is great' (Ps. 34.4 [3]). See W&O 24.2f, g; Joüon 52d; F. Maass, 'טהר', in *TLOT*, II, pp. 482-86 (483).

justification within its immediate context through comparison of the piel of טמא in Leviticus 13. Thus in 13.3 we read, '...when the priest has looked at him [and seen that the infection is leprous] he shall *pronounce him impure* (וְטִמֵּא אֹתוֹ)'.[5]

The second use of the piel is its more common 'factitive' use, that is, the action of making pure, purifying.[6] This occurs in two passages in the priestly literature. In the first, Aaron cleanses the altar from the impurities of the Israelites by means of the blood of the bull and goat purification offerings: 'And [Aaron] shall sprinkle some of the blood upon [the altar] with his finger seven times, and purify it (וְטִהֲרוֹ) and hallow it from the impurities of the people of Israel' (Lev. 16.19).[7] The second passage is Numbers 8. טהר occurs here four times, beginning with the command to Moses to purify the Levites: 'Take the Levites from among the people of Israel, and purify them (וְטִהַרְתָּ אֹתָם)' (Num. 8.6). Among the various rites required to accomplish this, two are particularly connected with the action of Moses or Aaron, namely, sprinkling with the water for impurity and the offering of a purification and burnt offering. Thus v. 7a continues, 'And thus you shall do to them, to purify them (לְטַהֲרָם): sprinkle the water of cleansing upon them...', and v. 21b, referring to the offering of the purification and burnt offerings (v. 12), concludes the rite as follows, '...and Aaron made atonement for them to purify them (לְטַהֲרָם)'.[8]

---

5. Cf. also Lev. 13.11, 15 with 13.13, 17; 13.20, 22 with 13.23; 13.25, 27 with 13.28; 13.30 with 13.34, 37. While the rendering 'to pronounce pure' differs from that of 'to purify' (for which see immediately below), it is best to see these two renderings as belonging to the same continuum of meaning. For while the priest in Lev. 13 was simply acknowledging a condition already present, there was a sense in which his declaration made the person's or object's state of purity or impurity official. Thus even though the mark of leprosy might have already disappeared, the person was not allowed re-entry into the camp until the priest sanctioned their purity. In this regard the priest can still be understood to be making the infected person or object pure or impure, though perhaps on a lesser scale than the rendering 'to purify'.

6. In his summary of his massive study on the piel, Ernst Jenni (*Das hebräische Pi'el. Syntaktisch-semasiologische Untersuchung einer Verbalform im Alten Testament* [Zürich: EVZ-Verlag, 1968], p. 275) states, 'Die Bedeutung des Pi'el ist nicht die eines (im Laufe der Zeit mannigfach abgeschwächten) Intensivs oder eines (mit dem Hif'il praktisch gleichbedeutenden) Kausativs, sondern es drückt das Bewirken des dem Grundstamm entsprechenden adjektivisch ausgesagten Zustandes aus'. See the English summary of Jenni in W&O 24.1f, h, i.

7. For the relationship between purification and consecration in Lev. 16.19, see n. 47 below.

8. The remaining instance is in v. 15, which refers back to the means of purification identified above: 'And after that the Levites shall go in to do service at the tent of meeting. So you will cleanse them (וְטִהַרְתָּ אֹתָם) and offer them as a wave offering, for they are wholly given to me from among the people of Israel...' (vv. 15-16a).

Finally, the hithpael of טהר is also used in two chapters with a factitive sense, this time reflexively. The first of these is with reference to the purification of the Levites in Numbers 8. There is some question as to the translation of the hithpael in 8.7, and therefore the Hebrew is cited in full:

וְכֹה־תַעֲשֶׂה לָהֶם לְטַהֲרָם הַזֵּה עֲלֵיהֶם מֵי חַטָּאת וְהֶעֱבִירוּ
תַעַר עַל־כָּל־בְּשָׂרָם וְכִבְּסוּ בִגְדֵיהֶם וְהִטֶּהָרוּ׃

The RSV translates as follows: 'And thus you shall do to them, to cleanse them: sprinkle the water of expiation upon them, and let them go with a razor over all their body, and wash their clothes and cleanse themselves'. The JPSV, however, takes the hithpael passively instead of reflexively, and translates the second half of the verse as follows: '...and let them go over their whole body with a razor, and wash their clothes; thus they shall be cleansed'. While the latter translation is not impossible,[9] Milgrom argues that a reflexive sense seems more likely in view of the fact that וְהִטֶּהָרוּ here appears to refer to the ritual bathing that often follows laundering. In support he notes, 'It is obvious for purposes of purification [that] laundering without bathing would be self-defeating (cf. Num. 19.19; Lev. 15.5-13)'.[10] More explicitly, however, he points out that bathing follows laundering in other purification rites: '[T]he prescribed sequence for the purification of the corpse-contaminated person is sprinkling, laundering, and bathing [Num. 19.19]; bathing is also the final act in the purification of the leper (Lev. 14.8)'.[11] To this it may be added that bathing follows sprinkling, shaving, and laundering in Leviticus 14, the same order found in Num. 8.7 above. For these reasons, then, it seems likely that וְהִטֶּהָרוּ should be translated reflexively, and that it refers to the Levites cleansing themselves by means of ritual bathing.

The other use of טהר in the hithpael occurs in Leviticus 14, where the participle occurs twelve times as a reference to 'him that is to be purified' of leprosy.[12]

To sum up, טהר occurs in the qal to describe the state of purity that someone is in or has arrived at. In the piel, טהר occurs with two different usages. In the first, it functions declaratively. In these instances the priest is the subject of the verb and he declares that someone is clean (Lev. 13.6, 17, 23, etc.). In the second, the piel has a factitive function. Here the priest, or Moses, is the subject of the verb; the objects of cleansing can be both inanimate (the altar; Lev. 16.19) and animate (the Levites; Num. 8.6); and

---

9. For the passive sense of the hithpael, see Joüon 53i; see also the use of the hithpael participle in Lev. 14 (see n. 12 below).
10. Milgrom, *Numbers*, p. 62.
11. Milgrom, *Numbers*, p. 62.
12. Verses 4, 7, 8, 11, 14, 17, 18, 19, 25, 28, 29, 31.

the means of cleansing is either blood (Lev. 16.19; Num. 8.21) or the water for impurity taken together with other rites (perhaps including sacrifice; Num. 8.7a with vv. 8-13). Finally, טהר also occurs in the hithpael, where it is used in Numbers 8 to describe the Levites cleansing themselves via ritual bathing (v. 7b), and in Leviticus 14 in participial form to describe 'him that is to be purified' of leprosy.

4.1.2. חטא[13]

חטא is used in the piel in two distinct ways. In the first usage, which occurs in three passages, חטא is used with the meaning 'to offer a purification offering': 'Then [Aaron] presented the people's offering, and took the goat of the purification offering which was for the people, and killed it, and offered it as a purification offering (וַיְחַטְּאֵהוּ) like the first' (Lev. 9.15).[14]

In the second usage, which also occurs in three passages, חטא is used with the privative sense, 'to de-sin',[15] which may be translated with 'to decontaminate' or 'to cleanse'.[16] In the first passage, the object that is cleansed is the altar, the subject of the verb is Moses, and the means of cleansing is the blood of the purification offering: 'And Moses killed [the bull of the purification offering], and took the blood, and with his finger put it on the horns of the altar round about, and cleansed the altar (וַיְחַטֵּא אֶת־הַמִּזְבֵּחַ)...' (Lev. 8.15a).[17] In the second passage, the object of cleansing is a house that

---

13. חטא occurs in the qal, piel, hiphil and hithpael, though only its occurrences in the piel and hithpael relate to cleansing.

14. See also Exod. 29.36 and Lev. 6.19 (26). For Exod. 29.36 see n. 17. For this use of the piel see Joüon 52d.

15. W&O gives the following examples of this use of the piel: לְדַשְּׁנוֹ, 'to clear it (the altar) of fat' (Exod. 27.3); לִבַּבְתִּנִי, 'You (fem.) have taken away my heart' (Song 4.9). See W&O 24.4f; Joüon 52d.

16. The rendering 'to decontaminate/to cleanse' as opposed to 'to de-sin' is in recognition of the fact that חטא is used with reference to impurity, not just sin (e.g. Lev. 14.49; Num. 19.12 [hithpael]). At the same time, however, it does not appear that the ancient Israelites saw sin and impurity as two unrelated spheres. The Day of Atonement ceremony, for example, speaks of being cleansed (טהר) from sin (חַטָּאָה) (Lev. 16.30) and of atonement (כפר) being made for both impurity (טֻמְאָה) and transgression (פֶּשַׁע) (Lev. 16.16). The relationship between sin and impurity is considered more fully in Chapter 5.

17. Exegetes are divided on which of the two translations—'to cleanse' or 'to offer a purification offering'—is most appropriate for חטא in Exod. 29.36a. Milgrom (*Leviticus 1–16*, p. 279) translates, 'Each day you shall sacrifice a bull as a purification offering, and you shall cleanse the altar (וְחִטֵּאתָ עַל־הַמִּזְבֵּחַ) by performing purgation upon it...' (see also Paul Garnet, 'Atonement Constructions in the Old Testament and the Qumran Scrolls', *EvQ* 46.3 [1974], pp. 131-63 [143]). The RSV, however, translates, 'And every day you shall offer a bull as a sin offering for atonement. Also you shall offer a sin offering for the altar (וְחִטֵּאתָ עַל־הַמִּזְבֵּחַ), when you make atonement for it...' (see also Kiuchi, *Purification Offering*, pp. 95-96; Houtman, *Exodus*, p. 548). This latter understanding of

has been 'healed' of leprosy, the subject of the verb is once again the priest, and the means of cleansing is the blood of an animal, together with water, which is sprinkled upon the house:

> And [the priest] will take to cleanse the house (לְחַטֵּא אֶת־הַבַּיִת) two small birds, with cedarwood and scarlet stuff and hyssop, and shall kill one of the birds in an earthen vessel over running water, and shall take the cedarwood and the hyssop and the scarlet stuff, along with the living bird, and dip them in the blood of the bird that was killed and in the running water, and sprinkle the house seven times. Thus he shall cleanse the house (וְחִטֵּא אֶת־הַבַּיִת) with the blood of the bird, and with the running water, and with the living bird, and with the cedarwood and hyssop and scarlet stuff. (Lev. 14.49-52)

In both instances, then, the priest is the one who cleanses an object, and in both instances the blood of an animal is used.

In the third passage, the context of which is corpse impurity, people as well as objects are cleansed, the subject of the verb is not a priest but simply a person that is clean, and the water for impurity is the means of cleansing:

> For the unclean they shall take some ashes of the burnt purification offering, and running water shall be added in a vessel; then a clean person shall take hyssop, and dip it in the water, and sprinkle it upon the tent, and upon all the furnishings, and upon the persons who were there, and upon the one who touched the bone, or the slain, or the dead, or the grave; and the clean person shall sprinkle upon the unclean on the third day and on the seventh day; thus on the seventh day he shall cleanse him (וְחִטְּאוֹ), and he shall wash his clothes and bathe himself in water, and at evening he shall be clean. (Num. 19.17-19)

Finally, there are three passages in which חטא also occurs with a privative sense, this time in the hithpael. The first of these is in Numbers 8, where the Levites are said to cleanse themselves: 'And the Levites cleansed themselves (וַיִּתְחַטְּאוּ הַלְוִיִּם), and washed their clothes...' (Num. 8.21a).[18] It would appear that חטא here refers to cleansing brought about by the water for impurity.[19] This finds support from the next two passages, both of which use

---

חטא seems more likely than the meaning 'to decontaminate', for in that case one would expect וְחִטֵּאתָ אֶת־הַמִּזְבֵּחַ (as in Lev. 8.15; see also Lev. 14.49, 52; Ezek. 43.20, 22, 23; 45.18), but not וְחִטֵּאתָ עַל־הַמִּזְבֵּחַ as we have here. See Kiuchi, *Purification Offering*, pp. 95-96.

18. With Milgrom (*Numbers*, p. 65), it may be assumed that a ritual bathing also follows the laundering: 'Bathing is omitted, but it is implied whenever laundering is required. A person who eats from a carcass must bathe and launder (Lev. 17.15-16). Lev. 11.40 describes a similar case and there, too, bathing is omitted (twice), as in the rest of the same chapter (vv. 11, 25, 28), because it is taken for granted.' See also the comments above on Num. 8.7.

19. Numbers 8.7 uses the phrase מֵי חַטָּאת, whereas the phrase מֵי נִדָּה is used in Num. 19 (vv. 9, 13, 20, 21) and 31.23. It seems likely, however, that these are referring to the same thing; see above, as well as comments of Milgrom, *Numbers*, p. 61.

4. *The Verb* כִּפֶּר *in Contexts of Impurity*

חטא in the hithpael in the context of cleansing people and/or objects with the water for impurity. Thus in Numbers 19, where the person who is unclean from a corpse is warned to cleanse himself lest he be cut off, the water for impurity is the primary means of cleansing:

> He who touches the dead body of any person shall be unclean seven days; he shall cleanse himself (יִתְחַטָּא) with [the water] on the third day and on the seventh day, and so be clean; but if he does not cleanse himself (וְאִם־לֹא יִתְחַטָּא) on the third day and on the seventh day, he will not become clean. Whoever touches a dead person, the body of any person who has died, and does not cleanse himself (וְלֹא יִתְחַטָּא), defiles the tabernacle of the LORD, and that person shall be cut off from Israel... (Num. 19.11-13a; see also v. 20)

חטא appears to be used in the same way in the third passage, Numbers 31, where persons and objects are once again being cleansed from corpse impurity, and where חטא is again conjoined with the water for impurity:

> 'Encamp outside the camp seven days; whoever of you has killed any person, and whoever has touched any slain, purify yourselves (וְהִתְחַטְּאוּ) and your captives on the third day and on the seventh day. You shall purify (תִּתְחַטְּאוּ)[20] every garment, every article of skin, all work of goats' hair, and every article of wood.' And Eleazar the priest said to the men of war who had gone to battle: 'This is the statute of the law which the LORD has commanded Moses: only the gold, the silver, the bronze, the iron, the tin, and the lead, everything that can stand the fire, you shall pass through the fire, and it shall be clean. Nevertheless it shall also be purified (יִתְחַטָּא) with the water for impurity; and whatever cannot stand the fire, you shall pass through the water.' (Num. 31.19-23)

In sum, the verb חטא occurs in purification contexts as follows. In the piel, it occurs with two distinct usages: (1) with the meaning 'to offer a purification offering' (Exod. 29.36; Lev. 6.19 [26]; 9.15); and (2) with a privative meaning, that is, 'to cleanse'. When used privatively, the cleansing is done either by the priest (or Moses) upon unclean objects by means of blood (Lev. 8.15; 14.49-52), or by a clean person upon unclean objects and people by means of the water for impurity (Num. 19.17-19). The hithpael of חטא also occurs with a privative use, and refers to the cleansing of people (Num. 8.21; 19.12, 13, 20; 31.19) or objects (Num. 31.20, 23) with special water.

4.1.3. טהר *and* חטא

It is hard to distinguish a difference in meaning when comparing the factitive occurrences of טהר ('to purify/purify oneself'; piel or hithpael) with the privative occurrences of חטא ('to cleanse/cleanse oneself'; piel or hithpael).

---

20. Milgrom (*Numbers*, p. 328 n. 40) notes that this could also be rendered 'cleanse for yourselves', a usage of the hithpael found (with different verbs) in 33.54 and 34.10 (Milgrom cites GKC on the latter of these; see GKC 54f[c]).

To begin, the piel of both verbs always takes a direct object (טהר: Lev. 16.19; Num. 8.6, 7, 15, 21; חטא: Lev. 8.15; 14.49, 52; Num. 19.19). Second, whether in the piel or hithpael, the object of the verb can be either animate (טהר: Num. 8.6, 7, 15, 21; חטא: Num. 19.19; 31.19) or inanimate (טהר: Lev. 16.19; חטא: Lev. 8.15; 14.49, 52; Num. 31.20, 23). Third, the cleansing can occur by means of blood (טהר: Lev. 16.19; חטא: Lev. 8.15), or by means of special water (טהר: Num. 8.7; חטא: Num. 8.21; 19.12, 13, 20; 31.19, 20, 23). Fourth, the subject of the verb can be the priest (or Moses) (טהר: Num. 8.6, 7a; חטא: Lev. 8.15; 14.49, 52; but note the one use of חטא in the piel where the subject is a clean person: Num. 19.19), or the party in need of cleansing (טהר: Num. 8.7b; חטא: Num. 8.21; 19.12, 13, 20; 31.19).

If there is any difference between them, it may simply be that the factitive use of טהר describes purification from a more positive perspective ('to make pure') whereas the privative use of חטא describes the same from a more negative perspective ('to de-sin', that is, 'to cleanse'). Given the similarities outlined above, however, it would seem that the factitive use of the piel and the hithpael of טהר and the privative use of the piel and hithpael of חטא are more or less synonymous.

4.1.4. כִּפֶּר and חטא טהר

Given the synonymous usage of טהר and חטא, it comes as no surprise that these terms manifest the same similarities and differences when compared with כִּפֶּר. To begin, there is no doubt that כִּפֶּר in purification contexts is clearly related in meaning to the factitive uses of טהר in the piel or hithpael and the privative uses of חטא in the piel or hithpael. This is perhaps most explicit for טהר in Num. 8.21, where it occurs in conjunction with כִּפֶּר: 'Aaron made atonement for [the Levites] to cleanse them' (וַיְכַפֵּר עֲלֵיהֶם אַהֲרֹן לְטַהֲרָם). It is equally evident for חטא in Lev. 14.52-53, which concludes the rite for cleansing a leprous house as follows: 'Thus [the priest] shall decontaminate the house with the blood of the bird and with the running water (וְחִטֵּא אֶת־הַבַּיִת בְּדַם הַצִּפּוֹר וּבַמַּיִם הַחַיִּים)...so he shall effect atonement for the house (וְכִפֶּר עַל־הַבָּיִת), and it shall be clean (וְטָהֵר)' (Lev. 14.52-53). Further similarities may also be mentioned though. To begin, כִּפֶּר occurs in contexts where both people (Lev. 12.7-8; 14.20) and objects (Lev. 14.53; 16.16) are being purified: 'And the priest will atone for her and she will be pure' (וְכִפֶּר עָלֶיהָ הַכֹּהֵן וְטָהֵרָה) (Lev. 12.8b);[21] 'And [the priest] will make atonement for the house, and it shall be pure' (וְכִפֶּר עַל־הַבַּיִת וְטָהֵר) (Lev. 14.53b). Moreover, as with most instances of טהר and חטא, the priest is the subject of כִּפֶּר (Lev. 14.18, 20, 21; 15.15, etc.). Finally, the means of

---

21. See also Lev. 14.20, 53; 15.15, 30 (though the verb טהר does not occur in Lev. 15, the context obviously implies that purity is the result).

כִּפֶּר in these contexts is that of blood (e.g. Lev. 16.15-16, 19-20, etc.),[22] which is also true of טהר in Lev. 16.19, and of חטא in Lev. 8.15 and 14.52.[23]

There are also important differences, however, that exist between these terms in purification contexts. To begin, whereas טהר and חטא in the piel are always followed by a direct object, and never a preposition,[24] כִּפֶּר is predominantly followed by the prepositions עַל or בַּעַד.[25] This is due to the fact that טהר and חטא simply refer to cleansing a person or object (who are thus the direct object of these verbs), whereas כִּפֶּר is used to refer to the execution of a rite carried out by the priest *on behalf of* someone or something (and hence the use of the prepositions). Thus Levine states that 'The cultic texts understood the verb *kippēr* primarily in a functional, or technical sense: "to perform rites of expiation", rather than: "to cleanse"'.[26] Similarly,

---

22. The above verses are some of the most explicit in making direct mention of the blood; other verses simply mention the sacrifice that is made (e.g. Lev. 12.6-8), though it is understood that the sacrifice is effective because of the blood rite involved.

23. These similarities between טהר, חטא, and כִּפֶּר prove problematic to Janowski's thesis on atonement. As noted above (see the opening comments to Chapter 2, and especially §2.2.1), Janowski understands atonement to refer to the dedication of the life to the holy. In keeping with this, Janowski interprets the application of blood to the sanctuary and its sancta as a dedication of life to the holy, and not as something that cleanses sin or impurity. This is problematic, however, insofar as the text explicitly conjoins the application of blood with the *cleansing* of the sanctuary and its sancta, for example, Lev. 8.15 and 16.19 (cf. Ezek. 43.20, 22). In a footnote responding to this, Janowski (*Sühne*, p. 241 n. 287) states that cultic atonement is a *removal* of sin. He argues, however, that this is not because sancta become *cleansed*, but because the application of the blood is a dedication of substituted life which breaks the connection between sin and punishment: 'Selbstverständlich ist kultische Sühne auch *Beseitigung der Sünde*, sie ist es aber nicht deshalb, weil das Heiligtum "rituell gesäubert", "gereinigt" wird, sondern deshalb, weil durch die Applikation des חַטָּאת-Blutes an Altar und Heiligtum eine *stellvertretende Lebenshingabe* vollzogen wird, durch die der Sünde-Unheil-Zusammenhang aufgehoben wird...' This, however, is special pleading, and contradicts the plain meaning of the text: the altar is the direct object of חטא (Lev. 8.15), טהר (Lev. 16.19), and קדש (Lev. 16.19) when describing the effects of the application of the blood of the purification offering to it. Moreover, given the defiling nature of sin (see §3.1.1), it would not be surprising that an act of cleansing is involved in the annulling of the connection between sin and punishment (the *Sünde-Unheil-Zusammenhang*). This is not to argue that atonement is exhausted by the sense of 'cleanse' or 'purge' (see the final discussion and translation of כִּפֶּר in §5.2 below), but that an element of cleansing is involved that Janowski does not properly account for. For further critique of Janowski, see §2.2.1 above.

24. The one exception is Exod. 29.36, where חטא is followed by עַל. The meaning of חטא here, however, is 'to offer a purification offering'. See above, n. 17.

25. Indeed, כִּפֶּר is followed by עַל or בַּעַד over sixty times in the priestly literature, compared to only three instances where it is followed by a direct object marker (Lev. 16.20, 33 [× 2]). See the Appendix for כִּפֶּר constructions and further discussion.

26. Levine, *Presence of the Lord*, p. 64.

Elliger writes that כפר occurs in the priestly literature with the meaning 'to carry out a rite' that frees a person or object from sin and impurity.[27]

Second, while טהר and חטא can occur in the hithpael with the one in need of cleansing as subject, and while חטא occurs once with a clean person as subject (Num. 19.19), כפר only takes the priest, or Moses (Lev. 8.15), as subject.

Third, and perhaps most significantly, while טהר and חטא can occur in contexts where either blood or water is the means of cleansing, כִּפֶּר only occurs in contexts where blood is involved, that is, where a sacrifice is made. Thus while it is possible for the Levites or the corpse-contaminated person to cleanse themselves with water (טהר: Num. 8.7; חטא: Num. 8.21; 19.12, 13, 20; 31.19, 20, 23), it is never said that a person 'atones' (כִּפֶּר) themselves, or any other object, by means of water.[28] This in turn suggests that, in purification contexts, there is something about sacrifice that is fundamental to the meaning of כִּפֶּר. Moreover, given that the blood of the sacrifice is clearly linked in with purification (Lev. 14.52-53; 16.15-16, 19-20), and given that the blood rites are central to the act of sacrifice, it would appear that it is the blood of sacrifice in particular that is fundamental to the meaning of כִּפֶּר in these contexts.

---

27. 'Es ist klar, daß כִּפֶּר bei P in aller Regel heißt einen Ritus vollziehen, der eine Person oder Sache von Sünde und Unreinheit befreit und vor ihrer Auswirkung schützt' (Elliger, *Leviticus*, p. 71).

28. One could argue, perhaps not altogether convincingly, that the omission of the verb כִּפֶּר in these contexts is simply incidental. In support of this, it could be noted that the verb כפר does occur in a sin context where no blood is involved, namely, Lev. 5.11-13. This passage prescribes that a person who is too poor to bring a purification offering of birds may bring an offering of flour instead, by which the priest will make atonement (כִּפֶּר) for them so that they may be forgiven (v. 13). If it is possible for the verb כפר to occur in a sin context that does not involve blood, then it would seem equally possible that it could also occur in a purification context that does not involve blood, and that the omission of כִּפֶּר in Num. 8, 19, and 31 is simply incidental. While this possibility is granted, it is also noted that Lev. 5.11-13 is clearly an exception to the rule that blood sacrifice is the typical requirement in these contexts. A non-blood offering is allowed only as a last resort for economic necessity. The exact same principle seems to be at work in such contexts as Num. 19, where the requirement of individual sacrifices from everyone who had been impacted by corpse impurity—which in most cases would involve a large extended family who would become impure during the process of mourning their loved one—would place a severe financial strain upon the relatives of the deceased. In short, Num. 19 appears to be another 'exception', for the sake of economic necessity, to the common way in which major impurities were dealt with (see further n. 69 below). Thus even if the omission of כִּפֶּר were incidental in such places as Num. 19, it would not take away from the point being made above, namely, that there is something about sacrifice, and in particular the blood of a sacrifice, that is fundamental to the verb כִּפֶּר in purification contexts.

4. *The Verb* כִּפֶּר *in Contexts of Impurity*

On the one hand, then, כִּפֶּר is not an exact synonym of טהר or חטא, since it appears that sacrifice and sacrificial blood are central to it in a way that they are not with טהר and חטא.[29] On the other hand, however, כִּפֶּר does include an element of purification, and its translation in purity contexts should reflect this. Drawing these similarities and differences together, then, it may be said that כִּפֶּר refers to a sacrificial rite, carried out by the priest on behalf of the person or object in need of cleansing, that results in that person or object becoming pure. While the following will require some modification at the end of the chapter, כִּפֶּר may provisionally be translated in purification contexts with 'to effect purgation': 'And the priest will effect purgation for her (וְכִפֶּר עָלֶיהָ הַכֹּהֵן) and she will be pure (וְטָהֲרָה)' (Lev. 12.8b).[30]

Diagrammatically, the relationship between these three verbs in purification contexts where כִּפֶּר is involved may be presented as follows:

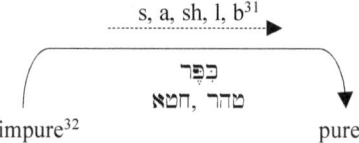

29. For Lev. 14.48-53 see n. 31.
30. As noted in the Introduction, further support for this rendering may be found in Akkadian *kuppuru*, which is also used in cultic contexts to refer to purification. In this way, the Akkadian evidence furnishes a helpful *illustrative* example of the semitic root *kpr* used in the D stem to refer to cultic purification, though as a matter of proper methodology it must be stated that the Akkadian evidence is not *determinative* for the meaning of כִּפֶּר.
31. In this, and subsequent diagrams, s = sacrifice; a = anointing (with blood, blood and oil, or water for impurity); sh = shaving; l = laundering; b = bathing. On the one hand, all of these rites occur at one point or another in conjunction with persons or items that require כִּפֶּר for purification. On the other hand, the only rite that occurs every time in the כִּפֶּר-contexts is that of sacrifice, implying again that there is something about sacrifice, and in particular the blood of sacrifice, that is central to the meaning of כִּפֶּר (see further §6.1.2). This finds confirmation in the one exception, namely, the bird that is slain in Lev. 14.48-53 for the 'leprous house'. Technically, this is not a sacrifice, insofar as the bird is not offered upon the altar. This exception, however, only proves the rule, since the text makes clear that it is the *blood* of this bird which cleanses the house (Lev. 14.51-52). חטא and טהר are placed next to each other in recognition of the fact that they are near synonyms (see §4.1.3); כִּפֶּר is placed close to these terms in recognition of the similarities it shares with them, and yet on a different line in recognition of the differences between it and the other two terms.
32. People or objects with a major impurity obviously start in an impure state. It is less obvious, though, that the Levites in Num. 8 were 'impure'. The need for their purification, however, is probably due to the fact that they were preparing for service in the sanctuary, where the everyday purity of lay people was insufficient (e.g. Num. 3.10; 8.19). Thus while not impure in the same way as one with a major impurity, the Levites were still viewed as those in need of cleansing (see also n. 62 below and discussion in §4.4.1).

We will return to this diagram below once we have had the chance to consider texts involving consecration (קדשׁ), and how the verb כִּפֶּר relates to קדשׁ in these instances.

4.2. *Consecration and* כִּפֶּר

4.2.1. קדשׁ

The verb קדשׁ occurs in the priestly literature in the qal, niphal, piel, hithpael, and hiphil. Each of these will be considered in turn.

In the qal, קדשׁ is used to refer to a person or object being or becoming holy.[33] In some instances, consecration comes about simply through contact with another item that is holy: 'The priest who offers [the purification offering] shall eat it; in a holy place it shall be eaten, in the court of the tent of meeting. Whoever touches its flesh shall become holy (כֹּל אֲשֶׁר־יִגַּע בִּבְשָׂרָהּ יִקְדָּשׁ)...' (Lev. 6.19-20a [26-27a]; see also Exod. 29.37; 30.29; Lev. 6.11 [18]).[34] In another instance, Aaron, his sons, and all their garments become

---

33. Occurrences: Exod. 29.21, 37; 30.29; Lev. 6.11 (18), 20 (27); Num. 17.2-3 (16.37-38).

34. Levine (*Leviticus*, p. 41) understands קדשׁ here and in the other relevant verses (Exod. 29.37; 30.29; Lev. 6.11 [18]) to refer to the necessity of being in a holy state. Thus he translates the opening phrase of the above verse as follows: 'Anyone who is to touch its flesh must be in a holy state'. He refers to his earlier comments on 6.11 (18), where he explains that the meaning of the verse is 'simply...that only consecrated persons may have contact with sacrificial materials, a notion that reinforces the opening of the verse: Only Aaronide priests may partake of the sacrifices' (*Leviticus*, p. 38). In further support, Levine (*Leviticus*, p. 38) cites Hag. 2.11-13, which seems to indicate that holiness was not contagious (Levine actually cites Mal. 2.11-13 by mistake; cf. Levine, *Numbers 1–20*, p. 419, where he has Haggai instead). While it is possible from a grammatical standpoint that יִקְדָּשׁ in these verses is meant to indicate that whoever touches these objects is to be in a holy state ('he *shall* be holy'), it seems more likely that it is referring to becoming holy, that is, that contact with the holy item communicates holiness to the person or object that touches it (so Elliger, *Leviticus*, pp. 79-80, 97; Wenham, *Leviticus*, pp. 113, 121; Milgrom, *Leviticus 1–16*, pp. 443-46). In support, Milgrom (*Leviticus 1–16*, p. 446) notes the phrase כָּל־הַנֹּגֵעַ בְּ־ יִקְדָּשׁ finds its antonym in the phrase כָּל־הַנֹּגֵעַ בְּ־ יִטְמָא, where יִטְמָא clearly means 'he will become impure' (e.g. Lev. 11.24, 26, 27, 31, 36, 39; 15.10, 11, 21, 23, 27). Moreover, the fact that holiness is indeed contagious is demonstrated in Ezek. 46.20: 'And he said to me, "This is the place where the priests shall boil the guilt offering and the purification offering, and where they shall bake the cereal offering, in order not to bring them out into the outer court and so communicate holiness to the people (לְקַדֵּשׁ אֶת־הָעָם)"' (Milgrom, *Leviticus 1–16*, p. 444). Finally, with reference to Hag. 2.11-13, it may be noted that the question is not whether holy items are directly contagious (as in the passages under consideration here), but whether they are contagious at a second remove (Milgrom, *Leviticus 1–16*, p. 445; note further that some impurities are likewise only contagious in a direct manner, and not at a second remove; see Wright's discussion on the communicability of impurity and the

holy after a series of sacrifices and anointings, culminating with the blood of a ram and the anointing oil being sprinkled upon them: 'Then you shall take part of the blood that is on the altar, and of the anointing oil, and sprinkle it upon Aaron and his garments, and upon his sons and his sons' garments with him; and he and his garments shall be holy (וְקָדַשׁ הוּא וּבְגָדָיו), and his sons and his sons' garments with him' (Exod. 29.21). Finally, the censers of those who rebelled with Korah become holy due to their being presented before the LORD:

> Tell Eleazar the son of Aaron the priest to take up the censers out of the blaze; then scatter the fire far and wide. For they are holy (כִּי קָדֵשׁוּ), the censers of these men who have sinned at the cost of their lives; so let them be made into hammered plates as a covering for the altar, for they presented them before the LORD; therefore they are holy (כִּי־הִקְרִיבֻם לִפְנֵי־יְהוָה וַיִּקְדָּשׁוּ). Thus they shall be a sign to the people of Israel. (Num. 17.2-3 [16.37-38])

In the niphal, קדשׁ has three different uses. In the first, it is simply the passive of the qal, and is used in Exodus 29 to refer to the tent of meeting becoming holy from the presence of the LORD: 'It shall be a continual burnt offering throughout your generations at the door of the tent of meeting before the LORD, where I will meet with you, to speak there to you. There I will meet with the people of Israel, and it shall be sanctified by my glory (וְנִקְדַּשׁ בִּכְבֹדִי)' (vv. 42-43). In the second use, the niphal refers to treating the LORD as holy: 'So you shall keep my commandments and do them: I am the LORD. And you shall not profane my holy name, but I will be treated as holy among the people of Israel (וְנִקְדַּשְׁתִּי בְּתוֹךְ בְּנֵי יִשְׂרָאֵל)...' (Lev. 22.31-32a).[35] Here the reference is not to the LORD becoming holy, which he is by nature, but rather to paying due respect to that holiness by keeping his commandments. Finally, the niphal is used in Numbers 20 to refer to the LORD showing himself to be holy: 'These are the waters of Meribah, where the people of Israel contended with the LORD, and he showed himself holy among them (וַיִּקָּדֵשׁ בָּם)' (v. 13). In this instance, Moses and Aaron failed to treat the LORD as holy (הִקְדִּישׁ, v. 12; see further below for hiphil); as a result, the LORD showed himself to be holy through judgment, in this instance, forbidding Moses and Aaron entry into the Promised Land.[36]

קדשׁ occurs most frequently in the priestly literature in the piel and predominantly with a factitive use. In this regard, both people and objects are 'consecrated' or 'sanctified', that is, made holy. In many of these instances, קדשׁ occurs in the context of a specific rite. For example, a major feature of

---

diagrams therein [*Disposal of Impurity*, pp. 179-219, helpfully summarized in Milgrom, *Leviticus 1–16*, pp. 953-68]).

35. Leviticus 10.3 could be using נקדשׁ in this sense, but see n. 36.
36. Wenham, *Numbers*, p. 151; Wenham cites Lev. 10.3 as another instance of the LORD showing himself to be holy through judgment (cf. also Num. 14.21-23).

the rites for consecrating the tabernacle and its contents, as well as Aaron and his sons, is anointing them or sprinkling them with the holy anointing oil:

> Then Moses took the anointing oil, and anointed the tabernacle and all that was in it, and consecrated them (וַיְקַדֵּשׁ אֹתָם). And he sprinkled some of it on the altar seven times, and anointed the altar and all its utensils, and the laver and its base, to consecrate them (לְקַדְּשָׁם). And he poured some of the anointing oil on Aaron's head, and anointed him, to consecrate him (לְקַדְּשׁוֹ). (Lev. 8.10-12; see also Exod. 30.29-30; 40.9-13; Num. 7.1)

At a later point in the same rite we read that another sprinkling was carried out upon Aaron and his sons, this time making use of blood as well as oil: 'Then Moses took some of the anointing oil and of the blood which was on the altar, and sprinkled it upon Aaron and his garments, and also upon his sons and his sons' garments; so he consecrated Aaron and his garments (וַיְקַדֵּשׁ אֶת־אַהֲרֹן אֶת־בְּגָדָיו), and his sons and his sons' garments with him' (Lev. 8.30; see also Exod. 29.21, 33). And in Lev. 16.19 there is a consecration that involves the application of blood alone, with no mention of oil: 'And he shall sprinkle some of the blood upon [the altar] with his finger seven times, and cleanse it and consecrate it from the uncleannesses of the people of Israel (וְטִהֲרוֹ וְקִדְּשׁוֹ מִטֻּמְאֹת בְּנֵי יִשְׂרָאֵל)'.[37]

Other rites aside from anointing or sprinkling were also involved in consecration. In Exodus 28, again describing the consecration of Aaron and his sons, the special garments made for them were an important part of the consecration process: 'And you shall speak to all who have ability, whom I have endowed with an able mind, that they make Aaron's garments to consecrate him (לְקַדְּשׁוֹ) for my priesthood' (v. 3; see also v. 41). Further, it also appears that one could consecrate something by means of waving it, for example, the breast of ordination:

> And you shall take the breast of the ram of Aaron's ordination and wave it for a wave offering before the LORD; and it shall be your portion. Thus you shall consecrate the breast of the wave offering (וְקִדַּשְׁתָּ אֵת חֲזֵה הַתְּנוּפָה), and the thigh of the priests' portion, which is waved, and which is offered from the ram of ordination, since it is for Aaron and for his sons. (Exod. 29.26-27)[38]

In other instances, however, the piel occurs with a factitive sense without there being any specific rite in the immediate context. In these cases, the verb refers to a person being consecrated by the LORD, which is in turn a ground for that person acting a certain way. Thus in Leviticus 22 we read:

---

37. See also Exod. 29.36-37 and Lev. 8.15, and discussion in n. 43 below.
38. See also Num. 8.13-14, where the result of 'waving' the Levites is that they become set apart to the LORD: 'And you shall cause the Levites to attend Aaron and his sons, and shall offer them as a wave offering to the LORD. Thus you shall separate the Levites from among the people of Israel, and the Levites shall be mine.'

> So you shall keep my commandments and do them: I am the LORD. And you shall not profane my holy name, but I will be treated as holy among the people of Israel (וְנִקְדַּשְׁתִּי בְּתוֹךְ בְּנֵי יִשְׂרָאֵל); I am the LORD who sanctifies you (אֲנִי יְהוָה מְקַדִּשְׁכֶם), who brought you out of the land of Egypt to be your God: I am the LORD. (Lev. 22.31-33)

Here the LORD set the people of Israel apart for himself when he brought them up out of Egypt, and their actions are to reflect this consecrated status, that is, they are to keep his commandments.[39]

Finally, the piel appears to have the sense of 'to treat as holy' in two instances. In Leviticus 25, the people of Israel are commanded to treat the Jubilee year as holy, in much the same way as they are commanded to treat the Sabbath as holy: 'And you shall treat the fiftieth year as holy (וְקִדַּשְׁתֶּם אֵת שְׁנַת הַחֲמִשִּׁים שָׁנָה), and proclaim liberty throughout the land to all its inhabitants...' (Lev. 25.10a; cf. Exod. 20.8: 'Remember the Sabbath day to treat it as holy [לְקַדְּשׁוֹ]'). This would also seem to be the sense of the verb in Lev. 21.8: '[The priests] shall not marry a harlot or a woman who has been defiled; neither shall they marry a woman divorced from her husband; for the priest is holy to his God. You shall treat him as holy (וְקִדַּשְׁתּוֹ), for he offers the bread of your God...' (vv. 7-8a). Given that it is the LORD who actually consecrates the priests (Lev. 21.15; 22.9), קדשׁ is best understood here in the sense 'to treat as holy', perhaps with the implication that the people were not to allow priests to marry just anyone.[40]

קדשׁ only occurs three times in the hithpael in the priestly literature. In one of these instances it is used with reference to making oneself holy by means of a rite. The context here is that of the people preparing themselves for a miracle of the LORD on the following day: 'And say to the people, "Consecrate yourselves for tomorrow (הִתְקַדְּשׁוּ לְמָחָר), and you shall eat meat' (Num. 11.18a). Based on Exodus 19, where the people had to be consecrated for the appearance of the LORD on the third day, it would seem that this consecration would involve laundering of clothes (19.10, 14), abstaining from sexual relations (19.15), and perhaps bathing as well (cf. 19.10, 14

---

39. See also 20.7-8: 'Consecrate yourselves therefore, and be holy (וְהִתְקַדִּשְׁתֶּם וִהְיִיתֶם קְדֹשִׁים); for I am the LORD your God. Keep my statutes, and do them; I am the LORD who sanctifies you (אֲנִי יְהוָה מְקַדִּשְׁכֶם)'. See also Exod. 31.13; Lev. 21.8b, 15; 22.9, 32.

40. Milgrom (*Leviticus 17–22*, p. 1808) notes that the rabbis cite two opinions on this point. The first is the one identified above, namely, 'Israel is responsible for the priest's maintaining his holy status, even if he is unwilling (*Sipra* Emor 1.13)' (see also Hartley, *Leviticus*, p. 348). This view connects the command of v. 8 closely with v. 7. The second understanding views v. 8 as a more general command to show the priest respect, for example, '"The school of R. Ishmael taught: (Give him precedence) to open proceedings, to say grace first, and to choose his portion first" (*b. Giṭ.* 59b; cf. 1QS 6.3-4, 8)' (Milgrom, *Leviticus 17–22*, p. 1809).

with 29.1, 4). In the other two instances there is no specific rite in the immediate context. Rather, the people's consecration is to manifest itself in their obedience to the LORD's commands:

> For I am the LORD your God; consecrate yourselves (וְהִתְקַדִּשְׁתֶּם), therefore, and be holy, for I am holy. You shall not defile yourselves with any swarming thing that crawls upon the earth. For I am the LORD who brought you up out of the land of Egypt, to be your God; you shall therefore be holy, for I am holy. (Lev. 11.44-45; see also Lev. 20.7)

Because the LORD has set the people apart as his own, and because he is holy, they were to consecrate themselves, that is, live lives in keeping with the holiness of their God.

Finally, קדש also occurs numerous times in the hiphil. There are three main contexts in which it occurs. In the first, the people of Israel are said to consecrate something to the LORD: 'When a person consecrates their house as holy to the LORD (וְאִישׁ כִּי־יַקְדִּשׁ אֶת־בֵּיתוֹ קֹדֶשׁ לַיהוָה), the priest shall value it as either good or bad; as the priest values it, so it shall stand' (Lev. 27.14; see also Exod. 28.38; Lev. 22.2-3; 27.15-19, 22, 26). It is not stated explicitly whether a rite was involved in this process, though it is possible that this consecration takes place by means of a vow (cf. Lev. 27.1-2).

In the second context, it is the LORD who is the subject, and who consecrates Israel to himself: 'For all the first-born are mine; on the day that I slew all the first-born in the land of Egypt, I consecrated for my own all the first-born in Israel (הִקְדַּשְׁתִּי לִי כָל־בְּכוֹר בְּיִשְׂרָאֵל), both of people and of beast; they shall be mine: I am the LORD' (Num. 3.13).

Lastly, the hiphil is used in two instances with the meaning 'to treat as holy'. Both of these verses refer to the waters of Meribah, where Moses and Aaron disobeyed the LORD, and in this way did not treat him as holy: 'And the LORD said to Moses and Aaron, "Because you did not believe in me, to treat me as holy in the eyes of the people of Israel (לְהַקְדִּישֵׁנִי לְעֵינֵי בְּנֵי יִשְׂרָאֵל), therefore you shall not bring this assembly into the land which I have given them"' (Num. 20.12; see also 27.14).

By way of summary, קדש is used in the following ways in the priestly literature. In the qal, קדש refers to being or becoming holy. It was seen that the means of consecration could involve rites such as anointing with blood and oil (Exod. 29.21). In other instances, however, no rite is involved, and consecration could result simply from contact with holy items (Exod. 29.37; 30.29; Lev. 6.11 [18], 19-20a [26-27a]) or, in the case of the censers, from being presented before the LORD (Num. 17.2-3 [16.37-38]).

In the niphal, קדש is used in three distinct ways. In the first, it functions as a simple passive of the qal, and is used to refer to the tent of meeting becoming holy from the presence of the LORD (Exod. 29.43). In the second, it refers to the LORD being treated as holy by Israel, as demonstrated by obedience to his commands (Lev. 22.32). In the last, it refers to the LORD showing himself to be holy via judgment (Num. 20.13).

With the piel, קדשׁ is used predominantly with a factitive use, that is, to refer to consecrating. The objects of consecration could be either people or objects. In many instances, the consecration comes about by means of a special rite, be it anointing with oil alone (Exod. 30.29-30; 40.9-13; Lev. 8.10-12; Num. 7.1), with blood and oil (Exod. 29.21, 33; Lev. 8.30), with blood alone (Lev. 16.19), through the donning of special garments (Exod. 28.3, 41), or through waving something before the LORD (Exod. 29.26-27). In all of these instances, people are the subject of קדשׁ. In other instances, however, no rites are specified. In many of these, the LORD is the subject, and he is said to have consecrated the people of Israel for himself by delivering them from Egypt, as a result of which they were to live holy lives (Lev. 22.31-33; cf. Exod. 31.13; Lev. 20.7-8; 21.8b, 15; 22.9, 32). Finally, there are two instances where the Israelites are commanded to treat something or someone as holy, namely, the year of Jubilee (Lev. 25.10) and the priests (Lev. 21.8).

In the hithpael, קדשׁ was seen to have two uses. In the first, it refers to consecrating oneself by means of bathing, laundering, and abstaining from physical relationships (Num. 11.18; cf. Exod. 19.10, 14-15, and 29.1, 4). In the second, the people are again to consecrate themselves, though no specific rite is mentioned. Instead, the consecration is to manifest itself in obedience to the LORD's commands (Lev. 11.44-45; 20.7).

Finally, the hiphil of קדשׁ was seen to be used in two ways. In the first, it refers simply to consecrating. This could be done by the people to an object (Exod. 28.38; Lev. 22.2-3; 27.14, 15-19, 22), perhaps by means of a vow (cf. Lev. 27.14 with 27.2), and was done by the LORD to the first-born during the last plague of the Exodus (Num. 3.13). In the second, the hiphil is used with the meaning 'to treat as holy'. In these instances, it is said that Moses and Aaron failed to treat the LORD as holy due to their disobedience (Num. 20.12; 27.14).

4.2.2. קדשׁ and כפר

Just as it was seen above that כפר was related to טהר and חטא in purification contexts, so too it may be seen that כפר is related to קדשׁ in consecration contexts. Thus in the consecration of Aaron and his sons we read, '[Aaron and his sons] shall eat those things by which purgation was effected (אֲשֶׁר כֻּפַּר בָּהֶם) to ordain them and to consecrate them (לְמַלֵּא אֶת־יָדָם לְקַדֵּשׁ אֹתָם)...' (Exod. 29.33a). 'Those things' in this verse refers to the ram of ordination which was offered on their behalf, the blood of which was placed and sprinkled upon them (vv. 20-21). A few verses later, with the consecration of the altar, the כפר-rite is again a central element:

And every day you shall offer a bull as a purification offering for atonement (עַל־הַכִּפֻּרִים); and you shall offer a purification offering upon the altar[41] when you effect purgation for it[42] (וְחִטֵּאתָ עַל־הַמִּזְבֵּחַ בְּכַפֶּרְךָ עָלָיו); and you will anoint it,[43] to consecrate it (וּמָשַׁחְתָּ אֹתוֹ לְקַדְּשׁוֹ). Seven days you shall effect purgation for[44] the altar (תְּכַפֵּר עַל־הַמִּזְבֵּחַ), and consecrate it (וְקִדַּשְׁתָּ אֹתוֹ), and the altar shall be most holy... (Exod. 29.36-37bα)[45]

Similarly, the כִּפֶּר-rite in Leviticus 16 also leads to the consecration of the altar:

41. For this translation of וְחִטֵּאתָ עַל־הַמִּזְבֵּחַ see above, n. 17.
42. Or: '...effect purgation upon it'. See n. 83 below and discussion in the Appendix.
43. Is this anointing done with the blood of the sacrifice, or did the priest at this point use the holy anointing oil? The text does not specify. On the one hand, because מָשַׁח is used predominantly in conjunction with the oil it might be assumed that the phrase 'and you will anoint it' refers to anointing with oil, and that it is this, and not the כִּפֶּר-rite, which results in the altar's consecration. On the other hand, however, it can be noted that the preceding verses detail the consecration of Aaron and his sons, and state that both the blood of the sacrifice as well as the anointing oil were used for their consecration (Exod. 20.20-21). Moreover, as Lev. 16.19 indicates, it was the blood of the purification offering that was used to consecrate the altar (see discussion below). And finally, the parallel text in Lev. 8.15 mentions only the blood of the sacrifice as that which cleanses and consecrates the altar. It is therefore likely that מָשַׁח in Exod. 29.36 refers to the application of the blood of the purification offering.
44. See n. 42 above.
45. See also the parallel in Lev. 8.15: 'And Moses killed [the purification offering], and took the blood, and with his finger put it on the horns of the altar round about, and purified (וַיְחַטֵּא) the altar, but the blood he poured out at the base of the altar; thus he consecrated it (וַיְקַדְּשֵׁהוּ) by effecting purgation for it (לְכַפֵּר עָלָיו)' (or: 'by effecting purgation upon it'; see n. 42 above). For this rendering of the infinitive (לְכַפֵּר) see also Wenham, *Leviticus*, p. 135. Milgrom (*Leviticus 1–16*, p. 524) argues against this rendering on two grounds: (1) '...one is hard put to justify the existence of an instrumental *lamed*; *lĕkappēr*, as indicated by its Exod. 29.36 counterpart...is intended to be understood infinitively'; (2) it is wrong to think that the blood of the purification offering can simultaneously decontaminate from impurity as well as consecrate, for the realms of impurity and holiness are incompatible. 'This necessitates two discrete processes: first decontamination and then consecration. Decontamination takes place with the blood of the purification offering and consecration with the anointment oil...' With regard to the first point, it may be noted that the existence of an instrumental *lamed* is not in doubt. Joüon notes that the 'infinitive with ל is very often used after a verb to express an action which gives more details about or explains the preceding action; it is then equivalent to the Latin gerund in *-do*, e.g. *faciendo* = Eng. *by doing*' (124o). To translate וַיְקַדְּשֵׁהוּ לְכַפֵּר עָלָיו in Lev. 8.15 with 'thus he consecrated it *by performing purgation* for it' is in perfect keeping with this use of the infinitive. As for his second point, Milgrom (*Leviticus 1–16*, p. 1037) later argues that the blood in Lev. 16.19 serves both to purify the altar from impurity as well as to consecrate it, and it should therefore be no problem to see the same taking place here.

Then [Aaron] shall go out to the altar which is before the LORD and effect purgation for it (וְכִפֶּר עָלָיו),[46] and shall take some of the blood of the bull and of the blood of the goat, and put it on the horns of the altar round about. And he shall sprinkle some of the blood upon it with his finger seven times, and purify it and sanctify it from the impurities of the people of Israel (וְטִהֲרוֹ וְקִדְּשׁוֹ מִטֻּמְאֹת בְּנֵי יִשְׂרָאֵל). (Lev. 16.18-19)[47]

In each of these instances, the כִּפֶּר-rite has been a central element of the consecration that has taken place, thus establishing a close relationship between כִּפֶּר and קדשׁ.

At the same time, however, כִּפֶּר and קדשׁ manifest important differences. First, קדשׁ in the piel is always followed by the direct object, and refers simply to the consecration of that object. כִּפֶּר, on the other hand, is predominantly followed in these contexts by the prepositions עַל or בְּעַד,[48] due to the fact, as noted above, that it refers to the performance of a rite that is executed on behalf of someone or something.[49]

Second, כִּפֶּר occurs only in the piel (or pual; Exod. 29.33) in consecration contexts and only takes the priest or Moses as subject. קדשׁ, however, can occur in the hithpael, where the person is to consecrate themselves (Num. 11.18). Moreover, while priests are often the subject of קדשׁ in the piel, non-priests can be too, such as the Nazirite who consecrates his head (Num. 6.11) or the people of Israel as a whole who are to consecrate the Jubilee year (Lev. 25.10).

Finally, כִּפֶּר always occurs in conjunction with a sacrifice in these contexts. As was seen above, however, קדשׁ is used to indicate consecration taking place in a wide variety of contexts, in most of which sacrifice plays no part—for example, anointing with oil alone (Exod. 40.9-13; Lev. 8.10-12; Num. 7.1), donning special garments (Exod. 28.3, 41), waving something before the LORD (Exod. 29.26-27), or coming into contact with something that is holy (Exod. 29.37; Lev. 6.11 [18], 20 [27]). This is perhaps the most fundamental difference of all, and directly implies that sacrifice is central to the meaning of כִּפֶּר, though not to the meaning of קדשׁ.[50]

On the one hand, then, כִּפֶּר is not a synonym of קדשׁ, whether קדשׁ occurs in the piel or in any other form, since כִּפֶּר always includes the idea of

---

46. See n. 42 above.
47. With reference to the relationship between טהר and קדשׁ here, Milgrom (*Leviticus 1–16*, pp. 522, 1037) suggests that a two-step process is involved, which may be reflected in the two different blood rites: first the altar is daubed (נתן; v. 18), which purifies it, and then it is sprinkled (הזה; v. 19), which consecrates it.
48. See above, n. 25.
49. See above, §4.1.4.
50. Indeed, as seen in n. 51 below, it is the blood of sacrifice in particular that seems to be a central part of כִּפֶּר in these contexts.

sacrifice, whereas קדשׁ does not. On the other hand, however, it may be said that in consecration contexts, כִּפֶּר refers to a sacrificial rite, carried out by the priest on behalf of the person or object in need of consecration, that results in that person or object becoming holy. In this regard, כִּפֶּר does contain elements of consecration as part of its sense. For reasons that become apparent in the following, the same rendering of כִּפֶּר given above for purification contexts will be maintained for the moment in consecration contexts —namely, 'to effect purgation' (as opposed to 'to effect consecration').

As a diagram, the relationship between כִּפֶּר and קדשׁ in consecration contexts where כִּפֶּר is involved may be presented as follows:

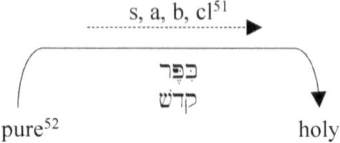

51. s = sacrifice; a = anointing (with blood, or with blood and oil); b = bathing; cl = clothing. Again, it may be noted on the one hand that all these rites occur in conjunction with people or objects that require כִּפֶּר for consecration. It may be noted on the other hand, however, that the only rites that occur every time in these כִּפֶּר-contexts are those of sacrifice and anointing with blood, suggesting once more that there is something about sacrifice, and in particular the blood of sacrifice, that is central to the meaning of כִּפֶּר (see also again §6.1.2). כִּפֶּר and קדשׁ are placed close to each other in recognition of the fact that they have some similarities; at the same time, they are on separate lines in recognition of the fact that there are significant differences between them.

52. This diagram assumes that the altar was in a pure state before it was consecrated in Exod. 29.36-37; Lev. 8.15; and 16.19. For 16.19, see n. 47 above, where it was suggested that וְטִהֲרוֹ וְקִדְּשׁוֹ was a two-stage process, that is, first cleansing, then consecrating. This could equally be the case in Exod. 29.36, which mentions offering a purification offering (for cleansing; cf. parallel in Lev. 8.15: וַיְחַטֵּא אֶת־הַמִּזְבֵּחַ) and anointing, with consecration seemingly connected with the latter of these. In all three instances, then, the כִּפֶּר-rite effected both purification and consecration (cf. Lev. 16.19 with 16.20; Exod. 29.36 with 29.37; for לְכַפֵּר in Lev. 8.15, see above, n. 45). A further question is why the altar is in need of cleansing in Exod. 29.36-37, since no specific impurity is mentioned in the immediate context. Earlier Jewish explanations have been surveyed by Milgrom (*Leviticus 1–16*, pp. 521-22): one of the leaders gave a gift for the tabernacle's construction which was taken by force; one of the people gave to the tabernacle's construction unwillingly; the builders of the tabernacle may have polluted it; or Aaron and his sons might have committed an inadvertent sin during their week in the tabernacle. Milgrom himself favors the last of these, though in that case it is not clear why the blood is not brought into the shrine (Lev. 4.3-7; for a survey of modern explanations, see Kiuchi, *Purification Offering*, pp. 41-43). Alternatively, it may simply be that the altar was already pure, but that, like the Levites in Num. 8, it was in need of further cleansing due to its presence in the tabernacle (see n. 32 above and n. 62 below).

4.3. Purification, Consecration, and כִּפֶּר

The results of the above study on כִּפֶּר in both purification and consecration texts may be presented schematically in two different ways. The diagram immediately below acknowledges that holiness is of a higher grade than purity, and thus shows the relationship between them progressively:[53]

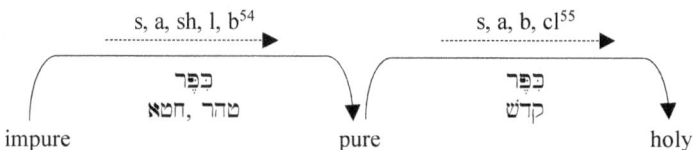

At the same time, there is a great deal of similarity between becoming pure and becoming holy. This can be seen through both negative and positive comparisons with כִּפֶּר.

Negatively, the three main differences between the use of כִּפֶּר when compared with טהר and חטא are the same three differences between the use of כִּפֶּר and קדשׁ.[56] (1) כִּפֶּר is predominantly followed by עַל or בַּעַד, whereas טהר, חטא, and קדשׁ are not.[57] Indeed, when these last three verbs occur in the piel they are always followed by a direct object, something that is only rarely true for כִּפֶּר.[58] (2) כִּפֶּר only ever has Moses, Aaron, or a priest as the subject. טהר, חטא, and קדשׁ, however, all have occurrences where the subject is not Moses, Aaron, or a priest, but a lay Israelite or a Levite.[59] (3) Finally, while כִּפֶּר always occurs in purification and consecration contexts where blood is involved (i.e. where a sacrifice is made), טהר, חטא, and קדשׁ do not: purification (טהר, חטא) can be accomplished with the application of water, and consecration (קדשׁ) can be accomplished by anointing with oil, donning special garments, and so on.

---

53. This chart is an adaptation of that originally proposed by Wenham (*Leviticus*, p. 26; see also p. 19) and then slightly modified by Jenson (*Graded Holiness*, p. 26).
54. See above, n. 31.
55. See above, n. 51.
56. Cf. §4.1.4 and §4.2.2 above.
57. Again, for Exod. 29.36 see n. 17.
58. See n. 25 above.
59. 'And thus you shall do to [the Levities] to cleanse them: sprinkle the water of expiation upon them, and let them go with a razor over all their body, and wash their clothes and cleanse themselves (וְהִטֶּהָרוּ)' (Num. 8.7); 'And the clean person shall sprinkle upon the unclean on the third day and on the seventh day; thus on the seventh day he shall cleanse him (וְחִטְּאוֹ), and he shall wash his clothes and bathe himself in water, and at evening he shall be clean' (Num. 19.19); 'And the Levites cleansed themselves (וַיִּתְחַטְּאוּ הַלְוִיִּם), and washed their clothes...' (Num. 8.21a); 'And that same day he shall consecrate his head (וְקִדַּשׁ אֶת־רֹאשׁוֹ) and shall dedicate to the LORD his days as a Nazirite...' (Num. 6.11b-12a).

Positively, the similarity between purification and consecration is seen in that some of the same rites occur alongside of the כִּפֶּר-rite in both purification and consecration contexts, for example, anointing with blood, or bathing. The similarities between purification and consecration are especially apparent when the purification of the leper is compared with the consecration of the priests: in both instances the one to be cleansed/consecrated is brought to the door of the tent of meeting (Lev. 14.11; Exod. 29.4); blood is put upon the right earlobe, thumb, and big toe of the one being cleansed/consecrated (Lev. 14.14; Exod. 29.20); and oil is then also applied (Lev. 14.15-18; Exod. 29.21). These similarities between becoming pure and becoming holy come into sharper focus when the relationship between purity and holiness, and how כִּפֶּר is involved in accomplishing either, is presented in parallel fashion:

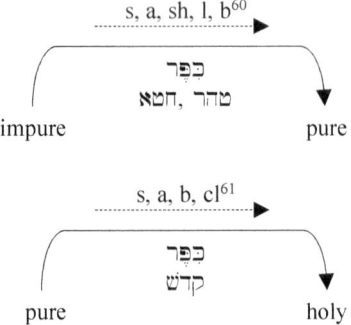

In short, the difference between purification and consecration is one of degree more than substance—that is, both refer to cleansing, with consecration being a more intense form of cleansing than purification.[62] In either

---

60. See above, n. 31.
61. See above, n. 51.
62. See also Péter-Contesse (*Lévitique 1–16*, p. 243), who states that everything that is holy is necessarily pure, though everything that is pure is not necessarily holy. The relative aspect of impurity to purity may be diagrammed as follows:

impurity   *purity*

But when holiness is added to the spectrum, the diagram changes:

impurity   *purity*   *holiness*

As argued further below, this understanding of the relationship between the pure state and the holy state helps to explain the numerous regulations that prohibit 'clean' people from certain cultic activities, foods, and places, since, from the perspective of the holy, even a clean person is in some respects impure.

instance, then, כִּפֶּר refers to a rite of purgation (i.e. sacrifice) which results in the cleansing of the person or object, be it to make them pure (חטא, טהר), or to make them holy (קדשׁ). The tentative translation in either context, then, is 'to effect purgation', with the understanding that consecration is a much more intense form of purgation than purification.

4.4. כִּפֶּר, *Purgation, and* כֹּפֶר

In the last chapter, it was seen that the verb כִּפֶּר is used in sin contexts to express the effecting of a כֹּפֶר-payment on behalf of the sinner, which results in the sinner being forgiven. In this chapter, it has been seen that the verb כִּפֶּר is used in purification and consecration contexts to express the effecting of purgation on behalf of a person or object, which results in that person or object being purified or consecrated.

It was also seen in the last chapter, however, that sin *pollutes*, and for this reason it was argued that the idea of purgation is probably still involved in the sense of כִּפֶּר in sin contexts. In the following, it is argued that impurity *endangers*, and for this reason the idea of כֹּפֶר may very well be included in the sense of כִּפֶּר in purification and consecration contexts. We will begin by considering those contexts involving purification, and then turn to consider those involving consecration.

4.4.1. *Purification and* כִּפֶּר

When כִּפֶּר occurs in a purification context, it is most often to cleanse a person or object from a major impurity. For this reason, we begin with a brief outline of the various grades of impurities in order to set the context of the discussion.

Impurities may be placed on a continuum between two poles: minor impurities and major impurities.[63] These poles are determined based on the type of rite required for cleansing, the duration of the impurity, and the degree of its contagion.[64] Minor defilements are those which are typically cleansed via bathing and/or laundering,[65] which last one day, and which are not contagious. People or objects with minor defilements include those who have touched or carried an unclean carcass (Lev. 11.24-28), those who have been touched by a corpse-defiled person (Num. 19.22), those who have

---

63. The word 'continuum' is used above due to the impurity of the corpse-contaminated person and menstruant, which fall in between minor and major impurities (see the above discussion and n. 69 below).

64. So Jenson, *Graded Holiness*, pp. 225-26.

65. The word 'typically' is used because in some instances it is not clear that the person had to bathe or launder, only that they had to wait until sunset (see Lev. 11.24, 27).

entered, slept, or eaten in a diseased house (Lev. 14.46-47), and those who have had sexual intercourse (Lev. 15.18).[66]

By way of contrast, major defilements require several more rites for cleansing. Thus alongside of bathing and laundering we also find shaving, sprinkling with the water for impurity, anointing with oil or blood, and the sprinkling of blood.[67] Most importantly, the cleansing of a major impurity always involves sacrifice, something that is never found with a minor impurity. Further differences between major and minor impurities are that major impurities also last at least seven days and can contaminate other people or objects.[68] People with major defilements include those with a skin disease (Lev. 13–14), a new mother (Lev. 12), or a male or female with a discharge (Lev. 15.13-15, 28-30).[69] What may be noted from the above, however, is that one of the distinguishing features of a major impurity is the requirement of sacrifice, as a result of which the verb כִּפֶּר occurs within the context of these impurities.

---

66. For a more comprehensive list of those with minor impurities, see Jenson, *Graded Holiness*, p. 225.

67. We also find that the metallic items from the spoil are to be passed through the fire as well as sprinkled with the water for impurity (מֵי נִדָּה; Num. 31.21-24).

68. For the contagion of major impurities, see especially the illustrations in Wright (*Disposal of Impurity*, pp. 179-219; summarized in Milgrom, *Leviticus 1–16*, pp. 953-68).

69. Jenson, *Graded Holiness*, p. 226. In between these poles is the impurity of the person who touches a corpse (Num. 19.11-22) and of the menstruant (Lev. 15.19-24). The impurity of the person who touches a corpse is like the major impurities in that it lasts for seven days and can contaminate other people or objects (Num. 19.11, 22). It differs in that it is not cleansed by the sacrifice of the individual, but by the 'water for impurity' (מֵי נִדָּה; Num. 19.9), which seems to be an admixture of water and ashes from a purification offering that has previously been made. Naturally, it would not be feasible to require the normal purificatory rites for major impurities in Num. 19, since whole families would be affected by the death of a loved one, and it would be an excessive burden to require every member to bring sacrifices (it would be a similar burden in Num. 31 to require sacrifices of all the men of an army, as well as of their captives, who had come into contact with the dead). In these instances, the water had its purifying effect due to its admixture with the ashes of an animal slaughtered and burned by the priest (vv. 1-10, 17). Milgrom (*Numbers*, pp. 438-43) understands this chapter to refer to a burnt purification offering, and Wenham (*Numbers*, p. 146) notes that the water would have contained all of the elements of a purification offering. In this regard, it may still be possible to classify this impurity as a major impurity, though with a cleansing rite that is somewhat of an exception to the rule (see also n. 28 above). The impurity of the menstruant also lasts seven days and can contaminate other people or objects (Lev. 15.19-24) but requires no sacrifice at all for its cleansing (perhaps again due to economic considerations?). It is generally assumed that the menstruant would need to bathe and launder (Milgrom, *Leviticus 1–16*, pp. 934-35; Jenson, *Graded Holiness*, p. 226; Wright, *Disposal of Impurity*, p. 191 n. 44). This would also be the case for the man who lies with the menstruant and comes into contact with her menstrual discharge (Lev. 15.24).

4. *The Verb* כִּפֶּר *in Contexts of Impurity*

With this backdrop in place, we now turn to consider why כִּפֶּר in purification contexts might involve not only purgation, but also elements of כֹּפֶר. Two considerations are worthy of note in this regard. First, as Milgrom has argued, those who suffer from a major impurity defile the sanctuary and its sancta, even if they have not had direct contact with them. This is evident from the following: (1) the tabernacle is defiled from impurities in the adytum, even though no one is allowed in there (Lev. 16.16);[70] and (2) those suffering from a major impurity must bring a purification offering; as the blood of this offering has a purifying function (Lev. 8.15), and as it is placed upon the sanctuary and its sancta, it follows that the sanctuary and its sancta have been polluted by the major impurity and are in need of cleansing.[71]

---

70. Milgrom, 'Israel's Sanctuary', p. 394.
71. Milgrom, 'Israel's Sanctuary', p. 391. Leviticus 15.31 reads as follows: 'Thus you shall keep the people of Israel separate from their uncleanness, lest they die in their uncleanness by defiling my tabernacle that is in their midst'. This passage has been taken to mean that uncleanness does not defile the tabernacle unless it is not dealt with properly. Thus Kiuchi (*Purification Offering*, p. 61) states, '[Lev. 15.31] hardly implies that the uncleanness dealt with in Lev. 15.2-30 defiles the tabernacle. Rather, what v. 31 says is that when the rules in vv. 2-30 are not kept, that defiles the tabernacle' (see also Hartley, *Leviticus*, p. 213). And again: the 'pollution [of the tabernacle] is caused by failure to undergo the prescribed cleansing procedures, not by the person contracting uncleanness' (Kiuchi, *Purification Offering*, p. 62). While Kiuchi is correct in stating that defilement of the tabernacle would result if the rules were not followed, this does not necessarily imply that the tabernacle was defiled only when the rules were not properly followed. This is evidenced by the comparable situation in Num. 35.30-34, which addresses the pollution of the land caused by bloodshed: 'If any one kills a person, the murderer shall be put to death on the evidence of witnesses; but no person shall be put to death on the testimony of one witness. Moreover you shall accept no ransom for the life of a murderer, who is guilty of death; but the murderer shall be put to death. And you shall accept no ransom for the one who has fled to their city of refuge, that they may return to dwell in the land before the death of the high priest. Thus you shall not pollute the land in which you live; for blood pollutes the land (וְלֹא־תַחֲנִיפוּ אֶת־הָאָרֶץ אֲשֶׁר אַתֶּם בָּהּ כִּי הַדָּם הוּא יַחֲנִיף אֶת־הָאָרֶץ), and no atonement can be made for the land, for the blood that is shed in it, except by the blood of the one who shed it. You shall not defile the land (וְלֹא תְטַמֵּא אֶת־הָאָרֶץ) in which you live, in the midst of which I dwell; for I the LORD dwell in the midst of the people of Israel' It is seen here on the one hand that the blood of the slain pollutes the land, and that the only means of addressing this is the blood of the slayer (v. 33). In the case of the inadvertent slayer, however, their blood was not required: instead, he or she was allowed to live in a city of refuge until the death of the high priest (v. 32). Despite the fact that the inadvertent slayer was not required to die, it is important to note at this point that the defilement of the land has not been fully redressed, as shown by the fact that the inadvertent slayer is not allowed to leave the city until the death of the high priest (v. 32). As long as this regulation is followed, the full consequence of the land's defilement—which elsewhere is the expulsion of those dwelling in it (Lev. 18.24-28)—is suspended.

The second consideration is simply that the defiling of sancta is a sin of the most serious consequences in the priestly literature. Thus the priests are warned, 'If any one of all your descendants throughout your generations approaches the holy things, which the people of Israel dedicate to the LORD, while he has an uncleanness, that person shall be cut off from my presence: I am the LORD' (Lev. 22.3); and again, after a series of warnings to the priests about not approaching the holy gifts while unclean: 'They shall therefore keep my charge, lest they bear sin for it and die thereby when they profane it: I am the LORD who sanctifies them' (22.9).[72]

In short, it is not simply that the person is defiled. Rather, through their impurity they have also (inadvertently) defiled sancta, a sin of the most serious consequences. It thus stands to reason that the verb כִּפֶּר in these contexts does not simply refer to cleansing; in keeping with its use elsewhere in the context of inadvertent sin—it also refers to ransom (כֹּפֶר) (see Chapter 3 above). Stated differently, the major pollutions do not only *defile*, they also *endanger*, and thus the כִּפֶּר-rite must cleanse the impurity (purgation) and rescue the endangered person (כֹּפֶר).[73]

True, it was never the intent of the parturient, leper, or the one suffering from a flow to defile the sanctuary or its sancta. This is granted. Nonetheless, even the inadvertent defiling of sancta was considered sinful, as is made clear by the case of the Nazirite in Numbers 6:

On the other hand, however, the Israelites are warned not to disregard this regulation and allow the inadvertent slayer to return home before the death of the high priest lest they defile the land—even though it is technically defiled already! In short, it would appear that inadvertent defilement did not bring about the judgment of the LORD, so long as the regulations for dealing with the pollution were followed. In the same way it is equally possible that the defilements of Lev. 15.2-30 (or of Lev. 12–15, depending upon how large a context 15.31 has in view) did pollute the tabernacle, but that the LORD's judgment of this was suspended as long as the Israelites dealt with the source of this defilement appropriately. When they did not, however, they were held fully responsible and were subject to the LORD's judgment (death).

72. See also the warnings of Num. 3.10; 8.19; 18.3-5, 7, 22.

73. It might be argued that כִּפֶּר does not refer to purgation *and* כֹּפֶר, but that כִּפֶּר itself refers simply to purgation, the *result* of which may be כֹּפֶר. In response, it may be noted that there are several different verbs for purification, but that cleansing from major impurities always involves sacrificial atonement. As a result, there is something unique about the cleansing represented by the verb כִּפֶּר. Given the similarities between the end result of major impurities seen in this chapter and the inadvertent sins of Chapter 3 (see §5.2 below), and given that כִּפֶּר was seen in Chapter 3 to be related strongly to כֹּפֶר, it seems very likely that the unique element of כִּפֶּר at work in contexts of major impurities is also that of כֹּפֶר. In other words, this is not any type of purgation that is taking place; this is כֹּפֶר-purgation. See also further arguments in §5.2 below.

> And if a person dies very suddenly (בְּפֶתַע פִּתְאֹם) beside him [i.e. the Nazirite], and he defiles his consecrated head, then he shall shave his head on the day of his cleansing; on the seventh day he shall shave it. On the eighth day he shall bring two turtledoves or two young pigeons to the priest to the door of the tent of meeting, and the priest shall offer one for a purification offering and the other for a burnt offering, and make atonement for him, *because he sinned* by reason of the dead body (וְכִפֶּר עָלָיו מֵאֲשֶׁר חָטָא עַל־הַנָּפֶשׁ). (Num. 6.9-11a)

The situation envisaged here is one in which the holy head of the Nazirite has been defiled by corpse contamination. The inadvertency of the situation is indicated by the suddenness of the death (בְּפֶתַע פִּתְאֹם), that is, the Nazirite did not purposefully expose himself to corpse contamination; instead, the event came about unexpectedly and in a manner outside of his control. Nonetheless, from the priestly perspective, the Nazirite has sinned, and is in need of atonement: '...and [the priest will] make atonement for [the Nazirite], *because he sinned* by reason of the dead body (וְכִפֶּר עָלָיו מֵאֲשֶׁר חָטָא עַל־הַנָּפֶשׁ)' (v. 11). Granted, the sin in view in this instance is the defiling of the Nazirite's head, and the text does not explicitly address the defiling of the sanctuary itself or its sancta. Nonetheless, the fact remains from this passage that the inadvertent defiling of a holy item (the Nazirite's head) was considered a sin in the priestly system, and therefore in need of redressing. Given that major impurities also defile holy items (namely, the sanctuary and its sancta), it may be concluded that those suffering from a major impurity are in the same place as the Nazirite, namely, as those who have sinned inadvertently. As a result, it would seem that כִּפֶּר in these contexts refers not only to an act of purgation, as argued above, but that it also refers to the principle of כִּפֶּר, in keeping with its use in contexts of inadvertent sin elsewhere.

Finally, there is one purification situation where כִּפֶּר is involved and yet where there is no major impurity mentioned, namely, the purifying of the Levites in Numbers 8.[74] In this context, the Levites are received by the LORD

---

74. This is labeled as a purification context, and not a consecration context, for the following reasons: (1) the verbs employed here are those of cleansing (טהר; vv. 6, 21; חטא; v. 21), not consecration (קדש); (2) unlike Aaron and the priests, no holy anointing oil is used (Exod. 29.7, 21), but instead the water for impurity (v. 7); (3) whereas Aaron and his sons put on new clothes as part of their consecration (29.5-9), the Levites simply wash the clothes that they have (v. 21) (see Gray, *Numbers*, p. 79; see also Levine, *Numbers 1–20*, p. 273; Wenham, *Numbers*, p. 96; Milgrom, *Numbers*, p. 61).

At the same time, it may also be noted that the purity of the Levites is of a higher grade than that of the Israelites, as indicated by the fact that they are able to be involved in the service of the tabernacle in ways that would otherwise be fatal to a normal Israelite (Num. 8.19). The Levites thus appear to have a grade of purity somewhere in between that of the everyday purity of a lay Israelite and that of the holiness of the priests. Again,

in place of the first-born of Israel and are given to Aaron and his sons for work in the service of the tabernacle (vv. 16-19; see also 3.5-9). In preparation for this service, the Levites have to undergo certain purification rites, such as being sprinkled with the water for impurity, shaving themselves, and laundering their clothes (v. 7). What is more, however, they are also required to offer a purification offering and a burnt offering, the purpose of which was to atone (לְכַפֵּר) for them: 'Then the Levites shall lay their hands upon the heads of the bulls; and you shall offer the one for a purification offering and the other for a burnt offering to the LORD, to atone for the Levites (לְכַפֵּר עַל־הַלְוִיִּם)' (v. 12).

It is clear in this context that the meaning of כִּפֶּר is tied in with purification: '...and Aaron offered [the Levites] as a wave offering before the LORD, and Aaron *made atonement* for them *to cleanse* them (וַיְכַפֵּר עֲלֵיהֶם אַהֲרֹן לְטַהֲרָם)' (v. 21). Exactly what the Levites are being cleansed from is not identified in this text, though given the fact that the natural purity of the lay person is as impurity relative to the holy sanctuary,[75] it may simply be this natural lack of relative purity that is in mind. In any case, it is cleansing that the Levites need and the כִּפֶּר-rite is a necessary element in accomplishing this.

While כִּפֶּר is clearly tied in with purification in these contexts, it also appears that it is related to כֹּפֶר. To be specific, since the tabernacle is the dwelling of the LORD, those who come into contact with it risk suffering the LORD's wrath. This is due to the fact, noted above, that the natural purity of people is as impurity relative to the holiness of the LORD.[76] As a result, the כִּפֶּר-rite served not only to cleanse, but also to ransom from certain death.[77] Indeed, the ransoming aspect of כִּפֶּר in Numbers 8 is underscored when the parallel between the Levites and the sacrificial bulls is considered.[78]

On the one hand, the Israelites lay their hands upon the Levites (v. 10), who are then given to Aaron 'to make atonement for (וּלְכַפֵּר עַל) the Israelites, that there may be no plague among the Israelites by their coming near to the sanctuary' (v. 19). Significantly, the sense of כִּפֶּר here is tied in very much with the idea of 'ransom' (כֹּפֶר), since the goal of the atonement is the

---

due to the use of טהר and חטא in this chapter, it is discussed in the context of purification, though this discussion could be put in the following section on consecration without affecting the observations and conclusions on כִּפֶּר above.

75. See above, nn. 32 and 62.
76. Again, see nn. 32 and 62.
77. As noted above, there is no specific sin or impurity mentioned that has caused the life of the Levite to be threatened; it is simply the general impurity of people, which results in death for those who approach the holiness of the LORD improperly. See the discussion following as well as Num. 18.2-5, 22.
78. Cf. Milgrom, *Numbers*, pp. 369-71.

4. The Verb כִּפֶּר in Contexts of Impurity

prevention of the LORD's wrath.[79] Exodus 30 provides a helpful parallel in this regard. In this text the Israelites take a census. Not only does the census put them at risk of experiencing *a plague* from the LORD (Exod. 30.12; cf. Num. 8.19), but the verb כִּפֶּר is used here to refer to the effecting of a כֹּפֶר-payment, as evidenced by the occurrence of the phrase 'ransom for his life' (כֹּפֶר נַפְשׁוֹ) in Exod. 30.12, paralleled by 'to ransom/make atonement for your lives' (לְכַפֵּר עַל־נַפְשֹׁתֵיכֶם) in v. 16:

> The LORD said to Moses, 'When you take the census of the people of Israel, then each shall give a *ransom for his life* (כֹּפֶר נַפְשׁוֹ) to the LORD when you number them, *that there be no plague among them* (וְלֹא־יִהְיֶה בָהֶם נֶגֶף) when you number them... And you shall take the atonement money from the people of Israel, and shall appoint it for the service of the tent of meeting; that it may bring the people of Israel to remembrance before the LORD, so as *to make atonement for your lives* (לְכַפֵּר עַל־נַפְשֹׁתֵיכֶם).' (Exod. 30.12, 16)[80]

כִּפֶּר in these instances thus refers to the effecting of a כֹּפֶר payment.

On the other hand, however, it may also be noted that immediately after the Israelites lay their hands on the Levites (Num. 8.10) to atone for them (לְכַפֵּר עַל־בְּנֵי יִשְׂרָאֵל; v. 19), the Levites lay their hands on the sacrificial bulls so that the bulls may atone for the Levites (לְכַפֵּר עַל־הַלְוִיִּם; v. 12).[81] Though the analogy eventually breaks down (the Levites are not sacrificed on the altar), the parallels are still significant, and suggest that as the Levites served to ransom the Israelites from the wrath of the Lord, so too the bulls ransom the Levites from that same wrath. In short, the כִּפֶּר-rite for the Levites in Numbers 8 serves not simply to purify them, but to ransom their lives from certain death, and in this way to effect כֹּפֶר for them.[82]

4.4.2. *Consecration and* כִּפֶּר

Since כִּפֶּר only occurs in consecration contexts which involve the contents of the tabernacle or those who work within it (i.e. Aaron and his sons), the comments made above on the purification of the Levites—who were also preparing for tabernacle work—may be profitably carried over to the

---

79. Milgrom, *Numbers*, p. 370.

80. One may also compare Num. 25.6-13 where Phinehas performs כִּפֶּר for the idolatrous Israelites by slaying Zimri and the Midianite woman, thus checking the plague that had spread among the people, and 2 Sam. 21.1-14, where David must perform כִּפֶּר for the bloodguilt of Saul, which has resulted in a famine on the land (Milgrom, *Numbers*, p. 370). In each instance, those who are subject to the LORD's wrath (Exod. 30.12-16), or who are presently experiencing it (Num. 25.6-13; 2 Sam. 21.1-14), require that כִּפֶּר be made for them, that is, the effecting of כִּפֶּר on their behalf.

81. Milgrom, *Numbers*, p. 369.

82. See n. 73 above for further clarification on the relationship between purification and ransom.

instances of consecration where כִּפֶּר occurs. In short, the person or object for which the כִּפֶּר-rite is effected is in need not only of cleansing, but of a כִּפֶּר-arrangement as well.[83]

4.5. *Summary*

The purpose of this chapter has been to consider the verb כִּפֶּר in purification and consecration contexts. It began with an examination of the verbs used in purification contexts (viz. טִהַר and חִטֵּא) and then compared these with each other and with כִּפֶּר. It was seen that the factitive occurrences of טהר (piel or hithpael) and the privative occurrences of חטא (piel or hithpael) were more or less synonymous. Due to their synonymous nature, these terms manifested the same similarities and differences when compared with כִּפֶּר. On the one hand, both verbs appeared in close conjunction with כִּפֶּר, and it was concluded that כִּפֶּר does involve an element of purification in these instances. On the other hand, it was also seen that these terms differed from כִּפֶּר in at least three ways: (1) טִהַר and חִטֵּא in the piel are always followed by a direct object, not a preposition,[84] while כִּפֶּר is predominantly followed by the prepositions עַל or בְּעַד;[85] this was due to the fact that the first two terms refer simply to purification, while כִּפֶּר refers to a rite that is executed on behalf of the person or object in need of purification; (2) טהר and חטא can occur in the hithpael with the one in need of cleansing as subject, and חטא occurs once with a clean person as subject (Num. 19.19), while כִּפֶּר only takes the priest, or Moses (Lev. 8.15), as subject; (3) טהר and חטא can occur in contexts where either blood or water is the means of cleansing, while כִּפֶּר only occurs in contexts where blood is involved, that is, where a sacrifice is made. This last point was seen to be especially important, since it suggests that there is something about sacrifice, and more specifically, the

---

83. A possible objection in this regard is that this would make impersonal objects, such as the altar, in need of a כִּפֶּר-arrangement, which at first glance seems unlikely. In response, it may be noted with Kiuchi (*Purification Offering*, p. 91) that personal and impersonal objects are often treated similarly in the priestly material with respect to purification and consecration: 'The priestly writer(s) hardly distinguishes between human and non-human objects in the contexts of purification and sanctification. For instance, Aaron and the priests ought to be holy just like the altars (cp. Exod. 29.33 with 29.37). Also not only Aaron and the priests but also their garments are said to become holy (Exod. 29.21). Similarly, the ritual procedure for the leper (Lev 14.2ff.) resembles closely that for a house infected by disease (Lev 14.49ff.).' In sum, because personal and impersonal objects are often treated similarly in the priestly material with respect to purification and consecration, it presents no special problem to see impersonal objects as being in need of a כִּפֶּר-arrangement. See further the discussion in the Appendix.

84. Again, for Exod. 29.36, see n. 17.

85. See above, n. 25.

blood of sacrifice, that is fundamental to the meaning of כִּפֶּר in purification contexts. It was concluded that in purification contexts, כִּפֶּר refers to a sacrificial rite, carried out by the priest on behalf of the person or object in need of cleansing, that results in that person or object becoming pure. The verb was thus tentatively translated with 'to effect purgation'.

The next verb to be considered and compared with כִּפֶּר was קדשׁ, the verb used in consecration contexts. As with טהר and חטא above, it was seen that קדשׁ occurs in close conjunction with כִּפֶּר, and that כִּפֶּר does involve an element of consecration in these instances. It was further noted, however, that קדשׁ also manifested the same three differences with כִּפֶּר as did טהר and חטא above: (1) קדשׁ in the piel is always followed by the direct object, and refers simply to the consecration of that object, while כִּפֶּר is predominantly followed in these contexts by the prepositions עַל or בַּעַד;[86] (2) קדשׁ occurs with non-priests as subject of the verb, while כִּפֶּר only occurs in these contexts with priests or Moses as subject; (3) קדשׁ is used to indicate consecration taking place in a wide variety of contexts, in most of which sacrificial blood plays no part, while כִּפֶּר only occurs in conjunction with a sacrifice and anointing with blood in these contexts. Once more, this was seen to be especially significant, insofar as it suggests that sacrifice, and in particular the blood of the sacrifice, is central to the meaning of כִּפֶּר, though not to the meaning of קדשׁ. It was then concluded that in consecration contexts, כִּפֶּר refers to a sacrificial rite carried out by the priest on behalf of the person or object in need of consecration. As a result of the rite, that person or object becomes holy. Given the similarities between purification and consecration contexts, it was suggested that the consecration of a person or object was also a cleansing (though of a more intense manner than purification contexts). For this reason it was again suggested that the verb כִּפֶּר could tentatively be rendered with 'to effect purgation' in these contexts.

Finally, it was considered whether the rendering 'to effect purgation' was sufficient. The basic conclusion was that an element of כֹּפֶר was probably also involved in the use of כִּפֶּר in these contexts. In the context of purification from a major impurity, it was argued that a כֹּפֶר is necessary since the person with a major impurity had defiled the tabernacle (albeit unintentionally), which put them in the same position as one who had committed an inadvertent sin, namely, in a position of needing a כֹּפֶר (see Chapter 3). In the context of those preparing for service in the tabernacle, be it those who were purified (namely, the Levites) or those who were consecrated (namely, Aaron and his sons), it was argued that the lives of those entering such service were put at risk due to the general impurity of people relative to the holy, and that consequently the כִּפֶּר-rite not only cleansed them, it also

---

86. Again, see above, n. 25.

ransomed their lives from certain death. In short, the כִּפֶּר-rite in these contexts accomplished both purgation and ransoming.

Having considered the use of כִּפֶּר to address sin in the previous chapter, and to address impurity in this chapter, we now turn to consider the relationship between sin and impurity, and how clarifying this relationship might provide insight into the meaning of כִּפֶּר.

Part III

SIN, IMPURITY, AND כִּפֶּר

5

THE RELATIONSHIP BETWEEN SIN AND IMPURITY AND ITS RELEVANCE TO כִּפֶּר

In Parts I and II we have focused on the meaning of כִּפֶּר in sin contexts (Chapters 1 to 3) and in contexts involving purification and consecration (Chapter 4). In those contexts involving sin, it was seen that the emphasis of כִּפֶּר is the effecting of a כֹּפֶר-payment on behalf of the guilty. At the same time, however, it was also noted that inadvertent sins would appear to pollute sancta, implying that the כִּפֶּר-rite might refer to purgation as well. In those contexts involving purification or consecration, it was seen that the emphasis of כִּפֶּר is that of purging impurity. In instances of purification from major impurity, however, it was argued that כִּפֶּר might also refer to the effecting of a כֹּפֶר-payment, since those who had a major impurity defiled the sancta, thus leaving them in the same position as the inadvertent sinner (viz. in need of a כֹּפֶר). It was likewise argued that כִּפֶּר could also refer to a כֹּפֶר-payment in instances of consecration (i.e. in those instances where people were preparing for service in the tabernacle), since in their natural state they were not pure enough for such service and would risk immediate death if they tried. For this reason, the כִּפֶּר-rite not only cleansed them, it also rescued their lives from certain destruction, and in this way effected כֹּפֶר for them. In all of these cases, then, it was suggested that כִּפֶּר refers both to the effecting of a כֹּפֶר-payment and to purgation, that is, it refers both to rescuing from punishment and to cleansing impurity.

This is in fact not surprising, given that the priestly literature understands sin and impurity to be closely related. The Day of Atonement rituals, for example, were meant to atone (כִּפֶּר) for both sin *and* impurity:

> ...thus [the priest] shall make atonement (וְכִפֶּר) for the holy place, because of the uncleannesses (מִטֻּמְאֹת) of the people of Israel, and because of their transgressions (וּמִפִּשְׁעֵיהֶם), all their sins (לְכָל־חַטֹּאתָם)... (Lev. 16.16a)

Moreover, several texts speak of *sins* which have a *polluting* effect

> 'Do not defile yourselves (אַל־תִּטַּמְּאוּ) by any of these [sexual sins], for by all these the nations I am casting out before you defiled themselves (נִטְמְאוּ); and the land became defiled (וַתִּטְמָא הָאָרֶץ)... (Lev. 18.24-25a)

> I myself will set my face against [the one who gives his children to Molech], and will cut him off from among his people, because he has given one of his children to Molech, defiling (טַמֵּא) my sanctuary and profaning (וּלְחַלֵּל) my holy name. (Lev. 20.3)

> You shall not thus [i.e. by accepting ransom for a murderer] pollute (וְלֹא־תַחֲנִיפוּ) the land in which you live; for blood pollutes (יַחֲנִיף) the land, and no atonement can be made for the land, for the blood that is shed in it, except by the blood of the one who shed it. You shall not defile (וְלֹא תְטַמֵּא) the land in which you live... (Num. 35.33-34a)

And finally, people are not *cleansed* simply of *impurities*, but also of *sins*:

> For on this day shall atonement be made for you, to cleanse you (לְטַהֵר אֶתְכֶם); from all your sins you shall be clean before the LORD (מִכֹּל חַטֹּאתֵיכֶם לִפְנֵי יְהוָה תִּטְהָרוּ). (Lev. 16.30)

While the relatedness of sin and impurity in the priestly system has been evident, clarifying the exact nature of this relationship has proved more difficult. This problem is especially evident with the verb כִּפֶּר, which occurs in both contexts, and yet which is difficult to translate the same way in each. The focus of Part III (Chapter 5), therefore, is to consider the relationship between sin and impurity with special reference to the use and translation of the verb כִּפֶּר.[1] We will begin by looking at the relationship between sin and impurity by itself. The most thorough analyses in this regard remain those of David Hoffmann and Adolph Büchler (writing near the beginning of the twentieth century), and David Wright and Jonathan Klawans (writing at the end of the twentieth century and the beginning of the twenty-first century). Our discussion will begin with an overview and analysis of these authors. The insights gained from this analysis, and in particular from the work of Wright, will then serve as the basis for considering why כִּפֶּר occurs in each of these contexts and how best to translate it.

---

1. A related area, which has received much attention lately but which is beyond the scope of this chapter, is the relationship between sin and impurity in ancient Judaism. Jacob Neusner has been one of the most prolific writers in this regard; see, for example, his *The Idea of Purity in Ancient Judaism* (Leiden: E.J. Brill, 1973); *A History of the Mishnaic Law of Purities* (22 vols.; Leiden: E.J. Brill, 1974–77); *Purity in Rabbinic Judaism: A Systemic Account* (Atlanta: Scholars Press, 1994). An important critique of Neusner's understanding of the relationship between sin and impurity in ancient Judaism and its relationship to the biblical material can be found in Milgrom, *Leviticus 1–16*, pp. 1004-1009. For a more recent analysis of the ideas of sin and impurity in ancient Judaism, and how they relate to one another, see Jonathan Klawans, 'Idolatry, Incest, and Impurity: Moral Defilement in Ancient Judaism', *JSJ* 29 (1998), pp. 391-415, and *Impurity and Sin in Ancient Judaism* (Oxford: Oxford University Press, 2000). A précis of this last work can be found in Klawans, 'The Impurity of Immorality in Ancient Judaism', *JJS* 48 (1997), pp. 1-16. For further references to literature dealing with sin and impurity in ancient Judaism, see Klawans, *Impurity and Sin*, p. 163 n. 1.

5. *The Relationship between Sin and Impurity*

5.1. *Approaches to the Relationship between Sin and Impurity*

5.1.1. *David Hoffmann*[2]

Hoffmann, drawing upon earlier rabbinic teaching, divides impurities into two groups.[3] The first of these, טומאת הקדושות (or טומאת הנפשות), stands in opposition to holiness (i.e. holy living) and is brought about by sinful behavior, for example, seeking out mediums or spiritists.[4] (It is for this reason that some scholars have described this type of impurity as 'moral' impurity.[5]) It is important to note that to Hoffmann this type of impurity is not simply symbolic, but a real, 'concrete' impurity, which separates the defiled person from God.[6] Moreover, Hoffmann states that there is no means of purification for this type of impurity.[7]

The second type of impurity, טומאת הגויות, stands in opposition to purity (as opposed to holiness), and is the focus of the majority of the laws in Leviticus 11–15.[8] This type of impurity does not result from sin; rather, the sources of this type of impurity are dead people and animals, various flows (e.g. the blood of the parturient or the person suffering genital discharges), and leprosy.[9] (In contrast to 'moral' impurity, then, this type of impurity has been labeled 'ritual' or 'levitical' impurity.[10]) Hoffmann also distinguishes this type of impurity from moral impurity in that it can be cleansed by means of an act of purification.[11] Finally, whereas moral impurity is an impurity that results from sin, Hoffmann understands ritual impurity to be an impurity that symbolizes sin. Thus the three sources of impurity outlined above symbolize three different types of sin: (1) the impurity that comes from dead

---

2. D. Hoffmann, *Das Buch Leviticus* (2 vols.; Berlin: M. Poppelauer, 1905–1906).
3. Hoffmann, *Leviticus*, I, pp. 303-304; see also p. 340.
4. Hoffmann, *Leviticus*, I, p. 303, and *Leviticus*, II, p. 59.
5. See Büchler (§5.1.2) and Klawans (§5.1.3), below.
6. Thus on Lev. 19.31: אל תבקשו וגו׳, suchet und befraget sie nicht; denn ihr würdet euch durch solches Treiben nur verunreinigen, und zwar nicht blos symbolisch, sondern concret... Ihr würdet dadurch eure Person, Körper und Seele, von Gott ab- und dem Wahne und der Unsittlichkeit zuwenden' (Hoffmann, *Leviticus*, II, p. 59).
7. Hoffmann, *Leviticus*, I, p. 303.
8. Hoffmann (*Leviticus*, I, pp. 303-304) includes the animals of Lev. 11 in the first category of impurity, stating that they are listed with impurities of the second type in Lev. 11–15 only because many of these animals can produce this second type of impurity after their death (p. 304).
9. Hoffmann, *Leviticus*, I, p. 315. See a slightly different breakdown of the sources of the second type of impurity on p. 304, where he includes purification implements ('Reinigungs-Utensilien') such as the water for impurity (Num. 19.21) or the goat sent into the wilderness (Lev. 16.26) as further sources of impurity.
10. See Büchler (§5.1.2) and Klawans (§5.1.3), below.
11. Hoffmann, *Leviticus*, I, pp. 303-304.

people and animals symbolizes sin against God; (2) the impurity that comes from various flows (e.g. the blood of the parturient or the person suffering genital discharges) symbolizes sin against oneself; and (3) the impurity that comes from leprosy symbolizes sin against other people (social sins).[12]

Positively, Hoffmann does well to distinguish between those impurities which arise from moral wrongdoing (e.g. seeking out mediums) and those which arise from amoral circumstances (e.g. dead corpses). As will become evident in the following, this bipartite distinction of impurity is axiomatic to more recent discussions of impurity.

At the same time, however, Hoffmann's bipartite distinction is not distinct enough. To be specific, Hoffmann's schema does not differentiate between impurity that arises from intentional sins and that which arises from unintentional sins.[13] As will become evident below in the discussion of David Wright (§5.1.4), this distinction is crucial, and inattention at this point actually obscures the relationship between sin and impurity. Moreover, while Hoffmann is correct to identify a relationship between 'ritual impurity' and sin, his suggestion of a symbolic correspondence between the three sources of ritual impurity and three different types of sin is unconvincing, primarily because there is a lack of objective criteria given to support the distinctions made.

5.1.2. *Adolph Büchler*[14]

Like Hoffmann, though using different terminology, Adolph Büchler also sees a bipartite division in the realm of impurity, distinguishing between 'levitical' and 'moral' impurity.[15] He contrasts these differing types of impurity in four ways. First, moral impurities, as their name suggests, are the

---

12. Hoffmann, *Leviticus*, I, p. 315. In support of this correspondence between sin and impurity, he begins by noting that the sins which cause God's glory to depart are called impurities (citing Lev. 16.16 [p. 315]). He later underscores his position by noting that the prophets describe cleansing from sin by using the same language as the priestly literature does when describing cleansing from impurity: 'Einen klaren Beweis, dass die Unreinheit nichts Anderes als ein Bild der Sünde ist, sehen wir darin, dass die Propheten für die Reinigung von der Sünde dieselben Ausdrücke gebrauchen, welche die Thora für die Reinigung von der levitischen Unreinheit gebraucht. "Badet euch, reinigt euch!" "Ich werde auf euch reines Wasser sprengen, und ihr werdet rein werden von allen euren Sünden" ', p. 318).

13. For the impurity that results from unintentional sins, see §3.1.1 above.

14. Adolph Büchler, *Studies in Sin and Atonement in the Rabbinic Literature of the First Century* (New York: Ktav, 1928).

15. See Büchler, *Studies in Sin*, Chapter 3 ('The Defiling Force of Sin in the Bible'), pp. 212-69. Büchler was not consistent in his use of terms, and sometimes referred to moral impurity as 'spiritual' or 'religious' defilement (Klawans, *Impurity and Sin*, p. 6, citing Büchler, *Studies in Sin*, pp. 214, 229).

5. *The Relationship between Sin and Impurity*

result of some moral lapse, whereas levitical impurities are not.[16] Second, moral impurities are cleansed via punishment, while levitical impurities are cleansed ritually (i.e. by bathing, laundering, etc.).[17] Third, moral impurities are not contagious, whereas levitical impurities can be.[18] Finally, the biblical use of impurity language to discuss 'moral' impurity is symbolic or figurative, whereas this is not the case with 'levitical' impurities.[19]

Despite the difference in terminology, the general similarities between Büchler and Hoffmann are obvious: there is a bipartite division of impurity, the first type of which results from moral wrongdoing, while the second type arises from amoral conditions. Moreover, Büchler is similar to Hoffmann in stating that moral impurity is not capable of being cleansed via priestly

---

16. Thus one of Büchler's (*Studies in Sin*, p. 220) proofs that the defilement of the land in Num. 35.33-34 is 'moral' impurity, and not to be compared with the 'levitical' impurity of the camp in Num. 5.3 and Deut. 23.15 (14), is that the impurities of the latter two involve no moral indiscretion. So on Deut. 23 he comments: 'No crime of any kind, no sin of immorality or of a forbidden marriage was committed, the soil is not declared to be defiled, and no punishment to expiate the deed or the condition of the land is imposed upon the man concerned. Not a sinful act, but the presence of the levitically unclean person in the camp is here offensive to the God of Israel who is present among his people.'

17. In discussing the defilement of the land that comes about through sexual sin (Lev. 18.1-23), idolatry (Ezek. 36.17, 18; Isa. 30.22), and sacrificing children to Molech—defilement which Büchler classifies as moral defilement—he notes (*Studies in Sin*, p. 216) that 'none of the ways and methods of purification known from the Pentateuch was applied in the removal of [such] impurity, but instead the complete vomiting out of the Canaanites, and later on of the Israelites themselves'. Later, in commenting upon the effect of the 'moral impurity' of idolatry upon the land (Ezek. 22.3-4), he notes that the uncleanness is consumed by the dispersion of the people (v. 15): 'The defilement conveyed by one of the two grave sins attaches itself to the perpetrators of it, and when, as a punishment, God scatters the sinners among the nations, He purges their sins…' (p. 225).

18. In discussing the moral impurity of evil lips, Büchler (*Studies in Sin*, p. 235) comments: 'It need not be especially emphasized that, though the terms of levitical uncleanness were figuratively applied to moral impurity, the ideas of levitical defilement were not transferred to the contamination by sin. Not even the gravest crime, like that of murder, would prevent the sinner from approaching the altar and seizing its horns (Exod. 21, 14; cf. 1 Reg. 1, 50-53; 2, 28-31), and he did not defile thereby the Sanctuary and its altar; and many a man soiled with sins entered the Temple to confess his transgression before God and to pray for forgiveness.'

19. Büchler (*Studies in Sin*, p. 237) comments: 'There was, certainly, in the minds of the prophets and Psalmists nothing to connect the character of sin with that of levitical impurity, except that the inward effect of the moral and religious contamination of the heart was illustrated by the outward defilement of the body, and the estrangement from God and his will by the physical separation from His Sanctuary, the terms defile, unclean, polluted, uncleanness and filth being applied *figuratively* to grave transgressions' (emphasis added).

means, while levitical impurity can be. He is also more specific at this point, however, arguing that while moral impurity cannot be cleansed via normal priestly means, it can be cleansed by means of punishment.[20] Büchler is also more specific than Hoffmann when he states that moral impurity is not contagious, whereas ritual impurity can be. Finally, Büchler differs from Hoffmann in seeing the impurity that results from moral impurities as metaphorical, and not literal.[21] This last point is addressed by Klawans and is considered in more detail in the following section.

Unfortunately Büchler, like Hoffmann, fails to make a distinction between the impurity that arises from unintentional sins and that which arises from intentional sins, nor does he discuss the differences between minor levitical impurities and major levitical impurities. This is perhaps because the main goal of the relevant chapters is to prove that there is a distinction to be made between 'levitical' and 'moral' impurity, and thus little attention is given to the distinctions within these categories. Nonetheless, this lack of specificity results in important similarities between the realms of sin and impurity remaining unnoticed.

5.1.3. Jonathan Klawans

One of the most thorough recent attempts to describe the relationship between sin and impurity is that of Jonathan Klawans.[22] Klawans follows the general approach to the relationship between sin and impurity taken by Hoffmann and Büchler, and it is for this reason that his work is considered ahead of the earlier work of Wright.[23] His analysis is far more extensive than that of Hoffmann or Büchler, however, and for this reason it will be considered in some detail.

Like Hoffmann and Büchler, Klawans also distinguishes between two types of impurity. The first, 'ritual impurity', 'results from direct or indirect contact with any of a number of natural sources including childbirth (Lev. 12.1-8), scale disease (Lev. 13.1–14.32), genital discharges (Lev. 15.1-33)',

20. See above, n. 17.
21. See the use of 'figuratively' in nn. 18 and 19 above. Klawans (*Impurity and Sin*, p. 174 n. 73) acknowledges that Büchler does describe moral impurity as figurative in some contexts, but argues that this is not always the case; as, for example, in his discussion of 'the defilement of the land by the three cardinal sins' (citing Büchler, *Studies in Sin*, pp. 221-30). Even here, however, Büchler (*Studies in Sin*, p. 226) says that the defilement of bloodshed is 'in parallelism with "filth"' and 'applied figuratively' in Ezek. 24.6-9, 11. It might be that Büchler was not consistent on this point.
22. Klawans, 'Impurity of Immorality'; 'Idolatry, Incest, and Impurity'; and *Impurity and Sin in Ancient Judaism*. The discussion above will interact predominantly with the last of these, which is the most thorough and which incorporates the insights of the first two articles.
23. For Klawans's interaction with Wright, see n. 50 below.

and so on, or 'comes about as a by-product of certain purificatory procedures (e.g. Lev. 16.28; Num. 19.8)'.[24] This type of impurity has three distinct characteristics: '(1) The sources of ritual impurity are generally natural and more or less unavoidable.[25] (2) It is not sinful to contract these impurities.[26] And (3) these impurities convey an impermanent contagion'.[27] Resolution of this type of impurity comes about through various purificatory procedures, 'from waiting until sundown, to bathing bodies, washing clothes, and performing sacrificial rites'.[28]

Klawans labels the second type of impurity as 'moral impurity'. It is *moral* impurity because it 'results from what are believed to be immoral acts', and it is moral *impurity* because it 'results from committing certain acts so heinous that they are explicitly referred to in biblical sources as defiling', namely, 'sexual sins (e.g. Lev. 18.24-30), idolatry (e.g. Lev. 19.31; 20.1-3), and bloodshed (e.g. Num. 35.33-34)'.[29] Such behaviors 'bring about an impurity that *morally*—but not *ritually*—defiles the sinner (Lev. 18.24), the land of Israel (Lev. 18.25; Ezek. 36.17), and the sanctuary of God

---

24. Klawans, *Impurity and Sin*, p. 23.

25. Commenting later upon this point, Klawans (*Impurity and Sin*, p. 24) notes: 'The "more or less" is important here, because certain contacts are relatively avoidable: in Leviticus 11.43, for instance, Israelites are urged not to defile themselves with certain impure animals. But, discharge, disease, and death are, alas, unavoidable. And as has been noted, some impurities are not only unavoidable, but obligatory. Israelites are obligated to bury their dead, though priests are allowed to contract corpse impurity only in certain cases (Lev. 21.1-4). Yet even priests, along with all Israelites, are obligated to reproduce (Gen. 1.28; 9.7). And of course priests are obligated to perform cultic procedures that leave them defiled as a result.'

26. Klawans (*Impurity and Sin*, p. 24) notes that 'this idea proceeds logically from the observations drawn above', since natural processes such as menstruation cannot be prohibited (he cites Tikva Frymer-Kensky, 'Pollution, Purification, and Purgation in Biblical Israel', in Carol L. Meyers and M. O'Connor [eds.], *The Word of the Lord Shall Go Forth: Essays in Honor of David Noel Freedman in Celebration of his Sixtieth Birthday* [Winona Lake, IN: Eisenbrauns, 1983], pp. 399-414 [403]; E.P. Sanders, *Jewish Law from Jesus to the Mishnah: Five Studies* [London: SCM Press, 1990], pp. 140-42; and David P. Wright, 'The Spectrum of Priestly Impurity', in Gary A. Anderson and Saul M. Olyan [eds.], *Priesthood and Cult in Ancient Israel* [JSOTSup, 125; Sheffield: JSOT Press, 1991], pp. 150-81 [157]).

27. Klawans, *Impurity and Sin*, p. 23. With reference to this last point, Klawans (p. 25) notes that some impurities gained through contact can last until sundown (e.g. Lev. 15.5, 21), while more severe impurities can last up to a week (e.g. Num. 19). When someone suffers a defiling condition (e.g. leprosy or childbirth) the impurity could last longer (e.g. 33 or 66 days for childbirth; Lev. 12.4, 5). Nonetheless, 'we hear of no form of ritual impurity that does not have purificatory procedures... Even when long-lasting, the status of ritual defilement is an impermanent one' (p. 26).

28. Klawans, *Impurity and Sin*, p. 26.

29. Klawans, *Impurity and Sin*, p. 26.

(Lev. 20.3; Ezek. 5.11)',[30] which in turn results in the expulsion of the people from the land (Lev. 20.3; Ezek. 5.11).[31]

Klawans then delineates five specific differences between moral and ritual defilement:

> (1) Whereas ritual impurity is generally not sinful, moral impurity is a direct consequence of grave sin. (2) Whereas ritual impurity often results in a contagious defilement, there is no contact-contagion associated with moral impurity... (3) Whereas ritual impurity results in an impermanent defilement, moral impurity leads to a long-lasting, if not permanent, degradation of the sinner and, eventually, of the land of Israel.[32] (4) Whereas ritual impurity can be ameliorated by rites of purification, that is not the case for moral impurity; moral purity is achieved by punishment, atonement, or, best of all, by refraining from committing morally impure acts in the first place.[33] (5) In addition to these phenomenological differences, there are also terminological distinctions drawn in the texts themselves. Although the term impure (טמא) is used in both contexts, the terms 'abomination' (תועבה) and 'pollute' (חנף) are used with regard to the sources of moral impurity, but not with regard to the sources of ritual impurity.[34]

These differences are then summarized in the following chart:[35]

Impurity Type	Source	Effect	Resolution
Ritual	Bodily flows, corpses, etc.	Temporary, contagious impurity	Bathing/waiting
Moral	Sins: idolatry, incest, murder	Desecration of sinners, land, and sanctuary	Atonement or punishment, and ultimately exile

Having summarized these differences, Klawans goes on to consider moral impurity more closely in an effort to support the distinctions made above. He begins by summarizing the biblical evidence which illustrates that sexual immorality, idolatry, and murder do indeed defile the sinner, the sanctuary, and the land, and then seeks to establish that this impurity is of a different order than ritual impurity.[36] He notes, for example, that it is clear from Leviticus 18 that sexual sins defile the sinner (vv. 24, 30) as well as the land (vv. 25-28), whereas 'Ritual impurity, in contrast, is never conveyed to, or

---

30. Klawans, *Impurity and Sin*, p. 26 (emphasis his).
31. Klawans, *Impurity and Sin*, p. 26.
32. Citing Frymer-Kensky, 'Pollution', pp. 406-407. See below, however, for evaluation of this comment.
33. This comment implies that atonement is not required for ritual impurity; his summary chart implies the same. See discussion below and n. 46.
34. Klawans, *Impurity and Sin*, p. 26.
35. Klawans, *Impurity and Sin*, p. 27.
36. Klawans, *Impurity and Sin*, pp. 27-31.

5. *The Relationship between Sin and Impurity* 147

contracted from, the land'.[37] After arguing the same for contexts of idolatry and murder, Klawans describes moral impurity and its effects as follows:

> Moral impurity is best understood as a potent force unleashed by certain sinful human actions. The force unleashed defiles the sinner, the sanctuary, and the land, even though the sinner is not ritually impure and does not ritually defile... As a result of this defilement, the sinners and the land experience a degradation in status.[38]

Moreover, this degradation also differs from the defilement of ritual impurity in that it is more or less permanent:

> The Holiness Code gives no indication of any methods for the removal of these defilements. Ablutions, as we have seen, are not efficacious here. The Day of Atonement service involves the purgation of the altar and shrine, which removes the stain left by sin upon the sanctuary (Lev. 16.11-19). This service also includes other sacrifices which atone for the people (16.20-22). But these sacrifices do not appear to purify grave sinners, or the land upon which the grave sins were committed. Such sinners either live out their lives in a degraded state (like the guilty adulteress) or suffer capital punishment (like apprehended murderers). The land, it appears, likewise suffers a permanent degradation.[39]

For all of these reasons, Klawans maintains a sharp distinction between ritual impurity and moral impurity. At the same time, however, he stresses that there is one way in which they are similar, namely, both impurities are *real*. Klawans notes that moral defilement is 'commonly understood by scholars as either metaphorical or figurative',[40] that is, 'no real defilement or purification is actually taking place', simply a figurative or metaphorical one.[41] To Klawans, however, this view is unjustified, as each type of impurity has serious ramifications. He argues:

> In the case of ritual impurity, a real, physical process or event (e.g., death or menstruation) has a perceived effect: impermanent contagion that affects people and certain objects within their reach. In the case of moral impurity, a real, physical process or event (e.g., child sacrifice or adultery) has a different perceived effect: a noncontagious defilement that affects persons, the land, and the sanctuary. In both cases, the impurity is conveyed by contact: ritual impurity is conveyed by direct and indirect human contact, and moral impurity is conveyed to the land by sins that take place upon it. In both cases, moreover, there are practical legal ramifications. The ritually impure person

---

37. Klawans, *Impurity and Sin*, p. 27.
38. Klawans, *Impurity and Sin*, p. 30.
39. Klawans, *Impurity and Sin*, p. 30. As noted further below, this last statement requires modification in the light of Num. 35.33 (cf. also Deut. 21.8-9).
40. Klawans, *Impurity and Sin*, p. 32 (and see nn. 72 and 73 there for references).
41. Klawans, *Impurity and Sin*, p. 33.

must keep away from sacred things, and in some cases must be barred from certain precincts. The morally impure person may be subject to capital punishment... When the land has been defiled to a great extent, then its people are exiled. Though the sources and modes of transfer of moral and ritual impurity differ, we are dealing, nonetheless, with two analogous *perceptions of contagion*, each of which brings about effects of legal and social consequence.[42]

In sum, Klawans presentation may be considered in terms of two main arguments: (1) there is a clear distinction between ritual impurity and moral impurity; (2) at the same time, these share in common the fact that both are real, and, in particular, that moral impurity is not figurative, but just as real as ritual impurity.

As for the first of these, the distinction between ritual and moral impurity is generally agreed upon, and Klawans has demonstrated on the whole that these are not the same. At the same time, however, questions may be raised with the third distinction that Klawans proposes. It is as follows: 'Whereas ritual impurity results in an impermanent defilement, moral impurity leads to a long-lasting, if not permanent, degradation of the sinner and, eventually, of the land of Israel'.[43] Numbers 35.33, however, indicates that the land may be purified from the defilement of homicide when the blood of the slayer is spilled upon it. The degradation in this instance is thus not permanent, nor is it necessarily long-lasting.

A further critique may also be made of the chart that Klawans provides to summarize the differences between ritual and moral impurity. In particular, the chart fails to make important and necessary distinctions within the realms of ritual and moral impurity. The bottom half of the chart, for example, which deals with moral impurity, only lists three sins—idolatry, incest, and murder—which pollute. With the exception of homicide, which may be either intentional or unintentional (Num. 35), these sins are all intentional and flagrant transgressions—what Klawans labels as 'grave' sins.[44] And yet the priestly literature is very concerned about *unintentional* sins (בִּשְׁגָגָה) that also pollute (Lev. 4.1–5.13); it would thus seem proper to add these texts to the chart as a source of moral impurity,[45] and to specify that sacrificial atonement is called for in these instances.

---

42. Klawans, *Impurity and Sin*, p. 34 (emphasis his).
43. Klawans, *Impurity and Sin*, p. 26, citing Frymer-Kensky, 'Pollution', pp. 406-407.
44. Klawans, *Impurity and Sin*, p. 26.
45. The defiling nature of these sins has been argued most thoroughly by Jacob Milgrom (see the discussion in §3.1.1; see below for the similar conclusions of Wright, n. 58). Klawans (*Impurity and Sin*, pp. 14-15; see also his summary on p. 41) is aware of Milgrom's discussion in this regard, though he neither refutes Milgrom's position, nor incorporates the sins of Lev. 4.1–5.13 into his discussion.

5. *The Relationship between Sin and Impurity* 149

A similar distinction can be made in the top half of the chart, which deals with ritual impurities. As set out by Klawans, the top half of the chart indicates that ritual impurity is resolved via bathing or waiting. While this may be true of *minor* impurities, *major* impurities always require sacrificial atonement, just as is required of the unintentional sins in Lev. 4.1–5.13.[46] In short, sacrificial atonement is a necessary aspect of addressing major ritual impurities as well as unintentional moral impurities.

This leads to a final observation. By failing to make distinctions within the realms of ritual and moral impurity, important similarities between the two realms are not identified. In particular, it has just been noted that major ritual impurities and inadvertent moral impurities both require sacrificial atonement. The reason for this similarity is explored further below in the discussion of Wright, and is indeed crucial to a proper understanding of כִּפֶּר. For the moment, however, it is enough to note *that the same ritual procedure (sacrifice) is prescribed for the cleansing of the ritual impurity that stems from a major impurity and for the moral impurity that stems from unintentional sin*. This is not to imply that Klawans is incorrect in distinguishing between moral and ritual impurity; it is simply to clarify that there are similarities between the two realms of impurity that his more general breakdown does not identify.

The major support for Klawans' second argument above (viz. that moral impurity is real and not simply metaphorical) comes from the fact that moral impurity, like ritual impurity, has tangible effects (viz. upon the sinner, land, and sanctuary).[47] As noted above, it is less clear that this is a permanent or even long-lasting degradation, as Klawans argues, since Numbers 35 indicates that land defiled by murder can be cleansed by the blood of the murderer (v. 33; cf. Deut. 21.8-9). Nonetheless, Klawans overall thesis in this regard seems correct. Indeed, by pointing out that both types of impurity bring about 'effects of legal and social consequence',[48] Klawans underscores

---

46. For the occurrence of sacrifice with major impurities, see above, §4.4.1; see also §5.1.4 below. To be fair, Klawans (*Impurity and Sin*, p. 26) does acknowledge earlier that sacrificial rites are part of the procedure for cleansing ritual impurity, though for some reason he does not include this in his chart.

47. Klawans (*Impurity and Sin*, p. 41) states in his conclusion: 'Moral impurity cannot profitably be understood as either metaphorical or figurative. Even though [the] moral defilement described in Leviticus 18 is of a different sort than the ritual impurity described in Leviticus 11–15, the sinners, land, and sanctuary are defiled by these sins in a very substantial way. This defilement, in turn, brings about tangible results for sinners, the sanctuary, and the land. Sinners are subject to a permanent debasement, if not capital punishment. The sanctuary is subject to defilement along the lines drawn by Jacob Milgrom. Regarding the land, if the defilement becomes severe enough, the people are exiled from it. In the final analysis, the biblical traditions that articulate the concept of moral impurity can and should be taken at face value: sin does indeed defile, in its own way.'

48. Klawans, *Impurity and Sin*, p. 34.

that though their original sources may differ, the end result of each can be similar in the deleterious effects they produce, a point to which we return immediately below.

Thus far, Hoffmann, Büchler, and Klawans have all identified various aspects of the differences between ritual and moral impurity. Unfortunately, none of these discussions adequately address how the priestly distinctions between major and minor impurities, as well as between intentional and unintentional sins, relate to the relationship between ritual and moral impurity. For this reason, we now turn to consider an important article by David P. Wright, who incorporates the differences between minor and major impurities, as well as unintentional and intentional sins, in his discussion of the relationship between ritual and moral impurity.

5.1.4. *David P. Wright*[49]

Though Wright also divides impurities into two main types, he leaves the vocabulary of 'ritual/levitical' and 'moral' behind, opting instead for the labels 'tolerated' and 'prohibited'.[50] The chart below, reproduced from Wright, displays this division graphically, as well as the finer distinctions made within these two larger divisions.[51] The lowest grades of impurity are on the left side of the chart, increasing in severity as one moves to the right:

---

49. See especially Wright, 'Spectrum'. This builds upon his earlier article, 'Two Types of Impurity in the Priestly Writings of the Bible', *Koroth* 9, Special Issue (1988), pp. 180-93. See also his 'Unclean and Clean (Old Testament)', in *ABD*, VI, pp. 729-42.

50. In critique of the regular nomenclature of 'ritual/levitical' and 'moral' impurity, Wright ('Spectrum', p. 152 n. 1) explains: 'A careful examination of all impure situations in the priestly rules shows that even the "moral" impurities are "cultic" or "ritual" in part. As we will see in this study, a sort of pollution still arises from these conditions, which requires sacrificial rectification. The term "levitical" essentially means "priestly" and hence confuses matters since "moral" impurity is also a concern of priestly legislation. In other words, the priestly moral impurity can still be called "levitical".' Wright ('Unclean and Clean', pp. 736-37, and 'Two Types', pp. 181-82) had earlier used the term 'permitted' instead of 'tolerated', but given that 'these impurities are allowed, [although] they are not necessarily encouraged' ('Spectrum', p. 158), Wright changed to the term 'tolerated', which is less neutral than 'permitted'. Klawans (*Impurity and Sin*, p. 17), however, finds both terms equally unsatisfactory, since 'many of the defilements so described result not just from permitted activities, but also from activities that are obligatory, including procreation and burial', and since 'What is commanded [in these instances] is not merely "tolerated"; it is, rather, "right and proper", to use Sander's phrase' (the reference here is to Sanders, *Jewish Law*, p. 151). In this regard, Klawans has properly identified that the term 'tolerated' does not apply to all of the *actions* that result in these impurities, for example, procreation. Nonetheless, from the perspective of the *impurity* that results, Wright's terms properly identify that some impurities are allowed (i.e. they are 'tolerated'), while others are not (i.e. they are 'prohibited').

51. Wright, 'Spectrum', p. 153.

5. *The Relationship between Sin and Impurity* 151

Tolerated		Prohibited	
(no distinction between unintentional and intentional)		unintentional	intentional
no sacrifices	individual ad hoc sacrifices	individual, sometimes communal, ad hoc sacrifice	Day of Atonement sacrifices
pollution of person	pollution of sanctuary (outer altar) and person	pollution of sanctuary (outer altar or shrine); 'ritual' personal pollution if deriving from tolerated impurity	pollution of sanctuary (adytum, shrine, outer altar), sometimes land; 'moral' pollution of persons; 'ritual' personal pollution if from tolerated impurity
non communicable to profane; hence, restriction only from sanctuary and sacred	communicable to profane; hence, restriction from the sanctuary and other sacred matters and restriction from or within the (profane) habitation	potential removal from life; restriction from sanctuary and sacred, and sometimes from habitation (if communicable to profane) if the sin derives from a tolerated impurity[52]	removal from life: *kārēt* or capital penalty; in some cases exile; restriction from sanctuary and sacred, and sometimes habitation if sin derives from a permitted impurity (until the penalty takes effect)

Tolerated impurities 'are those usually called "ritual" impurities and are the focus of the priestly (specifically P's) treatment of impurity'.[53] They are dealt with most specifically in Leviticus 11–16 and Numbers 19, and arise from events that are normal to every day life, for example, having a baby (Lev. 12) or coming into contact with the dead (Num. 19); their origin is thus amoral.[54]

These impurities are graded according to three factors: (1) the means required for cleansing them (sacrifice is not required for lesser grades, but is

---

52. The original reads, '…if the sin derives from a tolerated purity'. In a private communication, Wright has indicated that the last word should read 'impurity', and for this reason it has been corrected in the above.
53. Wright, 'Spectrum', p. 151.
54. Wright ('Spectrum', p. 154) does include here some impurities which are prohibited, for example, 'eating or touching some…impure animal carcasses' (for his reasoning, see pp. 165-69). For the difficulty in classifying the dietary laws, and an overview of different approaches, see Klawans, *Impurity and Sin*, pp. 31-32.

required for higher grades); (2) the extent of pollution, that is, whether the pollution did not defile the sanctuary (lesser grades) or whether it did extend to the sanctuary as well (higher grades); and (3) the communicability of the pollution, that is, whether it was non-communicable to the profane sphere, and thus allowed within the camp (but not the sanctuary), or whether it was communicable to the profane, and thus prohibited from both the sanctuary and, in some instances, the camp as well.[55]

As opposed to tolerated impurities, which arise from amoral situations, prohibited impurities are those 'arising from sinful situations', and are parallel to what the above authors called moral impurities.[56] The type of impurity resulting from these situations can be classified according to whether the sin was unintentional (column three) or intentional (column four).

One example of unintentional sin that causes impurity is inadvertently delaying purification from a tolerated impurity, which in turn results in the defilement of the sanctuary (Lev. 5.2-3).[57] Similarly, Leviticus 4 speaks of more general inadvertent sins which also result in the pollution of the sanctuary.[58] In either case, however, the sanctuary is polluted, and is cleansed by the bringing of a purification offering.

Examples of intentional sins that cause impurities include, among others, sacrifice to Molech (Lev. 20.2-5), 'purposefully polluting sacred items, such as touching or eating sacrifices while impure' (7.19-21; 22.3-7), and sexual sins (18.6-23).[59] The consequence of such sins is more severe with respect to both the guilty party and the sanctuary. With respect to the guilty party, the penalty is *kareth*, the premature death of the sinner;[60] no personal sacrifice is

---

55. Wright ('Spectrum', p. 157) notes: 'Some laws require the exclusion of [communicable] impurity from the area of the habitation, while others seem to allow some communicable impurities to remain within the habitation though under restrictions. The rationale behind this seems to be that were communicable impurity given free rein in the habitation, which is generally pure, other impurities would be generated from the communicable impurity and would threaten the sacred, either the sanctuary or the sacred things that happened to be present in the habitation.' Further details may be found in Wright, *Disposal of Impurity*, pp. 163-247. An example of communicable impurity allowed within the camp would be the menstruant, whose impurity is a lesser grade with reference to not needing sacrifice and not polluting the sanctuary (hence column one of the chart), but a higher grade with reference to the fact that it is highly communicable (hence column two of the chart; this in turn explains why the bottom box in column two of Wright's chart overlaps with column one, namely, there are communicable impurities [column two] that do not require sacrifice [column one]; see Wright, 'Spectrum', p. 156 n. 2).

56. Wright, 'Spectrum', p. 151.
57. Wright, 'Spectrum', p. 159.
58. Wright, 'Spectrum', p. 160. See above, §3.1.1.
59. Wright, 'Spectrum', pp. 161-63.
60. See discussion above, §1.2.2.

allowed, due to the intentionality of the sin.⁶¹ With respect to the sanctuary, Wright follows Milgrom in stating that it is the most holy place that is defiled (and not simply the outer altar), arguing that the 'rebellious deeds' that the most holy place is cleansed of in Lev. 16.16 are the intentional and unrepented of sins of the Israelites.⁶²

Like Hoffmann, Büchler, and Klawans, then, Wright distinguishes between those impurities that arise from amoral situations and those that arise from immoral situations. Significantly, however, Wright goes one step further by discussing the differing types of ritual ('tolerated') impurity and the differing types of moral ('prohibited') impurity, thus allowing similarities between ritual and moral impurity to become more evident (similarities already adumbrated in Chapters 3 and 4 above). In particular, Wright's analysis underscores the similarities between tolerated sacrificial impurities (column two) and prohibited unintentional impurities (column three), both of which defile the sanctuary and both of which require a sacrificial כִּפֶּר-rite.⁶³ As will be seen, these similarities, taken together with the observations of Chapters 3 and 4, are fundamental to an understanding of how to approach the verb כִּפֶּר.

5.2. כִּפֶּר *in the Priestly Literature*

With Wright's observations in hand, the question of the meaning of כִּפֶּר in the priestly literature may now be returned to, drawing together the results of Chapters 3 and 4 above. In particular, given the similarities between column two and column three that Wright has helped to identify, how should כִּפֶּר be understood in each?⁶⁴

---

61. As noted above (Chapter 1, n. 46), it would appear that some intentional sins may be repented of (e.g. Lev. 5.20-26 [6.1-7]). Whether this includes any of the sins enumerated above is less clear.

62. Wright, 'Spectrum', p. 163; see Milgrom, *Leviticus 1–16*, pp. 256-58, 1034, 1044. It may be questioned whether the text allows for this type of specificity with regard to the nature of the transgressions of the Israelites mentioned in Lev. 16.16, though this does not affect Wright's overall argument.

63. Wright ('Spectrum', pp. 164-65) comments: 'Notably, the distinction between tolerated sacrificial impurities and prohibited unintentional impurities is very thin in certain respects. Simple inadvertent delay of impurity puts one over the line from tolerated to prohibited impurity, and both categories require sacrifices for purification of the sanctuary.'

64. Column one of Wright's chart is not relevant since minor impurities do not require a כִּפֶּר-rite for cleansing, and column four of Wright's chart deals with brazen and intentional sins, for which a כִּפֶּר-rite is typically not prescribed. A possible exception for column four is the Day of Atonement (Lev. 16). If Wright's understanding of the Day of Atonement is correct, then the use of כִּפֶּר here would be very similar to its use in column

154   *Sin, Impurity, Sacrifice, Atonement*

In Chapter 3 it was noted that כִּפֶּר may be translated with 'to effect כֹּפֶר' in contexts of inadvertent sin (column three of Wright's chart). In Chapter 4 it was noted that כִּפֶּר may be translated with 'to effect purgation' in contexts of major impurity (column two). It was also noted in these chapters, however, that inadvertent sin (column three) defiles the sanctuary, implying that כִּפֶּר also refers to some element of purgation in contexts of sin (§3.1). The translation 'to effect כֹּפֶר' does not adequately account for this. In the same way, it was also noted that the person suffering from a major impurity (column two) has (unintentionally) defiled the sanctuary, thus placing him in the same position as an inadvertent sinner and in turn implying that כִּפֶּר also refers to some element of כֹּפֶר in contexts of major impurity (§4.4). In this instance, the translation 'to effect purgation' does not adequately account for this.

This leads to the following proposal: כִּפֶּר in these situations is best understood as referring to כֹּפֶר-purgation, that is, the כִּפֶּר-rite not only *purges* sin and impurity, it does so by means of a כֹּפֶר-arrangement (blood sacrifice) that rescues the impure person or sinner from the judgment of the Lord.⁶⁵ This understanding of כִּפֶּר fully accounts for the similarities between major impurities and inadvertent sins in the priestly system, namely, that major impurities and inadvertent sins both endanger (requiring כֹּפֶר) and pollute (requiring purgation), and that both require a sacrificial כִּפֶּר-rite (i.e. כֹּפֶר-purgation).⁶⁶

The fact that the verb כִּפֶּר can refer to כֹּפֶר-purgation is not only a logical conclusion from the study above, it also finds support in the use of the verb in Num. 35.30-34.⁶⁷ Numbers 35.6-29 deals with the cities of refuge and who may legitimately go there, namely, those who have unintentionally slain another. Verses 30-34, which conclude the chapter, read as follows:

> If anyone kills a person, the murderer shall be put to death on the evidence of witnesses; but no person shall be put to death on the testimony of one witness. Moreover you shall accept no ransom (כֹּפֶר) for the life of a murderer, who is

---

three, at least with respect to the Israelites who did not commit the sin. This is because the כִּפֶּר-rite would serve both to deliver the Israelites from the wrath of the LORD and to cleanse the sanctuary.

65. In the next chapter we turn to consider why it is that sacrificial blood is able to have this dual function.

66. See below, n. 76, for discussion of how to translate כִּפֶּר in these instances.

67. It is granted that this passage does not fit into column three, even though an inadvertent sin is addressed (Num. 35.32; see vv. 22-25). The reason for this appears to be that the inadvertent sin of murder is so serious that not even animal sacrifice can atone for it: only the blood of the slayer, or the death (and therefore blood?) of the high priest, will do (vv. 32-33). The passage is still relevant to the present discussion, however, insofar as it is using the verb כִּפֶּר in the context of an inadvertent sin which pollutes.

guilty of death; but the murderer shall be put to death. And you shall accept no ransom (כֹּפֶר) for the one who has fled to their city of refuge, that they may return to dwell in the land before the death of the high priest. You shall not thus pollute the land in which you live; for blood pollutes the land, and no atonement can be made for the land, for the blood that is shed in it (וְלָאָרֶץ לֹא־יְכֻפַּר לַדָּם אֲשֶׁר שֻׁפַּךְ־בָּהּ), except by the blood of the one who shed it. You shall not defile the land in which you live, in the midst of which I dwell; for I the LORD dwell in the midst of the people of Israel.

The thrust of the passage is straightforward. Verse 30 states that a murderer must be executed, provided there is more than one witness to the crime.[68] Verse 31 then states that when a person is found to be guilty of murder, no ransom payment (כֹּפֶר) can be accepted on their behalf.[69] Though not stated here, a ransom payment was often some payment of silver.[70] Verse 32 goes on to clarify that a ransom payment cannot be accepted even when the murder was unintentional, and thus even the unintentional slayer is not allowed to leave their city of refuge.[71] The reason that כֹּפֶר may not be accepted is given in v. 33: murder pollutes the land (just like sexual immorality [Lev. 18.25]). The severity of this is such that no כִּפֶּר can be effected for the land by a כֹּפֶר of silver; it is only a כֹּפֶר of blood that will כִּפֶּר the land, namely, the blood of the slayer: 'for blood pollutes the land, and no כִּפֶּר can be made for the land, for the blood that is shed in it, except by the blood of the one who shed it' (וְלָאָרֶץ לֹא־יְכֻפַּר לַדָּם אֲשֶׁר שֻׁפַּךְ־בָּהּ כִּי־אִם בְּדַם שֹׁפְכוֹ, v. 33). To receive anything less than this would be to leave the pollution of the land unaddressed, a situation which was inconceivable given that the LORD dwelt in the midst of it (vv. 33-34).

The relationship between כִּפֶּר and כֹּפֶר in this passage is self-evident. As noted by Milgrom:

---

68. On the execution of the murderer, see Gen. 9.6; Exod. 21.12-14; Lev. 24.12.
69. Whether or not this verse implies that ransom was being accepted in Israel at this point in time in the case of murder has been commented on above (§2.1.1.3) and is not relevant to the present discussion.
70. Though not in the context of murder, see Exod. 30.11-16, where the phrase כֹּפֶר נַפְשׁוֹ (v. 12), which is paralleled in our text by כֹּפֶר לְנֶפֶשׁ (v. 31), is a payment of a half shekel of silver (v. 13). See the discussion above in §2.1.1 for this and other כֹּפֶר-texts. For a narrative example of כֹּפֶר in the context of murder, see 2 Sam. 21.1-9, where the land is suffering a famine because of Saul's slaying of the Gibeonites (v. 1). As a result, David calls the Gibeonites and asks them, 'What should I do for you? And with what can I effect ransom (וּבַמָּה אֲכַפֵּר) that you may bless the heritage of the LORD?' (v. 3). That David was offering some sort of ransom payment by this statement is evident in the Gibeonites' response: 'It is not a matter of silver or gold between us and Saul or his house…' (v. 4). In the end, the only ransom suitable—as in Num. 35.33—was blood, namely, that of Saul's sons (v. 6).
71. That is, until the death of the high priest (see Num. 35.25, 28).

There are... cases in which the ransom [i.e. כֹּפֶר] principle is clearly operative. (1) The function of the census money (Exod. 30.12-16) is lĕkapppēr 'al-napšōtêkem 'to ransom your lives' (Exod. 30.16; cf. Num. 31.50): here the verb kippēr must be related to the expression found in the same pericope kōper napšô 'a ransom for his life' (Exod. 30.12). (2) The same combination of the idiom kōper nepeš and the verb kippēr is found in the law of homicide (Num. 35.31-33). Thus in these two cases, kippēr is a denominative from kōper, whose meaning is undisputed: 'ransom' (cf. Exod. 21.30).[72]

In this instance, a normal כֹּפֶר (i.e. a payment of silver) was insufficient to כִּפֶּר the land; only a כֹּפֶר of blood (i.e. the blood of the slayer) would suffice. In executing the slayer, and thus effecting כִּפֶּר, the sufficient ransom for the land would be paid and its defilement would be taken care of.

What is particularly important to note, however, is that while כִּפֶּר here does refer to the payment of a suitable ransom, *the intended result of the כִּפֶּר-action—that is, the payment of a suitable כֹּפֶר—is that of cleansing*, since it is the *pollution* and *defilement* of the land that is being addressed. In short, כִּפֶּר here refers to כֹּפֶר-purgation.[73]

---

72. Milgrom, *Leviticus 1–16*, p. 1082.

73. In an important article on Lev. 17.11, Schwartz ('Prohibitions', p. 56) argues that '[Lev. 17.11] is the only place in which the כִּפֶּר-action attributed to blood has the sense of ransom rather than purification'. Recognizing that Num. 35.31-33 would also seem to use כִּפֶּר in this way, Schwartz (p. 56 n. 1) offers the following comments: 'In vv. 31-32... the noun כֹּפֶר is, of course, "ransom", "payment". In v. 33, however... the word יְכַפֵּר not only echoes the כֹּפֶר of the preceding verses; it is also, and primarily, the antithesis of תַּחֲנִיפוּ... יַחֲנִיף, in which case it means "purge, purify". The play on words is that כֹּפֶר "ransom" cannot מְכַפֵּר "purify" the land of the blood of the innocent; only the blood of the homicide can accomplish this.' In this way Schwartz holds that כִּפֶּר in v. 33 refers solely to purification. While Schwartz's article as a whole is extremely insightful, the above comments may be questioned on two grounds. First, even leaving Num. 35 aside, it does not seem to be the case that Lev. 17.11 is the only verse where the כִּפֶּר-action attributed to blood refers to ransom, as demonstrated above in Chapter 3 for כִּפֶּר in Lev. 4–5 (Schwartz has followed Milgrom on the translation of כִּפֶּר in Lev. 4–5, for which see Chapter 3, n. 23), and as suggested in Chapter 4 for כִּפֶּר in contexts of major impurities (see §4.4 above). Second, Schwartz has correctly identified that one element of כִּפֶּר in Num. 35.33 is that of purification. He is also correct in stating that a כֹּפֶר cannot do this, though it is important to note at this point that it is not a כֹּפֶר in general that the text refers to, but a כֹּפֶר of silver (for which reason the text specifies 'you will not take a ransom' [וְלֹא־תִקְחוּ כֹפֶר] [vv. 31-32]; see also the comments above and cf. 2 Sam. 21.3-6 [n. 70 above], where King David cannot ransom the act of murder with silver but only with blood). For this reason, Schwartz's comments above could be more accurately stated as follows: 'The play on words is that [a] כֹּפֶר "ransom" [*of silver*] cannot מְכַפֵּר "purify" the land of the blood of the innocent; only the blood of the homicide can accomplish this'. In this regard, the blood of the slayer not only cleanses, it also rescues the land (and its inhabitants) from the judgment of the LORD; it is thus a ransom payment that cleanses, but a ransom payment nonetheless. Indeed, this is the reason that כִּפֶּר 'echoes' the word

5. *The Relationship between Sin and Impurity* 157

This understanding of כִּפֶּר as כֹּפֶר-purgation may profitably be applied to the translation of כִּפֶּר in columns two (Lev. 12–15) and three (Lev. 4–5) of Wright's chart. As noted above, those suffering from a major impurity (column two) are in need of purgation. In that their impurity has also defiled the sanctuary, however, putting them at considerable risk of suffering punishment, some element of ransom is also expected. Translating כִּפֶּר with 'to effect כֹּפֶר-purgation' accounts for both of these needs. Similarly, those who have committed an inadvertent wrong (column three) are in need of ransom. In that their sin has also defiled the sanctuary, however, which must be cleansed, some element of purgation is also expected. Once more, translating כִּפֶּר with 'to effect כֹּפֶר-purgation' satisfies both of these elements.[74]

If this understanding of כִּפֶּר strikes the modern ear as peculiar, it is perhaps because the discussion of sin and impurity has tended to focus on the starting point of each: sin starts from moral wrongdoing, while impurity starts from amoral causes (e.g. childbirth). In this way, sin and impurity appear to be two separate spheres. When the ending point of sin and impurity are compared, however, and in particular the ending point of an unintentional sin and a major impurity, the spheres overlap: the unintentional sinner and the person suffering a major impurity need to effect both כֹּפֶר and purgation.[75] The verb used to describe this dual event is כִּפֶּר.[76]

כֹּפֶר here (Schwartz, 'Prohibitions', p. 56 n. 1), namely, because כִּפֶּר refers to both ransom and purgation.

74. Again, in the next chapter we consider why it is that blood is able to have this dual function. It might be responded that כִּפֶּר is different in columns two and three insofar as the result of כִּפֶּר in Lev. 12–15 is purification (טָהֵר) while in Lev. 4–5 it is forgiveness (סָלַח). The reason for this, however, is simply that the starting point in each instance is different: in Lev. 12–15 the starting point is the impurity of the person, and thus the focus of the text is that the כִּפֶּר-rite results in cleansing; in Lev. 4–5 the starting point is the sin of the person, and thus the focus of the text is that the כִּפֶּר-rite results in forgiveness. In terms of the end point, however, columns two and three are the same: the כִּפֶּר-rite results in ransoming the offerer as well as cleansing impurity and sin. At most, it could be said that the emphasis in column two is upon purgation, while the emphasis in column three is upon כֹּפֶר, though כִּפֶּר in either column has both כֹּפֶר and purgation in view.

75. For how this relates to those not suffering a major impurity (Levites, Aaron, and the priests), see §4.4.1 and §4.4.2 above.

76. Naturally, it is extremely unwieldy in English to translate כִּפֶּר with 'to ransom-purgate'. Unfortunately, there is no one English term which incorporates all of these elements. The verb 'to expiate' focuses more on cleansing or removing guilt/sin or pollution, without necessarily including the idea of appeasement or ransom, while the verb 'to propitiate' has the opposite problem of focusing on appeasement or ransom but not necessarily cleansing. It is suggested that the translator make use of the verb 'to atone' with an explanatory footnote that atonement involves elements of both ransoming and purging.

5.3. Summary

The purpose of this chapter has been to consider the relationship between sin and impurity, and how a better understanding of this relationship could shed insight into the meaning of כִּפֶּר. In the first half of the chapter, therefore, four important contributions to the relationship between sin and impurity have been surveyed. The first three were those of D. Hoffmann, A. Büchler, and J. Klawans, each of which makes a similar distinction between 'ritual' or 'levitical' impurity and 'moral' impurity. This distinction is based on several differences evident in the two types of impurity, the foremost of which is that ritual impurity results from amoral causes (e.g. childbirth), whereas moral impurity—as its name suggests—has its root in moral wrongdoing (e.g. murder, idolatry, or sexual immorality).[77]

While these discussions were helpful in providing a broad description of the relationship between sin and impurity, they did not address some of the specific distinctions within the categories of ritual and moral impurity that are important for a proper understanding of the relationship between the two spheres. For this reason the work of D. Wright was then considered. It was seen that Wright not only distinguishes between ritual and moral impurities[78] —he also makes a distinction between minor and major ritual impurities, and between inadvertent and intentional moral impurities. These distinctions are presented graphically in a four-columned chart, with each column corresponding to a different category and increasing in degree of pollution from left to right: minor ritual pollution (column one), major ritual pollution (column two), inadvertent moral pollution (column three), intentional moral pollution (column four). This chart was especially helpful in making clear important similarities between major impurities (column two) and inadvertent sins (column three), namely, that both defile the sanctuary and both require a sacrificial כִּפֶּר-rite.[79] Indeed, these similarities, taken together with the observations of Chapters 3 and 4, prove fundamental to understanding how to approach the verb כִּפֶּר.

The second half of the chapter thus turned to consider the meaning of כִּפֶּר in these contexts. It was noted on the one hand that כִּפֶּר may be translated with 'to effect כֹּפֶר' in contexts of inadvertent sin (column three of Wright's chart), and with 'to effect purgation' in contexts of major impurity (column two). It was noted on the other hand, however, that neither of these translations was sufficient, insofar as inadvertent sin also polluted (requiring

---

77. For further distinctions see the discussion above.
78. Wright's nomenclature is different ('tolerated' instead of 'ritual', and 'prohibited' instead of 'moral') but his basic bipartite division is the same (see n. 50 above for his critique of these other labels).
79. See n. 63 above.

5. *The Relationship between Sin and Impurity* 159

purgation) and major impurities also endangered (requiring ransom). For this reason, it was proposed that כִּפֶּר in these situations is best understood as referring to כֹּפֶר-purgation, that is, the כִּפֶּר-rite not only *purges* sin and impurity, it does so by means of a כֹּפֶר-arrangement (blood sacrifice) that rescues the impure person or sinner from the judgment of the Lord. It was noted that this understanding of כִּפֶּר fully accounts for the similarities between major impurities and inadvertent sins in the priestly system, namely, that major impurities and inadvertent sins both endanger (requiring כֹּפֶר) and pollute (requiring purgation), and that both require a sacrificial כִּפֶּר-rite (i.e. כֹּפֶר-purgation).

This understanding of כִּפֶּר was further supported by reference to Num. 35.30-34, where כִּפֶּר occurs in the context of a polluting sin.[80] It was seen on the one hand that there is in this passage a strong relationship between the noun כֹּפֶר (vv. 31-32) and the verb כִּפֶּר (v. 33), such that כִּפֶּר referred to the executing of a כֹּפֶר-payment on behalf of the guilty party. Significantly, however, it was also seen that the כִּפֶּר action would have to address the *pollution* of the land. As a result, כִּפֶּר in this instance refers not only to the execution of a כֹּפֶר-payment, but also to one which has purifying effects, that is, כִּפֶּר refers to כֹּפֶר-purgation.

The chapter concluded by noting on the one hand that the starting points of major impurities and inadvertent sins are different: major impurity starts from amoral causes whereas sin starts from moral wrongdoing. It noted on the other hand, however, that the ending points are the same: both of these endanger (requiring כֹּפֶר) and both of these defile (requiring purgation). In either case, therefore, the person presenting the sacrifice needs to effect both כֹּפֶר and purgation. The verb used to describe this dual event is כִּפֶּר.

---

80. See above, n. 67.

Part IV

כָּפֶר AND THE ROLE OF BLOOD

6

A Consideration of the Role of Blood in Sacrificial Atonement, with Special Reference to Leviticus 17.11

In Part III (Chapter 5) it was argued that in the contexts of major impurities and inadvertent sins, the כִּפֶּר-rite effected both כֹּפֶר and purgation, and that the verb כִּפֶּר in these contexts referred to כֹּפֶר-purgation. This leads quite naturally to the question: Why is the כִּפֶּר-rite able to fulfill this dual role of כֹּפֶר and purgation?

The answer has already been hinted at above in the discussion of Numbers 35: it is the blood that both ransoms and purifies. The purificatory power of blood is quite evident: it has already been seen in Chapter 4 and is illustrated in such texts as Lev. 8.15 and 16.19. What of the ransoming power of blood? In contexts of sin (Chapter 3), it was argued that the sacrificial כִּפֶּר-rite accomplished ransom for the sinner. Central to the sacrificial כִּפֶּר-rite in these contexts are the blood rites, suggesting in turn that blood is central to the accomplishing of ransom. Similarly, in contexts of impurity (Chapter 4), it was argued that the sacrificial כִּפֶּר-rite not only accomplished purification, but also ransom. Once more, the blood rites are central to the sacrificial כִּפֶּר-rite in these contexts, implying again that blood is central to the accomplishing of ransom.

What is directly implied in the above contexts about the ransoming power of blood is stated explicitly in Lev. 17.11, one of the rare verses in the priestly literature in which the theory behind sacrificial atonement is expressed: 'For the life of the flesh is in the blood, and I myself have given it to you upon the altar to make atonement (כִּפֶּר) for your souls; for *it is the blood* that makes atonement, by means of the life'. If the atonement (כִּפֶּר) referred to in this verse is characterized by ransom, then it is strong support that blood does indeed have power to ransom.

There exists, however, significant debate as to the exact meaning of several elements of this verse, and, consequently, of the verse as a whole. The present chapter therefore begins with an exegesis of the verse, starting with a consideration of the place of the verse in Leviticus 17, and then proceeding to consider the individual parts of the verse. Moreover, though this verse has traditionally been understood to refer to the role of blood in atoning sacrifices in general, it has been argued more recently that it applies only to the peace offering, and consequently sheds no light upon the rationale of the other offerings. For this reason, the exegesis of the verse will be followed by a consideration of its application, that is, whether it speaks of the peace offering exclusively or of atoning sacrifice more generally. Having considered the exegesis and application of the verse, we will then return to our original question of why the כִּפֶּר-rite is able to fulfill the dual role of accomplishing כִּפֶּר and purgation.

6.1. *Leviticus 17.11*

6.1.1. *Introduction*

Leviticus 17 consists of an introductory formula (vv. 1-2) followed by five separate sections, the first four of which begin with some variation of the formula אִישׁ אִישׁ מִבֵּית/מִבְּנֵי יִשְׂרָאֵל (וּמִן־הַגֵּר הַגָּר/אֲשֶׁר־יָגוּר בְּתוֹכָם) אֲשֶׁר..., followed by a verb in the imperfect (vv. 3-7, 8-9, 10-12, 13-14), and the last of which begins with וְכָל־נֶפֶשׁ אֲשֶׁר, followed by a verb in the imperfect (vv. 15-16).[1] These five sections, and especially the first four, are thematically united by their common concern of how the blood of animals is to be dealt with.[2] Verses 10-12, coming in the midst of these five sections, serve as

---

1. Schwartz, 'Prohibitions', pp. 36-43 (37-41); see also Elliger, *Leviticus*, p. 219; Adrian Schenker, 'Das Zeichen des Blutes und die Gewißheit der Vergebung im Alten Testament: Die sühnende Funktion des Blutes auf dem Altar nach Lev. 17.10-12', *MTZ* 34 (1983), pp. 195-213 (198); Hartley, *Leviticus*, p. 265. The reason for the switch from אִישׁ אִישׁ in vv. 3-14 to וְכָל־נֶפֶשׁ in v. 15 is not entirely clear, though אִישׁ and נֶפֶשׁ alternate elsewhere, for example, Lev. 22.5-6. Schwartz ('Prohibitions', p. 41) suggests that the use of וְכָל־נֶפֶשׁ אֲשֶׁר תֹּאכַל in this verse 'is designed to resume the כָּל נפשׁ מכם לא תאכל of the third paragraph's [i.e. vv. 10-12] motivational section (v. 12aβ), which is itself an echo of בנפשׁ האכלת את הדם (v. 10bα), and which is further echoed in the fourth section's paraphrase דם כל בשׂר לא תאכלו (v. 14aβ)'. He then sees this to be 'further evidence of the interconnection of the third, fourth and fifth paragraphs'. Schwartz ('Prohibitions', p. 41 n. 3) also notes that נֶפֶשׁ 'tends to appear…in laws pertaining to eating and drinking', citing in support Exod. 12.4, 16; and Lev. 7.26 [*sic*; read 7.27?], as well as 'the expression עִנָּה נפשׁ "to fast", literally, "to deprive the throat" (Lev. 16.29, 31; 23.27, 29; Num. 30.14; Isa. 58.3), the opposite of which is הַשְׂבִּיעַ נפשׁ (Isa. 58.10-11; Ps. 107.9)' (other laws regarding eating and drinking that use נֶפֶשׁ include Lev. 7.18, 20, 25; 17.12, though אִישׁ may also be used in these contexts—e.g. Lev. 17.10; 22.4, 14).

2. So Erhard S. Gerstenberger (*Leviticus: A Commentary* [trans. Douglas W. Stott; Louisville, KY: Westminster/John Knox Press, 1996], p. 235): 'This present section is concerned primarily with how one deals with blood'. The last section (vv. 15-16) states that anyone who eats meat from an animal that died naturally or that was killed by another animal must launder their clothes and bathe in water (v. 15) in order to avoid bearing their sin (v. 16). While the blood of the animal is not explicitly mentioned here, it has often been observed that the flesh of such an animal would still have the blood in it

a foundation for what precedes and what follows. Verses 3-9, for example, give instructions that sacrifices are to be offered only on the altar, though the full rationale for this does not come until v. 11 (viz. that the altar is the place God has designated for these rites to occur). Similarly, vv. 13-14 prohibit the blood of hunted animals from being eaten, with the explanation of v. 11 being repeated in v. 14, namely, that the life of the flesh is in the blood.[3] It is to a closer examination of this central and foundational section that we now turn.

6.1.2. *Verses 10-12*

A וְאִישׁ אִישׁ מִבֵּית יִשְׂרָאֵל וּמִן־הַגֵּר הַגָּר בְּתוֹכָם אֲשֶׁר יֹאכַל כָּל־דָּם
 וְנָתַתִּי פָנַי בַּנֶּפֶשׁ הָאֹכֶלֶת אֶת־הַדָּם וְהִכְרַתִּי אֹתָהּ מִקֶּרֶב עַמָּהּ

B כִּי נֶפֶשׁ הַבָּשָׂר בַּדָּם הִוא וַאֲנִי נְתַתִּיו לָכֶם עַל־הַמִּזְבֵּחַ לְכַפֵּר עַל־נַפְשֹׁתֵיכֶם
 כִּי־הַדָּם הוּא בַּנֶּפֶשׁ יְכַפֵּר

A' עַל־כֵּן אָמַרְתִּי לִבְנֵי יִשְׂרָאֵל כָּל־נֶפֶשׁ מִכֶּם לֹא־תֹאכַל דָּם וְהַגֵּר הַגָּר
 בְּתוֹכְכֶם לֹא־יֹאכַל דָּם

> A If anyone of the house of Israel or of the strangers that sojourn among them eats any blood, I will set my face against the person who eats blood, and will cut [that person] off from among their people.
>
> B For the life of the flesh is in the blood; and I have bestowed[4] it to you upon the altar to make atonement for your lives; for it is the blood that makes atonement, by means of[5] the life.
>
> A' Therefore I have said to the people of Israel, 'No person among you shall eat blood, neither shall any stranger who sojourns among you eat blood'.

(A. Noordtzij, *Leviticus* [trans. R. Togtman; Bible Student's Commentary; Grand Rapids: Zondervan, 1982], pp. 178-79; Schwartz, 'Prohibitions', p. 42; Hartley, *Leviticus*, p. 277; Wenham, *Leviticus*, p. 246). This might in fact explain why the eater of the flesh becomes unclean (Hartley, *Leviticus*, p. 277; Wenham, *Leviticus*, p. 246), though it is also possible that the uncleanness mentioned in this verse comes about simply through contact with a dead animal, which was polluting in itself (11.39-40) (Wenham, *Leviticus*, p. 246).

3. For the centrality of Lev. 17.10-12 in this pericope, see Schenker, 'Das Zeichen', p. 198; Schwartz, 'Prohibitions', pp. 42-43; and Milgrom, *Leviticus 17–22*, pp. 1448-49.

4. Milgrom (*Leviticus 1–16*, p. 707) notes, 'A survey of P shows that wherever the subject of *nātan* is God, it means "bestow, appoint, assign" (e.g. Num. 8.19…; 18.8, 19; cf. also Gen. 1.29; 9.3; Lev. 6.10; 7.34; 10.17; Num. 35.6).' As supported in the following, the rendering 'bestow' seems to be most appropriate in this context. The theological significance of the fact that God himself has given the blood to the Israelites for atonement has been commented on insightfully by Schwartz, 'Prohibitions', pp. 50-51; Schenker, 'Das Zeichen', pp. 201-202; and Janowski, *Sühne*, p. 247. Schwartz ('Prohibitions', p. 51), for instance, writes, 'What our clause does, in its unique, metaphorically graphic way, is to take a set phrase, the "placing" of the blood on the altar, and to reverse the conceptual direction of the action: "It is not you who are placing the blood on the altar for me, for my benefit, but rather the opposite: it is I who have placed it there for you—for your benefit".'

5. See the discussion below for this translation.

Verses 10-12 are chiastic in structure, consisting of a prohibition against eating blood[6] (A; v. 10), the grounds for this prohibition (B; v. 11), and a repetition of the prohibition (A'; v. 12).[7]

Of these three verses, v. 11 has received the most attention, insofar as it appears to explain the rationale of blood as it relates to atonement.

As noted by Elliger, v. 11 actually gives two grounds for the prohibition against eating blood.[8] The first of these is simply that the life (נֶפֶשׁ) is in the blood: 'For the life of the flesh is in the blood...' (v. 11aα).[9] The reasoning seems to be that since the blood contains the life of the animal, and since it is wrong to consume the life of an animal, it is therefore wrong to consume the blood of an animal (cf. v. 14; Gen. 9.4; Deut. 12.23).

With regard to why it is wrong to consume the life of an animal, it has been noted on the one hand that this is due to the fact that all life belongs to God. So Noordtzij writes, 'The life of all creatures is the property of God, and human beings therefore have no claim on this'.[10] The continuation of the verse supports this understanding, where the LORD says, '...and *I myself* have given it [i.e. the blood] to you (וַאֲנִי נְתַתִּיו לָכֶם)', implying in turn that the LORD is the one who 'owns' the blood.

Conjoined with this reason, and perhaps based upon it, is the more general respect for the life of animals found in the Old Testament. The earlier verses of Leviticus 17 are an illustration of this, in that those who slaughter a domestic animal, but do not bring it to the sanctuary to present it as a sacrifice, are said to have 'shed blood' (דָּם שָׁפָךְ; v. 4), a formula frequently used to describe the slaying of another human (Gen. 37.22; Num. 35.33;

---

6. As argued by Milgrom ('A Prolegomenon to Leviticus 17.11', in *Studies in Cultic Theology and Terminology*, p. 99), the phrase 'to eat blood' most likely refers to eating meat with the blood in it. See Gen. 9.4, 'Only you shall not eat flesh with its life, that is, its blood (אַךְ־בָּשָׂר בְּנַפְשׁוֹ דָמוֹ לֹא תֹאכֵלוּ)', and Deut. 12.23, 'Only be sure that you do not eat the blood; for the blood is the life, and you shall not eat the life with the flesh (וְלֹא־תֹאכַל הַנֶּפֶשׁ עִם־הַבָּשָׂר)'.

7. Schenker, 'Das Zeichen', p. 196; Milgrom, *Leviticus 17–22*, p. 1469.

8. Elliger, *Leviticus*, p. 220; followed by Janowski, *Sühne*, p. 245; and Schenker, 'Das Zeichen', p. 196.

9. Or: 'For the life of the flesh is the blood...' See the discussion below of the *beth essentiae* understanding of the בְּ in v. 11b.

10. Noordtzij, *Leviticus*, p. 177; see also Notker Füglister, 'Sühne durch Blut. Zur Bedeutung von Leviticus 17, 11', in Georg Braulik (ed.), *Studien zum Pentateuch* (Festschrift Walter Kornfeld; Wien: Herder, 1977), pp. 143-64 (150-51) (he entitles the relevant section 'The Blood belongs to Yahweh'); Elliger, *Leviticus*, p. 228 (though Elliger holds that the prohibition may also stem from an animistic-totemistic view of life in which people feared somehow incorporating a foreign soul into themselves through the consumption of its blood; see p. 228); Luigi Moraldi, *Espiazione sacrificale e riti espiatori nell'ambiente biblico e nell'Antico Testamento* (Rome: Pontificio Istituto Biblico, 1956), p. 238.

Deut. 21.7; 1 Kgs 2.31; 2 Kgs 21.16; 24.4; 1 Chron. 22.8, etc.).[11] Further similarities between human life and animal life have been noted by Milgrom, who writes, 'An animal also has a *nepeš* (Gen. 9.10; Lev. 11.10, 46; 24.18; Num. 31.28); ...it is responsible under the law (Gen. 9.5; Lev. 20.15-16; cf. Exod. 21.28-32) and is a party to God's covenant (Gen. 9.9-10; Lev. 26.6, 22; cf. Hos. 2.20)'.[12] Due to this high view of animal life, its blood, in which its life is found, is to be treated with the utmost respect, that is, if not for sacrificial use (and thus put upon the altar; Lev. 17.11), then poured out upon the ground (and so returned to the earth; Deut. 12.16, 24; 15.23). In short, because all life, and thus all blood, belongs to the LORD, humans are not to appropriate life by eating blood, but are instead to treat the blood with the utmost respect.

The second ground for the prohibition on the consumption of blood is that God has granted the blood for a unique purpose, namely, for performing the בִּכֶּפֶר-rite upon the altar: '...and I myself have bestowed it to you upon the altar to make atonement for your lives' (v. 11aβ). This ground acknowledges that the LORD, as the owner of the blood, has granted that it may be used by the Israelites. It immediately clarifies, however, that it has been given to them for one specific purpose: the making of atonement. For this reason, any other use of the blood (e.g. eating it) is strictly forbidden, for it falls outside of the scope of use that the LORD intended.[13]

Though v. 11aα and v. 11aβ are separate grounds for the prohibition against consuming blood, they are definitely related, and for this reason are brought together in the third clause of the verse, v. 11b. Thus Schwartz comments:

> ...clause 1 says that the blood is the seat of the נֶפֶשׁ; clause 2 says that the blood is designated לכפר; clause 3 combines the two and says that the blood בנפשׁ יכפר... This third clause does more than merely summarize. It provides the logical connection between clause 1 and clause 2; it says that clause 2 is true *because of* clause 1. How does blood מכפר? בנפשׁ...[14]

He illustrates this with the following layout of the verse:[15]

---

11. Noted by Milgrom, *Leviticus 1–16*, p. 710.
12. Milgrom, *Leviticus 1–16*, p. 712.
13. For the theological implications of the fact that God is the one who has ordained this means of atonement, see above, n. 4.
14. Schwartz, 'Prohibitions', p. 47 (emphasis his). See also Kiuchi, *Purification Offering*, pp. 104-105; Adalbert Metzinger, 'Die Substitutionstheorie und das alttestamentliche Opfer mit besonderer Berücksichtigung von Lev. 17, 11', *Bib* 21 (1940), pp. 159-87, 247-72, 353-77 (260, 266, 271-72). Schenker ('Das Zeichen', p. 198) calls v. 11b the conceptual center of the passage ('die Pupille in der Iris des Auges').
15. Schwartz, 'Prohibitions', p. 47.

כִּי נֶפֶשׁ הַבָּשָׂר בַּדָּם הִיא   וַאֲנִי נְתַתִּיו לָכֶם עַל־הַמִּזְבֵּחַ לְכַפֵּר   עַל־נַפְשֹׁתֵיכֶם

כִּי   הַדָּם הוּא בַּנֶּפֶשׁ יְכַפֵּר

Thus the life-containing blood of the animal (v. 11aα), which God himself has given to the Israelites to atone (כִּפֶּר) for their lives (v. 11aβ), is able to do this בַּנֶּפֶשׁ (v. 11b).[16] This leads naturally to three fundamental questions about this verse. First, what is the meaning of כִּפֶּר in this verse? Second, since the goal of כִּפֶּר is accomplished בַּנֶּפֶשׁ, what is the meaning of the בְּ in the phrase כִּי־הַדָּם הוּא בַּנֶּפֶשׁ יְכַפֵּר? And third, which sacrifices are in view here whose blood בַּנֶּפֶשׁ יְכַפֵּר? A consensus is building in answer to the first question, and it will therefore occupy us only briefly. The second question is much more debated and will therefore need to be examined in greater depth. Finally, while there is a general consensus in answer to the third question, it has received renewed attention more recently, and will therefore also be examined in more detail.

6.1.3. *The Meaning of* כִּפֶּר *in Leviticus 17.11*

It is commonly agreed that the atonement referred to by the verb כִּפֶּר in Lev. 17.11 is characterized by ransom.[17] This finds support in the phrase לְכַפֵּר עַל־נַפְשֹׁתֵיכֶם in v. 11aβ, which occurs in only two other instances (Exod. 30.15-16; Num. 31.50), and which has the meaning 'to ransom your lives' both times. As noted by Milgrom, this is especially clear in Exodus 30, where the results of the כִּפֶּר action in vv. 15-16 are earlier described with the phrase כֹּפֶר נַפְשׁוֹ ('a ransom for his life').[18] Given this usage of the phrase elsewhere, then, it would seem reasonable that כִּפֶּר also refers to ransoming in this verse. Much more highly debated, however, is the meaning of the בְּ in v. 11b.

6.1.4. *The Meaning of* בְּ *in the Phrase* כִּי־הַדָּם הוּא בַּנֶּפֶשׁ יְכַפֵּר *in Leviticus 17.11b*

Verse 11b reads as follows: כִּי־הַדָּם הוּא בַּנֶּפֶשׁ יְכַפֵּר. One of the fundamental questions for the meaning of this phrase is the translation of the בְּ in בַּנֶּפֶשׁ. A related question is whether נֶפֶשׁ refers to the animal that is offered or to the worshipper who offers it.

---

16. This directly implies that it is the *life* of the animal that is central to its effecting of atonement (and not, for example, the *cost* of the animal).

17. Levine, *Leviticus*, p. 115; Milgrom, *Leviticus 1–16*, pp. 707-708; *idem*, *Leviticus 17–22*, p. 1474; Schwartz, 'Prohibitions', p. 55 and n. 1; Wenham, *Leviticus*, p. 115; Budd, *Leviticus*, p. 248.

18. Milgrom, *Leviticus 1–16*, p. 708; he refers further to the same combination of נֶפֶשׁ + כֹּפֶר and כִּפֶּר in Num. 35.31-33. That לְכַפֵּר עַל־נַפְשֹׁתֵינוּ also refers to a ransom in Num. 31.50 is evident from the fact that the context is the same as Exod. 30, namely, the taking of a census.

6. A Consideration of the Role of Blood 169

With regard to the function of the בְּ, three main proposals have been put forth. To begin, some understand the בְּ to be the *beth pretii*. In this regard, נֶפֶשׁ is taken to refer to the life of the human, as opposed to the life of the animal, and v. 11b is thus translated, '...it is the blood that makes atonement for one's life'.[19] A second group understands the בְּ to be *beth essentiae*, and so translate, '...it is the blood, as life, that effects expiation'.[20] In distinction from the *beth pretii* approach, נֶפֶשׁ in this instance refers to the life of the animal. Finally, a large number of translations and scholars understand the בְּ to be instrumental, and so translate, '...for it is the blood that makes atonement, by reason of/means of the life'.[21] As with the *beth essentiae* approach, נֶפֶשׁ in this instance refers to the life of the animal. Each of these positions will be considered in turn.

The *beth pretii* occurs in contexts where one item is given 'for' or 'in exchange for' another, for example, 'I will serve you seven years *for* Rachel (בְּרָחֵל)' (Gen. 29.18); '...and [Joseph's brothers] sold Joseph to the Ishmaelites *for* twenty [shekels] of silver (בְּעֶשְׂרִים כָּסֶף)' (Gen. 37.28).[22] Leviticus 17.11b would then be translated, 'it is the blood that makes atonement *for* one's life'.[23]

In support of this understanding of the בְּ, it is usually noted that Exod. 21.23 and Lev. 24.18 state the talionic principle with the phrase נֶפֶשׁ תַּחַת נֶפֶשׁ,

---

19. NIV; H. Cazelles, *Le Lévitique* (La Sainte Bible; Paris: Cerf, 1958), pp. 84-85; Noordtzij, *Leviticus*, p. 177.

20. JPSV; Ernst Jenni, *Die hebräischen Präpositionen. I. Die Präposition Beth* (Stuttgart: W. Kohlhammer, 1992), pp. 84-86; Füglister, 'Sühne', p. 145 (or *beth instrumenti*); Milgrom, 'Prolegomenon', pp. 96-98 (though changed to instrumental in *idem, Leviticus 1–16*, p. 706; *idem, Leviticus 17–22*, pp. 1478-79); Léopold Sabourin, 'Nefesh, sang et expiation (Lv 17.11, 14)', *ScEc* 18 (1966), pp. 25-45 (25) (or *beth instrumenti*); Ehrlich, *Randglossen. Zweiter Band*, p. 60; Gerstenberger, *Leviticus*, p. 234.

21. RSV; NASV; Metzinger, 'Substitutionstheorie', pp. 270-72; Gese, 'The Atonement', p. 107; Moraldi, *Espiazione*, p. 240; Janowski, *Sühne*, p. 245; Füglister, 'Sühne', p. 145 (or *beth essentiae*); Garnet, 'Atonement Constructions', p. 139; Dillmann, *Exodus und Leviticus*, p. 538 (or locative); Elliger, *Leviticus*, p. 218; Schwartz, 'Prohibitions', p. 47 n. 2; Milgrom, *Leviticus 1–16*, p. 706 (correcting Milgrom, 'Prolegomenon', pp. 96-98); *idem, Leviticus 17–22*, pp. 1478-79; Kiuchi, *Purification Offering*, pp. 105-106; Hartley, *Leviticus*, p. 261; Schenker, 'Das Zeichen', p. 198; Sabourin, 'Nefesh', p. 25 (or *beth essentiae*); Kurtz, *Sacrificial Worship*, pp. 71-72.

22. GKC 119p; see also W&O 11.2.5d, and, most extensively, Jenni, *Präpositionen*, pp. 150-60.

23. See n. 19 above. Brichto ('On Slaughter and Sacrifice', p. 23), while holding that the בְּ here is *beth pretii*, argues that taking the life of an animal required expiation, and thus understands נֶפֶשׁ to refer to the animal's life, so translating, '...for it is the blood which serves to *kipper* in exchange for the life [taken]' (for his full argument on Lev. 17.11, see pp. 22-29). Brichto's position is considered in more detail along with Milgrom's in §6.1.5 below.

whereas Deut. 19.21 states the same principle using נֶפֶשׁ בְּנֶפֶשׁ.²⁴ This then opens up the possibility that the בְּ is used in the same way in this instance, that is, that the blood (= life) of the animal is given *in exchange for/in place of* the life of the person. In this regard, the animal's life-blood becomes a substitute for that of the offerer.

This understanding of the בְּ would in turn work well with the use of כֹּפֶר in this verse. As noted above, כֹּפֶר in this instance is best translated with 'to ransom', implying that the blood serves as a כֹּפֶר for the life of the worshipper. Insofar as a כֹּפֶר serves as a mitigated penalty in place of a greater one, it would be fitting for the בְּ to be indicative of this substitution: '…for it is the blood that ransoms [i.e. serves as a כֹּפֶר for] one's life'. In short, this view emphasizes the substitutionary nature of sacrificial blood: the blood (= the life) of the animal is given as a substitute for the life (נֶפֶשׁ) of the worshipper.

By way of evaluation, Füglister notes that while the *beth pretii* is a possibility in this instance, the appeal to the use of בְּ in the talionic formula of Deut. 19.21 is not decisive, since the one clear occurrence of this formula in the priestly literature, Lev. 24.20, makes use of תַּחַת instead of בְּ.²⁵ Janowski further points out that the appeal to the talionic formula in Exod. 21.23, Lev. 24.18, and Deut. 19.21 is muted by the difference in the formulas, namely, כִּי־הַדָּם הוּא בַּנֶּפֶשׁ (Lev. 17.11) as opposed to נֶפֶשׁ תַּחַת/בְּנֶפֶשׁ (Exod. 21.23; Lev. 24.18; Deut. 19.21).²⁶ Further, the substitutionary element suggested by לְכַפֵּר עַל־נַפְשֹׁתֵיכֶם in v. 11aβ is not conclusive support for the *beth pretii* understanding, since, as becomes evident below, the *beth essentiae* and *beth instrumenti* views are also compatible with the idea of substitution suggested by the idea of ransom. Finally, the נֶפֶשׁ in v. 11b is most likely a reference to the life of the animal, and not that of the worshipper. This was already discussed above in Schwartz's layout of the verse, where it was seen that נֶפֶשׁ in v. 11aα and כֹּפֶר in v. 11aβ are combined together in v. 11b, implying that the נֶפֶשׁ in v. 11b is the same as it is in v. 11aα, namely, that of the animal. Kiuchi, citing Janowski, further underscores this flow of thought by noting that 'there is a chiasmus of נֶפֶשׁ and דָּם between v. 11aα and v. 11b'.²⁷ This observation may now be combined with Schwartz's layout of the verse as follows:

---

24. Cazelles, *Le Lévitique*, p. 85 n. a; Brichto, 'On Slaughter and Sacrifice', p. 28 n. 20.
25. Füglister, 'Sühne', p. 145. See also Janowski, *Sühne*, p. 244.
26. Janowski, *Sühne*, p. 244.
27. Kiuchi, *Purification Offering*, p. 105; see Janowski, *Sühne*, p. 245.

In sum, while the *beth pretii* view is possible grammatically, neither of the two grounds of support cited in its favor are overly strong, and the referent of נֶפֶשׁ in v. 11b is most likely that of the sacrificial animal.

A second understanding of the בְּ in v. 11b is that it is functioning as a *beth essentiae*. Generally stated, this means that what follows the בְּ is equivalent to, or somehow explicates, that which precedes it:[28] 'to give the land *as* an inheritance' (לָתֵת אֶת־הָאָרֶץ בְּנַחֲלָה; Num. 36.2); 'I appeared to Abraham, to Isaac, and to Jacob, *as* God Almighty' (...וָאֵרָא אֶל־אַבְרָהָם בְּאֵל שַׁדָּי; Exod. 6.3).[29] With this understanding of the בְּ, Lev. 17.11b is then translated, '...it is the blood, *as* life, that effects expiation'.[30]

In favor of this understanding of the בְּ, Jenni notes that Lev. 17.14b equates the blood with the life: '...for the life of every creature is its blood' (כִּי נֶפֶשׁ כָּל־בָּשָׂר דָּמוֹ הוּא).[31] This equation of blood and life in turn lends itself to understanding the בְּ in both Lev. 17.11a and 17.11b as *beth essentiae*, that is, 'for the life of the flesh *is* the blood' (כִּי נֶפֶשׁ הַבָּשָׂר בַּדָּם הוּא), and, 'for it is the blood, *as* life, that effects expiation' (כִּי־הַדָּם הוּא בַּנֶּפֶשׁ יְכַפֵּר).[32] Further, this understanding of the בְּ in v. 11b is in keeping with the fact that נֶפֶשׁ in v. 11b appears to refer to the life of the sacrificial animal. Finally, it was noted above that the idea of ransom that is represented by the verb כִּפֶּר in this context suggests that the life of the animal is in some way substituting for the life of the offerer.[33] The *beth essentiae* understanding of the בְּ is

---

28. Joüon (133c n. 3) writes, '[The] old, rather unclear expression [*beth essentiae*] probably means that the noun introduced by the בְּ belongs to the *essence* (in the broad sense) of the thing which is being talked about, or it may point to the function of the preposition as a link between the subject and predicate of an equational clause. The expressions *Bet of identity* and *pleonastic Bet* are also found.' See also Jenni, *Präpositionen*, p. 79.

29. See Jenni, *Präpositionen*, p. 79; GKC 119i. For further examples see W&O 11.2.5e; GKC 119i; and especially Jenni, *Präpositionen*, pp. 79-89.

30. JPSV. See also references in n. 20 above.

31. Jenni, *Präpositionen*, p. 84; see also Deut. 12.23: '...for the blood is the life' (כִּי הַדָּם הוּא הַנָּפֶשׁ).

32. Jenni, *Präpositionen*, p. 85. Jenni (p. 85) also reads the בְּ in v. 14a as *beth essentiae*: 'for the life of all flesh is its blood as its life' (כִּי־נֶפֶשׁ כָּל־בָּשָׂר דָּמוֹ בְנַפְשׁוֹ הוּא) (see also Füglister, 'Sühne', pp. 145-46). It is important to note in this regard that by translating the בְּ in v. 11a as *beth essentiae*, as opposed to the common localized translation of the בְּ (i.e. 'for the life of the flesh is *in* the blood'), Jenni diffuses the argument *contra* the *beth essentiae* view that since there is a distinction between flesh and blood in v. 11a, there cannot be an equation of them in v. 11b (e.g. Janowski, *Sühne*, p. 245). Rather, in Jenni's view, both v. 11a and v. 11b equate blood and life.

33. Though Schwartz goes with an instrumental understanding of the בְּ, he is very clear that the relatedness of כִּפֶּר in this verse to the notion of 'ransom' directly implies that a substitution is taking place: 'Consider the paradox in this: on the one hand, [Lev. 17.11] is a clear expression of the idea of measure for measure embodied in the talionic demand, expressed by Priestly law in the phrase נֶפֶשׁ תַּחַת נֶפֶשׁ—"life for life" (Lev. 24.18).

completely compatible with this: '…and I have bestowed [the blood] upon the altar to ransom your souls, for it is the blood, as life, that ransoms' (i.e. that ransoms by serving as a substitute for the life of the offerer).

It may of course be noted that the equation of life and blood in v. 14b does not preclude other possibilities for the בְּ in v. 11 aside from *beth essentiae*, for example, *beth instrumenti*. All in all, however, there is no reason why the *beth essentiae* cannot be a possibility in Lev. 17.11b: it is possible from a grammatical perspective, is consistent with understanding נֶפֶשׁ in v. 11b to refer to the sacrificial animal, and works well with the understanding of כִּפֶּר identified above.

The last (and most prevalent) view is that the בְּ in v. 11b is functioning as a *beth instrumenti*.[34] This use of the בְּ occurs when the בְּ indicates the instrument with which, or the means by which, something is done: 'They strike *with* the rod (בַּשֵּׁבֶט יַכּוּ)' (Mic. 4.14 [5.1]); 'Therefore I swear to the house of Eli that the iniquity of Eli's house shall not be atoned *by means of* sacrifice or offering (אִם־יִתְכַּפֵּר עֲוֹן בֵּית־עֵלִי בְּזֶבַח וּבְמִנְחָה) forever' (1 Sam. 3.14).[35] In Lev. 17.11b, this would then give the sense: '…because it is the blood that makes atonement *by means of* the life'.[36]

The primary support for this position comes from the fact that in every other occurrence of the phrase כִּפֶּר בְּ—with the exception of three locative references (Lev. 6.23 [6.30]; 16.17, 27)—the בְּ is instrumental (Gen. 32.21; Exod. 29.33; Lev. 5.16; 7.7; 19.22; Num. 5.8; 35.33; 1 Sam. 3.14; Isa. 27.9; Prov. 16.6).[37] This fact is significant, and a strong point in favor of an

---

Man has somehow incurred a debt of his life, his נֶפֶשׁ, and this is what he gives—a נֶפֶשׁ. On the other hand it is a rejection, or at least an alleviation, of the very same talionic demand, since the נֶפֶשׁ that man offers here is not his own, nor even actually that of an animal, but merely a כֹּפֶר—a substitute, an exchange which God is willing to receive in place of the real thing' (Schwartz, 'Prohibitions', pp. 56-57). Indeed, in a footnote to this comment Schwartz (p. 57 n. 1) goes on to suggest that it is the implication of substitution in this verse which has actually led some scholars to deny the connection between כפר and כֹּפֶר: '…one of the reasons scholars have labored so arduously at proposing other interpretations of how blood serves לכפר על נפשתיכם, and have often ignored the obvious derivation from כֹּפֶר, has been their reluctance to admit that the idea of vicarious sacrifice, indeed, vicarious *self*-sacrifice, might be at work here… The medievals were not so troubled; see Rashi (תכפר על הנפש); תבוא הנפש ותכפר על הנפש; similarly Ibn Ezra.' As noted above, however, Schwartz does not apply this understanding of כִּפֶּר to any sacrificial context outside of Lev. 17.11, for evaluation of which see §5.2, n. 73.

34. See above, n. 21.

35. GKC 119o; W&O 11.2.5d. For further examples see GKC 119o; W&O 11.2.5d; and most extensively Jenni, *Präpositionen*, pp. 118-49.

36. Hartley, *Leviticus*, p. 261; Elliger, *Leviticus*, p. 218. See further references above in n. 21.

37. Schwartz, 'Prohibitions', p. 47; Kiuchi, *Purification Offering*, p. 105; Dillmann, *Exodus und Leviticus*, p. 538; Milgrom, *Leviticus 1–16*, p. 706; idem, *Leviticus 17–22*, p. 1478; Füglister, 'Sühne', pp. 145-46 n. 11.

instrumental use of the בְּ in this phrase. Moreover, as with the *beth essentiae* view, the *beth instrumenti* position is consistent with understanding נֶפֶשׁ in v. 11b to refer to the sacrificial animal. Finally, this understanding of the בְּ also works well the ransoming nature of כִּפֶּר identified above: '…and I have bestowed [the blood] upon the altar to ransom your souls, for it is the blood that ransoms by means of the life'.[38]

In sum, from a grammatical perspective, the בְּ in Lev. 17.11b could be either a *beth pretii*, a *beth essentiae*, or a *beth instrumenti*. The last two of these are favored over the *beth pretii* approach insofar as they are in keeping with the more likely understanding that נֶפֶשׁ in v. 11b is a reference to the animal's life. Of these two, the *beth instrumenti* view finds strong support in the fact that when the phrase כִּפֶּר בְּ– occurs elsewhere, the בְּ is instrumental, or occasionally locative, but never used as a *beth essentiae*.

Having stated the above, however, it may also be noted that the meaning of v. 11b as a whole does not seem to differ greatly from the *beth instrumenti* understanding to the *beth essentiae* understanding. For this reason, some scholars are content to say that the בְּ could be translated either way, without producing any notable change in the meaning of the phrase.[39] Indeed, whether one states that blood atones *by means of* the life it contains, or whether one states that the blood atones *as* life, it is clear that the atoning function of the blood is grounded in its relation to the life of the animal, that is, *the blood is able to atone because of the life it contains*.

Pulling this together with the observations above on the meaning of כִּפֶּר (§6.1.3), v. 11 may now be translated as follows: 'For the life of the flesh is in the blood, and I myself have bestowed it to you upon the altar to ransom your lives, for it is the blood that ransoms by means of/as the life'. Indeed, this understanding of the verse is in perfect keeping with the observations above on כֹּפֶר (§2.1.3), which was seen to be a legally or ethically legitimate payment which delivers a guilty party from a just punishment that is the right of the offended party to execute or to have executed. The acceptance of this payment is entirely dependent upon the choice of the offended party, it is a lesser punishment than was originally expected, and its acceptance serves both to rescue the life of the guilty and to appease the offended party, thus restoring peace to the relationship. In this regard the life (נֶפֶשׁ) of the offerer is *ransomed* by means of the life (נֶפֶשׁ) of the animal, which is a payment that the offended party (the LORD) has agreed to (and indeed,

---

38. See again the comments of Schwartz ('Prohibitions', pp. 56-57): '…the נֶפֶשׁ that man offers here is not his own…but merely a כֹּפֶר—a substitute, an exchange which God is willing to accept in place of the real thing'.

39. Füglister, 'Sühne', p. 145; Sabourin, 'Nefesh', p. 25. Note that Milgrom was able to change from a *beth essentiae* view ('Prolegomenon', p. 96) to a *beth instrumenti* view (*Leviticus 1–16*, p. 706) without altering his overall understanding of the passage.

provided),⁴⁰ which is less than the penalty the offerer originally expected (viz. their own life), and which both rescues the offerer and restores peace to their relationship with the LORD.

With the above understanding of Lev. 17.11 in hand, we now turn to consider the third question raised above, namely: Which types of sacrifice, whose blood serves as a ransom, are in view in Lev. 17.11?

6.1.5. *Which Types of Sacrifice are in View in Leviticus 17.11?*
Many commentators, both ancient and modern, have seen the theological rationale of this verse as one that is relevant to all atoning sacrifices.⁴¹ This understanding has been challenged, however, by Jacob Milgrom and Herbert Brichto, both of whom have argued that this verse refers exclusively to the peace offering.⁴² Because Milgrom's work is the more extensive of the two, it will be the focus of consideration, though some comment will be reserved for Brichto's work as well.

Milgrom's analysis of Lev. 17.11 essentially involves six points, the first four of which set up a problem in the text, and the last two of which provide the resolution to the problem. Milgrom's first point may be summarized as follows: the people referred to in Lev. 17.11 are guilty of a capital offense, and the sacrificial blood they present is thus for the purpose of ransoming their lives (לְכַפֵּר עַל־נַפְשֹׁתֵיכֶם).⁴³ Milgrom finds support for this point in the phrase לְכַפֵּר עַל־נַפְשֹׁתֵיכֶם. He begins by stating that in a legal context, 'expressions compounded with [the word נֶפֶשׁ] often imply that life is at stake (e.g. Judg. 5.18; 12.3; 1 Sam. 19.5)'.⁴⁴ He finds further support in the fact that the only other two occurrences of the phrase לְכַפֵּר עַל־נַפְשֹׁתֵיכֶם have a

---

40. See the comments above in n. 4 on the phrase 'I myself have bestowed it to you' (v. 11).
41. For a discussion of Lev. 17.11 in early Jewish and Christian literature, see Metzinger, 'Substitutionstheorie', pp. 366-74. For modern applications of this verse to sacrifice in general, see, among others, Levine, *Leviticus*, pp. 115-16; Kurtz, *Sacrificial Worship*, p. 71; Kiuchi, *Purification Offering*, p. 103; Angel M. Rodriguez, *Substitution in the Hebrew Cultus* (Berrien Springs, MI: Andrews University Press, 1979), pp. 237-41; Wenham, *Leviticus*, pp. 61, 245; Hartley, *Leviticus*, pp. 274-75; Budd, *Leviticus*, pp. 247-48; and Martin Noth, *Leviticus* (trans. J.E. Anderson; London: SCM Press, 1965), p. 132 (originally published as *Das dritte Buch Mose, Leviticus* [Das Alte Testament Deutsch, 6; Göttingen: Vandenhoeck & Ruprecht, 1962]). The major exceptions in this regard are Milgrom and Brichto, for which see immediately below.
42. Milgrom, 'Prolegomenon', pp. 96-103; repeated with slight changes in Milgrom, *Leviticus 1–16*, pp. 706-13. In *Leviticus 17–22*, pp. 1472-79, Milgrom adds further points of clarification and responds to various critiques that have been raised against his proposal. The discussion below interacts with his two most recent works. For Brichto's work, see 'On Slaughter and Sacrifice', pp. 19-28, and the discussion below.
43. Milgrom, *Leviticus 1–16*, p. 708.
44. Milgrom, *Leviticus 1–16*, p. 707.

capital offense in view, namely, a census (Exod. 30.11-16; Num. 31.48).[45] Finally, he notes that the verb כִּפֶּר in Exod. 30.11-16 'must be related to the expression found in the same pericope *kōper napšô* "a ransom for his life" (Exod. 30.12)', a combination also found in Num. 35.31-33.[46] This suggests to Milgrom that כִּפֶּר is a denominative of כֹּפֶר in these two cases, which in turn implies 'that all texts that assign to *kippēr* the function of averting God's wrath'—such as Lev. 17.11—'have *kōper* in mind'.[47] All of the above, then, suggests to Milgrom 'that in Lev. 17.11, Israelites have become liable to death before God and the purpose of the sacrificial blood is *lĕkappēr 'al-napšōtêkem* "to ransom your lives"'.[48]

In his second point, Milgrom argues that the sacrifice in view in this pericope as a whole would appear to be the non-expiatory peace offering.[49] To support this, Milgrom appeals first to the phrase 'you will not eat blood', which occurs four times in this pericope and which is a reference to eating meat with the blood in it.[50] Since the peace offering was the only sacrifice eaten by the Israelites, it therefore stands to reason that Leviticus 17 is dealing with peace offerings. In further support, Milgrom notes that vv. 10-14 comprise two laws (vv. 10-12, 13-14) which together form a unity. 'Because the second deals with wild animals—hunted, obviously, for their meat and not for sport (*'āšer yē'kēl*)—the first law undoubtedly also speaks of the flesh of edible animals; these, however, are not game but domestic animals, which, according to H, must be sacrificed at the altar.'[51] Once more, then, it may be concluded 'that Lev. 17.11 does not concern itself with all sacrifices, but refers only to the one sacrifice whose flesh is permitted to be eaten by the laity',[52] namely, the peace offering.[53]

Milgrom proceeds to point out, however, that this conclusion leads to two problems. The first is that the peace offering would then have an expiatory role even though it 'never functions as a *kippūr!*'[54] Indeed, Leviticus only

---

45. Milgrom (*Leviticus 1–16*, p. 708) argues that the capital nature of this offense is indicated by the fact that the purpose of the atonement money 'is explicated by the clause "that no plague shall come upon them in their being counted" (Exod. 30.12b)'.
46. Milgrom, *Leviticus 1–16*, p. 708.
47. Milgrom, *Leviticus 1–16*, p. 708.
48. Milgrom, *Leviticus 1–16*, p. 708.
49. Milgrom, *Leviticus 1–16*, pp. 708-709.
50. Milgrom, *Leviticus 1–16*, pp. 708-709; see above, n. 6.
51. Milgrom, *Leviticus 1–16*, p. 709.
52. Milgrom, *Leviticus 1–16*, p. 709.
53. Though see the comments below.
54. Milgrom, *Leviticus 1–16*, p. 709; Milgrom will later argue that Ezek. 45.15, 17 do assign an atoning function to the peace offering (p. 1478 [correcting his comments in *Leviticus 1–16*, p. 709]), which he sees as only giving further support to his argument that the peace offering in Lev. 17 is also atoning.

identifies the purification, guilt, and burnt offerings as expiatory, but not the peace offering. How then can it be expected to have an expiatory role in this passage?

The second problem, which Milgrom briefly identifies, is that the sin that is to be expiated here is a capital offense against God, for which there can be no expiation:[55]

> In the Priestly laws...there is no sacrificial expiation for capital crime or, for that matter, for any deliberate violation. The presumptuous sinner is banned from the sanctuary because he 'acts defiantly (*běyād rāmâ*)...reviles the LORD...has spurned the word of the LORD and violated his commandment' (Num. 15.30-31; contrast vv 24-29).[56]

Thus Milgrom's first point above (i.e. that the people referred to in Lev. 17.11 are guilty of a capital offense) combined with his second point (i.e. that the sacrificial blood given in this instance to ransom their lives is that of the peace offering) faces two contradictions: '1. The *šĕlāmîm* is the one sacrifice that has no *kippûr* function. 2. No sacrifice can expiate a deliberate sin, not to speak of a capital crime!'[57]

In answer to these problems, Milgrom responds with his last two points. The first of these is that 'animal slaughter is murder except at an authorized altar (vv. 3-4)'.[58] In support, Milgrom appeals to v. 4b, where it is said of the one who slaughters at an *unauthorized* altar: 'blood guilt shall be reckoned to that man: he has shed blood (דָּם יֵחָשֵׁב לָאִישׁ הַהוּא דָּם שָׁפָךְ)'. Milgrom argues that these are 'precise legal terms, which define and categorize the guilt', noting that the idiom *šāpak dām* 'is the well-attested accusation of murder' (Gen. 9.6; Num. 35.33; 1 Sam. 25.31, etc.), and that 'the *niph'al* of *ḥšb* "be reckoned", is the declaratory statement in P and H for designating a cultic act as either acceptable or unacceptable to God (Lev. 7.18; Num. 18.27, 30; cf. Ps. 106.31)'.[59]

Having argued that animal slaughter is murder except at an authorized altar, Milgrom proceeds to his final point, which he takes together with his above point as a resolution of the two contradictions identified earlier: 'The resolution of both objections is found in the opening law of this chapter: animal slaughter is murder except at an authorized altar (vv. 3-4). Verse 11 offers the remedy: the blood ransoms the offerer's life and clears him of the charge of murder.'[60] In short, the blood of the peace offering is functioning

---

55. Milgrom, *Leviticus 1–16*, pp. 708-10.
56. Milgrom, *Leviticus 1–16*, p. 710.
57. Milgrom, *Leviticus 17–22*, p. 1474.
58. Milgrom, *Leviticus 17–22*, p. 1474, and *Leviticus 1–16*, pp. 710-11.
59. Milgrom, *Leviticus 1–16*, p. 710.
60. Milgrom, *Leviticus 17–22*, p. 1474, and *Leviticus 1–16*, pp. 710-11.

6. *A Consideration of the Role of Blood* 177

in an atoning manner here, insofar as it is ransoming the offerer for the crime of murder, that is, of killing the sacrificial animal.

Once again, Milgrom has supplied an incredibly creative and new approach to a much-discussed text. Despite this creativity, however, Milgrom's proposal appears unlikely. In particular, Milgrom's thesis depends upon vv. 10-12 being restricted to discussing the peace offering alone (his second point above). It should be noted, however, that it is not simply the blood of the peace offering that is in view in v. 10: 'If anyone of the house of Israel or of the strangers that sojourn among them eats *any* blood (אֲשֶׁר יֹאכַל כָּל־דָּם), I will set my face against the person who eats blood, and will cut that person off from among their people'. Milgrom's own comments on the phrase 'any blood' in this verse are instructive:

> Since the blood of game is the topic of the next law (vv. 13-14), one might argue that 'any blood' in this verse refers to only sacrificial animals. The rabbis, however, claim that this blood prohibition is total: it includes non-sacrificial animals as well (*Sipra* Aḥare, par. 3.3; *b. Ker.* 4b). This view is corroborated by the occurrence of the same phrase in another attestation of the blood prohibition (7.27 [*sic*; read 7.26]), which contains the added words *lā'ôp wĕlabbĕhēmâ* 'of birds and beasts', a phrase intended to include every *nonsacrificial* category: game, blemished animals, and carcasses.[61]

Verse 10 is thus a general prohibition against eating blood; it is not limited to the peace offering alone.[62]

Verse 11 then proceeds to provide two grounds for this general prohibition. The first is that the blood contains the life (v. 11aα). In keeping with the broad view of v. 10, this statement is true of the blood of all animals, not just sacrificial ones, and certainly not just the blood of the peace offering. As also noted above in §6.1.2, the reason that the life of an animal may not be consumed is due not only to the general respect for life found in the Old Testament, but also to the fact that God himself is the owner of life. Indeed, it is God's ownership of the life that leads to the second ground of v. 11, namely, 'and I myself have bestowed it to you upon the altar to ransom your lives' (v. 11aβ). In other words, the LORD has indeed granted that the Israelites may make use of the blood of animals; however, this use is very restricted, namely, solely for the making of atonement (and not for eating).

In short, then, v. 10 takes its eyes off of the peace offering to make a general prohibition against the consumption of the blood of *any* animal, sacrificial or not. Verse 11 then provides two grounds for this general prohibition: (1) the blood of animals contains its life, which may not be consumed, and (2) there is only one purpose that the LORD has allowed the Israelites to use

---

61. Milgrom, *Leviticus 17–22*, pp. 1470-71 (emphasis added).
62. The same is argued by Schwartz, 'Prohibitions', p. 44.

animal's blood for, namely, making atonement. There is thus no obligation to read v. 11 with specific reference to the peace offering. Rather, the text simply affirms that there is only one legitimate use for blood, namely, for the making of atonement. In this light, it is most natural to read this verse with reference to the sacrifices in Leviticus that accomplish atonement, that is, the purification, guilt, and burnt offerings.[63] This leads to a second point.

With reference to the traditional view that Lev. 17.11 is not addressing the peace offering but rather atoning sacrifice in general, Milgrom writes as follows:

> [This] interpretation...must be rejected out of hand. Why should the blood of the ḥaṭṭā't and 'āšām, the exclusive expiatory sacrifices, brought for *inadvertent* wrongs, ransom the offerer's life? What capital crime has he committed to warrant the forfeit of his life? In particular, as I argued thirty years ago,[64] is the new mother, whose 'ōlâ and ḥaṭṭā't offerings expressly expiate on her behalf (wĕkipper 'ālêhā, 12.7, 8), deserving of death because she had a baby?[65]

The first two questions may be considered together, before turning to the third.

The underlying assumption of Milgrom's first two questions is that one's life is never at risk due to an inadvertent sin. It would be true to say that one never *has* to forfeit their life for inadvertent sin, as is evident from the provisions made for unintentional sin in Leviticus 4 and 5, and especially in the contrast in Numbers 15 between the inadvertent sinner, for whom atonement (כִּפֶּר) and forgiveness (סָלַח) are possible (vv. 22-29), and the high-handed sinner, who is cut off (כָּרַת) from their people (vv. 30-31). Nonetheless, as discussed in §1.3 above, the fact that the inadvertent sinner may be forgiven by means of atonement does not mean that their life is *never* at risk. Indeed, as seen above in Chapter 3, the כִּפֶּר-rite in contexts of inadvertent sin is characterized by the *ransoming* of the sinner, that is, the giving of a legally

---

63. For those coming to a similar conclusion *contra* Milgrom, see also Schenker, 'Das Zeichen', p. 209; Frank H. Gorman, *The Ideology of Ritual: Space, Time and Status in the Priestly Theology* (JSOTSup, 91; Sheffield: JSOT Press, 1990), pp. 184-87; Schwartz, 'Prohibitions', pp. 58-60; Hartley, *Leviticus*, p. 275; Rendtorff, *Leviticus*, p. 169. There is some question as to whether or not the peace offering should be included in the list of atoning sacrifices. It may be noted that כִּפֶּר is never conjoined with the peace offering in the priestly literature, nor are the two conjoined frequently elsewhere, implying that atonement is not its primary function. That it can have an atoning function, however, finds support in Ezek. 45.15, 17 (so Rodriguez, *Substitution*, p. 228; Janowski, *Sühne*, p. 191 n. 30; Milgrom, *Leviticus 17–22*, p. 1478 [see n. 54 above]). In short, the peace offering can have an atoning function, though since this does not appear to be its major purpose, it is not included in the list of atoning sacrifices above.

64. See Jacob Milgrom, 'The Function of the ḥaṭṭā't Sacrifice', *Tarbiz* 40 (1970), pp. 1-8 (Hebrew).

65. Milgrom, *Leviticus 17–22*, p. 1475 (emphasis his).

legitimate ransom payment (כֹּפֶר) that acts as a mitigated penalty. Within this context, forgiveness functions as an expression of agreement to and acceptance of the ransom payment (כֹּפֶר). In short, it is not that the inadvertency of the sin means that there is no punishment to face; rather, the inadvertency of the sin means that the sinner is able to escape the expected punishment (i.e. death) by means of a כֹּפֶר-payment (i.e. the atoning sacrifice) which has been agreed to by the offended party (i.e. the LORD).

This in turn sets the proper context for answering Milgrom's third question, namely, whether the new mother is deserving of death because she had a baby. This problem has already been discussed to some extent in §4.4.1 and §5.2 above. As noted there, Milgrom himself argues that the new mother has defiled the tabernacle by giving birth. In the priestly system, however, defiling the sanctuary is a sin that leads to death (Lev. 15.31; Num. 19.13, 20). Naturally, it was not the new mother's intent to defile the tabernacle, and in this regard the sin may be classified as inadvertent. Like any other inadvertent sin, therefore, the new mother is able to escape from the penalty that her sin would normally incur (death) by means of the כֹּפֶר-payment agreed to by the offended party, that is, the atoning sacrifices stipulated by the LORD (Lev. 12.6-8). The case of the new mother is thus not a substantial reason to reject the traditional understanding of Lev. 17.11.

Similar to Milgrom, Herbert Brichto also argues that Lev. 17.11 has reference exclusively to the peace offering and not to the other atoning sacrifices. Like Milgrom, Brichto argues that slaughtering a (domestic) animal at any place except the tabernacle constitutes an act of murder,[66] and that the immediate context of Lev. 17.11 deals with the peace offering.[67] In addition, Brichto states that the בְּ in the phrase כִּי־הַדָּם הוּא בַּנֶּפֶשׁ יְכַפֵּר (v. 11b) is not a *beth essentiae*, but rather a *beth pretii*, or, as he calls it, a '*bet* of exchange', appealing to the interchange of בְּ and תַּחַת in the talionic formulas.[68] Brichto is unique, however, in arguing that נֶפֶשׁ here does not refer to the life of the offerer, since 'this latter element is already present in the verse in the plural of *nepeš* governed by the preposition *'al*: *'al napšōtēkem* "for/on behalf of your lives"'.[69] Instead, it refers to the life of the animal. Finally, he proceeds to argue that the word כִּפֶּר in this phrase is a denominative of כֹּפֶר; it thus refers to the effecting of a composition payment, which he defines as follows:

---

66. Brichto, 'On Slaughter and Sacrifice', p. 24.
67. 'We are...in complete agreement with Milgrom in rejecting the widely-held view that the function here of the altar-blood to *kipper* "for your lives" defines the purpose of all sacrificial blood; for, as he puts it, the contextual *šelāmîm*-sacrifices "have nothing to do with sin"' (Brichto, 'On Slaughter and Sacrifice', p. 27; see also p. 25).
68. Brichto, 'On Slaughter and Sacrifice', p. 28.
69. Brichto, 'On Slaughter and Sacrifice', p. 27.

An imbalance between two parties (individuals, families, clans or larger social groupings) results from a damage or deprivation inflicted upon one by the other. Equilibrium is restored by a process which consists of a transfer of something of value (a person, an animal, or a commutation of such in the form of commodity or currency) from the injuring party to the injured. The acceptance of this value-item by the latter, itself termed 'the composition' (as is the process itself also), serves to 'compose' or settle the difference.[70]

Having made the above points, he states the following conclusions:

1. The *kōper* is the *quid* in the *quid pro quo* of the compository transaction. Let us render this *quid* as 'the compository element/payment'.
2. The preposition *beth* in the word *bannepeš* is the *beth* of exchange, the *pro* in the *quid pro quo*. Let us render it 'in composition for'.
3. The *nepeš* governed by the preposition *beth* is not life as an abstraction nor the life of a person. Rather, this 'life', this *nepeš* is the *quo* in the *quid pro quo*, that is, the life of the victim, of the animal slaughtered.[71]

This in turn leads to his final translation of Lev. 17.11b: 'For it is the blood which serves as *kōper*, compository payment, for the life (taken)'.[72]

Brichto is correct that כִּפֶּר in this verse refers primarily to the effecting of a composition (or ransom) payment. His restriction of this verse to the peace offering, however, appears incorrect, as does his understanding of the word בַּנֶּפֶשׁ in v. 11b. Since these points have already been addressed in various sections of the discussion above, the following may be briefly noted. First, it has already been noted that v. 10 introduces a more general prohibition against the eating of *any* blood, and in so doing takes its eyes off of the peace offering in particular.[73] Verse 11 then provides two grounds for this general prohibition, one of which is that there is only one purpose the LORD has allowed the Israelite's to use blood for, namely, atonement. Verse 11 is thus better read as a general reference to those sacrifices in Leviticus which accomplish atonement. Second, with reference to the meaning of the בְ in the word בַּנֶּפֶשׁ, it has been noted above that the appeal to the interchange between בְ and תַּחַת in the talionic formulas is not conclusive, due to the fact that the formulas in Exod. 21.23, Lev. 24.18, and Deut. 19.21 all differ from the formula in this verse, and due further to the fact that Lev. 24.18, the only other priestly instance of the talionic formula, uses תַּחַת and not בְ. It may be further noted in this regard that Brichto provides no substantial critique of

---

70. Brichto, 'On Slaughter and Sacrifice', pp. 27-28.
71. Brichto, 'On Slaughter and Sacrifice', p. 28.
72. Brichto, 'On Slaughter and Sacrifice', p. 28.
73. Brichto ('On Slaughter and Sacrifice', p. 23) translates v. 10 as follows: 'Yes, any man of Israel's line, or of the alien residing among them, *who at all* partakes of the blood (אֲשֶׁר יֹאכַל כָּל־דָּם)' (emphasis added). There is no apparent justification for this translation, especially in view of Lev. 7.26-27.

the other positions: he makes the surprising comment that the *beth essentiae* category is one 'whose very existence is without basis',[74] and his only remark on the *beth instrumenti* view is as follows: 'A more reasonable treatment of the preposition governing *nepeš* [than that of the *bet essentiae* view] is, as Levine proposes, *bet pretii* "of price". The alternative suggestion, that it is *beth instrumenti*, would be a response to the demurrer that a commercial usage is not quite apposite to the sacral context.'[75] It is not entirely clear whether this last comment is to be taken positively or negatively. If taken positively, this last comment would mean that the *beth instrumenti* was an option in his view. If taken negatively, it is not clear why he disagrees with this view, which has substantial support in the frequent occurrence of the phrase בְּכֶפֶר־. Finally, as also noted above, the most likely referent of נֶפֶשׁ in v. 11b is the offerer and not the animal.

6.2. *Summary and Conclusion*

In sum, then, the most compelling understanding of Lev. 17.11 is the traditional one, namely, that Lev. 17.11 identifies a general theological principle that applies to the atoning sacrifices: the life-blood of the sacrificial animal atones for the life of the offerer.

Thus far the following conclusions on Lev. 17.11 have been reached. First, as noted by many scholars today, כֹּפֶר in this verse is best taken in the sense of 'ransom'. In this regard, the life-containing blood of the animal serves as the ransom for the life of the offerer. Second, the בְּ in the phrase כִּי־הַדָּם הוּא בַּנֶּפֶשׁ יְכַפֵּר could be translated either as a *beth instrumenti* or *beth essentiae*. The verse as a whole is thus translated: 'For the life of the flesh is in the blood, and I myself have bestowed it to you upon the altar to ransom your lives, for it is the blood that ransoms by means of/as the life'. Third, *contra* Milgrom and Brichto, this verse does not refer exclusively to the peace offering. Instead, the traditional reading of the verse, and in particular of v. 11b, is correct, that is, it is stating a general theological principle that applies to all atoning sacrifices, namely, the purification, guilt, and burnt offerings.[76]

---

74. Brichto, 'On Slaughter and Sacrifice', p. 26; cf. above, n. 29, and especially Jenni, *Präpositionen*, pp. 79-89! Brichto's comment is based in part upon a misreading of GKC (Janowski, *Sühne*, p. 245 n. 310). In a footnote to the comment cited above, Brichto ('On Slaughter and Sacrifice', p. 26 n. 18) writes, 'See, for example, Gesenius-Kautzsch-Cowley, 119i, for the examples which are so dubious as to receive characterization as "the בְּ *essentiae* of the earlier grammarians"'. Read in context, however, GKC's comment is not pejorative, but simply a means of identifying this particular use of the בְּ.
75. Brichto, 'On Slaughter and Sacrifice', p. 27.
76. For the peace offering, see above, n. 63.

With this in hand we may now return to the question with which this chapter began, namely: Why is the כִּפֶּר-rite able to fulfill the dual role of כֹּפֶר and purgation? The answer is simply that the blood of the animal that is sacrificed in the כִּפֶּר-rite contains life, and life-containing blood both ransoms and purifies. The purifying power of blood has been noted above in Chapter 4 (see §4.1.1 and §4.1.2) and is illustrated in Lev. 8.15 and 16.19. The ransoming power of blood was implied above by the centrality of blood to the ransom-effecting כִּפֶּר-rites discussed in Chapters 3 and 4. To the implications of these two chapters is now added the explicit statement of Lev. 17.11 identified in this chapter, namely, that the blood of atoning sacrifices does indeed ransom the life of the sinner. Finally, the power of blood to both ransom and purify is not only a logical implication of the above, it is also evident from the discussion of Num. 35.30-34 in the last chapter (§5.2), where life-blood functions in this dual way.

A final comment is in order. It may be asked: If כִּפֶּר refers primarily to 'ransom' in Lev. 17.11, does this not undermine the thesis that it refers to both ransom and purgation elsewhere? By no means. As noted above in Chapter 5, the emphasis of כִּפֶּר in some contexts (such as those addressing inadvertent sin [Chapter 3]) is upon ransom (כֹּפֶר), while the emphasis in other contexts (such as those addressing major impurity [Chapter 4]) is upon purgation.[77] The emphasis of Lev. 17.11 is in keeping with the former of these. In either context, however, it was seen that the end point of sin and impurity is the same: both endanger (requiring ransom) and both pollute (requiring purgation). As a result, it is not simply כֹּפֶר that is needed in some instances and purgation that is needed in others, but כֹּפֶר-purgation that is needed in both. In short, due to the similar ending points of sin and impurity, even when the emphasis is upon ransom (כֹּפֶר), it is a purifying ransom that is in view, and even when the emphasis is upon purgation, it is a ransoming-purgation that is in view. The verb that describes this dual event is כִּפֶּר, and the ability of the כִּפֶּר-rite to accomplish this dual event is due to the blood of the sacrifice which both ransoms and purifies.

---

77. It was suggested that this difference is due to the different starting points of sin and impurity; see further Chapter 5, n. 74.

7

Conclusion

The main title of this work derives from the fact that the priestly literature describes instances where both *sin* and *impurity* require *sacrifice* for *atonement* (כִּפֶּר). This fact leads to two questions. First: Why does the verb כִּפֶּר appear in contexts of both inadvertent sin and major impurity in the priestly literature? This question is the focus of Parts I–III (Chapters 1 to 5). The answer to this question leads to a second, namely: Why is sacrifice able to fulfill the dual function of כִּפֶּר and purgation? This question is the focus of Part IV (Chapter 6). The main conclusions and contributions of this study may be organized under the answers to these two questions. As the first question is the focus of Parts I–III of the study, its answer will naturally be longer than that of the second.

1. *Why does the verb כִּפֶּר appear in contexts of both inadvertent sin and major impurity in the priestly literature?* More specifically, while a verb for atonement is not surprising in contexts of sin, why does it also occur in contexts of impurity, which is often the result of amoral circumstances (such as having a baby)? This question is especially focused with reference to the translation of the verb כִּפֶּר.

In sin contexts, כִּפֶּר has traditionally been translated with 'to atone/ expiate' or 'to perform atonement/expiation'. While the nature of this atonement has been variously understood, it is argued in Part I (Chapters 1 to 3) that כִּפֶּר is related to כֹּפֶר in meaning and refers to the execution of a כֹּפֶר-payment on behalf of the offerer. The necessity of כֹּפֶר in sin contexts was established in Chapter 1, where it is argued that there is a connection between sin and punishment. In particular, this study has argued that even inadvertent sins may be followed by punitive consequences, and will ultimately result in death if not properly addressed. For this reason, even the inadvertent sinner is endangered, and therefore in need of a ransom.

Having established the necessity of כֹּפֶר for the inadvertent sinner, and anticipating that כִּפֶּר is related to כֹּפֶר in sin contexts, the term כֹּפֶר was examined in Chapter 2. This led to the definition of כֹּפֶר as a legally or ethically legitimate payment that delivers a guilty party from a just punishment that is the right of the offended party to execute or to have executed. It is further noted that the acceptance of this payment was entirely dependent upon the choice of the offended party. Finally, it was also seen that the כֹּפֶר was a lesser punishment than was originally expected, and that its acceptance serves to rescue the life of the guilty on the one hand and to appease the offended party on the other.

Having established that the inadvertent sinner is in need of a כֹּפֶר (Chapter 1), and having defined the term (Chapter 2), the study next argued that כִּפֶּר does indeed refer to the effecting of a כֹּפֶר-payment in sin contexts (Chapter 3). That כִּפֶּר can be used to refer to effecting a כֹּפֶר-payment was already established in Chapter 2 with reference to such passages as Exod. 30.12-16 and Num. 35.31-33. That it is used in this way in contexts of inadvertent sin was established in Chapter 3 through an examination of the term סָלַח and the phrase נָשָׂא עָוֹן, both of which describe the results of כִּפֶּר in sin contexts. Significantly, both of these describe results which are in keeping with the nature of כֹּפֶר. Thus the verb סָלַח, which describes the results of כִּפֶּר in the well-known phrase (וְכִפֶּר עָלָיו הַכֹּהֵן מֵחַטָּאתוֹ/עַל־חַטָּאתוֹ אֲשֶׁר־חָטָא, וְנִסְלַח לוֹ) need not refer to the removal of all penalty, but may be used to refer to the substitution of a mitigated penalty. This was seen through a consideration of Numbers 14, where the LORD's decision to forgive (סָלַחְתִּי) the people is expressed in the substitution of a mitigated penalty (non-entry into the land) for a much more severe penalty (immediate destruction by plague, being disinherited). In this way, סָלַח was seen to be an expression of the כֹּפֶר-principle. The same was seen to be true for the phrase נָשָׂא עָוֹן in Exod. 28.38, Lev. 10.17, and 16.22. In each of these instances the offended party (the LORD) prescribed a special means (a כֹּפֶר) by which the penalty of sin could be avoided. By executing the כֹּפֶר-rite (the purification offering [Lev. 10.17]; the scapegoat [Lev. 16.22]), or simply by wearing the golden plate (Exod. 28.38), the sin is borne away (נָשָׂא עָוֹן), and the guilty party is no longer subject to punishment.

In short, sinners who bring a sacrifice are *endangered* because of their sin. The sacrifice thus serves to ransom them, delivering them from punishment and appeasing the offended party. This in turn suggested that the traditional rendering of כִּפֶּר with 'to atone' is appropriate in these contexts, with the understanding that atonement refers to the effecting of a ransom payment (כֹּפֶר) on behalf of the offerer.

Two further considerations, however, were raised at this point. First, it was argued in Chapter 3, following Jacob Milgrom, that inadvertent sins do not simply endanger; like impurities, they also *pollute*. This was supported on the one hand from the fact that one may pollute the sanctuary without having direct contact with it (e.g. Lev. 20.3), which in turn suggested that

7. Conclusion

the sins of Leviticus 4 and 5 may also pollute the sanctuary, even if direct contact with it is not involved. It was supported on the other hand by the fact that one of the functions of the purification offering is the cleansing of the sanctuary and its sancta (Lev. 16.16, 19, 33; see also 8.15). The requirement of the purification offering in Leviticus 4 and 5 thus suggested that these sins have resulted in the contamination of the sanctuary. These facts in turn implied that כִּפֶּר might also refer to purification, and not simply to ransom (כֹּפֶר), in these contexts.

The second consideration that was raised at this point was how כִּפֶּר is to be translated in contexts of impurity, where no wrong has been done. It is not immediately clear, for example, why a new mother would need to be 'ransomed' for giving birth to a baby. Part II (Chapter 4) therefore concentrated on the meaning of כִּפֶּר in contexts of impurity. This was done through a comparison of כִּפֶּר with the three verbs that it occurs in conjunction with in these contexts, namely, טהר, חטא, and קדש. The first two of these verbs, טהר and חטא, are used in contexts of purification, that is, where a person or object is moving from an impure state to a pure state. It was seen that these verbs occur in close conjunction with כִּפֶּר and that כִּפֶּר does include elements of purification in these instances. This led to a tentative translation of כִּפֶּר with 'to effect purgation' in purification contexts. At the same time, it was also seen that כִּפֶּר is not synonymous with these terms, and in particular, that while טהר and חטא can occur in contexts where either blood or water is the means of cleansing, כִּפֶּר only occurs in contexts where blood is involved, that is, where a sacrifice is made. This in turn suggested that there is something about sacrifice, and in particular the blood of sacrifice, that is fundamental to the meaning of כִּפֶּר in purification contexts.

The last verb, קדש, is used in consecration contexts. As with טהר and חטא above, it was seen that קדש also occurs in close conjunction with כִּפֶּר, and that כִּפֶּר does involve an element of consecration in these instances. This would in turn suggest a translation of כִּפֶּר in these contexts with 'to effect consecration'. It was argued, however, that consecration is best understood as an intense form of purification. That is to say, though the person or object that is being consecrated might already be 'pure' (טָהוֹר), this purity is as impurity *relative to the state of holiness*. As a result, the person or object is still in need of cleansing. For this reason, כִּפֶּר was still tentatively translated with 'to effect purgation' in these contexts, with the acknowledgment that this cleansing is a more intense form of cleansing than purification by itself. It was once again identified, however, that כִּפֶּר is not synonymous with קדש in these contexts. In particular, קדש is used to indicate consecration taking place in a wide variety of contexts, in most of which sacrificial blood plays no part, while כִּפֶּר only occurs in consecration contexts in conjunction with a sacrifice and anointing with blood. This again suggested that sacrifice, and in particular the blood of sacrifice, is central to the meaning of כִּפֶּר, though not to the meaning of קדשׁ.

On the one hand, then, it was concluded that in contexts of purification and consecration כִּפֶּר refers to a sacrificial rite carried out by the priest on behalf of the person or object in need of cleansing that results in that person or object becoming pure or holy. The verb was thus tentatively translated with 'to effect purgation' in these contexts.

On the other hand, however, it was also concluded that the term כִּפֶּר is not an exact synonym of other terms for purifying (טהר, חטא) or consecrating (קדשׁ). In particular, there is something about sacrifice, and especially the blood of sacrifice, that sets כִּפֶּר apart. This last observation will be returned to below in addressing the second main question of this study.

Having identified the purificatory nature of כִּפֶּר, Chapter 4 proceeded to argue that כִּפֶּר in these instances likely involves an element of כֹּפֶר as well. In the context of purification from a major impurity, for example, it was argued that a כֹּפֶר is necessary since the person with a major impurity has defiled the tabernacle (albeit unintentionally). This then puts them in the same position as one who has committed an inadvertent sin, and thus in need of a כֹּפֶר. In the context of those preparing for service in the tabernacle, be it those who are purified (the Levites) or those who are consecrated (Aaron and his sons), it was argued that the lives of those entering such service are put at risk due to the general impurity of people relative to the holy. Consequently, the כִּפֶּר-rite not only cleanses them, it also ransoms their lives from certain death. In short, impurity does not simply *pollute*; like sin, it also *endangers*, and כִּפֶּר must address both of these elements in purification contexts. This was seen as an important corrective to more recent studies that have emphasized the purificatory elements of כִּפֶּר in purification contexts, without at the same time identifying the danger that this impurity results in.

The similarities between sin and impurity in Parts I and II lead us to consider the relationship between them in Part III (Chapter 5). Following Wright's analysis, the differing types of impurity and sin were compared in a four-columned chart, with each column corresponding to a different category and increasing in severity from left to right: minor ritual pollution (column one), major ritual pollution (column two), inadvertent moral pollution (column three), and intentional moral pollution (column four). This chart was especially helpful in making clear the similarities between major ritual pollution (column two) and inadvertent moral pollution (column three), similarities adumbrated in Chapters 3 and 4: in both instances the sanctuary and/or its sancta have been defiled, and in both instances a כִּפֶּר-effecting sacrifice is required.

These similarities, combined with the observations from Chapters 3 and 4, are fundamental to understanding how to approach the verb כִּפֶּר in each column. In sum, it was argued that כִּפֶּר is best translated with 'to effect כִּפֶּר-

purgation' in both columns two and three. This rendering is an implicit recognition that the ultimate results of major impurities and inadvertent sins are the same, namely, that each requires both *ransom* (כֹּפֶר) and *cleansing* (purgation). Stated differently, impurity not only *pollutes*, it also *endangers*, while sin not only *endangers*, it also *pollutes*. In either case, therefore, the person presenting the sacrifice needs to effect both כֹּפֶר and purgation. The verb used to describe this dual event is כִּפֶּר.

2. *Why is sacrifice able to fulfil the dual function of* כֹּפֶר *and purgation?* The answer to this question was found in the blood of the sacrifice, which both ransoms and purifies. The purifying power of blood was noted above in Chapter 4 (see §4.1.1 and §4.1.2) and is illustrated in Lev. 8.15 and 16.19. The ransoming power of blood was implied above by the centrality of blood to the ransom-effecting כִּפֶּר-rites discussed in Chapters 3 and 4. To the implications of these two chapters was added the explicit statement of Lev. 17.11 identified in Chapter 6, namely, that the blood of atoning sacrifices does indeed ransom the life of the sinner. Finally, the power of blood to both ransom and purify was not only a logical implication of the above, it was also evident from the discussion of Num. 35.30-34 in Chapter 5 (§5.2), where life-blood was seen to function in this dual way.

In sum, inadvertent sin and major impurity both require sacrifice for atonement. Since both inadvertent sin and major impurity endanger (requiring ransom) and pollute (requiring purgation), sacrificial atonement must both ransom and cleanse. The verb used to describe this dual event is the verb כִּפֶּר, and the power of the כִּפֶּר-rite to accomplish both is due to the lifeblood of the animal.

APPENDIX

כִּפֶּר AND ITS SYNTAGMATIC RELATIONS IN THE PRIESTLY LITERATURE

The term כִּפֶּר occurs in the priestly literature with the following syntagmatic relations:[1]

I. כִּפֶּר + עַל
   a. + impers. obj.[2]   Exod. 29.36, 37; 30.10a; Lev. 8.15; 14.53; 16.18[3]
   b. + pers. obj.   Exod. 30.15, 16; Lev. 1.4; 4.20, 31; 5.26 (6.7); 8.34; 10.17; 12.7, 8; 14.18, 20, 21, 29, 31; 16.10,[4] 30, 33; 17.11a; 23.28; Num. 8.12, 19, 21; 15.25, 28 (× 2); 17.11 (16.46), 12 (16.47); 25.13; 28.22, 30; 29.5; 31.50; Ezek. 45.15; 1 Chron. 6.34 (49); 2 Chron. 29.24[5]
   c. + pers. obj. + מִן   Lev. 4.26; 5.6, 10; 14.19; 15.15, 30; 16.34; Num. 6.11
   d. + impers. obj. + מִן   Exod. 30.10b; Lev. 16.16[6]
   e. + pers. obj. + עַל   Lev. 4.35; 5.13, 18
   f. + בְּ (instrumental)   Lev. 5.16; Num. 5.8
   g. + בְּ (instrumental) + עַל   Lev. 19.22

   1. The following chart is based upon that of Janowski, *Sühne*, pp. 186-87, followed in turn by Kiuchi, *Purification Offering*, p. 88. Due to the similarity in subject matter between the priestly material, Ezek. 40–48, and 'ChrG' (*chronistischen Geschichtswerk*), Janowski includes references from these last two books in his discussion, which is also followed in the above.
   2. All of the references following are to sancta, with the exception of Lev. 14.53, which refers to the 'leprous' house.
   3. See also Jer. 18.23; Ps. 79.9.
   4. For this verse see Chapter 3, n. 41.
   5. See also Neh. 10.34 (33).
   6. Though these constructions are formally the same, the מִן functions differently in each: '...*from* (or: *with*) (מִן) the blood of the purification offering of atonement he shall make atonement for it...' (Exod. 30.10b); '...thus he shall make atonement for the holy place, *because of* (מִן) the uncleannesses of the people...' (Lev. 16.16; for this use of מִן cf. Lev. 5.10 [אֲשֶׁר־חָטָא מֵחַטָּאתוֹ הַכֹּהֵן עָלָיו וְכִפֶּר] with Lev. 5.13 [וְכִפֶּר עָלָיו הַכֹּהֵן עַל־חַטָּאתוֹ אֲשֶׁר־חָטָא]).

II.	כִּפֶּר + impers. dir. obj. (sanctum)	Lev. 16.20, 33 (× 2);[7] Ezek. 43.20, 26; 45.20[8]
III.	כִּפֶּר + בְּעַד + pers. obj.	Lev. 9.7 (× 2); 16.6, 11, 17b, 24; Ezek. 45.17; 2 Chron. 30.18-19[9]
IV.	כִּפֶּר + בְּ	
	a. locative	Lev. 6.23 (30); 16.17a, 27
	b. instrumental	Exod. 29.33 (pual); Lev. 7.7; 17.11b; Num. 35.33 (pual)[10]
V.	כֻּפַּר (note pual) + לְ	Num. 35.33[11]

There is a broad consensus with regard to the meaning of the prepositions in I.b, c, e, f, g, III, IV, and V above. Thus עַל in I.b, c, e, f, and g is generally translated as 'for' or 'on behalf of'. This finds support in comparison with the use of בְּעַד in III: 'And the priest will atone *for them* (עֲלֵהֶם) [i.e. the people]' (Lev. 4.20); 'And [Aaron] will atone *on his behalf* (בַּעֲדוֹ) and *on behalf of* the people (וּבְעַד הָעָם)' (Lev. 16.24).[12] In IV.a the בְּ is translated with a locative sense ('to perform atonement in the holy place [בַּקֹּדֶשׁ]' [Lev. 6.23 (30)]), and in IV.b with an instrumental sense ('and the priest who performs atonement with it [יְכַפֶּר־בּוֹ] [i.e. the guilt offering]' [Lev. 7.7]. And in V, the לְ is translated with 'for': 'But for the land no atonement will be made (וְלָאָרֶץ לֹא־יְכֻפַּר)' (Num. 35.33).

There is less agreement, however, on how to translate the עַל in I.a and d, and on how to translate the direct object marker in II.[13] Each of these will be considered in turn.

---

7. Leviticus 16.32 has וְכִפֶּר הַכֹּהֵן without any object, though this is due to the fact that the rest of the verse is explicating הַכֹּהֵן; v. 33 then resumes the flow of thought and identifies that object (וְכִפֶּר אֶת־מִקְדַּשׁ).

8. Though not part of the sanctuary or its sancta, see also Gen. 32.21 (20); Deut. 32.43; 1 Sam. 3.14 (hithpael); Isa. 6.7 (pual); 22.14 (pual); 27.9 (pual); 28.18 (pual); 47.11; Pss. 65.4 (3); 78.38; Prov. 16.6 (pual), 14; Dan. 9.24.

9. See also Exod. 32.30.

10. See also I.f, g, V, and Gen. 32.21; 1 Sam. 3.14; 2 Sam. 21.3; Isa. 27.9; Prov. 16.6. For Lev. 17.11b, see §6.1.4.

11. This verse also has an instrumental בְּ. For כפר + לְ see also Deut. 21.8 (once piel, once nithpael); Ezek. 16.63 (piel). Other constructions include כפר + direct object + לְ (Isa. 22.14 [pual]) and כפר + direct object + בְּ (instrumental; Prov. 16.6 [pual]; 1 Sam. 3.14 [hithpael]).

12. There does not seem to be any real semantic difference between כִּפֶּר עַל and כִּפֶּר בְּעַד in these contexts. Milgrom (*Leviticus 1–16*, p. 578) argues that the choice of one over the other, however, is not without reason: "*'al* can refer only to persons other than the subject, but when the subject wishes to refer to himself *bě'ad* must be used (e.g. 16.6, 11, 24; Ezek. 45.22). This distinction is confirmed by Job 42.28 [*sic*; read 42.8]: "Offer a burnt offering for yourselves (*bě'adkem*) and Job, my servant, will intercede on your behalf (*'ălêkem*)"' (see Milgrom's earlier article, '*kipper 'al běadh*', *Leshonenu* 35 [1970], pp. 16-17 [Hebrew]).

13. All of the references in Group II above have the direct object marker except for Ezek. 43.20, which simply has a pronominal suffix (וְכִפַּרְתָּהוּ [i.e. the altar]); note v. 26,

In I.a and d the phrase כִּפֶּר עַל is followed by an impersonal object such as the altar or its horns, the holy place, the tent of meeting, or the 'leprous' house (Exod. 29.36, 37; 30.10a, b; Lev. 8.15; 14.53; 16.16, 18).[14] This has raised a question insofar as it is generally acknowledged that כִּפֶּר עַל followed by a personal object is best translated as 'to atone for' or 'to atone on behalf of' the person. It is not immediately evident to a modern reader, however, what it might mean to atone *for* or *on behalf of* an impersonal object such as the altar, other sancta, or a house. This problem has been answered in at least two different ways.

On the one hand, Jacob Milgrom holds that the עַל in these instances is best translated with 'on' or 'upon'. He renders Lev. 14.53, for instance, as follows: '…he shall release the live bird over the open country outside the city. Thus he shall perform purgation upon the house (וְכִפֶּר עַל־הַבָּיִת) and it shall be pure.'[15] This seems possible in most instances, insofar as the object of the preposition is often the recipient of some aspect of the כִּפֶּר-rite, for example, blood is sprinkled upon the leprous house (Lev. 14.51), or placed upon the altar (Exod. 30.10; Lev. 16.18).

On the other hand, Kiuchi argues that the עַל in these instances should be translated the same as it is when followed by a personal object (i.e. with 'for'). In support, Kiuchi notes that the idea of atoning for sancta, which might strike modern ears as peculiar, is in perfect keeping with the priestly system, which often treats both inanimate objects and people in the same way, at least from the perspective of purification and sanctification:

> The priestly writer(s) hardly distinguishes between human and non-human objects in the contexts of purification and sanctification. For instance, Aaron and the priests ought to be holy just like the altars (cp. Exod. 29.33 with 29.37). Also not only Aaron and the priests but also their garments are said to become holy (Exod. 29.21). Similarly, the ritual procedure for the leper (Lev. 14.2ff.) resembles closely that for a house infected by disease (Lev. 14.49ff.). In view of the priestly writer's general view of uncleanness it seems artificial to make a semantic distinction between עַל in כפר + עַל + sanctum and עַל in כפר + עַל + person.[16]

Both of these views, however, have challenges. The most difficult verse for Milgrom's view is Lev. 16.16a. Together with v. 15, it would read as follows:

---

though, which switches to the use of the direct object marker in referring to the same event (וְכִפְּרוּ אֶת־הַמִּזְבֵּחַ).

14. For 16.10, see again Chapter 3, n. 41.
15. Milgrom, *Leviticus 1–16*, p. 829. For other relevant verses see pp. 493, 528, 882, 1010, 1036.
16. Kiuchi, *Purification Offering*, p. 91.

> Then he shall kill the goat of the purification offering which is for the people, and bring its blood within the veil, and do with its blood as he did with the blood of the bull, sprinkling it upon the mercy seat (עַל־הַכַּפֹּרֶת) and before the mercy seat (וְלִפְנֵי הַכַּפֹּרֶת); thus he shall perform purgation upon the holy place (וְכִפֶּר עַל־הַקֹּדֶשׁ), because of the uncleannesses of the people of Israel, and because of their transgressions, all their sins...

Milgrom, however, does not appear comfortable with the phrase 'performing purgation upon the holy place'. Instead, he translates the עַל differently in this instance, treating it as though it were a direct object marker: 'Thus he shall purge the adytum (וְכִפֶּר עַל־הַקֹּדֶשׁ) of the pollution and transgressions of the Israelites, including all their sins...'[17] This would certainly be a rare usage of עַל, and unfortunately Milgrom provides no explanation of his translation in this regard. A more natural approach in this instance is to follow Kiuchi in treating the עַל here in the same way as with a personal subject: 'Thus he shall make atonement for the holy place, because of the uncleannesses of the people of Israel, and because of their transgressions, all their sins...'

For Kiuchi, the most difficult verse is Exod. 30.10a, which would read, 'Aaron shall make atonement for its horns (וְכִפֶּר אַהֲרֹן עַל־קַרְנֹתָיו) once a year...' While curious to the modern reader, however, this translation is not impossible, especially if the horns are seen here as a synecdoche for the altar. Indeed, the verse as a whole reads: 'Aaron shall make atonement for its horns once a year; he shall make atonement for it [עָלָיו; note singular] with the blood of the purification offering of atonement once a year throughout your generations. It is most holy to the LORD.' Having said the above, it must also be noted that this verse reads very naturally by translating כִּפֶּר עַל with 'to make atonement upon': 'Aaron shall make atonement upon its horns once a year; he shall make atonement upon it with the blood of the purification offering...'

In short, both of these renderings are a possibility, and one may therefore translate כִּפֶּר עַל + impersonal object with either 'to atone for' or 'to atone upon'. Does one of these translations enjoy preference over the other? On the one hand, it may be noted that in all of these contexts the impersonal objects are positively affected by the כִּפֶּר-rite. The translation 'to atone for' would seem to bring this out most clearly, is justified by Kiuchi's observations above that impersonal objects are often treated the same as personal objects with respect to purification and consecration, and is warranted by the most likely translation of כִּפֶּר עַל in Lev. 16.16. This perhaps tips the scales in favor of this rendering. On the other hand, however, even if כִּפֶּר עַל is translated with 'to atone upon', it is still clear from the larger context that the impersonal objects benefit from the כִּפֶּר-rite.

---

17. Milgrom, *Leviticus 1–16*, p. 1010.

192   *Sin, Impurity, Sacrifice, Atonement*

We turn finally to consider Group II, which contains four verses in which כִּפֶּר is followed by the direct object marker (Lev. 16.20, 33; Ezek. 43.26; 45.20) and one in which a pronominal suffix functions as the direct object (Ezek. 43.20). It may be noted that in each instance the direct object is not only impersonal, but also part of the sancta, namely, the holy place (הַקֹּדֶשׁ; Lev. 16.20; מִקְדַּשׁ הַקֹּדֶשׁ, v. 33), the tent of meeting (אֹהֶל מוֹעֵד; Lev. 16.20, 33), the altar (הַמִּזְבֵּחַ; Lev. 16.20, 33; Ezek. 43.20, 26), or the temple (הַבָּיִת; Ezek. 45.20). The different approaches taken to כִּפֶּר אֶת + impersonal object may be seen most clearly in the translation of Lev. 16.33, and in particular, the translation of כִּפֶּר אֶת in comparison with כִּפֶּר עַל in this verse. Two approaches may be noted, to which a third is put forward.

First, those who would maintain the rendering 'to atone' for כִּפֶּר have translated the אֶת in the same way as עַל: 'He shall make atonement for (אֶת) the sanctuary, and he shall make atonement for (אֶת) the tent of meeting and for (אֶת) the altar, and he shall make atonement for (עַל) the priests and for (עַל) all the people of the assembly' (RSV).[18] While it is certainly possible to atone *for* sancta (as has just been argued above), it is not clear that this translation does adequate justice to the interchange of כִּפֶּר אֶת and כִּפֶּר עַל.[19]

A second approach, which appears more able to do justice to the interchange of כִּפֶּר אֶת and כִּפֶּר עַל, is to translate כִּפֶּר with 'to purge'. Thus Milgrom translates: 'He shall purge the (אֶת) holiest part of the sanctuary, and he shall purge the (אֶת) Tent of Meeting and the (אֶת) altar; and he shall effect purgation for (עַל) the priests and for (עַל) all the people of the congregation' (Lev. 16.33).[20] While this does well in distinguishing between כִּפֶּר אֶת and כִּפֶּר עַל, however, the translation of כִּפֶּר with 'to purge' is

---

18. See also Hartley, *Leviticus*, p. 221; Dillmann, *Exodus und Leviticus*, pp. 531, 533; Kiuchi, *Purification Offering*, pp. 92-94 (see pp. 87-94 for his entire discussion on כִּפֶּר constructions); Janowski, *Sühne*, p. 229 (on Ezek. 43.20); NASV; NIV.

19. Though see n. 22 below. Kiuchi (*Purification Offering*, p. 92) notes that Lev. 16.16 has כִּפֶּר עַל followed by the sanctuary (וְכִפֶּר עַל־הַקֹּדֶשׁ) whereas 16.20 has כִּפֶּר אֶת followed by the sanctuary (וְכִלָּה מִכַּפֵּר אֶת־הַקֹּדֶשׁ). He then asks, 'Why does *kipper* take עַל in one case and אֶת in another? There is no obvious reason, except that כִּפֶּר אֶת is followed *only* by sancta…' (pp. 92-93 [emphasis his]). In other words, כִּפֶּר אֶת and כִּפֶּר עַל are synonymous here. While possible, another explanation is simply that כִּפֶּר אֶת and כִּפֶּר עַל are related but not synonymous. To be specific, one can '*kipper*' for (כִּפֶּר עַל) sancta (v. 16), as a result of which one has '*kippered*' the (כִּפֶּר אֶת) sancta (v. 20). In terms of the *end result* there is no difference; this does not mean, however, that עַל and אֶת are functioning in exactly the same way (see in this regard the second and third approaches to כִּפֶּר in Lev. 16.33 outlined below). Thus כִּפֶּר אֶת and כִּפֶּר עַל would be closely related but not synonymous. (In fairness to Kiuchi it should be noted that he is not arguing for the translation of כִּפֶּר עַל with 'to atone for' as much as he is arguing against the translation of כִּפֶּר with 'to purge'.)

20. Milgrom, *Leviticus 1–16*, p. 1011. See also Levine, *Leviticus*, p. 110; Wenham, *Leviticus*, p. 227; JPSV.

inadequate.²¹ Indeed, as this work has argued, elements of both ransom and purgation are involved in the priestly conception of כִּפֶּר.

This leads to a third proposal: 'He shall כִּפֶּר-purgate the (אֶת) holiest part of the sanctuary, and he shall כִּפֶּר-purgate the (אֶת) Tent of Meeting and the (אֶת) altar; and he shall effect כִּפֶּר-purgation for (עַל) the priests and for (עַל) all the people of the congregation' (Lev. 16.33). This rendering is able to distinguish between כִּפֶּר אֶת and כִּפֶּר עַל, as well as to identify the various elements that sacrificial כִּפֶּר represents. In short, כִּפֶּר followed by the direct object marker can be taken transitively, and refers in these verses to the כִּפֶּר-purgation of the sancta.²²

---

21. See especially §5.2.

22. For further details, and for more practical suggestions on the translation of כִּפֶּר, see §5.2 and n. 76. In keeping with this it may be noted that if one translates כִּפֶּר consistently with 'to atone', then Lev. 16.20 and 16.33 are somewhat problematic. This is because it is difficult to maintain the apparently transitive nature of כִּפֶּר אֶת in these verses, since English does not use the verb 'to atone' transitively in these contexts (one does not speak of 'atoning the sanctuary'). One helpful proposal for those wishing to maintain the translation 'to atone' is that of John Kleinig. In Lev. 16.33, for example, Kleinig (*Leviticus* [Concordia Commentary; Saint Louis, MO: Concordia Publishing House, 2003], p. 328) translates, 'He shall make atonement [to purge] the holiest part of the Holy Place, and he shall make atonement [to cleanse] the tent of meeting and the altar; he shall make atonement on behalf of the priests and all the people of the assembly' (additions his). Kleinig's translation has the advantage on the one hand of maintaining a distinction between כִּפֶּר אֶת and כִּפֶּר עַל, and on the other hand of allowing for elements of both כֹּפֶר and purgation to be represented (especially if the translator has noted that the verb 'to atone' includes elements of ransom and cleansing, as suggested in Chapter 5, n. 76).

BIBLIOGRAPHY

Alfrink, B., 'L'expression *ne'esap 'el 'amayw*', *OTS* 5 (1948), pp. 115-28.
Anderson, A.A., *2 Samuel* (WBC, 11; Waco, TX: Word Books, 1989).
Anderson, Gary A., and Saul M. Olyan (eds.), *Priesthood and Cult in Ancient Israel* (JSOTSup, 125; Sheffield: JSOT Press, 1991).
Averbeck, Richard E., 'כפר', in *NIDOTTE*, II, pp. 689-710.
Barr, James, 'Semantics and Biblical Theology—A Contribution to the Discussion', in *Congress Volume: Uppsala, 1971* (VTSup, 22; Leiden: E.J. Brill), pp. 11-19.
—*The Semantics of Biblical Language* (Oxford: Oxford University Press, 1961).
Barton, John, 'Natural Law and Poetic Justice', *JTS* NS 30 (1979), pp. 1-14.
Beekman, John, John Callow, and Michael Kopesec, *The Semantic Structure of Written Communication* (Dallas, TX: Summer Institute of Linguistics, 5th edn, 1981).
Brichto, Herbert Chanan, 'On Slaughter and Sacrifice, Blood and Atonement', *HUCA* 47 (1976), pp. 19-55.
Büchler, Adolph, *Studies in Sin and Atonement in the Rabbinic Literature of the First Century* (New York: Ktav, 1928).
Budd, Philip J., *Leviticus* (NCBC; Grand Rapids: Eerdmans, 1996).
—*Numbers* (WBC, 5; Waco, TX: Word Books, 1984).
Bullinger, E.W., *Figures of Speech Used in the Bible* (repr., Grand Rapids: Baker Book House, 1898).
Cazelles, H., *Le Lévitique* (La Sainte Bible; Paris: Cerf, 1958).
Cotterell, Peter, and Max Turner, *Linguistics and Biblical Interpretation* (London: SPCK, 1989).
Dillmann, August, *Die Bücher Exodus und Leviticus* (Leipzig: F. Hirzel, 3rd edn, 1880).
Durham, John I., *Exodus* (WBC, 3; Waco, TX: Word Books, 1987).
Ehrlich, Arnold B., *Randglossen zur hebräischen Bibel. Zweiter Band: Leviticus, Numeri, Deuteronomium* (repr., Hildesheim: Georg Olms Verlagsbuchhandlung, 1908–14).
Elliger, Karl, *Leviticus* (HAT, 4; Tübingen: J.C.B. Mohr, 1966).
Fahlgren, K.Hj., 'Die Gegensätze von *ṣĕdeqā* im Alten Testament', in Klaus Koch (ed.), *Um das Prinzip der Vergeltung in Religion und Recht des Alten Testaments* (repr.; Darmstadt: Wissenschaftliche Buchgesellschaft, 1972 [originally published 1932]), pp. 87-129.
Fensham, F.C., 'Liability of Animals in Biblical and Ancient Near Eastern Law', *JNSL* 14 (1988), pp. 85-90.
Finkelstein, J.J., *The Ox That Gored* (Philadelphia: American Philosophical Society, 1981).
Frymer-Kensky, Tikva, 'Pollution, Purification, and Purgation in Biblical Israel', in Carol L. Meyers and M. O'Connor (eds.), *The Word of the Lord Shall Go Forth: Essays in Honor of David Noel Freedman in Celebration of his Sixtieth Birthday* (Winona Lake, IN: Eisenbrauns, 1983), pp. 399-414.

Füglister, Notker, 'Sühne durch Blut. Zur Bedeutung von Leviticus 17, 11', in Georg Braulik (ed.), *Studien zum Pentateuch* (Festschrift Walter Kornfeld; Wien: Herder, 1977), pp. 143-64.
Garnet, Paul, 'Atonement Constructions in the Old Testament and the Qumran Scrolls', *EvQ* 46.3 (1974), pp. 131-63.
Gerleman, Gillis, 'Die Wurzel *kpr* im Hebräischen', in *Studien zur alttestamentlichen Theologie* (Heidelberg: Schneider, 1980), pp. 11-23.
Gerstenberger, Erhard S., *Leviticus: A Commentary* (trans. Douglas W. Stott; Louisville, KY: Westminster/John Knox Press, 1996). Originally published as *Das dritte Buch Mose: Leviticus* (Das Alte Testament Deutsch, 6; Göttingen: Vandenhoeck & Ruprecht, 1993).
Gese, Hartmut, 'Die Sühne', in *Zur biblischen Theologie. Alttestamentliche Vorträge* (BEvT, 78; Munich: Chr. Kaiser Verlag, 1977), pp. 85-106. ET, 'The Atonement', in *Essays on Biblical Theology* (trans. K. Crim; Minneapolis: Fortress Press, 1981), pp. 93-116.
Gordon, Cyrus H., *Ugaritic Literature* (Rome: Pontificio Istituto Biblico, 1949).
Gorman, Frank H., *The Ideology of Ritual: Space, Time and Status in the Priestly Theology* (JSOTSup, 91; Sheffield: JSOT Press, 1990).
Gray, George Buchanan, *Numbers* (ICC; Edinburgh: T. & T. Clark, 1903).
—*Sacrifice in the Old Testament* (Oxford: Clarendon Press, 1925).
Gray, John, 'Social Aspects of Canaanite Religion', in *The Legacy of Canaan: The Ras Shamra Texts and their Relevance to the Old Testament* (VTSup, 15; Leiden: E.J. Brill, 1965), pp. 170-92.
Greenberg, Moshe, 'Some Postulates of Biblical Criminal Law', in Menahem Haran (ed.), *Yehezkel Kaufmann Jubilee Volume* (Jerusalem: Magnes Press, 1960), pp. 5-28.
Hartley, John E., *Leviticus* (WBC, 4; Waco, TX: Word Books, 1992).
Herrmann, Johannes, *Die Idee der Sühne im Alten Testament. Eine Untersuchung über Gebrauch und Bedeutung des Wortes kipper* (Leipzig: J.C. Hinrichs, 1905).
—'ἱλάσκομαι, ἱλασμός', in *TDNT*, III, pp. 301-10.
Hertzberg, Hans Wilhelm, *I & II Samuel* (trans. J.S. Bowden; London: SCM Press, 1964). Originally published as *Die Samuelbücher* (Göttingen: Vandenhoeck & Ruprecht, 1960).
Hoffmann, D., *Das Buch Leviticus* (2 vols.; Berlin: M. Poppelauer, 1905–1906).
Houtman, Cornelis, *Exodus* (trans. Sierd Woudstra; 3 vols.; Leuven: Peeters, 2000).
Hugenberger, Gordon P., *Marriage as a Covenant: A Study of Biblical Law and Ethics Governing Marriage, Developed from the Perspective of Malachi* (VTSup, 52; Leiden: E.J. Brill, 1994).
Jackson, Bernard S., 'The Goring Ox', in *idem* (ed.), *Essays in Jewish and Comparative Legal History*, pp. 108-52.
—'Reflections on Biblical Criminal Law', in *idem* (ed.), *Essays in Jewish and Comparative Legal History*, pp. 25-63.
Jackson, Bernard S. (ed.), *Essays in Jewish and Comparative Legal History* (SJLA, 10; Leiden: E.J. Brill, 1975).
Janowski, Bernd, *Sühne als Heilsgeschehen. Studien zur Sühnetheologie der Priesterschrift und zur Wurzel KPR im Alten Orient und im Alten Testament* (Neukirchen–Vluyn: Neukirchener Verlag, 1982).
Jenni, Ernst, *Das hebräische Pi'el. Syntaktisch-semasiologische Untersuchung einer Verbalform im Alten Testament* (Zürich: EVZ-Verlag, 1968).

—*Die hebräischen Präpositionen*. Band 1. *Die Präposition Beth* (Stuttgart: W. Kohlhammer, 1992).
Jenson, Philip Peter, *Graded Holiness: A Key to the Priestly Conception of the World* (JSOTSup, 106; Sheffield: JSOT Press, 1992).
Joüon, Paul, 'Notes de lexicographie hébraïque', *Bib* 19 (1938), pp. 454-59.
Kiuchi, N., *The Purification Offering* (JSOTSup, 56; Sheffield: Sheffield Academic Press, 1987).
Klawans, Jonathan, 'Idolatry, Incest, and Impurity: Moral Defilement in Ancient Judaism', *JSJ* 29 (1998), pp. 391-415.
—*Impurity and Sin in Ancient Judaism* (Oxford: Oxford University Press, 2000).
—'The Impurity of Immorality in Ancient Judaism', *JJS* 48 (1997), pp. 1-16.
Kleinig, John W., *Leviticus* (Concordia Commentary; Saint Louis, MO: Concordia Publishing House, 2003).
Knierim, Rolf, *Die Hauptbegriffe für Sünde im Alten Testament* (Gütersloher Verlagshaus: Gerd Mohn, 1965).
—'אשׁם', in *THAT*, I, pp. 251-57.
Koch, Klaus, 'Gibt es ein Vergeltungsdogma im Alten Testament?', *ZTK* 52 (1955), pp. 1-42.
—*Die Priesterschrift von Exodus 25 bis Leviticus 16. Eine überlieferungsgeschichtliche und literarische Untersuchung* (FRLANT, 71; Göttingen: Vandenhoeck & Ruprecht, 1959).
Kurtz, Johann Heinrich, *Sacrificial Worship of the Old Testament* (trans. James Martin; Edinburgh: T. & T. Clark, 1863).
Landsberger, Benno, *The Date Palm and its By-Products according to the Cuneiform Sources* (*AfO* Beiheft, 17; Graz: Weidner, 1967).
Lang, B., 'כִּפֶּר *kipper*', in *TDOT*, VII, pp. 288-303.
Levine, Baruch A., *In the Presence of the Lord: A Study of Cult and some Cultic Terms in Ancient Israel* (SJLA, 5; Leiden: E.J. Brill, 1974).
—*Leviticus* (JPS; New York: Jewish Publication Society of America, 1989).
—*Numbers 1–20* (AB, 4a; New York: Doubleday, 1993).
Levinson, Bernard M., 'The Case for Revision and Interpolation', in *idem* (ed.), *Theory and Method in Biblical and Cuneiform Law: Revision, Interpolation and Development* (JSOTSup, 181; Sheffield: Sheffield Academic Press, 1994), pp. 37-59.
Lyons, John, *Semantics* (2 vols.; Cambridge: Cambridge University Press, 1977).
Maass, F., 'טהר', in *TLOT*, II, pp. 482-86.
—'כפר', in *THAT*, I, pp. 842-57.
Macholz, Christian, 'Das "Passivum divinum", seine Anfänge im Alten Testament und der "Hofstil"', *ZNW* 81 (1990), pp. 247-53.
Malul, Meir, *The Comparative Method in Ancient Near Eastern and Biblical Legal Studies* (Neukirchen–Vluyn: Neukirchener Verlag, 1990).
McKane, William, *Proverbs* (OTL; London: SCM Press, 1970).
McKeating, Henry, 'Sanctions against Adultery in Ancient Israelite Society, with Some Reflections on Methodology in the Study of Old Testament Ethics', *JSOT* 11 (1979), pp. 57-72.
Metzinger, Adalbert, 'Die Substitutionstheorie und das alttestamentliche Opfer mit besonderer Berücksichtigung von Lev 17, 11', *Bib* 21 (1940), pp. 159-87, 247-72, 353-77.

Milgrom, Jacob, *Cult and Conscience: The ASHAM and the Priestly Doctrine of Repentance* (SJLA, 18; Leiden: E.J. Brill, 1976).
—'The Function of the *Ḥaṭṭā't* Sacrifice', *Tarbiz* 40 (1970), pp. 1-8 (Hebrew).
—'Israel's Sanctuary: The Priestly Picture of Dorian Gray', *RB* 83 (1976), pp. 390-99.
—'*kipper 'al bĕadh*', *Leshonenu* 35 (1970), pp. 16-17 (Hebrew).
—*Leviticus 1–16* (AB, 3; New York: Doubleday, 1991).
—*Leviticus 17–22* (AB, 3A; New York: Doubleday, 2000).
—*Numbers* (JPS; New York: Jewish Publication Society of America, 1990).
—'A Prolegomenon to Leviticus 17.11', in *Studies in Cultic Theology and Terminology* (SJLA, 36; Leiden: E.J. Brill, 1983), pp. 96-103. Originally published in *JBL* 90 (1971), pp. 149-56.
—Review of *Sühne als Heilsgeschehen. Studien zur Sühnetheologie der Priesterschrift und zur Wurzel KPR im Alten Orient und im Alten Testament* (Neukirchen–Vluyn: Neukirchener Verlag, 1982), by Bernd Janowski, in *JBL* 104 (1985), pp. 302-304.
—*Studies in Cultic Theology and Terminology* (SJLA, 36; Leiden: E.J. Brill, 1983).
—*Studies in Levitical Terminology: The Encroacher and the Levite, the Term 'Aboda* (Berkeley: University of California Press, 1970).
Miller, Patrick D., Jr, *Sin and Judgment in the Prophets: A Stylistic and Theological Analysis* (SBLMS, 27; Chico, CA: Scholars Press, 1982).
Moraldi, Luigi, *Espiazione sacrificale e riti espiatori nell'ambiente biblico e nell'Antico Testamento* (Rome: Pontificio Istituto Biblico, 1956).
Neusner, Jacob, *A History of the Mishnaic Law of Purities* (22 vols.; Leiden: E.J. Brill, 1974–77).
—*The Idea of Purity in Ancient Judaism* (Leiden: E.J. Brill, 1973).
—*Purity in Rabbinic Judaism: A Systemic Account* (Atlanta: Scholars Press, 1994).
Nida, Eugene A., 'The Implications of Contemporary Linguistics for Biblical Scholarship', *JBL* 91 (1972), pp. 73-89.
Noordtzij, A., *Leviticus* (trans. R. Togtman; Bible Student's Commentary; Grand Rapids: Zondervan, 1982).
Noth, Martin, *Exodus* (trans. J.S. Bowden; London: SCM Press, 1966). Originally published as *Das zweite Buch Moses, Exodus* (Das Alte Testament Deutsch, 5; Göttingen: Vandenhoeck & Ruprecht, 1959).
—*Leviticus* (trans. J.E. Anderson; London: SCM Press, 1965). Originally published as *Das dritte Buch Mose, Leviticus* (Das Alte Testament Deutsch, 6; Göttingen: Vandenhoeck & Ruprecht, 1962).
Otto, Eckart, *Körperverletzungen in den Keilschriftrechten und im Alten Testament: Studien zum Rechtstransfer im Alten Orient* (Neukirchen–Vluyn: Neukirchener Verlag, 1991).
—*Rechtsgeschichte der Redaktionen im Kodex Ešnunna und im 'Bundesbuch': Eine Redaktionsgeschichtliche und rechtsvergleichende Studie zu altbabylonischen und altisraelitischen Rechtsüberlieferungen* (Göttingen: Vandenhoeck & Ruprecht, 1989).
Paul, Shalom M., *Studies in the Book of the Covenant in the Light of Cuneiform and Biblical Law* (VTSup, 18; Leiden: E.J. Brill, 1970).
Péter-Contesse, René, *Lévitique 1–16* (Geneva: Labor et Fides, 1993).
Péter-Contesse, René, and John Ellington, *A Handbook on Leviticus* (New York: United Bible Societies, 1992).

Phillips, Anthony, *Ancient Israel's Criminal Law: A New Approach to the Decalogue* (Oxford: Basil Blackwell, 1970).
—'Another Look at Adultery', *JSOT* 20 (1981), pp. 3-25.
Porter, J.R., *Leviticus* (CBC; Cambridge: Cambridge University Press, 1976).
Procksch, Otto, 'λύω', in *ThWB*, IV, pp. 329-37.
Rad, Gerhard von, *Old Testament Theology* (2 vols.; trans. D.M.G. Stalker; New York: Harper & Row, 1962–65).
Reiner, E., *Šurpu* (*AfO* Beiheft, 11; Graz: Im Selbstverlage des Herausgebers, 1958).
Rendtorff, Rolf, *Leviticus* (BKAT, 3; 3 vols.; Neukirchen–Vluyn: Neukirchener Verlag, 1985–92).
Rodriguez, Angel M., *Substitution in the Hebrew Cultus* (Berrien Springs, MI: Andrews University Press, 1979).
Sabourin, Léopold, 'Nefesh, sang et expiation (Lv 17.11, 14)', *ScEc* 18 (1966), pp. 25-45.
Sakenfeld, Katharine D., 'The Problem of Divine Forgiveness in Numbers 14', *CBQ* 37 (1975), pp. 317-30.
Sanders, E.P., *Jewish Law from Jesus to the Mishnah: Five Studies* (London: SCM Press, 1990).
Saussure, Ferdinand de, *Cours de linguistique générale* (Paris: Payot, 3rd edn, 1969 [1st edn 1916]).
Schenker, Adrian, '*kōper* et expiation', *Bib* 63 (1982), pp. 32-46.
—*Versöhnung und Widerstand. Bibeltheologische Untersuchung zum Strafen Gottes und der Menschen, besonders im Lichte von Exodus 21–22* (Stuttgart: Katholisches Bibelwerk, 1990).
—'Das Zeichen des Blutes und die Gewißheit der Vergebung im Alten Testament: Die sühnende Funktion des Blutes auf dem Altar nach Lev 17.10-12', *MTZ* 34 (1983), pp. 195-213.
Schötz, Dionys, *Schuld und Sündopfer im Alten Testament* (Breslau: Müller & Seiffert, 1930).
Schwartz, Baruch J., 'The Bearing of Sin in the Priestly Literature', in D.P. Wright, D.N. Freedman, and A. Hurvitz (eds.), *Pomegranates and Golden Bells: Studies in Biblical, Jewish and Near Eastern Ritual, Law and Literature in Honor of Jacob Milgrom* (Winona Lake, IN: Eisenbrauns, 1995), pp. 3-21.
—'The Prohibitions concerning the "Eating" of Blood in Leviticus 17', in Anderson and Olyan (eds.), *Priesthood and Cult*, pp. 34-66.
—'"Term" or Metaphor: Biblical נשׂא עון/פשׁע/חטא', *Tarbiz* 63 (1994), pp. 149-71 (Hebrew).
Selms, A. van, 'The Goring Ox in Babylonian and Biblical Law', *ArOr* 18 (1950), pp. 321-30.
Silva, Moisés, *Biblical Words and Their Meanings: An Introduction to Lexical Semantics* (Grand Rapids: Zondervan, 1983).
Speiser, E.A., 'Census and Ritual Expiation in Mari and Israel', *BASOR* 149 (1958), pp. 17-25.
Stamm, Johann Jakob, *Erlösen und Vergeben im alten Testament. Eine begriffsgeschichtliche Untersuchung* (Bern: A. Francke, 1940).
—'סלח', in *THAT*, II, pp. 150-60.
Stewart, William J., and Robert Burgess, *Collins Dictionary of Law* (Glasgow: Harper Collins, 1996).

Thiselton, Anthony C., 'Semantics and New Testament Interpretation', in I. Howard Marshall (ed.), *New Testament Interpretation: Essays on Principles and Methods* (Carlisle: Paternoster Press, 1992), pp. 75-104.
Toorn, K. van der, *Sin and Sanction in Israel and Mesopotamia: A Comparative Study* (Assen/Maastricht: Van Gorcum, 1985).
Unterman, Jeremiah, 'Redemption', in *ABD*, V, pp. 650-54.
Wenham, Gordon J., *Leviticus* (NICOT, 3; London: Hodder & Stoughton, 1979).
—*Numbers* (TOTC; Leicester: InterVarsity Press, 1981).
Westbrook, Raymond, 'Lex Talionis and Exodus 21, 22-25', *RB* 93 (1986), pp. 52-69.
—*Studies in Biblical and Cuneiform Law* (CahRB, 26; Paris: J. Gabalda, 1988).
Wierzbicka, Anna, *Lexicography and Conceptual Analysis* (Ann Arbor, MI: Karoma, 1985).
Wold, Donald J., 'The *kareth* Penalty in P: Rationale and Cases', *SBLSP* 1 (1979), pp. 1-45.
Wright, David P., *The Disposal of Impurity* (SBLDS, 101; Atlanta: Scholars Press, 1987).
—'The Spectrum of Priestly Impurity', in Anderson and Olyan (eds.), *Priesthood and Cult*, pp. 150-81.
—'Two Types of Impurity in the Priestly Writings of the Bible', *Koroth* 9, Special Issue (1988), pp. 180-93.
—'Unclean and Clean (Old Testament)', in *ABD*, VI, pp. 729-42.
Yaron, R., 'The Goring Ox in Near Eastern Law', in H.H. Cohn (ed.), *Jewish Law in Ancient and Modern Israel* (New York: Ktav, 1971), pp. 50-60.
Young, Norman H., 'C.H. Dodd, "Hilaskesthai" and his Critics', *EvQ* 48.2 (1976), pp. 67-78.
Zimmerli, Walther, 'Die Eigenart des prophetischen Rede des Ezechiel', *ZAW* 66 (1954), pp. 1-26.

INDEXES

INDEX OF REFERENCES

Hebrew Bible
Genesis
1.28	145	49.33	18		180
1.29	165	50.15-17	90	21.23a	51
4.13	20, 22, 23, 34	50.17-18	92	21.28-32	50, 53, 69, 72, 73, 167
6.5-7	11	50.17	89, 90	21.29	50, 69
6.14	48	50.18	90	21.30	6, 46, 47, 50, 51, 53, 55, 63, 64, 68, 69, 71-75, 156
9.3	165	*Exodus*			
9.4	166	6.3	171		
9.5	167	8.18	61		
9.6	155, 176	8.19	61		
9.7	145	8.23 ḥ	61	21.31	50
9.9-10	167	10.12-17	90, 91	21.32	50
9.10	167	10.17	89	21.35-36	30
19.13-14	11	12.4	164	22.4	27
19.15	21	12.5	27	22.9a	27
20.9	36	12.16	164	22.18-20	98
20.16	44, 45	13	62	23.8	58
20.17-18	36	13.11-15	62	25.17-18	91
25.8	18	14.53	188	27.3	109
25.17	18	16.18	188	28	98, 118
26.10	35	19	119	28.1-39	98
29.18	169	19.10	119, 121	28.3	118, 121
31.20 ET	44	19.14-15	121	28.35	13, 14
31.21	44	19.14	119	28.36-37	98
32.20 ET	73, 76, 189	19.15	119	28.38	92, 95, 98, 100, 120, 121, 184
32.20b	45	20.4	27		
32.21	73, 76, 172, 189	20.8	119	28.40-43	98
		20.20-21	122	28.41	118, 121
		21	53-55, 63	28.42-43a	21, 23
35.29	18	21.12-14	54, 155	28.43	13-15, 20, 41
37.22	166	21.13	54		
37.28	169	21.14	143	29	117
42–44	90	21.22-25	51	29.1	121
47.30	27	21.22	51	29.4	121, 126
		21.22b	51		
		21.23	169, 170,		

Index of References

29.5-9	131	30.13	53, 155	2.4b	27
29.7	131	30.14	53	4–5	87, 156, 157
29.20-21	121	30.15-16	168		
29.20	126	30.15	53, 75, 188	4	5, 24, 30-32, 36, 37, 40, 42, 43, 46, 88, 178, 185
29.21	116-18, 120, 121, 126, 131, 134, 190	30.16	6, 47, 53, 75, 133, 156, 188		
29.26-27	118, 121, 123	30.19	55	4.1–5.13	87, 88, 100, 148, 149
		30.20-21	13, 15		
29.33	6, 118, 121, 123, 134, 172, 189, 190	30.20	14		
		30.21	14, 55	4.2-23	30
		30.25	55	4.2	24
		30.29-30	118, 121	4.3-12	34, 36
29.33a	121	30.29	52, 116, 120	4.3-7	124
29.36-37b	122			4.3	24-26, 34-37, 39, 41
29.36-37	118, 124	30.30	92, 189		
29.36	109, 111, 113, 122, 124, 125, 134, 188, 190	30.31	155	4.13-21	34, 36
		30.32a	92	4.13-14	24, 30, 31, 33
		30.33	15		
		30.38	15	4.13-14a	27
		31.13	119, 121	4.13	24, 30, 33, 34, 36, 37, 39, 41
29.36a	109	31.14-15	14		
29.37	116, 120, 123, 134, 188, 190	31.14	13-16, 19		
		31.15	13, 14	4.14	27, 30, 33, 36
		32	91, 92		
29.42-43	117	32.1-10	11	4.20	5, 75, 80, 81, 85, 188, 189
29.43	120	32.25-28	13		
30	133, 168	32.31-32a	91		
30.10	96, 190	32.32-33	90	4.22-26	39
30.10a	188, 190, 191	32.32	89, 91	4.22-23a	28, 33
		32.35	13, 92	4.22-23	31, 32
30.10b	188, 190	33.2-3	90	4.22	24, 25, 30, 32, 33, 36, 40
30.11-16	52, 55, 71, 83, 155, 175	34	84, 85, 91		
		34.6-7	84, 91		
		34.7	89-91	4.23	24, 27, 28, 30-33, 36, 40
30.12-16	6, 47, 133, 156	34.9	90, 91		
		35.2	13, 14		
30.12-14	184	38.25-28	52	4.26	80, 81, 85, 188
30.12	6, 47, 52, 63, 69, 73-75, 133, 155, 156, 175	40.9-13	118, 121, 123		
				4.26b	3
				4.27-31	39, 42
		Leviticus		4.27-28a	28
		1.4	6, 53, 75, 97, 188	4.27-28	31, 32, 87
30.12b	175			4.27	24, 30, 32, 33, 36, 40
30.13-16	53	1.4b	97		

Leviticus (cont.)
4.28	24, 27, 28, 30-33, 36, 40	5.21-23a	29, 31	8.10-12	118, 121, 123
4.31	80, 81, 85, 188	5.23	24, 30-32, 34, 36	8.14	118
4.31b	44, 87	5.24	24, 25	8.15	88, 96, 110-14, 122, 124, 129, 134, 163, 182, 185, 187, 188, 190
4.32	87	5.25a	31		
4.35	80, 81, 188	5.26	6, 24, 25, 37, 80, 81, 188		
4.35b	87	6.1-7	24		
5	5, 24, 30, 31, 46, 88, 178, 185	6.1-7 ET	41, 42,		
		6.2-4a	29, 31	8.15a	109
		6.4 ET	30, 31	8.30	118, 121
		6.5 ET	24, 25	8.34	95, 188
		6.6a	31	8.35	13-15
5.1-4	31, 38	6.7 ET	24, 25, 80, 81, 188	9	94
5.1	20, 22-24, 38, 41, 42			9.7	189
		6.10	165	9.15	93, 109, 111
5.2-5	30, 31, 36, 40	6.11	116, 120, 123	10	93
5.2-4	24, 31, 38, 42	6.18	116	10.1-7	93
		6.18 ET	116, 120, 123	10.1-3	11
5.2-3	152			10.1-2	13, 14
5.2	24, 25, 39	6.19-20a	116, 120	10.2	14
5.3	24	6.19	109, 111	10.3	117
5.4	24	6.20	116, 123	10.6-7	13
5.5	24	6.22	29	10.6	14, 36
5.6	35, 85, 188	6.23	29, 172, 189	10.7	14
				10.8-15	93
5.10	80, 188	6.26 ET	109, 111	10.9	13-15
5.11-13	114	6.26-27a ET	116, 120	10.10	105
5.13	80, 81, 114, 188	6.27 ET	116, 123	10.16	93
		6.30 ET	172, 189	10.17	92, 93, 95, 98-100, 165, 184, 188
5.15	24	7.7	172, 189		
5.16	6, 80, 81, 172, 188	7.18	21, 23, 42, 164, 176		
5.17-19	37	7.19-21	152	10.17a	94
5.17-18a	37, 38	7.19	20	11–16	151
5.17-18	24	7.20	15, 18, 43, 164	11–15	141, 149
5.17	20, 22-24, 30, 31, 37, 39-42	7.21	15	11	141
		7.25	15, 164	11.10	167
5.18	6, 24, 80, 81, 188	7.26-27	180	11.11	110
		7.26	164, 177	11.24-28	127
5.19	24, 30, 37	7.27	15, 164, 177	11.24	116, 127
5.20-26	24, 41, 42, 153			11.25	110
		7.34	165	11.26	116
				11.27	116, 127

Index of References

11.28	110	14.11	108, 126	15.28-30	128
11.31	116	14.14	27, 108,	15.30	112, 188
11.32	106		126	15.31	13-15,
11.36	116	14.15-18	126		129, 130,
11.39-40	165	14.17	108, 188		179
11.39	116	14.18	108, 112	16	99, 122,
11.40	110	14.19	108, 188		153
11.44-45	120, 121	14.20	6, 106,	16.2	13-15
11.46	167		112, 188	16.6	189
12–15	130, 157	14.20b	3	16.9	97
12	43, 128,	14.21	112, 188	16.10	6, 92, 95-
	151	14.25	108		97, 99,
12.1-8	144	14.28	108		188
12.4	145	14.29	108, 188	16.11-19	147
12.5	145	14.31	108, 188	16.11	189
12.6-8	113, 179	14.46-47	128	16.13	13-15
12.7-8	112	14.48-53	115	16.15-16	113, 114
12.7	178, 188	14.49-52	110, 111	16.15	190
12.8	106, 178,	14.49	109, 110,	16.16	88, 96,
	188		112, 134,		109, 112,
12.8b	3, 112,		190		129, 142,
	115	14.51-52	115		153, 185,
13–14	128	14.51	190		188, 190-
13	106, 107	14.52-53	4, 112,		92
13.1–14.32	144		114	16.16a	139, 190
13.3	107	14.52	110, 112,	16.17	172
13.6	106, 108		113	16.17a	189
13.11	107	14.53	106, 112	16.17b	189
13.13	107	14.53	188, 190	16.18-19	123
13.15	107	14.53b	3, 112	16.18	96, 123,
13.17	107, 108	15	112		190
13.20	107	15.1-33	144	16.19-20	113, 114
13.22	107	15.2-30	129, 130	16.19	88, 107-
13.23	107, 108	15.5-13	108		109, 112,
13.25	107	15.5	145		113, 118,
13.27	107	15.10	116		121-24,
13.28	107	15.11	116		163, 182,
13.30	107	15.13-15	128		185, 187
13.34	106, 107	15.13	106	16.20-22	147
13.37	107	15.15	112, 188	16.20	3, 45, 113,
14	106, 108,	15.18	128		124, 189,
	109	15.19-24	128		192, 193
14.4	108	15.21	116, 145	16.21-22	95-97, 99,
14.7	108	15.23	116		100
14.8	106, 108	15.24	128	16.21	6, 20, 92
14.9	106	15.27	116		

Leviticus (cont.)						
16.22	20, 92, 95, 96, 99, 100, 184		179, 180, 181, 189	20.7-8	119, 121
		17.12	164, 166	20.7	120, 121
		17.12a	164	20.9-16	14, 24
		17.13-14	164, 165, 175, 177	20.9	13, 14
16.24	189			20.10-13	14
16.26	141	17.14	15, 166	20.10	13, 14, 56
16.27	172, 189	17.14a	164, 171	20.11	13, 14
16.28	145	17.14b	171, 172	20.12	13, 14
16.29	164	17.15-16	110, 164	20.13	13, 14
16.30	109, 140, 188	17.15	106, 164	20.14	13, 14
		17.16	20, 21, 23	20.15-16	14, 167
16.30a	4	18	146, 149	20.15	13, 14
16.31	164	18.1-23	143	20.16	13, 14
16.32	189	18.6-23	152	20.17-21	17, 24
16.33	3, 88, 113, 185, 188, 189, 192, 193	18.14	17	20.17	15, 17, 20, 21, 23, 24, 42
		18.15	112		
		18.16	17	20.18	17, 20, 42
16.34	188	18.24-30	145	20.19	20, 21, 23, 24, 42
17	163, 164, 166, 175	18.24-28	129		
		18.24-25a	139	20.20-21	17
17.1-2	164	18.24	145, 146	20.20	13, 14, 20, 21, 24, 41, 42
17.3-14	164	18.25-28	146		
17.3-9	165	18.25	11, 145, 155		
17.3-7	164			20.27	13, 14
17.3-4	176	18.29	15, 17	21.1-4	145
17.4	15, 166	18.30	146	21.7-8a	119
17.4b	176	19.7-8	21, 42	21.7	119
17.8-9	164	19.8	15, 20, 23, 42	21.8	119, 121
17.9	15			21.8b	119, 121
17.10-12	164-66, 175, 177	19.17	20, 21, 23 24	21.9	13, 14
		19.20-22		21.15	119, 121
17.10	15, 18, 164, 166, 177, 180	19.20	14	22	118
		19.22	24, 80, 81, 172, 188	22.2-3	120, 121
				22.3-7	152
17.10a	164	19.31	141, 145	22.3	15, 130
17.11	5, 42, 43, 86, 156, 163-69, 171, 173-80, 181, 182, 187	20.1-3	145	22.4	164
		20.2-5	152	22.5-6	164
		20.2-3a	17	22.9	13-15, 20, 21, 41, 119, 121, 130
		20.2-3	19		
		20.2	13, 14, 19		
		20.3	15, 18, 19, 88, 140, 146, 184		
17.11a	166-68, 170, 171, 177, 188			22.14	164
				22.16	20, 21, 24, 25
		20.5	15, 18		
17.11b	166-73,	20.6	15, 18	22.31-33	119, 121

22.31-32a	117	3.5-9	132	8.15-16a	107
22.32	119, 121	3.10	13, 14,	8.15	107, 112
23.27	164		115, 130	8.16-19	132
23.28	188	3.13	120, 121	8.19	53, 115,
23.29	15, 164	3.38	13, 14		116, 130-
24	189	3.40-51	62		32, 165,
24.12	155	3.46	62		188
24.14-15	21, 23, 24	3.48	62, 175	8.21	109, 111,
24.14	13	3.49a	62		112, 114,
24.15	20, 41	3.51a	62		131, 132,
24.16	13, 14, 41	4.15	13, 14		188
24.16a	14	4.18-20	16, 17	8.21a	110, 125
24.17	13, 14	4.18	15, 17	8.21b	107
24.18	167, 169-	4.19	13, 14, 17	9.13	15, 20, 21,
	71, 180	4.20	13-15		23, 42
24.20	170	5	24	11.1	11
24.21	13, 14	5.3	143	11.18	121, 123
24.23	13, 14	5.5-8	24	11.18a	119
25	64, 119	5.6	24	12.9-11	11
25.10	121, 123	5.7	24, 30	12.10	13
25.10a	119	5.8	172, 188	13–14	84
25.25	65	5.31	20, 21	13.31-33	84
25.26	64, 65	6	130	14	84, 85, 90,
25.29	64	6.9-11a	131		92, 100,
25.51	64	6.11	123, 131		184
25.52	64	6.11b-12a	125	14.1-37	13
26.6	167	7.1	118, 121,	14.1-3	84
26.14-33	11		123	14.4-5	84
26.22	167	8	107-109,	14.6-9	84
27.1-2	120		114, 124,	14.10	84
27.2	121		131	14.11-25	84
27.14	120, 121	8.6	107, 108,	14.11-12	11, 84
27.15-19	120, 121		112, 131	14.12	90
27.22	120, 121	8.7	108, 110,	14.13-16	84
27.26-27	62		112, 114,	14.17	85
27.26	120		125, 132	14.18-19	91
27.29	14	8.7a	107, 109,	14.18	84, 89-91
29.1	120		112	14.19	84, 91
29.4	120	8.7b	109, 112	14.20	84, 85
29.37	124	8.8-13	109	14.21-23	84, 117
		8.10	132, 133	14.22-23	11
Numbers		8.12	107, 132,	14.23a	84
1.3	52		133, 188	14.26-39a	84
1.51	13, 14	8.13-14	118	14.28-37	11
3	62, 78	8.14-19	53	14.32	42

Numbers (cont.)		18.1	20, 21, 42,	20.12	117, 120,
14.34	20, 21, 42		89, 92-94		121
14.37	14, 15	18.2-5	132	20.13	117, 121
15	13, 19,	18.3-5	130	21.5-6	11
	178	18.3	13-15, 42	21.6	13
15.22-29	178	18.7	13, 14,	25.1-9	13, 53
15.24-29	176		130	25.6-13	133
15.25	80, 81,	18.8	165	25.13	188
	188	18.15-17	62	27.14	120, 121
15.26	80	18.16	62	28.22	188
15.27-31	19	18.19	133, 165	28.30	188
15.27-29	19	18.22	13-15, 20,	29.5	188
15.28	80, 81,		21, 42,	31.5	188
	188		130, 132	30	81
15.30-31	19, 176,	18.23	20, 21, 89,	30.5	81
	178		92, 94	30.5 ET	81-83
15.30	13, 15	18.27	176	30.6	81-83
15.31	15	18.30	176	30.6 ET	81
15.32-36	13	18.32	13-15, 20,	30.8 ET	81, 83
15.32	19		21, 42	30.9	81, 83
15.35-36	14	19	110, 111,	30.12 ET	81, 83
15.35	14, 19		114, 128,	30.13	81, 83
16.25-35	11		145, 151	30.14	164
16.31-33	13	19.8	145	30.15 ET	20, 21, 81
16.35	13	19.9	108, 110,	30.16	20, 21, 81
16.37-38	117		128	31	114, 128
16.37-38 ET	116, 120	19.11-22	128	31.1-10	128
16.41-50 ET	15	19.11-13a	111	31.17	128
16.46-49 ET	13, 53	19.11	128	31.19-23	111
16.46 ET	188	19.12	109, 111,	31.19	111, 112,
16.47-48 ET	53		112, 114		114
16.47 ET	53, 188	19.13	15, 110-	31.20	111, 112,
16.49 ET	15		12, 114,		114
17	53		179	31.21-24	128
17.2-3	116, 117,	19.17-19	110, 111	31.23	110-12,
	120	19.19	108, 112,		114
17.6-15	15		114, 125,	31.28	167
17.10 ET	13-15		134	31.48-54	53
17.11-14	13, 53	19.20	15, 110-	31.50	6, 47, 53,
17.11	6, 53, 188		12, 114,		156, 168
17.12-13	53		179	31.52	53
17.12	188	19.21	110, 141	31.54	53
17.13 ET	13, 14	19.22	127, 128	32–33	154
17.14	15	20	111, 117	32.23	22, 34
17.25	13-15	20.10-12	13	32.33	22, 34
17.28	13, 14	20.11	13	33.54	111

Index of References

34.10	111		172, 176,	*Ruth*	
35	54-56,		189	2.20	65
	148, 149,	35.34	6, 54	3.9	65
	156	36.2	171	3.12	65
35.6-29	154			4	64
35.6	165	*Deuteronomy*		4.6	64
35.9-34	54	4.25-28	11	4.7	64
35.11	54	6.14-15	11	4.10	17
35.15	54	7.4	11		
35.16-21	13, 54	10.17	58	*1 Samuel*	
35.16-18	14	12.16	167	2.27-32	11
35.16	14	12.23	166	3.14	172, 189
35.17	14	12.24	167	5.6-10	53
35.18	14	13.2 ET	27	8.3	58
35.19	14, 65	13.3	27	12	58
35.21	14, 65	15.23	167	12.1-5	58
35.22-25	54, 154	16.19	58	12.3	57, 58
35.24	65	19	54, 55	15.23-25	90
35.25	65, 155	19.1-14	54	15.25	89
35.26-29	54	19.1-13	54	19.5	174
35.26-27	54	19.6	65	21.4 ET	105
35.28	54, 155	19.12	65	21.5	105
35.30-34	54, 83,	19.21	170, 180	21.5 ET	105
	129, 154,	21.7	167	21.6	105
	159, 182,	21.8-9	147, 149	24.5	35
	187	21.8	189	24.22	16
35.30-31	54	22.1-2a	27	25.14-31	90
35.30	13, 54,	23	143	25.24	22, 34
	155	23.14 ET	143	25.27	90
35.31-34	68, 69, 74	23.15	143	25.28	89, 90
35.31-33	6, 47, 156,	27.25	58	25.31	35, 176
	168, 175,	28.15-68	11	28.9-10	21
	184	32.30-31	51		
35.31-32	156, 159	32.43	189	*2 Samuel*	
35.31	6, 13, 14,			4.9	62
	54, 67, 69,	*Joshua*		6.6-7	15
	155	20.1-9	54	12.9-14	11
35.32	6, 54, 67,	20.3	65	14.11	65
	129, 154	20.5	65	21	31
35.33-34a	140	20.9	65	21,3	47
35.33-34	54, 143,			21.1-14	133
	145, 155	*Judges*		21.1-9	155
35.33	6, 54, 129,	2.13-15	11	21.1	12, 40,
	147-49,	3.7-8	11		155
	155, 156,	5.18	174	21.3-6	156
	159, 166,	12.3	174	21.3	155, 189

2 Samuel (cont.)		9.26-28	11	34.21 ET	39
21.4	155	10.33 ET	188	34.22-23	35
21.6	155	10.34	188	34.22	39
24	52, 53			37.28	17
24.10	35, 52	*Job*		37.38	17
24.15-17	53	5.20	62	38	35
24.15	53	6.23	62	38.2-11	35
		7.21	89, 90	38.2-5 ET	35
1 Kings		33.19-22	59	38.3-6	35
1.21	17	33.23-24	59	38.18 ET	35
1.50-53	143	33.23	59	38.18-19	35
2.28-31	143	33.24	59, 70	38.19	35
2.31	167	33.27-28	59	39.9	22, 34
2.32	11	33.27	59	41	35
8.31-40	11	33.28	59	49	55
9.6-9	11	36.16-20	58	49.5 ET	56
11.9-11	11	36.18	58	49.6	56
11.16	17	38.15	24	49.6 ET	56
14.10	17	42.8	189	49.7	56
14.31	17	42.28	189	49.7 ET	56
21.21	17			49.7-8 ET	55, 63, 64, 73
		Psalms			
2 Kings		5.10 ET	11	49.8-9a	56
17.6-18	11	5.11	11, 39	49.8-9	55, 63, 64, 73
21.16	167	5.20 ET	39		
24.4	167	6	35	49.8	56, 70
		7.8-16 ET	12	49.11 ET	56
1 Chronicles		7.9-17	12	49.12	56
6.34	188	11.5-6	11	49.14 ET	56
21.1-15	11	13.8	55	49.15	56
21.3	35	16.7	35	49.15 ET	56
22.8	167	19.14 ET	65	49.16	56
		19.15	65	55.18 ET	62
2 Chronicles		25.17-18	90	55.19	62
7.13-14	11	25.18	89	65.3 ET	189
19.10a	30	25.22	62	65.4	189
29.24	188	26.11	62	69.18 ET	65
30.18-19	189	31.5 ET	62	69.19	65
		31.6	62	78.35	65
Ezra		32	35, 90	78.38	189
9.13-14	11	32.1	45, 89	79.9	188
		32.4	90	85	90
Nehemiah		32.5	89, 90	85.2 ET	45, 89, 90
3.37	45	34.3 ET	106	85.3	45, 89, 90
4.5 ET	45	34.4	106	85.3 ET	90
6.11	188	34.19	35	85.4	90

102.4-11	35	44.6	65	4.5	89
106.31	176	44.24	65	4.6	89
107.9	164	47.11	46, 189	5.11	146
109.13	17	49.26	65	6.6	39
111.9	61	51.10-11	65	7.3	11
130.7	61, 62	51.11	62	7.8-9	11
149.3	35	53.4	99	11.6-12	11
		53.12	20, 22, 34	11.15	64
Proverbs		58.3	164	14.7-8	11
6.20-35	56	58.10-11	164	14.10	20
6.32-35	57	60.16	65	16.63	189
6.34-35	56	63.4	64	18.3	89
6.35	47, 57, 58,			18.19-20	20, 89
	67, 68, 71	*Jeremiah*		22.3-4	143
10.16	22, 34	2.3	39	22.4	11
12.2	11	3.1-3a	11	22.4a	25
13.8	67	4.4	11	22.13-15	11
16.6	172, 189	4.18	22, 34	22.15	143
16.14	73, 75, 76	5.3	11	23.49	20
17.23	58	9.11b-12a	93	24.6-9	144
21.18	59, 67	9.12b-13a ET	93	24.11	144
		15.21	62	25.12	25
Song of Songs		17.14	35	36.17	143, 145
1.14	48	18.8	22, 34	36.18	143
4.9	109	18.11	22, 34	43.20	3, 110,
4.13	48	18.23	44, 188		113, 189,
		22.13	13		192
Isaiah		25.24	64	43.22	110, 113
3.16-17	11	25.31	64	43.23	45, 110
9.13-14	11	25.32	64	43.26	3, 189,
10.5-6	11	25.48	64		192
22.14	189	31.11	65	44.10	20
24.6	39	32.7	64	44.12	20
24.20	22, 34	32.8	64	45.15	175, 178,
27.9	172, 189	50.34	65		188
28.18	189	51.5b	35	45.17	175, 178,
30.22	143				189
33.24	89, 90	*Lamentations*		45.18	110
35.9-10	65	3.38	22, 34	45.20	189, 192
41.14	65	3.39	22, 34	45.22	189
43.1-7	69	3.42-47	11	46.20	116
43.3-4	59, 70	4.6	22, 34	48.15	105
43.3	70				
43.4	70	*Ezekiel*		*Daniel*	
43.14	65	4.4	89	9.24	189

Hosea		3.2	11	Qumran	
1.4-5	11	4.6	61	*1QS*	
2.8-13 ET	11	5.12	57, 58	6.3-4	119
2.10-15	11			6.8	119
2.20	167	*Micah*			
5.12	12	1.3-7	11	Talmuds	
5.14	12	4.14	172	*b. Giṭṭin*	
5.15	35	5.1 ET	172	59b	119
8.13b-14	11	6	90		
10.1-2	11	6.13-16	11	*b. Keritot*	
10.2	39	7.18	89, 90	4b	177
13.14	65				
13.15–14.1	90	*Zephaniah*		*b. Yebamot*	
13.15-16 ET	90	1.2-6	11	78b	40
13.16 ET	39				
14.1	39	*Haggai*			
14.2 ET	89	2.11-13	116		
14.3	89				
		Zechariah			
Joel		11.5	35		
1.18	39	14.18-19	21, 22, 34		
Amos		*Malachi*			
1.3–2.5	11	1.6-11	98		
1.11a	94	2.1-3	98		

INDEX OF AUTHORS

Alfrink, B. 18
Anderson, A.A. 40
Averbeck, R.E. 45

Barr, J. 45, 49, 105
Barton, J. 12
Beekman, J. 49
Brichto, H.C. 2, 21, 46, 76, 169, 170, 174, 179-81
Büchler, A. 142, 144
Budd, P.J. 15, 24, 168, 174
Bullinger, E.W. 12
Burgess, R. 77

Callow, J. 49
Cazelles, H. 169, 170
Cotterell, P. 48, 49

Dillmann, A. 23, 36, 92, 94, 99, 169, 172, 192
Durham, J.I. 15

Ehrlich, A.B. 93, 169
Elliger, K. 2, 94, 95, 114, 116, 164, 166, 169, 172
Ellington, J. 25

Fahlgren, K.Hj. 22
Fensham, F.C. 50
Finkelstein, J.J. 50
Frymer-Kensky, T. 145, 146, 148
Füglister, N. 166, 169-71, 173

Garnet, P. 109, 169
Gerleman, G. 3
Gerstenberger, E.S. 164, 169
Gese, H. 2, 169
Gordon, C.H. 81
Gorman, F.H. 178

Gray, G.B. 3, 55, 131
Gray, J. 81
Greenberg, M. 56

Hartley, J.E. 25, 32, 36, 82, 94, 96, 119, 129, 164, 165, 169, 172, 174, 178, 192
Herrmann, J. 1, 2, 46, 67, 68
Hertzberg, H.W. 40
Hoffmann, D. 141, 142
Houtman, C. 51, 52, 98, 109
Hugenberger, G.P. 48, 49

Jackson, B.S. 50, 51, 55-57
Janowski, B. 1-4, 22, 25, 42, 45-47, 50, 67, 69-71, 82, 94, 95, 113, 165, 166, 169-71, 178, 181, 188, 192
Jenni, E. 107, 169, 171, 172, 181
Jenson, P.P. 105, 125, 127, 128
Joüon, P. 24, 25, 95, 96, 106, 108, 109, 122, 171

Kiuchi, N. 1, 31-33, 37, 82, 93, 94, 96, 97, 109, 110, 124, 129, 134, 167, 169, 170, 172, 174, 188, 190, 192
Klawans, J. 140, 142, 144-51
Kleinig, J.W. 193
Knierim, R. 12, 24, 25, 94
Koch, K. 11, 12, 22
Kopesec, M. 49
Kurtz, J.H. 2, 169, 174

Landsberger, B. 3
Lang, B. 2, 45, 68
Levine, B. 3-5, 23, 25, 37, 45, 46, 67, 81, 92, 94, 96, 113, 116, 131, 168, 174, 192
Levinson, B.M. 27
Lyons, J. 48, 105

Maass, F. 67, 106
Macholz, C. 82
Malul, M. 50
McKane, W. 56
McKeating, H. 57
Metzinger, A. 167, 169, 174
Milgrom, J. 3, 6, 14-19, 22-25, 27, 30-32, 34-39, 42, 43, 46, 47, 52, 67, 81, 82, 85, 87-89, 92-94, 96, 97, 108-11, 116, 117, 119, 122-24, 128, 129, 131-33, 140, 153, 156, 165-69, 172-78, 189-92
Miller, P.D. 12
Moraldi, L. 166, 169

Neusner, J. 140
Nida, E.A. 48
Noordtzij, A. 165, 166
Noth, M. 16, 174

Otto, E. 50

Paul, S.M. 50, 56
Péter-Contesse, R. 15, 23, 25, 30, 36, 82, 92, 94, 96, 126
Phillips, A. 57, 58
Porter, J.R. 16
Procksch, O. 47

Rad, G. von 22
Reiner, E. 40
Rendtorff, R. 24, 30, 32, 82, 178
Rodriguez, A.M. 174, 178

Sabourin, L. 169
Sakenfield, K.D. 84, 85

Sanders, E.P. 145, 150
Saussure, F. de 45
Schenker, A. 2, 46, 50, 67, 72-74, 164-67, 169, 178
Schötz, D. 44
Schwartz, B.J. 1, 2, 22-24, 156, 157, 164, 165, 167-69, 172, 173, 177, 178
Silva, M. 48
Speiser, E.A. 52
Stamm, J.J. 2, 44, 45, 47, 81, 82, 85
Stewart, W.J. 77

Thiselton, A.C. 48, 49
Toorn, K. van der 12, 25, 39, 40
Turner, M. 48, 49

Unterman, J. 55

Van Selms, A. 50

Wenham, G.J. 16-18, 23, 31, 36, 37, 55, 84, 85, 94, 105, 116, 117, 122, 125, 128, 131, 165, 168, 174, 192
Westbrook, R. 50, 51, 54, 55
Wierzbicka, A. 49
Wold, D.J. 16, 18
Wright, D.P. 16, 116, 117, 128, 145, 150-53

Yaron, R. 50
Young, N.H. 2

Zimmerli, W. 22, 89, 94

www.ingramcontent.com/pod-product-compliance
Lightning Source LLC
Chambersburg PA
CBHW070316230426
43663CB00011B/2152